Cases in Public Policy and Administration

Cases in Public Policy and Administration

By

Jay M. Shafritz

and

Christopher P. Borick

Routledge
Taylor & Francis Group

LONDON AND NEW YORK

First published 2011 by Pearson Education, Inc.

Published 2016 by Routledge
2 Park Square, Milton Park, Abingdon, Oxon OX14 4RN
711 Third Avenue, New York, NY 10017, USA

Routledge is an imprint of the Taylor & Francis Group, an informa business

ISBN: 9780205607426 (pbk)

Library of Congress Cataloging-in-Publication Data
Shafritz, Jay M.
    Cases in public policy and administration / by Jay M. Shafritz and Christopher P. Borick.
      p. cm.
    ISBN-13: 978-0-205-60742-6
    ISBN-10: 0-205-60742-X
    1. Public administration–United States.   2. Public administration.   3. Policy sciences.   4. Political planning—United States.   5. Political planning.   6. United States—Politics and government.   I. Borick, Christopher P.   II. Title.
    JK421.S52 2011
    320.60973–dc22

                                                              2009044810

Contents

Preface   xi

PART I **The Development of U.S. Public Administration   1**

CHAPTER 1 Sherlock Holmes and the Case of Scientific Management: How the World's Most Famous Detective Was a Pivotal Influence on the Development of U.S. Public Administration   1

CHAPTER 2 Muckrakers and Reformers to the Rescue: How the Progressive Movement Created Modern Public Administration from the Muck of Corruption, Indifference, and Ignorance   11

PART II **Public Policy Making   23**

CHAPTER 3 The Case for Understanding the Critical Role of Doctrine in Public Policy Making: "Seeing" Policy Evolve Through the Lenses of the Doctrinal Development Cycle   23

CHAPTER 4 Who Really Made the Decision to Drop the First Atomic Bomb on Hiroshima?: Was It President Harry S. Truman or His Advisors, the Chief Executive or His Team of Technical Experts?   35

PART III **The Machinery of Government   42**

CHAPTER 5 How the Ideas of an Academic Economist, Friedrich A. Hayek, Led to the Thatcher Revolution in Great Britain, Inspired the Reagan Revolution in the United States, and Pushed the World's Global Economy into Its Worst Crisis since the Great Depression of the 1930s   42

CHAPTER 6   From German Chancellor Otto von Bismarck to U.S. President Bill Clinton: How Political Leaders Created the Modern Welfare State Using Social Insurance as an Alternative to Socialism   55

PART IV   Intergovernmental Relations   70

CHAPTER 7   Gun Shows, Gun Laws, and Gun Totin': Second Amendment Fanatics Versus All Levels of Government   70

CHAPTER 8   The Politics—Administration Dichotomy Negated Again: How the Rove Doctrine Subordinated State, Local, and National Environmental Policy to the Service of the Republican Party   80

PART V   Ethics   87

CHAPTER 9   The Gas Chamber of Philadelphia: How a 1977 Incident at Independence Mall Illustrates the "Banality of Evil" Concept First Applied to Adolf Eichmann, the Nazi Holocaust Administrator   87

CHAPTER 10   The Red Ink of Orange County: When Is It Ethical for Public Treasurers to Gamble with Public Money? Only When You Win!   97

PART VI   Organization Theory   104

CHAPTER 11   Using Systems Theory to Understand How Sun Tzu Predictably Turned Concubines into Soldiers in Ancient China; and How Chaos Theory Explains Why Systems Are Ultimately Unpredictable Even When They Are Otherwise Understood   104

CHAPTER 12   Using William Shakespeare's Plays to Prove That He Was an Instinctive and Early Organization Theorist: Whether in a Beehive or the Court of Elizabeth I, He Knew How Honey (or Money) Got Things Done   114

PART VII **Organization Behavior 124**

CHAPTER 13 The Case of the Ubiquitous Chief of Staff: How a Job Invented by and Once Confined to the Military Escaped Its Uniformed Existence and Is Now Commonly Found in Government and Corporate Offices 124

CHAPTER 14 Organization Development in Hollywood War Movies: From John Wayne in *The Sands of Iwo Jima* to *G.I. Jane* and Beyond 132

PART VIII **Managerialism and Information Technology 139**

CHAPTER 15 George Orwell's Big Brother Is Bigger and Better than Ever: Not Only Is He Watching You, He Is Counting the Number of Times You Visit His Website, Taking Your Picture, Converting It to a Series of Numbers, and Destroying Your Anonymity! 139

CHAPTER 16 Did Al Gore Really Invent the Internet? And did Gore Lose the 2000 Presidential Election to George W. Bush by Threatening to Take Away the Internet? 146

PART IX **Strategic Management 153**

CHAPTER 17 How the U.S. Strategic Policy of Containment (of Communism in General and the Soviet Union in Particular) Gradually Evolved Just After World War II to Win the Cold War in 1989 153

CHAPTER 18 The Rand Corporation as an Exemplar: The Origins of and Increasingly Important Role of Strategic Think Tanks 167

PART X **Leadership 179**

CHAPTER 19 Implementing Strategy Through the Levels of Leadership and Strategic Optimism: How Strategic Leadership Invariably Devolves into Tactical Operations 179

CHAPTER 20   Was It Good Leadership for General Douglas Macarthur to Take His Staff with Him When He Abandoned His Army in the Philippines and Ran Away to Australia at the Beginning of World War II?   190

PART XI   **Personnel Management   200**

CHAPTER 21   Why Advancement in Public Administration Has Always Been an Essay Contest: Proofs from the Presidency and the Bureaucracy   200

CHAPTER 22   The Case for Mentoring Junior Managers with Executive Potential: How General Fox Conner Set a Young Dwight D. Eisenhower on the Path to the Presidency   211

PART XII   **Social Equity   220**

CHAPTER 23   Brown Reverses the Plessy Doctrine: How Thurgood Marshall Convinced The U.S. Supreme Court that Separate Is Inherently Not Equal, Laid the Legal Foundations for the Modern Civil Rights Movement, and Earned Himself an Appointment as the First African American Justice on That Supreme Court   220

CHAPTER 24   Government Regulation of Sex: Toward Greater Social Equity at Work Through Remedial Legislation, Judicial Precedents, and Sexual Harassment Prohibitions Written into Manuals of Personnel Rules   226

PART XIII   **Public Finance   237**

CHAPTER 25   Take Me Out to the Ball Game and You Buy the Ticket: The Case for Public Stadium Financing   237

CHAPTER 26   The Fall of the House of California: How the Richest State in the Country Cratered into Budgetary Chaos and a Fiscal Nightmare   242

PART XIV **Program Analysis and Evaluation 253**

CHAPTER 27 Why Florence Nightingale, the Famous Nurse
Who Pioneered the Graphic Presentation of
Statistical Data, Is the Now-Forgotten "Mother"
of Program Evaluation and PowerPoint®
Illustrations   253

CHAPTER 28 The Often Ridiculous Nature of Public Policy and Its
Analysis: Why It Is So Important to Allow for Ridicule
and to Consider the Ridiculous   260

INDEX   271

Preface

This collection of instructive stories on public policy and its administration follows an ancient tradition. Ever since prehistory, stories have been used by tribal elders to illustrate, indoctrinate, and educate. With the advent of writing, the stories, once memorized, were recorded for greater permanency. Thus Homer's two great works, *The Iliad,* on the Trojan War, and *The Odyssey,* on Ulysses' circuitous route home from that war, were first narrative poems, part of the rich oral tradition of ancient Greece. These were not just "fun" tales to listen to around the fireplace on a long winter's night. They offered serious instruction on how to conduct oneself as a warrior, on the nature of honor, on military strategy and tactics, and on how to deal with the gods that abounded in that world. Such stories were not mere entertainments, although they were certainly entertaining; they presented the crucial lessons of life as the ancient Greeks knew it.

THE CASE STUDY APPROACH

So it is not surprising that Greece was the society that produced the Western world's earliest histories, what we now call case studies, on the ebb and flow of war, on the nature of battles, and on political and institutional leadership. Ever since then, the study of political decision making and its subsequent administrative implementation has been undertaken by means of a case study, usually in the form of an in-depth analysis of a single subject such as a war or battle. Wars tend to make excellent case studies because, at least after they are over, they come with the three key ingredients all cases must have: a beginning, a middle, and an end.

Thucydides' *History of the Peloponnesian War* (404 BCE) is the progenitor of these military and political case studies. His *History* provides a full account of the war between the ancient Greek cities of Athens and Sparta. Thucydides made one of the most famous observations on what causes war: "What made war inevitable was the growth of Athenian power and the fear which this caused in Sparta." It is possible to discern in this one sentence recognition of what has subsequently been termed the security dilemma, a situation in which one state takes action to enhance its security, only to have this action seen as threatening by other states. The result is that the other states engage in countermeasures, which intensify the first state's insecurity. The dilemma arises from the fact that because of this process, actions taken to enhance security can actually end up diminishing it. There is also a dilemma for the second state in that if it regards the action as defensive and takes no countermeasures, it leaves itself vulnerable; whereas if it responds vigorously, it will exacerbate the first state's insecurity.

Although he was writing 2,500 years ago, Thucydides distilled the essence of the Cold War conflict between the United States and the former Soviet Union, the current security dilemma facing both Iran and Israel, and countless other international squabbles during the past two millennia. What makes a case useful is not just the information it supplies about itself, but the utility of its wider applicability. So, although Thucydides had no knowledge of the United States/Soviet Union conflict, the lessons of his case concerning ancient Athens and Sparta held universal truths.

This wider applicability of truths, ancient or not, is the essence of a good case. Thus a case is worth reading not just because it is a good story; but because it teaches something beyond itself. Mere entertainment does not suffice for a good case. For example, the story of David, a boy working as a shepherd in ancient Israel, may be interesting, but it is not a case that offers larger truths. However, the story of David versus Goliath is a classic case that has within it lessons of strategy, tactics, honor, fear, and asymmetrical warfare—all issues that are still relevant today.

Military colleges and general staffs have long used the case study method to review battles and study generalship. Generalship is not an occupation that gives its practitioners much of an opportunity to ply their trade. Thus most generals fight pitifully few battles. One of the prime reasons that Napoleon Bonaparte was so successful as a general and for so long was that he kept France almost continuously at war. Consequently, he was literally the most experienced general of his age by far—he fought almost sixty major engagements. Even though he lost the last one, Waterloo in 1815, you cannot take all those other victories away from him. Experience counts! And that is why case studies are so useful: They are the only way we know to duplicate cheaply some very expensive—in money and/or lives—experiences.

Wait, you say! What about simulations, whether as board games, interpersonal exercises, or computer games? All these are valid training techniques, but they are also just variants of the traditional case study that goes back to Thucydides, who, by the way, was also a general. Unfortunately, he lost the battle for a colony that the Athenians charged him with protecting from the Spartans. As punishment, he was exiled from Athens for twenty years. Fortunately, this gave him the time to write his classic book.

This same military case study technique is now widely used in a civilian context to examine how policy proposals become law, how programs are implemented, and how special interests affect policy development. College courses in business and public administration often use a case study approach. An entire course may consist of case studies (frequently combined into a casebook) of management situations to be reviewed. The goal is to inculcate experience artificially. Any manager rich with years of service will have had the opportunity to live through a lifetime of "cases." If life is, as it is often said, "one damn thing after another," then a career in business or public administration is, in a parallel sense, "one damn case after another." By having students study many cases, each of which may have occurred over many years, the case study course compresses both time and experience.

Case studies, in effect, allow students to live many lives, to replicate the cases that made up the lives of others. Thus relatively young students can gain much of the insight and wisdom of a manager who has had the equivalent of hundreds of years of experience. In theory, this makes them so wise beyond their years that employers will eagerly seek them out. In allowing students to borrow the experiences of others, case studies seek to solve the problem of creating on-the-job experiences in those who have no actual experience.

IN THE TRADITION OF THUCYDIDES

The modern case study as a specific vehicle for conveying social science research became fashionable in the period between the world wars. These case studies were inspired by the case history approach used in medical research. Now the term *case study* is used for a bewildering variety of presentations, some so methodologically rich that they sag with statistical analyses, others straight historical narratives that tell a story from beginning to end. Sometimes such cases are written specifically for teaching purposes and have only a beginning and a middle. The end, known to the instructor, is kept from the students until after a presumably lively class discussion allows students to come to their own conclusions that are then compared to the reality. Then, of course, there are legal cases, the precedent-setting opinions of judges used to teach law; these are not our concern here.

Within the fields of public policy and administration, two kinds of cases have emerged. The first is historical, much like those of Thucydides. They recount events and seek to draw lessons. The best of them are also gripping stories, with much of the dramatic suspense and surprising outcome of a novel. However, the case study format is also used as a way of framing and presenting the results of formal empirical research. Here observational or survey techniques yield quantitative data that can be validated by statistical methodologies, similar to formal experiments in the natural sciences and medicine. These latter types of case, used increasingly as the basis for research designs in public policy and administration, and also in doctoral dissertations, are not our concern either.

This book is a collection of historical cases—informal history presented as good stories or explanations of policy-making and/or administrative phenomena. Our efforts are unabashedly in the tradition of Thucydides in that we hope all our efforts are useful enough to have wider applicability. Although the cases are clearly concerned with public policy and its administration, they are written, as far as practical given the nature of the subject matter, in an informal journalistic manner. Even though we do not offer news as such, our case study format tends to follow the journalistic credo that a news story should contain these essential elements: who, what, why, when, where, and how.

A MESSAGE TO GARCIA

Case studies are not just explorations into techniques of how to accomplish this or that critical task; they must also be, at heart, inspirational. That is certainly what the Greeks expected of their cases. Readers today are still inspired by the story of *The Iliad* and the exploits of Ulysses depicted in *The Odyssey*. Cases ultimately must be able to inspire readers toward new achievements.

A modern, compared to ancient Greek, case that illustrates this inspirational aspect is Elbert Hubbard's (1856–1915) *A Message to Garcia* (1899). Hubbard, who is generally credited with first observing that "life is one damn thing after another," was an American publisher and writer. During the Spanish-American War, he learned of the exploits of Andrew Rowan, an Army officer sent behind enemy lines to Cuba to coordinate military efforts with the Cuban revolutionaries fighting for independence from Spain.

This tale of initiative in the face of daunting challenges exhorts the reader to take a similar "don't ask questions, get the job done" attitude toward his or her job. Rowan's job was to get a message through to Calixto Garcia (1839–1898), who had long been leading the fight for Cuban independence. Rowan's inventive way of overcoming of every obstacle—harsh jungles, smelly bandits, poisonous snakes, the usual—that got in his way becomes an inspirational saga, as written by Hubbard, that sold over 40 million copies and was known by practically every literate American throughout most of the first half of the twentieth century. It was required reading for U.S. officers in World Wars I and II; and large businesses bought copies in bulk for their managers. The very title, *A Message to Garcia,* became a catchphrase for accomplishment, for a "can do" attitude, for doing a difficult task despite all, and for demonstrating your worthiness as a member of your team.

Inspirational case studies come in many forms. For example, consider the inspirational nature of Shepherd Mead's *How to Succeed in Business Without Really Trying* (1952). This book, when made into a play, won the Pulitzer Prize for drama in 1967, despite the fact that it was really a Broadway musical comedy (made into a film in 1967). Nevertheless, it inspires. It inspires those who seek to rise in the corporate world to do so by sucking up to the big boss, to his ugly secretary, and to anyone else who needs sucking up to. Inspirational? Yes, to a limited number of suckers who don't realize that this case is a parody of the business world, but hardly widely applicable.

Real knights of the organizational realm earn their spurs by taking "a message to Garcia," by accomplishing something that is admirable. Widely known case studies such as *Garcia* illustrate, define, and project the character of a nation. The ancient Greeks might seek to emulate Ulysses' cunning, determination, and devotion to his family. Now the Americans, who always had famous heroes such as George Washington and Abraham Lincoln, suddenly had as a role model an ordinary man doing an extraordinary thing. This offering up of a role model—an exemplar to be admired and imitated—has always been one of the most important functions of a case study. Remember Ulysses.

ADVENTURE FOLLOWS

The cases in this book are in this tradition of narrative instruction, of narrative inspiration. Included are twenty-eight stories or explanations of public policy making and/or administrative phenomena. For the most part, these provide information that every student and practitioner should know. They were all (but one) written by the same team, so they have the same style and tone. If you liked reading the various editions of *Introducing Public Administration* by Jay M. Shafritz, E. W. Russell, and Christopher P. Borick, then this collection should have comparable appeal to you. The organization of this work has the same chapter arrangement as *Introducing Public Administration*, but the cases are all independent; they can be easily mixed or matched with any other core text.

Before a case can be of instructional value, it must be interesting enough for students to begin to read it, and then hold their attention. That is why, we have sought to create cases that highlight the great drama of public policy and the ingenuity of its concomitant administrators. As much as possible we sought out adventure. We wanted to tell thrilling stories that emphasized the true-life adventures of public policy makers and administrators.

Even though we start out with a story of the world's most famous fictional detective, the story is true because it deals with a fictional character's influence on real events. The only other major use of fiction is our use of Shakespeare's plays to understand organization theory (Chapter 12); snippets of fiction are used here and there to illustrate aspects of organization development (Chapter 14), government surveillance (Chapter 15), and policy analysis (Chapter 28).

Not all of the cases that follow are strictly historical. Certainly all the biographical cases are; but others are procedural in whole or in part because they do not so much provide a case as make the case for a process or way of thinking about public policy and its implementation. For example, Chapter 3 makes the case that doctrine is pivotal to understanding public policy, and Chapter 12 makes the case that Shakespeare's prose and poetry anticipated many of the findings of twentieth-century social scientists and organization theorists.

For the most part, we offer histories in the form of adventure stories that every student of public policy and administration should know. Readers will learn:

- How Lincoln Steffens and the muckrakers paved the way for the development of modern public administration (Chapter 2)

- How the decision was made by President Harry S Truman to drop the first atomic bomb on Japan in order to end World War II (Chapter 4)

- How the ideas of an academic economist and a famous novelist led to the recession that started in 2008 (Chapter 5)

- How the current U.S. welfare state was inspired by a German chancellor (Chapter 6)

- How a Nazi war criminal inadvertently provided the world with a lesson in bureaucratic ethics (Chapter 9)

- How Sun Tzu, in ancient China, understood the essentials of modern systems theory (Chapter 11)

- How Napoleon Bonaparte encouraged the job of chief of staff to escape from the military and live in contemporary civilian offices (Chapter 13)

- How Al Gore really deserves just a little bit of credit for inventing the Internet (Chapter 16)

- How an obscure state department bureaucrat wrote the policy of containment that allowed the United States to win the Cold War with the Soviet Union (Chapter 17)
- How the RAND Corporation was invented and, in turn, invented strategy for the nuclear age (Chapter 18)
- How gaining high office is so often an essay contest won by those who can write well, such as Woodrow Wilson, as well as by those who can cheat at writing well, such as John F. Kennedy (Chapter 21)
- How Dwight D. Eisenhower was started on the road to the presidency by a mentor he found in the Panamanian rainforest (Chapter 22)
- How Thurgood Marshall led the legal fight for civil rights and made it possible for Barack Obama to become president (Chapter 23)
- And how Florence Nightingale gathered statistics during the Crimean War that helped lead to contemporary program evaluation (Chapter 27)

The case topics were selected because we found them interesting. Sometimes we took a paragraph or two from our introductory text and developed it into a case. Sometimes we took a case that had been retired from the text (and now exists only in earlier editions) and expanded and updated it into a new case. More often we started from scratch with just the germ of an idea that we nurtured into a case.

ACKNOWLEDGMENTS

We would like to thank the following reviewers for their assistance on this book: Peter L. Cruise, Mary Baldwin College; Samuel T. Shelton, Troy University; and Allen Zagoren, Drake University. We are especially grateful to Jeffery K. Guiler of Robert Morris University for his many suggestions on the Sherlock Holmes chapter. Robert Seskin, the treasurer of the Siena Community Association, offered essential advice on the ethical mandates and fiduciary responsibilities of those who are stewards of public funds. Peter Foot of the Geneva Center for Security Policy offered invaluable assistance with earlier versions of Chapter 14, "Organization Development in Hollywood War Movies." This case originally appeared in Jay M. Shafritz and E. W. Russell, *Introducing Public Administration*, 2nd edition (New York: Longman, 2000); then in a revised version that appeared in *Public Voices*, Vol. 4, No. 2 (2000). This was also the situation with Chapter 12 on Shakespeare. The material originated in Jay M. Shafritz, *Shakespeare on Management: Wise Counsel and Warnings from the Bard* (New York: Birch Lane Press, 1992). Material from that work was adapted for an article, "Shakespeare the Organization Theorist," which appeared in the first issue of *Public Voices*, Vol. 1, No. 1 (Fall 1993). The current chapter is a new adaptation from the original source. We are also indebted to Albert C. Hyde, formerly of the Brookings Institution, who, being a resident of San Francisco, was uniquely situated to write Chapter 26 on the state of California's fiscal woes. Finally, we are happy to thank Eric Stano, Longman's political science editor, who helped to conceptualize this project and used his good offices to bring it to life.

This book has been a collaboration of two friends. Although we are separated by both generations and geography, we have a common interest in good stories that illustrate the subjects we have spent our academic lives teaching. We hope that our work provides readers with an interesting and insightful perspective on a field that touches so many aspects of our daily lives. Naturally, all omissions, mistakes, or other flaws that may be found herein are solely our responsibility. We are hopeful that this will find sufficient acceptance that subsequent editions will be warranted. Thus, suggestions for improvements and enhancements will always be welcome.

JAY M. SHAFRITZ
Professor Emeritus
Graduate School of Public and International Affairs
University of Pittsburgh
shafritz@yahoo.com

CHRISTOPHER P. BORICK
Political Science Department
Muhlenberg College
cborick@muhlenberg.edu

CHAPTER ONE

Sherlock Holmes and the Case of Scientific Management

HOW THE WORLD'S MOST FAMOUS DETECTIVE WAS A PIVOTAL INFLUENCE ON THE DEVELOPMENT OF U.S. PUBLIC ADMINISTRATION

PREVIEW

Mickey Mouse and Santa Claus are his only rivals to having the world's most instantly recognizable silhouette. Almost everyone in the literate world knows that a deerstalker cap on the head, a drooping pipe in the mouth, a short-caped overcoat on the shoulders, and a magnifying glass in the hand mean that Sherlock Holmes is afoot. The demand for Sherlock Holmes stories, both original and derivative, has been unrelenting ever since this intellectual action hero first appeared in London's *Strand Magazine* in 1891. Untold numbers of novels, stage plays, films, radio dramas, and television programs have used the Holmes character both seriously and in parody. However, the following case offers something that has never been seen before: Sherlock Holmes coming to life and taking his place on history's stage.

FROM FICTION TO HISTORY

This is a true story about something that is fundamentally untrue, the career of Sherlock Holmes. How can there be a true story about a fictional character invented by an amiable country doctor and alive only in the imaginations of his fans? "Elementary, my dear reader," as Holmes himself might say.

The truth of this story lies not in the existence of the character but in the influence the character has had on real events and real people. This is a case of a fictional detective being so influential that he has moved beyond the realm of literature and into the reality

1

of history. A few years after the Sherlock Holmes character was first presented to the public, he came to life not as a living individual but as a force in human events. As you will see, there is nothing supernatural afoot.

Although it rarely happens, it is unquestionably true that fictional characters can play critical roles in historical events. Perhaps the most telling single example of this phenomenon is Harriet Beecher Stowe's 1852 novel, *Uncle Tom's Cabin*. This depiction of the cruelty of slavery did much to create the political climate that led to the U.S. Civil War of 1861–1865. Consequently, when wartime President Abraham Lincoln met Mrs. Stowe for the first time in 1863, he said, "So you're the little woman who wrote the book that made this great war!"

Stowe wrote *Uncle Tom's Cabin* specifically as abolitionist propaganda, to influence the national debate over slavery, but Arthur Conan Doyle (1859–1930) did not have any such high motives in mind when he conceived Sherlock Holmes. The author was a struggling young physician with few patients and consequently a lot of time on his hands. His marginal medical practice gave him the free time to write a story about a new kind of detective, one who would treat crime as physicians treated disease: by combining modern science with ancient logic.

CONCEIVED AS POPULAR ENTERTAINMENT

Conan Doyle's goal was simply to write a popular entertainment that would supplement the income from his medical practice. In this he would be bitterly disappointed—if only initially. He had already published more than two dozen short stories, but he was unable to interest a regular publisher in the first Sherlock Holmes story, the novel, *A Study in Scarlet*. After several rejections, his only option was to sell it outright to a magazine—for only £25, less than $3,000 today. Thus Holmes made his debut as one feature among many in *Beeton's Christmas Annual* for 1887—hardly an impressive start for what would become the single most popular and best-loved literary creation of all time.

The novel proved popular enough that it appeared as a book in London in 1888 and in a U.S. edition in 1890. However, Conan Doyle made nothing from these books, as he had been required to assign all rights to *Beeton's*. Meanwhile, he went on to new writing projects that did not include Holmes. But then the United States came to the rescue, and Holmes was resurrected.

Because the United States did not have a law governing international copyrights until mid-1891, British authors, who conveniently wrote in English, were easily and frequently pirated. As a result, even though he was not paid for it, some of Conan Doyle's short stories as well as the first Holmes novel were more widely read in the United States than in Great Britain. While pirates in the publishing trade effectively steal from authors by not paying them with cash, they at least pay them the compliment of selling their work to an expanding audience.

Conan Doyle's growing reputation, following in large measure from this literary piracy, directly led to a momentous dinner invitation. The U.S. editor of *Lippincott's Monthly Magazine*, Joseph Marshall Stoddart, was in England in early 1889 seeking to commission new stories for both the U.S. edition of the magazine and a new English version that would be published simultaneously. Thus he invited two promising young authors to dine with him at the Langham Hotel in London: Conan Doyle and Oscar Wilde.

The buttoned-down provincial physician could hardly be more of a contrast to the flamboyant urbane wit long known for his outrageous dress. Nevertheless, the two seemed to get on splendidly with each other and with Stoddart. The dinner was such a success that by its end, each author had agreed to provide a new novel that would be first published in the magazine. Conan Doyle would produce another Sherlock Holmes adventure, *The Sign of the Four* (1890). His new friend Oscar Wilde, whose great plays were still to come, would create his classic, *The Picture of Dorian Gray* (1891).

This literary dinner was a satisfactory feast in every respect. Conan Doyle would later honor and advertise the Langham Hotel by giving it a role in several of his stories, including *The Sign of the Four*. This is an early example of what Hollywood now calls product placement.

Further food for the imagination is the oft-made suggestion that one of the characters in *The Sign of the Four,* Thaddeus Sholto, bears a decided resemblance to Wilde in that he described his house as "an oasis of art in the howling desert of South London," considered himself a man of "refined tastes," and sought to "seldom come in contact with the rough crowd." But we mustn't make too much of this, as Conan Doyle frequently took characteristics from people he knew and assigned them to his fictional characters. This was nowhere more true than with Holmes himself—whose powers of deduction were based on one of Conan Doyle's medical school professors, Joseph Bell, who could deduce the occupations of patients just by looking at their clothes, posture, complexion, and deformities. For example, someone with a notch in a tooth might be a tailor, because the notch was created by the constant biting off of thread. A man whose trousers were unusually worn down on the inner thigh might be a shoemaker, because that is where he held the shoe as he worked on it. This proclivity for taking a small fact and deducing from it a larger conclusion became one of the best-loved features of each Sherlock Holmes story.

The second Holmes novel enjoyed the same kind of limited success as the first—a respectable reception when it was included in a quality magazine, followed by equally respectable sales when it was published in book form. Nothing foretold the superstardom that was awaiting Conan Doyle's imaginary friend.

SHERLOCK HOLMES BECOMES A SUPERSTAR

Sherlock Holmes is the star not only of sixty stories (fifty-six short stories and four novels) by his creator, but of countless imitative stories and novels, stage plays, radio dramas, television series, and movies from the silent era onward.

This multimedia powerhouse, unique among literary characters, has spawned an enormous and ever-increasing number of articles and books that analyze his exploits and biography as if he were an actual historical figure. Indeed, today there are thousands of followers of the life and times of Holmes organized into local associations or societies across the globe, ranging from the equivalent of movie star fan clubs to the most serious academic groups. They continue to publish in print and on the Internet everything from trivia to very thoughtful academic papers.

Holmes, whose creator died in 1930, has never been more alive and active than he is today. After a few difficult years finding his audience, Holmes became a literary and cultural superstar in 1891 and has continued to sell well in bookstores and at the box office ever since. What did it? How did a character in two middling successful novels jump to superstar status almost overnight? The inherent merit of Conan Doyle's prose and the attractiveness of the character are obvious reasons. However, these reasons were fully obvious in the novels, so merit alone is not a sufficient explanation. In modern terms, the character had to be relaunched in a different format using a new medium. The format was the short story, and the medium was *Strand Magazine.*

Conan Doyle decided to put his unique character into a series of short stories that, although they would have continuing characters, would be complete in themselves. This avoided the problem so common with the serialization of long novels, such as those of Charles Dickens, that readers might be confused or lose interest if they missed an issue of the magazine.

Within only two weeks, Conan Doyle produced "A Scandal in Bohemia" (1891) and "The Red Headed League" (1891) and sent them off to the *Strand,* the most popular general-interest magazine in London. One key to the magazine's huge circulation was its policy of publishing pictures on almost every page. Thus, when the first Holmes stories were accepted, an illustrator was commissioned to draw scenes for the tales. The stories, with illustrations by Sidney Paget, were an immediate and enormous success. They made the Holmes stories, in effect, an early form of what is now called a graphic novel. Two dozen stories were completed over the next two years. They were then published as collections in two volumes: *The Adventures of Sherlock Holmes* (1892) and *The Memoirs of Sherlock Holmes* (1893).

The stories became immensely popular in the United States for the same reasons they were loved in England. However, another factor was also at work in the United States. Because of the copyright situation, cheap pirated editions of the collections were readily available. Newspapers as well as magazines freely published the stories, inadvertently giving them an aura of authenticity. After all, they were written as if they were first-person accounts from a distinguished British physician, Dr. John H. Watson. No wonder Holmes was thought to be real! Real or not, within a year of the first stories appearing, Holmes was one of the most famous imaginary faces on the face of the earth.

THE IMPORTANCE OF FAME

This worldwide fame is critical to the premise of this case, because it is Holmes's early and continuing superstar persona that facilitated one of the most significant developments of the twentieth century: the increase in manufacturing productivity and standard of living brought about through scientific management.

The first escapades of Sherlock Holmes and his friend, Dr. Watson, purportedly the author of the Holmes stories, appeared more than two decades before the theory of scientific management was first presented in 1910. To fully appreciate the significance of these dates, one must first appreciate the impact of Sherlock Holmes in his time. He was *big*. He was as big a phenomenon in his time as Elvis or the Beatles or Harry Potter in other times. He captured the attention of the international public so much that when Conan Doyle allowed Holmes to die after several dozen stories, he was forced, by popular demand, to resurrect him.

Although Sherlock Holmes never helped to start a war, he was instrumental in jump-starting one of the most pivotal peacetime events in world history. Holmes was the fictional brain behind the real-life business efficiency movement, eventually known as scientific management, of the early twentieth century.

So what has this got to do with public administration? Only that the public-sector version of this movement for business efficiency that grew out of scientific management in turn grew into the emerging field of public administration.

THE FIRST MODERN CONSULTANT

Sherlock Holmes is now so famous that describing someone as "a Sherlock Holmes" has long meant that he is a brilliant detective, just as describing someone as "a Napoleon" has long meant that he is a highly skilled military officer (or, perhaps, merely a short one). Holmes's fame is important here because of what he was famous for: in his own words from *A Study in Scarlet* (1887), "I have a trade of my own. I suppose I am the only one in the world. I'm a consulting detective." At first he was a singular figure in plying his trade, but he became the inspiration to untold thousands more who modeled themselves on him: some to detect crime as well as others who would detect and solve business problems.

Today consultants are common. Business and governments hire them for a vast variety of specialized skills—accounting, engineering, computer services, management, and even ethics. The first consultants were oracles, or fortune tellers, in ancient Greece. This same term was adopted by legal specialists in ancient Rome and eventually applied to medical experts in England—the doctors to whom general practitioners sent their patients with problems needing advanced skills. Conan Doyle was just such a general practitioner in England when the first Sherlock Holmes tale was published in 1887.

Because Holmes was the kind of detective to whom other detectives, members of the police as well as private investigators, turned to when they were stumped, Conan Doyle made him a self-described consultant. This is critically important, because Holmes was the first modern consultant of any kind outside the field of medicine.

Obviously, smart people have always consulted, have always given advice. However, Holmes was the first to set up shop—yes, at 221B Baker Street—to sell his brainpower, his ability to theorize rapidly and think creatively, for a living. As he put it in *A Study in Scarlet*, "I depend upon them [his theories of detection] for my bread and cheese." Holmes, in effect, created the world's first self-conscious consulting firm.

You don't have to take our word for it. No less a source than the monumental twenty-volume *Oxford English Dictionary*, the most authoritative and exhaustive source of the origins and definitions of English words, confirms this. If you look up "consultant" on page 800 of volume III of the second edition (1989), you will see that the first definition deals with those ancient Greek oracles. The second refers to those English medical specialists, Conan Doyle's colleagues, whose descendents are still practicing today. The third definition, however, reads as follows: "A person qualified to give professional advice or services, e.g. in problems of management or design; an advisor; also . . . a private detective." Then it literally cites a story in Arthur Conan Doyle's *Memoirs of Sherlock Holmes* (1893) as the original source of this modern usage. The specific reference is to a quote from "Silver Blaze" (1892), in which Colonel Ross asserts that "I am rather disappointed in our London consultant." By the end of the story, however, Colonel Ross would conclude that his consultant, Holmes, was "wonderful." Note that although this is the first use of the term *consultant* outside of ancient history and medicine, Holmes described himself as a "consulting detective" from his very first appearance in *A Study in Scarlet* (1887).

SHERLOCK HOLMES, SYSTEMS ANALYST

Holmes was the original crime scene investigator. Today's investigators, both on television and in real life, arrive on the scene and proceed to follow in Holmes's footsteps by systematically analyzing the physical evidence and drawing conclusions based on logical deductions.

The key word here is *system.* Although he never used the word, Holmes always took a holistic approach to a problem. He saw some of the pieces of a puzzle at a crime scene and, by using scientific methods and logical analysis, was able to come up with the missing pieces to get the whole picture.

Think of a problem such as a crime to be solved as a jigsaw puzzle. The placement of the last remaining piece becomes obvious once you have figured out the rest of the puzzle—that is, arranged the rest of the pieces properly. Then, as Holmes initially said in *The Sign of the Four* (1890), "When you have eliminated the impossible, whatever remains, however improbable, must be the truth." It is his systemic approach to problem solving that allows Holmes to discover the truth of a crime. This jigsaw puzzle approach to solving crimes is readily illustrated by Holmes in two of his most famous short stores: "The Red-Headed League" (1891) and "The Adventure of the Six Napoleons" (1904). In each case, Holmes works out the criminal's *modus operandi*—his method (his system) of operation—and is able to catch the miscreant in the act by anticipating his next step. Holmes, his systemic thinking flawless, is able simply to wait in the dark, with the police at his side, for the criminal to show up. As Holmes advised in *The Valley of Fear* (1914), "Everything comes in circles. . . . The old wheel turns, and the same spoke comes up. It's all been done before, and will be again."

FROM CRIME TO BUSINESS

Now the question is, how did Sherlock Holmes, a consulting detective, give birth to the modern hodge-podge of business consultants of every stripe? Because Holmes shone the spotlight on the job description of a consulting detective, he extended the notion of what a consultant was and could do.

If the fictional police could call in the fictional Holmes to help solve a case, then it was that much more acceptable for a real company to call in a real consultant to solve a management problem. And the more famous Holmes became with each new published adventure, the more often this happened. From its tiny beginnings in 1893, modern management consulting increasingly extended its reach into industry in direct response to Holmes's phenomenal popularity.

According to Frederick W. Taylor's biographer, Robert Kanigel, in 1893 Taylor "set out on a new career, as a management consultant, still an oddball way to make a living. There were management consultants before Taylor, but no one called them that." When Taylor ordered his new letterhead to read "Frederick Taylor, Consulting Engineer in Management," he was—whether he realized it or not—following in the wake of Sherlock Holmes, who was already world famous as the first "consulting detective." Business people who had read about this "consulting detective" would be more likely to hire and feel more comfortable using a "consulting engineer in management." It was Holmes who first taught the world what to expect from and how to use a consultant.

Solving crimes and solving production bottlenecks call for the same kinds of intellectual skills. The science of deduction applies in both instances. In one case, actual criminals are sought; in the other, it is criminal waste and inefficiency that must be removed from the society of the factory. By doing the first, Holmes paved the way for the second.

Early management consultants, often known as efficiency experts, were every bit as enamored of scientific methods as was Holmes. Indeed, they labeled their techniques scientific management only after Holmes had been enormously famous as a scientific detective for two decades. Holmes was their inspiration: first, as an exemplar of the scientific approach to problem solving; but second, and equally important, as a model of what a consultant could do. Thus Holmes gave legitimacy and created opportunity to all of the real-life business consultants who followed in his wake. The scientific managers who plied their trade in the shadow of Holmes' notoriety were very much in his debt for making their mutual profession—generic consulting, if you will—acceptable to business leaders and the public as a viable and useful occupation.

Just as Frederick W. Taylor, the preeminent apostle sometimes called the "father" of scientific management, was able to demonstrate that workers using different-sized shovels were more efficient at moving differing weights of coal, Holmes delights us with his ability to solve his mysteries by also pointing to what eventually seems to be obvious.

THE TRUE FATHER OF SCIENTIFIC MANAGEMENT

Despite what you may have heard about Frederick W. Taylor being the father of scientific management, paternity belongs to the man whose inspiration gave life and energy to the movement toward greater industrial efficiency that continues today. That man, that character, is Sherlock Holmes.

Holmes sought to make solving crimes a science. His techniques bypassed his colleagues in the police, who were still using old-fashioned detective methods such as a roundup of the usual suspects. As Holmes asserted in *The Sign of the Four* (1889), "Detection is, or ought to be, an exact science and should be treated in the same cold and unemotional manner." Similarly, Taylor and his associates disdained informal work rules and procedures for a formal scientific approach to solving the problems of organization and production. Holmes disdained the informality of police methods just as Taylor and friends disdained informal work procedures. However, Holmes's disdain came first and was known throughout the world for decades before Taylor had a national audience for his views. The point here is that practically everybody who could read, knew of Holmes's approach to problem solving. Taylor essentially took Holmes's basic idea and applied it to business.

Looking at the illustrious career of Sherlock Holmes, it can be deduced, as Holmes might, that Conan Doyle's fictional consulting detective paved the way for the introduction of the theories of scientific management and birth of the management consultant as we know the position today. After all, these early twentieth-century management reformers were certainly detectives. Their goal, however, rather than eliminating crime, was eliminating "wanton, wicked waste," according to Harrington Emerson, the "high priest of efficiency" in the business efficiency movement. Waste, meaning wasted time caused by using inefficient methods, costs money, so reducing waste means higher profits and, eventually, higher wages for workers as well.

Emerson, the consultant who achieved enormous cash savings for the Santa Fe Railroad between 1904 and 1907, caused a national sensation in 1910 when he testified before the U.S. Interstate Commerce Commission (ICC) that the nation's railroads could save "$1,000,000 a day" if they adopted scientific management methods. Consequently, the government should not allow the railroads to raise their rates, because the savings that could be achieved by installing scientific management methods would make raising rates unnecessary.

It was this series of ICC hearings that first made Frederick W. Taylor and scientific management almost as famous as Sherlock Holmes. Until then Taylor was unknown to the general public, and scientific management, as a phrase, did not exist. The process, previously called "shop management" by Taylor in his 1905 book on the subject, had to be rebranded.

The group of efficiency experts led by Taylor and Emerson who were to testify against the railroad rate increase knew that shop management was too dull and too old a phrase. Attorney Louis D. Brandeis (later a U.S. Supreme Court Justice), who arranged for the experts to testify, knew that the term *shop management* would not elicit much excitement or much needed publicity for their cause. So shortly before the hearings, he had the experts meet and agree on a new phrase that would summarize the totality of their efforts toward greater industrial efficiency. Thus *scientific management* was born in 1910 as a catch-phrase in a public relations campaign. This systematic effort to find the "one best way" of accomplishing any given task by discovering the fastest, most efficient, and least fatiguing production methods, rapidly became a secular religion—at least among business leaders. Its methods, similar to those used by Holmes to solve crimes, became gospel, and Taylor, because of his extensive lecturing and writings, was their preeminent prophet.

Why did Taylor become the name preeminently associated with scientific management? He initially thought that the phrase was too academic-sounding and off-putting to practical businessmen, but once it became a national sensation, he quickly embraced it. He immediately did a cut-and-paste job on his earlier articles and speeches and produced a small book, *The Principles of Scientific Management* (1911), which became an instant and continuous worldwide best seller. *The Principles* contain not one word about Sherlock Holmes, but because the methods and ideas of Holmes were "in the air," they made the *Principles* all the more acceptable to the practical business people who were Taylor's audience and customers.

Holmes's enormous popularity helped blaze the trail for the acceptance of scientific management. That this connection has not been noticed before is analogous to a situation in "Silver Blaze" (1892), when Holmes refers to "the curious incident of the dog in the night-time." When his companion exclaims, "The dog did nothing in the night-time," Holmes replies, "That was the curious incident."

So it is with the link between Holmes and scientific management. Neither a dog nor anyone else has been barking about this connection. However, it becomes glaringly obvious once the facts of the case are examined. You should now be able to conclude, as Dr. Watson did in "The Stock-Broker's Clerk" (1893), that, "[l]ike all Holmes' reasoning the thing seemed simplicity itself when it was once explained." As Holmes asserted in "A Scandal in Bohemia" (1891), the problem may be that "you see, but you do not observe." Many readers will be thoroughly familiar with both the historical facts of scientific management and the fictional stories of Sherlock Holmes that comprise this case. Although you may have seen much, you may not have yet observed how they knit together.

Without the pipe-smoking man in the deerstalker hat, it seems beyond a reasonable doubt that the independent management consultant selling modern scientific management methods would have taken much longer to become an essential part of business and public administration. Our basic contention is that scientific management, meaning in effect all modern management, grew up in the shadow of and under the influence of Sherlock Holmes. And there it remains.

A CASE OF CIRCUMSTANTIAL EVIDENCE

Of course, the case for the considerable influence of Sherlock Holmes in the development of the movement toward modern management is inherently a circumstantial one. Circumstantial evidence does not bear directly on a case in the way that eyewitness evidence does. Instead, it focuses on the attendant circumstances from which a judge or jury may infer facts or conclusions. You, the reader, are the judge and jury in this case. You must ultimately decide if the circumstantial case is convincing and compelling.

There is no choice but to take a circumstantial approach when the principle witness is fictional and all the historic witnesses, the pioneers of the movement toward scientific management, are long dead. But fear not as you trod this circumstantial path. According to Holmes in "The Adventure of the Noble Bachelor" (1892), "Circumstantial evidence is occasionally very convincing, as when you find a trout in the milk, to quote Thoreau's example." Holmes is quoting from the November 11, 1850, entry of Henry David Thoreau's published *Journal*. In the nineteenth century it was not uncommon on both sides of the Atlantic Ocean for farmers to increase the amount of milk they had to sell by diluting what came from the cow with what came from a local river. A "trout in the milk" was thus strong circumstantial evidence that this had happened.

Holmes also warns, however, in "The Boscombe Valley Mystery" (1891), "Circumstantial evidence is a very tricky thing. It may seem to point very straight to one thing, but if you shift your own point of view a little, you may find it pointing in an equally uncompromising manner to something entirely different." For example, the "trout in the milk" might be marinating in preparation for cooking. Fortunately, you will find nothing fishy about the circumstantial evidence case linking Holmes with scientific management.

FOR DISCUSSION

Does this case give too much, too little, or just enough credit to Sherlock Holmes as the instigator of the methods that led to the scientific management movement? Are the systematic methods of investigation pioneered by Sherlock Homes as valid and relevant today as when they were first published more than a century ago?

BIBLIOGRAPHY

Booth, Martin. *The Doctor and the Detective: A Biography of Sir Arthur Conan Doyle.* New York: St. Martin's, 1997.

Carr, John Dickson. *The Life of Arthur Conan Doyle.* London: John Murray, 1949.

Conan Doyle, Sir Arthur. *The New Annotated Sherlock Holmes.* Edited by Leslie S. Klinger. New York: W. W. Norton, 2005.

Higham, Charles. *The Adventures of Conan Doyle: The Life of the Creator of Sherlock Holmes.* London: Hamilton, 1976.

Kanigel, Robert. *The One Best Way: Frederick Winslow Taylor and the Enigma of Efficiency.* New York: Penguin, 1997.

Miller, Russell. *The Adventures of Arthur Conan Doyle.* New York: St. Martin's, 2008.

Nordon, Pierre. *Conan Doyle: A Biography.* New York: Holt, Rinehart and Winston, 1967.

Stashower, Daniel. *Teller of Tales: The Life of Arthur Conan Doyle.* New York: Henry Holt, 1999.

Taylor, Frederick W. *The Principles of Scientific Management.* New York: Harper Bros., 1911.

Wrege, Charles, and Ronald G. Greenwood. *Frederick W. Taylor: The Father of Scientific Management, Myth and Reality.* Homewood, IL: Business One Irwin, 1991.

CHAPTER TWO

Muckrakers and Reformers to the Rescue

HOW THE PROGRESSIVE MOVEMENT CREATED MODERN PUBLIC ADMINISTRATION FROM THE MUCK OF CORRUPTION, INDIFFERENCE, AND IGNORANCE

PREVIEW

Muck is what animals leave behind from their behinds. As it accumulates, it becomes increasingly unpleasant, especially when it is in a confined space such as a stable. Muck happens! Therefore, it must be shoveled or raked out periodically.

Most people are familiar with muck because they have stepped in it or have had to put up with a lot of it, but few have been able to rise above it to see its strong historical relationship to public administration. To be specific, contemporary U.S. public administration, as both an academic discipline and a professional practice, has its origins in the early twentieth-century investigative journalism of a group of reporters known to history as the muckrakers.

This story starts in 1906, when President Theodore Roosevelt figuratively put a muck rake into the hands of those investigative journalists who were gaining ever-increasing fame for exposing government corruption. For inspiration, Roosevelt called on John Bunyan (1628–1688), an English preacher and notorious nonconformist (meaning he did not conform to the teachings of the Church of England), who, while serving time in jail for his nonconformity, wrote *Pilgrim's Progress* (1678), a religious allegory that for centuries was one of the most widely read books in the English-speaking Protestant world.

THE TREASON OF THE SENATE

In a speech on April 16, 1906, President Theodore Roosevelt used Bunyan to attack journalists who were stirring up so much muck that he was concerned that some of it might land on him. He was specifically upset with a series of nine articles that began in the February 17, 1906, issue of *Cosmopolitan*, which examined the pervasive corruption of the U.S. Senate. Freelance journalist David Graham Phillips wrote, "Treason is a strong word, but not too strong, rather too weak to characterize the situation in which the Senate is the eager, resourceful, indefatigable agent of interests as hostile to the American people as any invading army could be, and vastly more dangerous."

Phillips's series, later published in book form as *The Treason of the Senate* (1906), exposed the corporate links of U.S. senators, who earned significant sums by serving on boards of directors and then contended that these fees could not possibly influence their senate votes. Substitute campaign contributions for director's fees and the situation is not too different from today.

However, Phillips was not attacking corrupt big city political bosses as other reporters had done; he was assaulting the honesty and integrity of many of Roosevelt's closest personal friends and Republican political allies in the Senate. So Roosevelt, perhaps concerned that he would suffer guilt by association, spoke out against the "treason" argument. He suggested that people recall, from Bunyan's *Pilgrim's Progress*, "the description of the Man with the Muckrake, the man who could look no way but downward with the muckrake in his hand; who was offered a celestial crown for his muckrake but who could neither look up nor regard the crown he was offered but continued to rake to himself the filth of the floor."

Then Roosevelt called for a time-out. He suggested that things may have gone too far, because "muckraking leads to slander that may attack an honest man or even assail a bad man with untruth. An epidemic of indiscriminate assault upon character does no good but very great harm." He concluded that "men with the muckrake are often indispensable to the well-being of society, but only if they know when to stop raking the muck." This was essentially a plea for press self-censorship.

Roosevelt's appeal backfired. Not only did it not stop or delay the muckraking, it unintentionally gave these reporters their now immortal title and made more citizens than ever anxious to read their details of governmental muck. As for Phillips himself, he became the man credited with creating the demand for the direct election of senators. The thinking was that if senators were elected by the citizens instead of the state legislatures, they might feel a greater sense of obligation to public rather than corporate interests. We all know how well that has worked out! And Phillips did not live to see his handiwork triumph, when the Seventeenth Amendment to the U.S. Constitution, mandating the direct election of senators, was ratified in 1913. In an instance of individualized press censorship, he was gunned down in 1911 on the streets of New York City by a disgruntled reader. Muckraking could be dangerous work.

FROM MUCKRAKING TO REFORM

Who were those journalists who wrote the exposés of business and government corruption that so annoyed the President? Some of the most famous muckrakers were Lincoln Steffens (1866–1936), who, in *The Shame of the Cities* (1904), found big cities such as

Philadelphia to be "corrupt and contented"; Ida M. Tarbell (1857–1944), who exposed the monopolistic practices of John D. Rockefeller and forced the breakup of Standard Oil; and Upton Sinclair (1878–1968), whose exposure of the poisonous practices of the meatpacking industry in *The Jungle* (1906) led to the passage of the Pure Food and Drug Act of 1906. Today, anyone who writes an exposé of governmental corruption or incompetence might be called a muckraker. Today's muckrakers avoid the term, preferring to be called investigative journalists, but they continue the practice.

Muckraking reached its height during the first decade of the twentieth century, but its practices went back decades and came about because of two parallel developments: massive

Contemporary cartoon from the Utica, New York, *Saturday Globe,* of President Theodore Roosevelt taking hold of the investigating muckrake while holding his nose. The original caption read, "A nauseating job, but it must be done." The stink of the meat scandal originated with Upton Sinclair's muckraking novel, *The Jungle* (1906). The book exposed the meatpacking industry's tendency to put rotten, putrefying meat, along with rats who had died from poisoning, into sausage that was sold to the public. For flavoring, large globs of rat dung, filthy water, and the occasional human finger, sometimes a whole arm, were added to the mix. This expose caused such a sensation that, within months, the federal government was forced to pass the Pure Food and Drug Act of 1906, which initiated federal government inspection of food sold in the United States. President Roosevelt can be said to be holding his nose for two reasons: (1) to cope with the stench of the foul meat and (2) to express his disapproval of the muckrakers. After all, he gave them that name in the first place in an effort to discourage their investigations. It is ironic that circumstances then forced him to start raking with them!
Source: Culver Pictures, Inc.

government corruption and the advent of mass-circulation periodicals such as big city newspapers and national magazines. The most famous muckrakers all published chapters of their now classic books in magazines such as *McClure's*, *Collier's*, and *Cosmopolitan*. The first two of these general-interest magazines are long gone, but *Cosmopolitan* lives on, having reinvented itself as a journal of romance and sexual adventure for young women.

Modern U.S. public administration as an academic discipline has its origins in the muck dug up by the investigative journalist "rakers," who encouraged the political involvement of administrative reformers and who, in turn, created the educational programs needed to prepare experts to institutionalize their reforms. In short, the muckrakers led to the reform movement, which led to the progressive movement, which led to academic departments of public administration. This sounds neat—too neat. The true story is, as with so much of real life, quite messy.

THE REFORM MOVEMENT

The chronology of the post–Civil War reform era is easily delineated. A variety of specific events and documents provide a convenient framework for analysis. However, the motivations of those who led the reform movement remain cloudy, lending themselves to considerable speculation. Historians tend to agree that the leaders of the movement represented a socioeconomic class that was both out of power and decidedly antagonistic to those elements of society who were in power. In simplistic terms, it was the WASP (white Anglo-Saxon Protestant) patricians versus the ethnic plebeians. The social upheavals that accompanied the Civil War left in its wake what Richard Hofstadter, in *The Age of Reform* (1955), described as a displaced class of old gentry, professional men, and the civic leaders of an earlier time:

> In their personal careers, as in their community activities, they found themselves checked, hampered, and overridden by the agents of the new corporations, the corrupters of legislatures, the buyers of franchises, the allies of the political bosses. In this uneven struggle they found themselves limited by their own scruples, their regard for reputation, their social standing itself. To be sure, the America they knew did not lack opportunities, but it did seem to lack opportunities of the highest sort for men of the highest standards. In a strictly economic sense these men were not growing poorer as a class, but their wealth and power were being dwarfed by comparison with the new eminences of wealth and power. They were less important, and they knew it.

This displacement, this alienation, did much to establish the "ins" versus the "outs" pattern of the politics of reform. Because the reformers blamed the professional politicians for their own political impotence, they struck at the source of their political strength—the spoils system. *Spoils* refers to what a military victor traditionally takes from a defeated enemy. By analogy, the *spoils system* was the widespread practice of awarding government jobs to political supporters, the victors, as opposed to awarding them on the basis of merit. Both sides abided by the "system." Consequently, the campaign slogan of the party out of power was often "Throw the rascals out," when all they really meant was that it was time for a change of rascals. According to Ari Hoogenboom, in *Outlawing the Spoils* (1961), "As a weapon they [the alienated gentry] used civil service reform, which would convert the public service from partisanship to political neutrality." Thus neither side would be able to place rascals in office, because only gentlemen such as themselves would qualify.

President Ulysses S. Grant inadvertently accelerated the demand for reform when, upon obtaining office, he not only excluded the old gentry from patronage appointments but also denied office to the editors of influential newspapers and journals. This was in contrast to Lincoln's policy of courting the press by bestowing lavish patronage on them. As a result, the press of both parties started speaking out, started exposing corruption, started "muckraking," more strongly than ever before in favor of reform.

Grant, a West Point graduate and career military officer, knew a great deal about tents and camping out. Despite this, he was unable to grasp the traditional folk wisdom that it is "better to have them (potential political adversaries) inside the tent pissing out than outside the tent pissing in." So Grant inadvertently encouraged muckraking journalists and their publishers to thoroughly expose his administration. They did such a good job of pissing all over Grant's administration that it was commonly considered the most corrupt administration in U.S. history—until the administration of Richard M. Nixon "redeemed" Grant with an even more corrupt group of fellow travelers. At least Grant was personally honest; you could not say that about Nixon.

Of course, the huddled polyglot masses of the country's growing urban centers had little concern for reforming the public service at any level of government. A sincere concern for honesty in public service has always been a luxury reserved for the middle and upper classes. The masses of the urban poor care deeply about the integrity of public office only if it proves to have some measurable and immediate effect on their lives.

Although the reform impetus might strike some as being a radical departure, its origins were essentially conservative; the economic elite wanted nothing more than to be nobly obligated (*noblesse oblige*) to perform public service—and at the highest possible levels. Rudely denied this rite of passage in a gentleman's life, they embraced reform with the traditional zeal of new converts everywhere.

There is no way to ascertain exactly what particular factors engendered a reform impetus in any given individual, but there is no doubt that the reform proposals themselves tended to benefit one segment of society at the expense of another. Although the reformers first achieved success on the national level, the class basis of the reform impetus was essentially an urban phenomenon—WASP suburbanites, dismayed at what the ethnic hordes were doing to "their" city, called for reform. And they made their call in the newspapers and magazines that they owned. It was a call heard by anyone with a few pennies to buy sensational stories of crime, corruption, incompetence, and bad odors from the public sewers and in the public service.

SOCIAL ADVANCEMENT THROUGH PUBLIC SERVICE

Public service has always been used by ascending groups in U.S. society as a vehicle for social advancement. Inevitably accompanying such changes has been a large measure of friction, distrust, and hostility. The continuity of this process is unbroken to this day. In this regard, there is no significant difference between the successors of President Andrew Jackson deposing the aristocratically tinged civil service to replace them with loyalists of common origin and today's displacement of white ethnic municipal officials with black stalwarts. Each ascendant group had a similar problem during the time that they dominated local public office. The groups that were displaced were quite vocal in indicating that the insurgents were grossly corrupt and using public office largely for their private gain and for the advantage of their peers. Although such utterances were typically attributed to such factors as racism and religious prejudice, the foundation on which the remarks were made—the venality of public officeholders—is essentially sound. There is no doubt that each succeeding power group used public office to their private advantage. This trend continues today in many jurisdictions.

As each succeeding social group took advantage of whatever the local political process could offer, they advanced themselves socially, sent their children to college, and moved to the suburbs, leaving the machine and its style of politics to the next cycle of immigrants. Now both physically and generationally removed from the political atmosphere from which they benefited, they felt comfortable viewing the present inhabitants of the buildings in which they were born as socially and morally inferior. Safely middle class, they could now afford to be reformers—especially now that reform was to be at somebody else's expense. The cycle was complete; they now felt as strongly about "those" people in the city as an earlier group had felt about their grandparents.

BUSINESS INTERESTS STEP UP

As the U.S. economy expanded during the last half of the nineteenth century, the orientation of the business community became less and less focused on parochial interests bounded by the neighborhood and more and more oriented toward urban, regional, national, and international markets. Economic determinists could well argue that the death knell of the spoils system was sounded when the ineptness of government began to hamper the expansion of business. It is noteworthy in this respect that the federal government made some efforts to institute merit system concepts in both the New York Post Office and the New York Customs House several years before the passage of the Pendleton Act of 1883, which introduced the merit concept into federal service. These preliminary reform measures, limited as they were, were a direct result of pressure from a business community that had grown increasingly intolerant of ineptness in the postal service and extortion on the waterfront.

With the ever-present impetus of achieving maximum public services for minimum tax dollars, the businessman was quite comfortable supporting reform. Support for reform was just one of a variety of strategies employed by business interests to have power pass from the politicos to themselves. The political parties of the time were almost totally dependent for a financial base on assessments made on the wages of their members in public office. The party faithful had long been expected to kick back a percentage of their salary in order to retain their positions. A good portion of the Pendleton Act and parallel laws at the state and local levels were devoted to forbidding this and other related methods of extortion.

With the decline of patronage, the parties had to seek out new funding sources. Business interests, then as now, were more than quite willing to assume this new financial burden and its concomitant influence. A similar gambit used at the municipal level was to change the form of legislative representation from one that was ward-based to one that conducted elections on a city-wide basis, which usually required far more substantial campaign funds. The business interests had an even greater advantage if there was a nonpartisan ballot. So once the reformers obtained city-wide elections of legislatures on nonpartisan ballots, getting a government that reflected their interests was just a matter of time and money.

With the end of the Civil War and the abolition of slavery, the immorality of our governing institutions became the great moral issue that was to inspire countless muckraking journalists and opposition politicians. It is difficult if not impossible to separate the moralistic from the political motivations of people. One can never truly know where moral indignation over patronage abuses and incompetent government ended and a not-disinterested concern for denying a power base to hostile political incumbents began. Nevertheless, the reform movement gradually evolved into the progressive movement. Indeed, the terms tend to be used interchangeably. It is perhaps best to think of the reform movement as the more all-encompassing term, as an effort at political revitalization that started several decades earlier than the progressive movement and that eventually subsumed it.

THE PROGRESSIVE MOVEMENT

The muckraking journalists were part of the reform movement that began after the Civil War, but they are most associated with the Progressive movement. Formally, this is a designation applied to the U.S. experience with the consequences of urbanization and industrialization that affected Western society in the decades between 1890 and 1920. Although the term has its origins in religious concepts that argued for the infinite improvability of the human condition rather than ordained class distinctions, by the end of the nineteenth century it had come to mean a religiously inspired responsibility of classes for one another and a willingness to use all government and social institutions to give that responsibility legal effect.

To a large extent the movement was a reaction to social Darwinism, Charles Darwin's (1809–1882) concept of biological evolution applied to the development of human social organization and economic policy. The major influence on U.S. social Darwinism was an Englishman, Herbert Spencer (1820–1903), who spent much of his career working out the application of concepts such as "natural selection" and "survival of the fittest" to his ideas of social science.

U.S. social Darwinists, generally speaking, held a wide range of theories, from an absolute rejection of the idea of government intervention in social development (meaning let the poor fend for themselves) to elaborate methods of developmental influence that could affect the various races into which they believed all humans, even Europeans, were divided (meaning let's educate the poor only well enough so that they can be servants and factory workers). The progressive movement was to a large extent an antidote to, and a repudiation of, the doctrines of social Darwinism.

In the United States, the progressive movement was most associated with the search for greater democratic participation by the individual in government, and the application of science and specialized knowledge and skills to the improvement of life. Politically, the movement reached its national climax in 1911, with the creation of the Progressive Party as an alternative to both the Republican Party professionals, who backed the incumbent, William Howard Taft (the only person to be both President of the United States [1909–1913] and Chief Justice of the Supreme Court [1921–1930]), and the Republican opponents of political machine politics and party regularity, who nominated former Republican President Theodore Roosevelt. The split in the Republican Party caused the Democratic candidate, Woodrow Wilson, to be elected in 1912. Wilson in fact represented many of the programs the progressives had supported (banking reforms, antitrust laws, and business regulation), but he did not support many of the progressive interests in national social policy (meaning he was an unabashed racist and hostile to the interests of African Americans).

The Progressives got their name from the fact that they believed in the doctrine of progress—that governing institutions could be improved by bringing science to bear on public problems. It was a disparate movement, with each reform group targeting a level of government, a particular policy, and so on. Common beliefs included that good government was possible and that "the cure for democracy is more democracy." And to achieve this, they only had to "throw the rascals out." At the national level, they achieved civil service reform, introduced the direct primary (an election in which political party nominees are selected directly by the voters), the initiative (a procedure that allows citizens, as opposed to legislators, to propose by ballot proposition the enactment of state or local laws), the referendum (a procedure for submitting proposed laws or state constitutional amendments to the voters for ratification), and the recall (a procedure that allows citizens to vote officeholders out of office between regularly scheduled elections). At the local level, they also spawned the commission and council-manager forms of government. Although the Progressive movement sought to offer solutions to many vexing social problems, these problems were often first identified and dug up by the muckrakers. And it was the Progressive influence that initially forged the fledgling discipline of public administration.

A DANGEROUS PROFESSION

Lincoln Steffens, arguably the single most influential of the muckrakers, got his start in the muck from what now would be called "tough love." Because his father was a prosperous West Coast businessman, Steffens was able to study first at the University of California, Berkeley; then on to Germany at the universities in Berlin, Heidelberg, and Leipzig; and then a further year of study in Paris and London. Finally back in New York he received a letter from his father that Steffens quotes in his *Autobiography* (1931): "By now you must know about all there is to know of the theory of life, but there's a practical side as well. It's worth knowing. I suggest that you learn it, and the way to study it, I think is to stay in New York and hustle." The father enclosed a check for $100 (then a substantial sum) and wished his son well in becoming self-supporting.

This admonition to "stay in New York and hustle" is one of the most succinct and best-known snippets of career advice in U.S. history. Because Steffens was so thoroughly overeducated and dressed so much like a European gentleman, he found it almost impossible to get any sort of suitable employment. In desperation, he accepted a job as a newspaper reporter, in 1892 a somewhat low-status occupation fit only for literary hustlers. Spurred on by a wife and new child, no one hustled better.

Ten years later he joined the staff of *McClure's Magazine* and inadvertently started muckraking when he crafted an article on corruption in St. Louis, where every vote by the city council was determined by a political boss who sold those votes to the highest bidder. None of this was secret, but local reporters could not write of it without fear for their lives. After "Tweed Days in St. Louis" was published in the October 1902 issue of *McClure's,* letters poured into the magazine with horror stories of corruption in other cities. Thus, subsequent articles exposed malfeasance in Minneapolis, Pittsburgh, Philadelphia, Chicago, and New York. When a collection of seven of these articles was published as *The Shame of the Cities* (1904), muckraking had its epic tome and would-be municipal reformers had their cause.

Steffens's lurid accounts of evil doings in the big city were followed by similar accounts by less well known scribblers. They showed that problems in one city were typically paralleled in others. On the whole, the articles created a sense of alarm, calls for a new sense of civic mindedness, and an end to "bossism." Steffens wrote in his *Autobiography* (1931) that "I did not intend to be a muckraker; I did not know I was one till President Roosevelt picked the name out of Bunyan's *Pilgrims Progress* and pinned it on us." Nevertheless, it was the work of Steffens and his kind that fostered the early developers of modern public administration by throwing so much light on a problem that it proved impossible for the civic-minded members of the community not to take action.

THE ADVENT OF PROFESSIONAL PUBLIC ADMINISTRATION

The reform movement that was part of the overall progressive effort developed a tactic to shed light on social problems. Private nonprofit organizations such as Hull House (founded in 1889; this was the best known of the "settlement houses," organizations run by the middle class for the benefit of the poor in Chicago) and the Institute of Public Administration (a private research organization founded in 1906 as the New York Bureau of Municipal Research, in New York City) conducted formal, methodological rigorous investigations of poor, often immigrant communities. The information gained from such social surveys was used to make policy recommendations for ameliorating the social and urban ills brought to light by the investigations. However, no matter how accurate and telling the social surveys were, nothing could be done to change conditions until government got involved.

Unfortunately, government, particularly bossism (an informal system of local government in which public power is concentrated in the hands of a central figure, called a political boss, who may not have a formal government position) of the day, was a big part of the problem. So the survey technique was turned on the bosses themselves in order to spur reform. According to Camilla Stivers (1998), "The first such investigation was launched in 1906 by the newly formed New York Bureau of Municipal Research. Blocked by Tammany Hall [a building in New York City, named after a Delaware Indian chief, whose name became a symbol of political machines because the New York County Democrats met in the building] from digging into municipal finance and accounting practices, the bureau decided to conduct an outdoor survey of city street cleaning and repair." Their results "documented the shocking state of the streets, marshaled evidence of the need for better administrative methods, and led to the forced resignation of the Manhattan borough president."

This was a different kind of muckraking, but muckraking nonetheless. Instead of reporters digging up scandals, there were structured studies of efficiency, really, studies (called surveys) of the current inefficiencies in government. This is why, public administration is derived from the scientific management movement, which was famously obsessed with efficiency and with finding the "one best way" of organizing work.

The success of this technique of embarrassing the bosses was quickly duplicated in other major cities: Philadelphia, Cincinnati, Chicago, Milwaukee, Minneapolis, Kansas City, and San Francisco among others. By 1916 there were twenty of these private bureaus, many inspired by the New York Bureau and often staffed by its former members. The bureaus were financially supported by businessmen, who realized that a more efficient government was not only a good thing in itself but would mean lower taxes on their municipal properties. For example, the work of the New York Bureau was initially funded by Andrew Carnegie and John D. Rockefeller, arguably the two wealthiest businessmen in the United States at the time. These bureaus had a variety of names. For example, Chicago had a Bureau of Public Efficiency, Detroit had a Bureau of Governmental Research, Los Angles had an Efficiency Commission, and Kansas City had a Public Service Institute.

The effects of the private municipal research bureaus led directly to the beginning of professional education in public administration. Jane Dahlberg, in her history of the New York Bureau of Municipal Research (1966), observes that the programs created to train people to conduct these reform-minded surveys evolved into the graduate programs in public administration that we have today. Indeed, the first such degree programs, at the University of Michigan (1914), Syracuse University (1924), and the University of Southern California (1928), were heavily staffed by people from the survey movement. And public policy studies (while always a part of history, political science, and law) were especially well nurtured by these and many other public administration programs.

For more than a hundred years now, academic and professional public administration has been nurtured by reformers and muckrakers. They have found institutional homes in newspapers, in academic departments, and in "good government" research organizations. As each new means of corrupting public office has been tried, it has, generally speaking, been exposed and forestalled. This is a never-ending cycle. Like zombies that never die, the corruptors still walk, and steal, among us. They must be found out and killed off, administratively speaking. Now it is your turn, dear reader, to jump into the circle, to continue with reform. Surely you did not accept or do not aspire to, a career in public service just to maintain the status quo. You must want to make things better. Therefore, you are a reformer who metaphorically has the blood of these early muckrakers and scientific management efficiency experts in your veins.

Always remember that the idealism associated with public administration goes far beyond the individual. The goal is the mystical one of building "a city upon a hill," an ideal

Two "street arabs" from Jacob A. Riis's *How the Other Half Lives* (1890). Riis was a muckraker with a camera. He documented the conditions in the slums of New York City with heart-wrenching photographs. Homeless, unwanted children known as "street arabs" (because they were urban nomads) roamed the streets by day pursuing careers of petty crime and slept in alleys and doorways at night. The boys in this photo are brothers, ten-year-old John and eight-year-old Willie. When they were picked up by the police, they said they "didn't live nowhere," had never gone to school, and could not read or write. Riis wrote that they had a twelve-year-old sister who "kept house for the father, who turned the boys out to beg, or steal, or starve." Riis's documentation of this "homeless army" of children helped foster charitable and governmental efforts to alleviate their plight. With his photographs of the conditions of the poor, he excelled at the primary tactic of the muckrakers and political reformers—putting the problem in the face of the middle class and politicians so that it could no longer be ignored.
Source: © Jacob August Riis/CORBIS. All rights reserved.

political community thoroughly fit for others to observe as an example. This phrase comes from John Winthrop, governor of the Massachusetts Bay Colony. In 1630 he wrote, "For we must consider that we shall be as a city upon a hill. The eyes of all people are upon us." This is a famous statement in Massachusetts history, and both Presidents John F. Kennedy and Ronald Reagan favored using it in speeches. It also illustrates how the nondenominational religious elements of public administration allow participants to gain satisfaction by becoming involved with an issue greater than themselves. Like it or not, the future of public administration, the fate of that "city upon a hill," is in your hands. Don't muck it up!

FOR DISCUSSION

Why were the classic muckrakers so influential in their own time and continue to be an inspiration to each new generation of reporters and public administrators? If you were given a budget and staff to investigate inefficiencies in your local government, where would you start to rake the muck with your own brand of survey research?

BIBLIOGRAPHY

Bausum, Ann. *Muckrakers.* Washington, DC: National Geographic, 2007.

Dahlberg, Jane. *The New York Bureau of Municipal Research: Pioneer in Government Administration.* New York: New York University Press, 1966.

Griffith, Ernest S. *A History of American City Government: The Progressive Years and Their Aftermath 1900–1920.* New York: Praeger, 1974.

Hofstadter, Richard. *The Age of Reform.* New York: Vintage Books, 1955.

——. *The American Political Tradition.* New York: Vintage Books, 1948.

Hoogenboom, Ari. *Outlawing the Spoils.* Urbana, IL: University of Illinois Press, 1961.

Miraldi, Robert, ed. *The Muckrakers: Evangelical Crusaders,* Westport, CT: Praeger, 2000.

Mosher, Frederick C., ed. *American Public Administration: Past, Present, Future.* University, AL: University of Alabama Press, 1976.

Riis, Jacob A. *How the Other Half Lives.* New York: Scribner's, 1890.

Shafritz, Jay M. *Public Personnel Management: The Heritage of Civil Service Reform.* New York: Praeger, 1975.

Steffens, Lincoln. *The Shame of the Cities.* New York: McClure, 1904.

——. *Autobiography.* New York: Harcourt, Brace, 1931.

Stivers, Camilla. "Municipal Research Bureaus." In *International Encyclopedia of Public Policy and Administration,* edited by Jay M. Shafritz. Boulder, CO: Westview Press, 1998.

——. "Survey Method." In *International Encyclopedia of Public Policy and Administration,* edited by Jay M. Shafritz. Boulder, CO: Westview Press, 1998.

Tarbell, Ida M. *The History of Standard Oil Company.* New York: Norton, 1966.

Weinberg, Arthur, and Lila Weinberg, eds. *The Muckrakers.* Urbana: University of Illinois Press, 1961.

CHAPTER THREE

The Case for Understanding the Critical Role of Doctrine in Public Policy Making

"SEEING" POLICY EVOLVE THROUGH THE LENSES OF THE DOCTRINAL DEVELOPMENT CYCLE

PREVIEW

Every aspect of human endeavor, from acting to zookeeping, has its philosophy, its fundamental beliefs that form its core of understanding. However, all philosophy is inherently intellectual. It is just a way of thinking. To actually do something with it, to turn thought into action or to make a policy, you need doctrine. A *doctrine* is a teaching. Note that it has the same Latin origins as *doctor* (originally a teacher). Doctrine is a mediating force between philosophy and policy. This case explains how doctrine takes philosophy, often so vague and theoretical, and makes it operational so that specific policies can be derived from it. Thus doctrine consists of the fundamental principles of how lives are to be lived or how things are to be done. However, it always reflects an underlying philosophy—whether of a political party, a religion, or an organization. When it is codified, it becomes a political party's platform, a religion's book of scripture, or an organization's manual of standard operating procedures. When things are to be done "by the book," it means that the doctrine—as written and as subdivided into lots of policies—is to be followed without deviation.

THE DOCTRINE OF REPUBLICANISM

Doctrine determines policy. A public policy is the implementation of a subset of a governing doctrine. The governing doctrine is necessarily an ideology, a comprehensive set of political beliefs about the nature of people and society. It is perhaps best thought of as an organized collection of ideas about the best way for people to live and about the most appropriate institutional arrangements for their societies. The term *ideology* first arose during the French Revolution of 1789 to refer to a school of thought, separate from religion, about how society should be managed.

In the United States, the governing doctrine is republicanism. Note the small "r." After all the speeches are made, after all the negative ads have appeared on TV, after all the soft money has been spent, and after all the votes have been counted, some people are elected. If they are elected as executives (president, governor, mayor, etc.), they can, upon taking office, make policy within their sphere of constitutional discretion. If they are elected as legislators, they join with other members of the assembly to make or obstruct policy. The whole point of the modern democratic process is to designate people to make policy—to make decisions—on behalf of their polity. Without the ritual of selection—of election—the process cannot be democratic. It is this ritual that gives the ultimately promulgated policies their legitimacy in the eyes of the people.

The founders of the United States were rightly suspicious of pure democracy because time and again throughout history, pure democracies degenerated into dictatorial tyrannies. This concern is as worrying today as it was then. Fareed Zakaria, the editor of *Newsweek International*, uses the term "illiberal [meaning nonfree] democracy" to describe the problematic democracies of the modern era, where elected leaders such as those, for example, in Russia and Venezuela, are regularly "ignoring constitutional limits on their power and depriving their citizens of basic rights." Elections alone will not guarantee a society's freedom. Something more is needed. And that thing, in the case of the United States, has been a strong republican governing structure.

President John Adams wrote in an April 15, 1814, letter, "Remember, democracy never lasts long. It soon wastes, exhausts, and murders itself. There never was a democracy yet that did not commit suicide." This well-justified fear of mobocracy led Adams and the other founders to create a republic, a form of government one step removed from democracy, which presumably protects the people from their own passions. In effect, what the founders bequeathed to the people of the United States was a doctrinal republican solution (the U.S. Constitution) to the problems posed by the adoption of democratic rule.

FROM DOCTRINE TO POLICY

Although doctrine is an extension of a broader philosophy, policy is derived from doctrine. For example, in some states, convicted murderers are executed; in others, they are sentenced to long prison terms. Some states allow for abortion on demand; in others it is severely restricted. Some states have high taxes and extensive public services; while others have lower tax rates and fewer public services. These actions, these results, these policies are all reflective of a governing doctrine, which, in turn, is derived from a political philosophy.

The relationship among philosophy, doctrine, and policy is shown in Figure 3.1.

Philosophy always comes first, because doctrine is derived from it; and, in turn, policy is derived from doctrine. However, doctrine is not immutable. It constantly

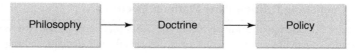

Figure 3.1 The Doctrinal Template

evolves, albeit sometimes very slowly, to reflect changing circumstance. Doctrine is always a response to historical experiences. Thus it becomes the common starting point for its revision. An inherent danger of doctrine is that it can eventually acquire a dogmatic status that resists changes that must be made to accommodate new technologies or new social conditions. This can have a constipating effect on the policy process—new policies must await a change in doctrine. This situation is illustrated in Figure 3.2, which takes the theoretical relationships in Figure 3.1 and makes them specific.

It is doctrine that establishes the principles of a political party and motivates its voters and supporters. Once it is in power, the party will seek to bend existing government programs, and create new ones, to reflect its doctrinal beliefs. In the United States, the most prevalent political philosophies are those of the Republican and Democratic Parties. The Republican Party has long been considered the conservative party in U.S. politics. Republicans tend to favor increased spending on defense, decreased spending on domestic programs, and a general reduction in the size of government by curtailing government regulation and privatizing selected government programs. The modern Democratic Party has had a reputation for being liberal, for appealing to low-income groups, for expanding civil rights protections, and for believing that government is a legitimate vehicle for solving social problems.

The doctrines of a political party are to be found in its platform, a statement of basic principles put forth at its national convention, to be adopted by its candidates in the election campaign. The platform, which does not formally bind either the party or its candidates, also contains specific short-term goals or proposals for legislation, known as planks. The planks of a party's political platform are often hotly contested at a national

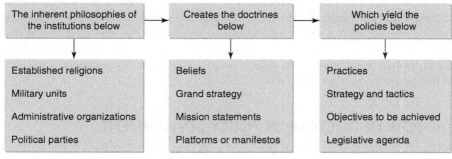

Figure 3.2 The Doctrinal Template with Specific Examples

Table 3.1 Comparing Political Party Platform Doctrines

Listed here are the essence of some planks of the 2008 platforms of the two major U.S. political parties. Note how each position on an issue reflects a doctrine calling for radically different policies.

Issue	*Republican Position*	*Democratic Position*
Abortion	Constrained as possible	Generally available
Tax cuts	Lower for all taxpayers	Lower for the middle class, higher for upper-level incomes
Affirmative action	End preferential treatment	Continue preferences
Social security	Restructure with individual investment accounts	Retain current system
Health care	Minimal Role for federal government	Expanded role for federal government
Homosexual rights	Opposes same-sex marriage	Supports same-sex marriage
Illegal immigrants	Should not be eligible for government benefits	Should be eligible for some government benefits

convention, as party ideologues seek to nail down their favorite planks and supporters of the likely nominees strive to make it so general that it will have wide appeal. Those who believe that "there's not a dime's worth of difference" between the two major parties should read their platforms. For example, the Republicans are pro-life, against minimum wage increases, and opposed to new taxes. The Democrats are pro-choice; want indexing applied to minimum wages, and are more open to raising taxes—especially on the wealthy. Table 3.1 presents more of their differences.

The ideals of a platform are often given a name that summarizes their intentions. For example, the New Deal refers to domestic programs and policies of the administration of President Franklin D. Roosevelt. The phrase comes from his acceptance speech at the Democratic National Convention on July 2, 1932, when he said, "I pledge to you, I pledge myself, to a new deal for the American people." The New Deal marked the beginning of "big government" in the United States. Its domestic programs, such as Social Security, minimum wages, child labor prohibitions, and government regulation of business, are now part of the fabric of U.S. life.

THE ROLE OF DOCTRINE IN POLICY DEVELOPMENT

All public policies have their origin in an underlying doctrine. This has been true throughout history. For example, among the first policy-related doctrines were maxims that had to do with the management of armies in peacetime and their deployment in wartime. Thus Confucius (551–479 BCE) in ancient China warned that "To lead an untrained people to war is to throw them away." Renatus Vegetius (fourth century CE), a contemporary analyst of the Roman army, reinforced this dicta: "Reason will convince us that what is necessary to be performed in the heat of action should constantly be practiced in the leisure of peace." This is no different than what is taught today.

Doctrine, which encompasses and provides direction for strategy, tactics, and principles, is a state's (or any large organization's) operating philosophy of policy development and administration—the accepted notions of how things are to be done. Doctrine is the tenets, principles, and practices that are turned to in times of uncertainty. It is the general theory that can be applied to practical problems. However, it is misleading to equate doctrine with theory. A theory, whether in politics or biology, is a body of principles that one can use to find solutions to new problems. A doctrine, in contrast, offers "correct" answers to anticipated problems. Thus the doctrines of a political party "dictate" the correct answers—meaning policies—to specific problems. If the problem is poverty, the Democrats may want more government welfare spending and the Republicans may want tax incentives for businesses to hire marginal workers. Both have the same goal (less poverty), but their doctrines offer differing policy solutions.

LEADING WITH DOCTRINE

Doctrine is a useful synonym for policy, but it is only used for policies of great import and as a way of signaling a nation's intentions. Nations, not individuals, lead with doctrine. By announcing to the world their policies and/or intentions, they seek to deter others from interfering with their vital interests. The first major use of the word in this context was the Monroe Doctrine, the assertion by President James Monroe in his 1823 State of the Union message that the Western Hemisphere was closed to colonization by European powers. In return, the United States promised not "to interfere in the internal concerns" of Europe. It takes only the slightest knowledge of World Wars I and II to realize that this was a promise that was not kept.

When a doctrine is revised and added to, the new policy may be known as a corollary. For example, there is a Roosevelt corollary to the Monroe Doctrine. This is President Theodore Roosevelt's assertion in his message to Congress of December 6, 1904, that "In the Western hemisphere the adherence of the United States to the Monroe Doctrine may force the United States, however reluctantly, in flagrant cases of wrongdoing or impotence, to the exercise of an international police power." Roosevelt, thus, extended Monroe's original prohibition against European intervention to include an assertion that the United States had the right to intervene in internal matters to end "chronic wrongdoing." Using this corollary, every U.S. president from Theodore Roosevelt to Calvin Coolidge dispatched U.S. Marines to Latin American or Caribbean nations.

Doctrinal policies, once rare, multiplied rapidly after World War II. The 1947 Truman Doctrine to resist Communist encroachment in Greece and Turkey was followed by the 1957 Eisenhower Doctrine, which originated when President Dwight Eisenhower requested congressional authority to provide military and economic aid to countries in the Middle East. This doctrine was later used as the legal basis for the U.S. intervention during the 1958 Lebanese Insurrection and differs from other presidential doctrines in that it was formally adopted as a joint resolution of the Congress.

The Johnson Doctrine was the rationale used by the administration of President Lyndon Johnson to justify its military intervention in the 1965–1966 Dominican Civil War. President Johnson claimed the "unilateral right of the United States to intervene militarily in any sovereign state of the hemisphere if . . . states were in danger of falling to the communists." Teddy Roosevelt would have approved.

The Nixon Doctrine was a policy enunciated in 1969 that sought to minimize the role of the United States as world policeman. The central thesis of the doctrine is that "America cannot—and will not—conceive all the plans, design all the programs, execute all the decisions and undertake all the defense of the free nations of the world. We will help where it makes a real difference and is considered in our interest." The Nixon Doctrine is best understood as an attempt to come to terms with the limits of U.S. power while avoiding a retreat into isolationism.

President Jimmy Carter's doctrine was announced in his 1980 State of the Union address to Congress: "An attempt by any outside forces to gain control of the Persian Gulf region will be regarded as an assault on the vital interests of the United States of America, and such as an assault will be repelled by any means necessary, including military force." The press labeled the statement the Carter Doctrine and characterized it as a reversal of the Nixon Doctrine. The policy was directed at the Soviets, because only they represented "any outside force" capable of gaining control of the Persian Gulf.

The Reagan Doctrine was the policy of President Ronald Reagan's administration (in conjunction with the Congress) of militarily supporting guerrilla insurgencies against Communist governments in Third World countries, such as Afghanistan, Angola, Cambodia, and Nicaragua. With the end of the Cold War and the demise of the Soviet Union, neither President George H. W. Bush nor President Bill Clinton felt the need to announce a major foreign policy doctrine. After all, the core purpose of an announced doctrine is to deter—and it seemed for a while there was nobody left to deter. Then came September 11, 2001, and once again a doctrine, the (George W.) Bush Doctrine, was called on to cope with new adversaries.

DEVIATING FROM DOCTRINE

Doctrine should not be followed slavishly. Policy makers and managers are expected to use their own experiences to deviate from established doctrine when that deviation will get the job done. Creative deviation is often the essence of leadership.

This can be illustrated by applying our doctrinal template shown in Figure 3.1 to a famous example. Prior to the Great Depression of the 1930s, the underlying philosophy of the U.S. economic system was capitalism. Its doctrine was *laissez-faire* (a hands-off style of governance), which led to a policy of noninterference with the ups and downs of the natural business cycle. This can now be applied to our doctrinal template, as shown in Figure 3.3.

The Depression was such a huge shock to the U.S. economy and political system, however, that President Franklin D. Roosevelt espoused the doctrine of the New Deal,

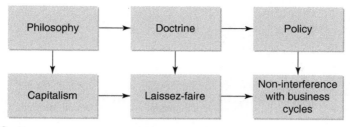

Figure 3.3 Economic Doctrine Prior to the New Deal

which led to welfare-state policies such as Social Security and the government regulation of business. This changed the schematic to one like that shown in Figure 3.4.

Of course, our schematic is a simplification of reality. Things as large as a national economy are always far more complicated than can be shown on a single diagram. Nevertheless, the schematic does illustrate the critical role that doctrine plays in policy development. The New Deal did permanently modify the nature of capitalism in the United States, by implementing literally hundreds of programs that led to policies that continue to influence the national economy.

Another example is President Harry S. Truman's doctrine of containment, which began in the late 1940s. This eventually led to the defeat of worldwide communism—even though it took another forty years. Its essence can be illustrated using our schematic as in Figure 3.5.

The useful thing about our schematic is that it can be applied to all policies. Just as all children must have biological parents, all policies are derived from doctrines that, in turn, originated in philosophies. The reason it is useful to think in terms of our schematic is that the thinking can go in either direction. If you know the policy, you can usually figure out where and how it originated. If you know the philosophy, you can usually predict the policies that will come from it.

Not all doctrines have catchy names that function as an overall label for a series of diplomatic, military, and/or legislative initiatives. Thus President Richard Nixon had lots of doctrinal names for individual problems: *détente* with the Soviet Union, *rapprochement* with China, and "Vietnamization" as a way of ending U.S. involvement in the Vietnam War.

Figure 3.4 New Deal Economic Doctrine

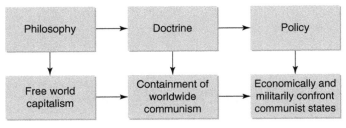

Figure 3.5   President Truman's Doctrine of Containment

Doctrines are seldom pure. Usually they contain varying elements of administrative reform, ideological zeal, religious fervor, and political cunning all wrapped up in a public relations package that makes them more attractive to the citizenry than would otherwise be the case. This is how the fascism of Nazi Germany and the communism of the Soviet Union were sold to the world. Genuine democracies avoid this trap because their doctrines are continuously being challenged by the loyal opposition, a free press, and an informed citizenry. Thus doctrine is always evolving in response to the political process and new research into the effectiveness of current programs.

The overarching terms for research into the efficacy of public policies that are derived from any given doctrine are policy analysis and program evaluation. Indeed, it could be argued that policy analysis itself has a doctrine. It is from the work of Jeremy Bentham that we trace the now often espoused doctrine of policy analysis: that government should strive to achieve the "greatest happiness for the greatest number." Now, happiness as a goal may sound a bit flip until you remember that the 1776 Declaration of Independence states that the United States was created in part so that its citizens would have the "unalienable right" to "life, liberty and the pursuit of happiness." Happiness is a most serious business as far as public policy goes.

THE DOCTRINAL DEVELOPMENT CYCLE

Doctrines resemble the paradigms of Thomas S. Kuhn (1922–1996). In his landmark book, *The Structure of Scientific Revolutions* (1970), Kuhn explained that as the natural sciences progressed, they amassed a body of ever-changing theory. Scientific advances were not based on the accumulation of knowledge and facts, but rather on a dominant paradigm (or model) used in any specific period to explain the phenomena under study. Rather than refuting previous theories, each paradigm would build on the body of relevant knowledge and theories. Once a paradigm was accepted by consensus among current scholars, it would last as long as it remained useful. Ultimately it would be displaced by a more relevant and useful paradigm; this process of replacement was Kuhn's "scientific revolution."

Kuhn first discovered his paradigms when he, as a graduate student in physics at Harvard, was asked to teach a course on the history of science for undergraduates. He realized that he had "never read an old document in science." After reviewing Aristotle's

Physics, he was startled to find how unlike it was to Isaac Newton's concepts of physics. Aristotle offered not an earlier version of Newton but an entirely different way of looking at the fundamentals of mass, speed, and gravity. This led Kuhn to conclude that science is not a steady, step-by-step, ever-upward accumulation of knowledge. Rather, as he explains in *The Structure,* it is "a series of peaceful interludes punctuated by intellectually violent revolutions." And when those revolutions occur, "one conceptual world view is replaced by another." The individuals who create such breakthroughs by inventing a new paradigm are "almost always . . . either very young or very new to the field whose paradigm they change. . . . These are the men [and women] who, being little committed by prior practice to the traditional rules of normal science, are particularly likely to see that those rules no longer define a playable game and to conceive another set that can replace them." This is why, the physics of Newton is so radically different from that of Aristotle. Newton's ideas didn't expand on those of Aristotle. Newton supplanted them with totally new ideas.

Although paradigms have their own time frames and contents, they overlap both in time and content because they are constantly evolving. In a parallel sense, doctrinal development in public policy and administration has been inherently cyclical. A successful innovation by reformers is followed by a period of increased effectiveness; at least until competing organizations adopt similar reforms. Over time, however, advancing technologies and changing environments allow the innovation to deteriorate relative to other arrangements, first to become less competent, then to become incompetent. After an innovative change remedies the problem, the cycle of competence and incompetence repeats. This "time lag" phenomenon is similar to the traditional boom-and-bust business cycle, with incompetence occurring when the cycle is in recession. Thus maintaining organizational competence is a never-ending struggle. And an understanding of this cycle is the key to understanding the ebb and flow of public policies. Doctrinal analysis goes beyond policy analysis because it analyzes not specific policies but how all policies rise and fall, live and die, are competent and then less than competent.

EVER-EVOLVING DOCTRINAL INNOVATIONS

Every doctrinal innovation designed to remedy previous incompetence, no matter how successful, contains within itself the seeds of future incompetence. This is similar to historian Arnold J. Toynbee's (1889–1975) view of military effectiveness following "a cycle of invention, triumph, lethargy and disaster." The "invention" is a new organizing doctrine, a new policy doctrine, or a doctrine for using a new technology. Thus incompetence occurs after an innovation grows old—becomes "lethargic"—and allows an organization's capabilities to lag behind those of competing organizations. This is eventually what happened to ancient Rome. This is why, Rome first rose—because it was extraordinarily innovative and thus effective in its military and administrative institutions, but then fell—because it lost the ability to be as administratively competent or militarily innovative as its competition.

This cyclical nature of doctrinal and policy development explains why competing organizations—whether armies, governments, or corporations—tend to look like each

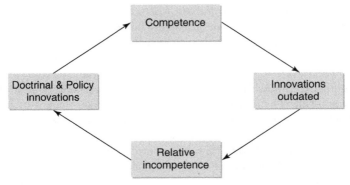

Figure 3.6 The Cyclical Nature of Doctrinal and Policy Development

other over time. Whenever an innovation earns a reputation for being successful, it is copied by others wishing to be equally successful. However, equality in structure and equipment is not always enough to ensure being a successful competitor. A famous example will illustrate. During the spring of 1940, Nazi Germany conquered France using tanks, planes, and troops in a *Blitzkreig* formation. Germany won despite the fact that France had not only more troops but also significantly more tanks that were of better quality. What made the difference was the fact that the Germans had a better doctrine for the use of their tanks—a doctrine they got from British and French officers whose innovative ideas on how tanks should be used were largely ignored in their own countries. So it didn't do the French much good in 1940 to make sure that they had more tanks than the Germans. The French only superficially reflected the German strength in tanks. True strength was in the doctrine on how to use tanks—in massed assaults as opposed to piecemeal support for infantry.

Just as tanks got a new paradigm when they were first used in massed assaults, so, too, with naval aviation. The world's navies first used aircraft by adding them to traditional battleships—catapults launched seaplanes, which could be hoisted back on board. In this role they were just extended lookouts. According to James Q. Wilson (1989), "The organizational innovation occurred when aviation was recognized as a new form of naval warfare and the aircraft were massed on carriers deployed in fast-moving task forces." Figure 3.6 illustrates the rise and fall of doctrinal competence.

THE DOCTRINAL TEMPLATE

Public policy can best be understood within its doctrinal context. To a large extent, doctrine is destiny, in both the intellectual and real worlds. Thus academic disciplines and the specializations within them have their own peculiar doctrinal lenses through which they see the policy world. Behaviorists in political science and the idealists in international relations all view the policy world from their unique perspectives. These doctrines often predispose what they see and consequently what policies they advocate.

Similarly, the real world of political doctrine often makes liberals see one thing and conservatives another when they are viewing the identical problem. For example, and overgeneralizing to make the point, liberals see rising crime rates and think government should create more public works jobs and expand welfare programs. Conservatives see the same thing and think that government should hire more police and build more prisons. Sometimes a doctrinal belief is upset by reality. This is illustrated by the saying that "a conservative is a liberal who has been mugged."

There are many examples of how new doctrinal paradigms have led to new policies. New thinking about how to defend the United States in its war on terrorism has led to the adoption of a preemptive as opposed to the more traditional reactive policy of defense. The national welfare system, which was based on entitlements, was radically reformed by means of a doctrine that requires greater personal responsibility. Big city policing that had been reactive changed to a proactive doctrine and saw crime dramatically reduced.

The doctrinal template is an easily solved puzzle. Since philosophy leads to doctrine which creates policy, you can work your way forward or backward along the template, depending on where you start. The doctrinal template is an artificially created intellectual construct designed to make it easier to "see" and understand public policy. The whole doctrinal approach is, in essence, just a set of "constructed" lenses that authors made up to serve a specific purpose—so that readers have a tool with which to view the public policies that surround them everywhere and every day.

FOR DISCUSSION

Why is there a direct relationship between a doctrine and the policies that flow from it? Is the "boom and bust" doctrinal development cycle inevitable, or can it be delayed or prevented?

BIBLIOGRAPHY

Confucius. *Analects.* London: Allen & Unwin, 1938.

Gladden, E. N. *A History of Public Administration,* 2 vols. London: Frank Cass, 1972.

Kuhn, T. S. *The Structure of Scientific Revolutions* (2nd ed., enlarged). Chicago: University of Chicago Press, 1970.

Lemann, Nicholas. "The Next World Order: The Bush Administration May Have a Brand-New Doctrine of Power." *New Yorker,* April 1, 2002.

Olasky, Marvin. *Compassionate Conservatism.* New York: Free Press, 2000.

Ott, J. Steven, and Jay M. Shafritz. "Toward a Definition of Organizational Incompetence: A Neglected Variable in Organization Theory." *Public Administration Review* 54 (July–August 1994).

———. "The Perception of Organizational Incompetence: A Serious Danger and a Complex Challenge for Management." In *The Challenge of Public Management in a Changing World,* edited by Arie Halachmi and Geert Bouckaert. San Francisco: Jossey-Bass, 1995.

Ricks, Thomas E., and Vernon Loeb. "Bush Developing Military Policy of Striking First: New Doctrine Addresses Terrorism." *Washington Post,* June 10, 2002.

Shafritz, Jay M., and Christopher P. Borick. *Introducing Public Policy.* New York: Longman, 2008.

Taylor, Frederick W. *The Principles of Scientific Management.* New York: Harper, 1911.

Wilson, James Q. *Bureaucracy.* New York: Basic Books, 1989.

Wren, Daniel A. *The Evolution of Management Thought,* 3rd ed. New York: Wiley, 1987.

Van Gelder, Lawrence. "Thomas S. Kuhn, Scholar Who Altered the Paradigm of Scientific Change Dies at 73," *New York Times,* June 19, 1996.

Vegetius Renatus, Flavius. *Vegetius: Epitome of Military Science.* Liverpool, UK: Liverpool University Press, 1993.

Zakaria, Fareed. *The Future of Freedom: Illiberal Democracy at Home and Abroad.* New York: W. W. Norton, 2003.

CHAPTER FOUR

Who Really Made the Decision to Drop the First Atomic Bomb on Hiroshima?

WAS IT PRESIDENT HARRY S. TRUMAN OR HIS ADVISORS, THE CHIEF EXECUTIVE OR HIS TEAM OF TECHNICAL EXPERTS?

PREVIEW

The decision to attempt to build a nuclear weapon was made by President Franklin D. Roosevelt early in World War II, when it was widely thought that Nazi Germany was also making such an effort. The United States did not know it had successfully created such a weapon until July 1945, when it was tested in New Mexico. This was several months after the defeat of Germany. So, with President Roosevelt dead, his successor, Harry S. Truman, had to make the decision of whether to use this weapon on Japan when it had been created to deter or use on Germany. This case deals with how the decision to use the fist nuclear bomb, the atomic bomb, was made.

THE POTSDAM DECLARATION

The last of the World War II summit meetings was held in the Berlin suburb of Potsdam in July 1945, ten weeks after Germany's surrender. Out of this came the Potsdam Declaration, a joint proclamation of the United States, Great Britain, and China issued on July 26, 1945, which stated that now that Germany had been "laid waste . . . the full application of our military power . . . will mean the inevitable and complete destruction of the Japanese armed forces and just as inevitably the utter devastation of the Japanese homeland." It then called "upon the government of Japan to proclaim now the unconditional surrender of all Japanese armed forces. . . . The alternative for Japan is prompt and utter destruction." Tokyo did not respond, perhaps because the Japanese mistook this simply as wartime propaganda.

Consequently, the Japanese city of Hiroshima was destroyed on August 6, 1945, by the first nonexperimental atomic bomb dropped from a U.S. B-29 bomber, the *Enola Gay* (affectionately named after the pilot's mother). More than 70,000 of Hiroshima's 200,000 residents were killed by the blast and firestorm. Thousands more died later from wounds and radiation. Eighty percent of the city's structures were destroyed when the bomb was exploded 1,000 feet in the air for maximum effect. Three days after the destruction of Hiroshima, a second atomic bomb was dropped on Nagasaki. Today, devices of this size are considered small in comparison to modern nuclear weapons.

THE CONTINUING CONTROVERSY

The decision to drop atomic bombs on Hiroshima and Nagasaki was controversial even at the time and has remained so. Even the scientists who developed the bombs disagreed over whether a weapon developed to use against Germany should be used against a country that had shown no inclination to build nuclear weapons. There was also disagreement about whether these bombs should be used against targets of slight military value, as well as the need for the second attack on Nagasaki. This first use of nuclear weapons was justified on the basis of the estimates of likely U.S. casualties during an invasion of Japan. Some critics have suggested that the bombing was not so much one of the final acts of World War II as it was one of the first acts of the Cold War against the Soviet Union—a warning to the Soviets that although the United States did not have the largest number of army divisions in Europe (the Soviets did, by far), the United States nevertheless had the biggest stick on the block, so to speak. One thing is absolutely certain: The bombing of Hiroshima and Nagasaki ended the war.

Japanese Emperor Hirohito's radio address to the Japanese nation, on August 15, 1945, acknowledged the effectiveness of the two bombs: "Despite the best that has been done by everyone . . . the war situation has developed not necessarily to Japan's advantage. Moreover, the enemy has begun to employ a new and most cruel bomb, the power of which to do damage is indeed incalculable, taking the toll of many innocent lives. . . . We have resolved to pave the way for a grand peace for all the generations to come by enduring the unendurable and suffering what is insufferable."

Thus the Emperor, who many historians believe was as guilty of war crimes as the Japanese generals executed after the war, was able to "use" the bombs to convince his government and people to surrender. Because he was the only unifying force in Japan, the Allies allowed him (after he renounced his divinity) to convert to a constitutional monarch, and all kept quiet about his criminal past—except the governments of Australia, China, and New Zealand, who thought he should be given a fast and fair trial, then hanged. Hirohito continued in his pose as the kindly elder statesman until his death in 1989. While his people had to endure "the unendurable" and suffer "what is insufferable," he did very well for himself—even though he had to give up being a god. His descendants have continued on as the constitutional monarchs of Japan. Significantly, they have not sought to reassert their divinity.

Controversy over the use of the bombs continues to this day. William Manchester wrote in his World War II memoir, *Goodbye, Darkness* (1980), "you think of the lives which would have been lost in an invasion of Japan's home islands—a staggering number of Americans but millions more of Japanese—and you thank God for the atomic bomb." This judgment is not universally shared, of course, and there has been much criticism of the United States for using the bomb without warning on a country that appeared to be on the verge of defeat.

According to Paul Fussell in *Thank God for the Atom Bomb* (1988):

> [Harvard economics professor] John Kenneth Galbraith . . . thinks the A-bombs were unnecessary and unjustified because the war was ending anyway. The A-bombs meant, he says, "a difference, at most, of two or three weeks." But at the time, with no indication that surrender was on the way. . . . Allied casualties were running to over 7,000 per week. Two weeks more means 14,000 more killed and wounded, three weeks more, 21,000. Those weeks means the world if you're one of those thousands or related to one of them. . . . What did he do in the war? He worked in the Office of Price Administration in Washington. I don't demand that he experience having his ass shot off. I merely note that he didn't.

Fussell, a severely wounded U.S. infantry veteran who actually had portions of "his ass shot off," saw considerable combat in World War II and has written extensively about what war means to the infantry. He is especially annoyed with policy analysts, of whom John Kenneth Galbraith is merely representative, who suggest that the atomic-bombs should not have been used when they were. He feels that the bombs, which made a military assault on Japan unnecessary, literally saved tens of thousands of U.S. lives. That is why he titled his book *Thank God for the Atom Bomb*—because as a lieutenant slated to lead a rifle platoon during the invasion of Japan, that is exactly how he felt.

THE DECISION

So who actually made the decision that led to the dropping of that first atomic bomb? Was it Albert Einstein (1879–1955), the German-born physicist whose special theory of relativity postulated that space and time are relative, not absolute? After winning the Nobel Prize in Physics in 1922, Einstein, for the rest of his life, was one of the world's most influential theoretical physicists. As a famous Jewish scientist, he was forced to flee Nazi Germany when Hitler came to power in 1933. His was the first major voice to call for the development of the atomic bomb. In a now-famous letter to President Franklin D. Roosevelt on August 2, 1939, Einstein wrote that "it may become possible to set up a nuclear chain reaction in a large mass of uranium, by which vast amounts of power and large quantities of new radium-like elements would be generated. . . . This new phenomenon would also lead to the construction of bombs, and it is conceivable—though much less certain—that extremely powerful bombs of a new type may thus be constructed." Years later, Einstein would say of his role in the development of the atom bomb, "If only I had known, I should have become a watchmaker" (*New Statesman*, April 16, 1965).

Or was it President Harry Truman? He wrote in his memoirs: "The final decision of where and when to use the atomic bomb was up to me. Let there be no mistake about it. I regarded the bomb as a military weapon and never had any doubt that it should be used." According to historian David McCullough, "Indeed, to have said no at this point and called everything off would have been so drastic a break with the whole history of the project, not to say the terrific momentum of events that summer, as to have been almost inconceivable." However, Truman was only incidentally the formal decision maker. Any responsible president, on being told, as Truman was, that the planned invasion of Japan would cost a quarter-million U.S. casualties, would have done the same.

LEGAL AUTHORITY VERSUS TECHNICAL ABILITY

Truman truly believed it was his decision, but he was no physicist and made no effort to understand the technical details of the bomb. He was totally dependent on his scientific advisors, who told him the bomb would work. Truman had the legal authority to make the decision. After all, he was the commander in chief. However, Truman lacked the technical ability to decide. Quite literally, he did not know what he was doing when he gave the order to destroy Hiroshima. And in our technological age, this is an everyday occurrence. It happens whenever most people start their car, turn on their television, or boot up their computer. We know how to use these products (just as Truman knew how to use the bomb), but most of us have no idea how they work. There is a massive disconnect between the ability to use a thing and the ability to understand it.

Don K. Price, a pioneering analyst of science policy, was the first to assert that decisional authority inexorably flowed from executive to technical offices. Consequently, a major distinction had to be made between the legal authority to make a policy decision and the technical ability to make the same decision. Price's work predated John Kenneth Galbraith's *The New Industrial State* (1967), in which Galbraith made a similar claim for the decisional processes of large corporations. This theme is destined to be a continuing one in the study of public policy and administration, involving the dilemmas of control of power, information, and technical expertise—what many writers have called the problem of technocracy.

Executives of all stripes increasingly need technical help in making policy decisions. This is hardly a new phenomenon. The characters in William Shakespeare's plays, as in real life, often have need of an expert, a friend, or a spouse who will help them make up their minds on some pressing policy issue. Was ever a wife more helpful than Lady Macbeth? When her husband seemed indecisive about undertaking the murder of King Duncan, in *Macbeth* (Act I, scene vii), she kindly reassures him:

MACBETH: If we should fail?

LADY MACBETH: We fail!
But screw your courage to the sticking place,
And we'll not fail.

Some readers have found a blatant lewdness in her instructions. There has been much speculation about just where Lady Macbeth thought the proper "sticking place" was for Macbeth's "courage." Nevertheless, her advice worked: Macbeth eventually became a very successful murderer, at least until the last act.

So who really made the decision to kill the king and get the play's plot rolling? Was it Macbeth or his lady? Was it the executive or his technical advisor? The same considerations apply to Truman's decision. And Truman's prime technical advisor, J. Robert Oppenheimer, the University of California physicist who directed the team of civilian scientists who built the bomb, suffered from much of the same postdecisional angst as did Lady Macbeth. Although he didn't go about figuratively washing the blood off his hands as Lady Macbeth did ("Out; damned spot!"), he suffered great remorse for his role in the deaths of so many.

So who really made the decision to drop the bomb? Was it Truman, who had the legal authority, or his "advisors," who had the technical ability to build the device and tell the president it would work? This is not an "old" question about a historical topic. Those exact same considerations, albeit in a different context, apply to a president's decision about building and deploying a missile defense system for the United States. And to hundreds of other more obscure decisions where the president must rely on the advice of experts.

POLICY ADVISORS

Of course, presidents as well as all other political executives have far wider sources of policy advice than just their staffs. On every contentious issue, opinions on what to do pop up seemingly everywhere—and at once. Journalists aspiring to the status of a national pundit offer analyses laced with quotes from Edmund Burke and Jeremy Bentham. Alas, their opinions may be worth no more than the dollar it costs to buy the newspaper in which they appear.

For greater depth, the undecided executive may turn to experts such as working professionals in the area of concern, university professors, and "think tank" thinkers. The immediate problem here is that they don't always agree on a course of action. Remember, at any major jury trial, both sides will bring in expert witnesses—esteemed men and women in their chosen fields. These learned individuals will then proceed to contradict each other—in effect, call each other fools, stupid, or worse. The jury then has the unenviable task of sorting out the truth from all the squabbling experts.

The classic statement on the advice of experts is contained in a letter the British Secretary of India, Lord Salisbury, wrote on June 15, 1877, to Lord Lytton, Viceroy of India: "No lesson seems to be so deeply inculcated by the experience of life as that you never should trust in experts. If you believe the doctors nothing is wholesome; if you believe the theologians nothing is innocent; if you believe the soldiers nothing is safe. They are all required to have their strong wine diluted by a very large admixture of insipid common sense."

This reliance on experts was the mistake that President John F. Kennedy made during the 1961 Bay of Pigs fiasco. The failed U.S.-sponsored invasion of Cuba by Cuban exiles was an embarrassment because it was an incompetent effort. The invasion was based on grossly wrong intelligence, was poorly planned and led, and lacked adequate air cover. Kennedy speechwriter Theodore C. Sorensen, in his biography of his old boss (1965), quotes the president assessing his judgment on the Bay of Pigs: "All my life I've known better than to depend on the experts. How could I have been so stupid, to let them go ahead?"

Kennedy was certainly neither stupid nor lacking in common sense. In this instance, however, he deferred to the experts. So always remember that looking to experts

Thirty-year-old Colonel Paul W. Tibbets, Jr., pilot of the B-29 he named the *Enola Gay,* having just returned from dropping the atomic bomb on Hiroshima, stands by his plane's front landing gear on August 6, 1945. Tibbets did not have the power to decide whether to drop the bomb. As the low man on the decisional totem pole, his duty (along with that of his crew) was just to do the actual dropping. Tibbets was selected for the mission because he was considered to be the best bomber pilot in the U.S. Army Air Corps. Not only had he led B-17 bombing missions over Europe, he was one of the test pilots for the B-29. Before being told of the historic mission in store for him, Tibbets was asked by a security officer if he had ever been arrested. According to Richard Rhodes (1986), "Tibbets considered the situation and decided to answer honestly to this stranger that he had been, as a teenager in North Miami Beach, caught *in flagrante delicto* in the backseat of a car with a girl." That sealed the deal. This was a test of his honesty. If he had lied at that moment, the *Enola Gay* would have been named after somebody else's mother. He named the plane after his mother (her maiden name was Enola Gay Haggard) because she told him that he wouldn't be killed if he became a pilot. Of course, lots of other mothers' sons and daughters were killed because he was such a good pilot. Brigadier General Tibbets retired from the U.S. Air Force in 1966, continued his career in civilian aviation, and died in 2007, never having expressed any regret, any remorse, or historical revisionism about doing his duty by dropping the bomb.
Source: © CORBIS. All Rights Reserved.

for advice may work—but often it may not. Truman, a serious reader of history, knew this lesson well. That is why, in his August 6, 1945, official announcement of the atomic explosion over Hiroshima, Japan, he said, "We have spent two billion dollars on the greatest scientific gamble in history—and won." And that was when two billion dollars was a lot of money for the federal government to spend.

FOR DISCUSSION

Did President Truman do the morally correct thing in deciding to drop atomic bombs on Japanese cities in order to end the war speedily? Can you think of other examples when executives commonly have the formal authority to make decisions but lack the technical expertise to fully understand what they are doing?

BIBLIOGRAPHY

Bix, Herbert P. *Hirohito and the Making of Modern Japan.* New York: HarperCollins, 2000.

Fussell, Paul. *Thank God for the Atomic Bomb.* New York: Summit Books, 1988.

———. *Wartime.* New York: Oxford University Press, 1990.

Galbraith, John Kenneth. *The New Industrial State.* Boston: Houghton Mifflin, 1967.

Keegan, John. *A History of Warfare.* New York: Knopf, 1993.

Manchester, William. *Goodbye, Darkness.* Boston: Little, Brown, 1980.

McCullough, David. *Truman.* New York: Simon & Schuster, 1992.

Price, Don K. *Government and Science.* New York: New York University Press, 1954.

———. *The Scientific Estate.* Cambridge, MA: Harvard University Press, 1965.

Rhodes, Richard. *The Making of the Atomic Bomb.* New York: Simon & Schuster, 1986.

Sorensen, Theodore C. *Kennedy.* New York: Harper & Row, 1965.

Truman, Harry S. *Memoirs*, vol. 1. New York: Doubleday, 1955.

CHAPTER FIVE

How the Ideas of an Academic Economist, Friedrich A. Hayek, Led to the Thatcher Revolution in Great Britain, Inspired the Reagan Revolution in the United States, and Pushed the World's Global Economy into Its Worst Crisis since the Great Depression of the 1930s

PREVIEW

In one of the most influential of all economics books, *The General Theory of Employment, Interest, and Money* (1936), John Maynard Keynes (1883–1946) wrote: "The ideas of economists and political philosophers, both when they are right and when they are wrong, are more powerful than is commonly understood. Indeed the world is ruled by little else. Practical men, who believe themselves to be quite exempt from any intellectual influences, are usually the slaves of some defunct economist." "Defunct" might be too strong a word here. Because while Friedrich A. Hayek (1899–1992) is certainly defunct, meaning "dead," he is far from defunct, meaning "finished." Indeed, when George W. Bush became the U.S. president in 2000, the ideas of this Austrian-born economist became exceedingly influential, so much so that they nearly caused the Free World economy to collapse into another Great Depression.

EARLY YEARS

After being educated at the University of Vienna, Friedrich A. Hayek produced pioneering work on business cycles. He became so acclaimed that in 1931, at age thirty-two, he effectively reached the top of his profession when he was appointed the Tooke Professor of Economic Science and Statistics at the University of London. He thrived in England, produced a series of papers on how capitalism's price system functions as an information-processing machine, and became a British subject in 1938. Nevertheless, when World War II broke out in 1939 and his academic peers, including his close friend Keynes, were offered significant positions in the civil service, he was blacklisted from such work because of his Austrian background. Austria had been incorporated into Germany the year before, and no German, even a forsworn one, could be trusted with war work—especially when he had been an Austrian artillery officer during World War I and had served with distinction, even being decorated for bravery. He only fought against the Italians; but still! This arbitrary exile from the defense of his new realm had the unintentional but beneficial effect of giving him the time to write what became his most enduring and influential book, *The Road to Serfdom* (1944).

Hayek's *Road,* written for a popular audience, argued that "the unforeseen but inevitable consequences of socialist planning create a state of affairs in which, if the policy is to be pursued, totalitarian forces will get the upper hand." To Hayek, state intervention in the economy in Great Britain and the United States differed only in degree, not in kind, from the fascism of Hitler and the communism of Stalin. The evil to be resisted was collectivism, whether it wore a swastika or not.

By asserting that allied economic policies were headed in the direction of Nazi policies, Hayek was being deliberately provocative and controversial. According to Hayek, "there is scarcely a leaf out of Hitler's [economic] book which somebody or other in England or America has not recommended us to take and use for our own purposes." Thus the "road" to serfdom was a collectivism that would ultimately lead to a Hitler-like totalitarianism. Consequently, open-market capitalism, a political system with minimal state planning and regulation, offered the only logical means to maintain prosperous and free societies.

Hayek's book, which can be condensed into five words—government planning leads to dictatorship—was an immediate best-selling sensation on both sides of the Atlantic. However, it made Hayek decidedly unpopular in a postwar Britain that was implementing the socialist agenda of the Labour Party. So, after a messy divorce that alienated him from even more friends and colleagues, Hayek moved "across the pond" to the University of Chicago.

In a world moving increasingly toward centralized planning, Hayek seemed more like a crank than a prophet during the next two decades. Thus many people were surprised when he was awarded the Nobel Prize in Economics in 1974. His body of work justifying and defending free-market capitalism became the foundation of the modern conservative movements on both sides of the Atlantic. Significantly, he inspired important disciples such as Margaret Thatcher and Ronald Reagan.

THE THATCHER REVOLUTION

In Margaret Thatcher's first speech as leader of the Conservative Party in Great Britain on October 10, 1975, she restated Hayek's core concept: "What we face today is not a crisis of capitalism but of socialism. No country can flourish if its economic and social life is dominated by nationalization and state control. The cause of our shortcomings does not, therefore, lie in private enterprise. Our problem is not that we have too little socialism. It is that we have too much."

Upon becoming Prime Minister of England in 1979, she then proceeded to dismantle much of the socialist state that had been created since World War II. Her Conservative Party's reprivatization of nationalized institutions and its privatization or outsourcing of many government functions became known as Thatcherism. To be sure, Thatcher was a disciple of Hayek. As she proudly boasted in her autobiography (1995),

Margaret Thatcher, before and after. At a 1995 book signing, the former British Prime Minister holds a copy of her autobiography, *The Path to Power* (1995). The photo on the book's cover shows her as a young woman, before she had read Hayek's *The Road to Serfdom*. (She was a chemistry major—not a politics major—at Oxford University.) The older woman holding her book has a face—and had a career—dominated by the ideas of Hayek. In her book she wrote of the doctrine she took from Hayek: that "each demand for security, whether of employment, income or social position, implied the exclusion from such benefits of those outside the particular privileged group—and would generate demands for countervailing privileges from the excluded groups." In such a socialist state, "everyone will lose." This is why, her mission in life became to roll back the British welfare state.
Source: © Russell Boyce/Reuters/CORBIS. All Rights Reserved.

all of her "general propositions favouring freedom" she had "imbibed at my father's knee or acquired by candle-end reading of [Edmund] Burke and Hayek." John Ranelagh reported that at a Conservative Party meeting in the late 1970s, when a colleague was arguing that "the middle way was the pragmatic path" for the party, Thatcher grabbed a book of Hayek's from her briefcase. Interrupting the speaker, she held Hayek's book up for the audience to see. Sternly, she said, "This is what we believe." Then, like any good disciple, she emphasized her point by loudly banging the book down on the table.

U.S. ECONOMIC POLICY BEFORE AND AFTER HAYEK

Until the 1960s, the premises of national economic policy, those established thirty years earlier by the New Deal of President Franklin D. Roosevelt, were largely unchallenged. Indeed, they were soon reinforced by the Great Society programs of the Lyndon B. Johnson Administration. However, high rates of federal taxation and seemingly ever increasing federal involvement with more and more aspects of life in the United States caused the American disciples of Hayek to rise up in protest.

The doctrinal template presented in Figure 5.1 reflects the economic policies of the New Deal and Great Society programs and the Democratic Party in general.

All national economies other than totalitarian tyrannies are necessarily mixed. Even the staunchest libertarian believes in the necessity of public programs for police, fire, and military protection. The economic liberalism (capitalism operating with a minimum of government restraint and regulation) espoused by Hayek, Reagan, and Thatcher still allowed welfare-state programs, but at a minimal level. Thus the safety net—social welfare programs that assure at least a subsistence standard of living—espoused by President Reagan was considered by his political critics to have too many holes in it—meaning that the benefits were not generous enough for those who wanted a more expansive welfare state.

The current debate over economic policy is one of degree. Because a mixed economy is a given, the doctrinal question is not whether there should be a safety net, but

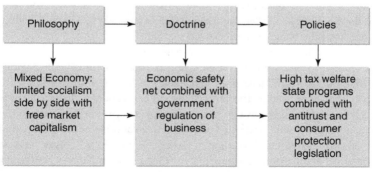

Figure 5.1 Economic Policies Derived From the New Deal

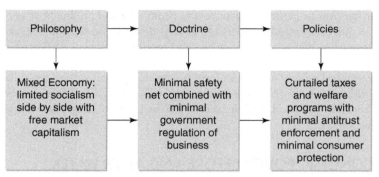

Figure 5.2   Economic Doctrines of Hayek, Reagan, and Thatcher

how large it should be—not whether there should be government regulation of business, but how much of it. The ensuing policies would reflect the new emphasis: expanding or contracting welfare benefits, more or less vigorous antitrust laws (statutes that limit the ability of businesses and unions to exercise monopoly control and to cause restraint of trade), and the enforcement of government regulations and consumer protection efforts. Figure 5.2 is the competing doctrinal template, one that, in contrast to Figure 5.1, reflects the economic world view of Hayek, Reagan, and Thatcher—and the U.S. Republican Party in general.

A CHOICE, NOT AN ECHO

It is generally agreed that contemporary policies of deregulation and minimal regulation have their origins in the 1964 presidential campaign of Senator Barry Goldwater (1909–1998). This blunt-speaking Republican from Arizona was hardly an intellectual force. His only major book, *The Conscience of a Conservative* (1960), was not only not much more than elongated pamphlet, it was ghost-written by L. Brent Bozell, Jr. (1926–1997), an editor of the *National Review*. Nevertheless, Goldwater was the national voice of the Republican conservatives in the early 1960s, when the Republican Party was dominated by so-called moderate Republicans—those who were willing to accept the results of the New Deal policies.

Conservatives like Goldwater wanted to repeal much of the New Deal. He offered what was referred to as a "choice, not an echo," meaningful (usually ideological) differences in what political candidates or parties stand for. In asserting, "I will offer a choice, not an echo," he announced in 1963 that he would be a candidate for president in 1964. Phyllis Schlafly (1924–) then gave the phrase wide currency when she used it as the title of her 1964 campaign polemic attacking both Republican and Democratic Party leaderships and national administrations. According to George Will (1987), "Conservatives had . . . the 'conservatives in the woodwork' theory . . . : One reason millions of Americans do not vote is that they are forced to choose between two liberals; give them a choice, not an echo, and conservatives will pour out of the woodwork, into voting booths."

Goldwater's 1964 presidential bid was the making of today's Hayek-inspired conservative movement for two reasons. First, Goldwater unabashedly said he wanted to repeal much of the New Deal. He wanted to reform Social Security, privatize the Tennessee Valley Authority (TVA), and end welfare as we then knew it. It is hard to assess how radical these ideas sounded at the time. Indeed, they made Goldwater seem like a madman. His public image as someone who could not be trusted with the public's business is illustrated by the story of a pollster who asked an elderly lady why she intended to vote against Goldwater. She replied, "because he wants to take away my TV." The pollster responded: "He only wants to privatize the TVA."

"Well, I'm not taking any chances."

Neither was the rest of the country. Goldwater lost the 1964 presidential election so overwhelmingly to President Lyndon Johnson that there was much talk of the total disintegration of the Republican Party—especially because Johnson's landslide brought into the Congress a significant number of new Democrats on his coattails.

THE REAGAN REVOLUTION

Nevertheless, Goldwater's ill-fated campaign put the issues of modern conservatism on the national agenda—only to see them soundly rejected. His campaign put something else on the national agenda as well: That "thing" was Ronald Reagan.

Reagan, a movie actor since the late 1930s, took part in the early introduction of Hollywood to labor organization and Democratic Party politics. He became a successful television promoter of General Electric products in the 1950s and joined the Republican Party. His active involvement in the 1964 presidential campaign of Barry Goldwater made him a major voice in national Republican politics. This led to Reagan's election as governor of California (1967–1975) and eventually to his successful 1980 presidential campaign against incumbent President Jimmy Carter, and his even more successful 1984 campaign for reelection against Walter Mondale.

The Reagan revolution consisted largely of the Goldwater agenda. The Reagan administration redefined domestic priorities and curtailed federal programs designed to solve social problems. As Reagan often said, "Government is not the solution to our problems. Government is the problem." This is the essence of Hayek. In other words, the national welfare would be better served with general economic prosperity, brought about by tax cuts, than with expanded welfare programs.

Reagan did not take just a page from Goldwater's book; he took the whole book. *The Conscience of a Conservative* became the modern conservative credo by describing what would later be known as the Reagan revolution. These ghost-written words of Goldwater represent the heartfelt truths of Reagan:

> I have little interest in streamlining government or making it more efficient for I mean to reduce its size. I do not undertake to promote welfare for I propose to extend freedom. My aim is not to pass laws, but to repeal them. It is not to inaugurate new programs, but to cancel old ones that do violence to the Constitution, or that have failed in their purpose, or that impose on the people an unwarranted financial burden.

That Ronald Reagan was also influenced by Hayek is beyond doubt. According to Martin Anderson (1988), Reagan read and studied the works of the "giants of the free market economy—Ludwig von Mises, Friedrich Hayek and Milton Friedman." Not only was Reagan an economics major in college, he read serious books on economics and political philosophy all his active life. In a June 22, 1983, speech, President Reagan succinctly and comically summarized Hayek's economic philosophy: "The principles of wealth creation transcend time, people, and place. Governments which deliberately subvert them by denouncing God, smothering faith, destroying freedom, and confiscating wealth have impoverished their people. Communism works only in heaven, where they don't need it, and in hell, where they've already got it."

The ascent to power of Thatcher in 1979 and of Reagan in 1981 created an informal trans-Atlantic coalition to advance Hayek's principles of less government and more market rule. The movement toward privatization and deregulation now had as its champions the two most influential political voices in the English-speaking world.

Deregulation is the lifting of restrictions on business, banking, industry, and other professional activities for which government rules were established and bureaucracies created to administer. The modern movement toward deregulation, which began during the Jimmy Carter administration under the leadership of Alfred Kahn at the Civil Aeronautics Board, was supported by both parties in the United States, but for different reasons. Republicans tended to support it because they were inclined to be philosophically hostile toward government interference with business in the first place. Democrats tended to support it because they felt that greater market competition would bring down prices for the consumer. Hayek's ideas were becoming bipartisan, at least to a degree.

President George H. W. Bush, on November 18, 1991, presented the Presidential Medal of Freedom to Hayek and said, "At a time when many saw socialism as ordained by history, he foresaw freedom's triumph. Over 40 years ago, Professor von Hayek wrote that 'the road to serfdom' was not the road to the future or to the political and economic freedom of man." According to Austin Furse, then White House Director of Policy Planning, "More than almost anyone else in the twentieth century, this guy was vindicated by the events in Eastern Europe"(*New York Times,* November 19, 1991).

John Cassidy reported in the *New Yorker* that as the frail, ninety-year-old Hayek was watching communism's fall on television in 1989, "he would beam benignly" and say to his son, "I told you so." On November 20, 1994, Hayek's close friend Milton Friedman was discussing the fiftieth-anniversary edition of *The Road to Serfdom,* just published by the University of Chicago Press (because Friedman had written a new introduction to it) on C-SPAN's *Booknotes* program. Friedman told host Brian Lamb, "Over the years I've gone around and asked people who had shifted from a belief in central government and socialism and what today goes by the name of liberalism what led them to shift, what led them to an understanding that that was a wrong road. Over and over again, the answer has been *The Road to Serfdom.*"

THE GEORGE W. BUSH REVIVAL OF THE REAGAN LEGACY

When President Ronald Reagan left office in 1989, he was succeeded by George H. W. Bush, who had been vice president for the previous eight years. Bush was never the ideologue that Reagan was. Indeed, Reagan selected him to be vice president in 1980 in large part to assuage the declining moderate wing of the Republican Party. Although Bush was from Texas, he grew up in Connecticut as the son of the U.S. senator from that state and never even lived in Texas until after serving in the Navy during World War II and graduating from Yale. Bush was really an Eastern establishment—meaning moderate—Republican, but his son, George W. Bush, grew up in Texas and consequently became a genuine Texas conservative.

When George W. Bush became president in 2001, he was determined to implement his conservative agenda, which to a large degree mirrored the policies of Reagan. Like Reagan, Bush increased defense spending massively while at the same time cutting taxes. This meant that domestic spending had to be seriously curtailed. Bush also, again following a Reagan refrain, placed a new emphasis on outsourcing government programs, privatizing Social Security, and expanding the role of the nonprofit sector in providing social safety net services. Bush learned from his father's mistakes. The father raised taxes and alienated his Republican base of support—and lost his bid for reelection. The son, however, did neither. He cut taxes, played to his base, and won reelection.

Goldwater, Reagan, and George W. Bush were strong advocates of public-choice policies. Their advocacy of the privatization of Social Security, the TVA, and other government programs proved this. They saw public-choice approaches as a radical way to reduce government spending, reduce government budgets, and reduce government itself. Hayek-inspired public-choice doctrine rejects the concept of the welfare state that emerged out of the New Deal: When private markets failed, the government had to step in to carry out the public interest, and the governmental level best suited to do this was the federal one.

Public choice as a theoretical approach in both economics and politics is inherently reactive—almost reactionary. It is a reaction to large government and high taxation (to pay for it), which calls for less government and concomitant lower taxes. It harkens back to the ideal of self-reliance, the notion that citizens should take care of their own economic needs and not be dependent on the government for the necessities of life. This was President Herbert Hoover's philosophy of "rugged individualism," which called for economic freedom and opposed paternalistic government welfare programs—which he thought undermined character.

THE THEORY OF PUBLIC CHOICE

Abraham Lincoln can be considered the first major public-choice theorist. In 1854 he wrote:

> The legitimate object of government is to do for a community of people, whatever they need to have done, but can not do, at all, or can not so well do, for themselves—in their separate, and individual capacities.
>
> In all that the people can individually do as well for themselves, government ought not to interfere.

What Lincoln was calling for, though he did not use the term, was a cost–benefit approach to ascertain whether goods and/or services should be provided collectively rather than individually. This is the test that James M. Buchanan and Gordon Tullock proposed for all public policies in their classic analysis, *The Calculus of Consent* (1962). They asked: "When will a society composed of free and rational utility-maximizing individuals choose to undertake action collectively rather than privately?" The answer is that the rational person takes collective action to obtain a collective good, anything of value (such as clean air, safe streets, or tax loopholes) that cannot be denied to a group member.

A group can vary from all of society to any subset of it. Economist Mancur Olson, in *The Logic of Collective Action* (1965), found that small groups are better at obtaining collective goods. The larger the potential group, the less likely it is that most will contribute to obtain the "good." Thus a particular industry is better able to obtain tax loopholes for itself than the general public is able to obtain overall tax equity.

The problem with collectively provided goods, those paid for by tax dollars, is that the demand will always exceed what can be supplied. After all, if something appears to be both desirable and "free," demand for it will only continue to rise. This leads to budget deficits and the kind of destruction illustrated by the story of the tragedy of the commons—an illustration of the principle that the maximization of private gain will not result in the maximization of social benefit.

Public-choice theory is very closely related to libertarianism, a pure form of the classical liberalism espoused by Hayek. This asserts that a government should do little more than provide police and military protection; other than that, it should not interfere—either for good or ill—in the lives of its citizens. A major intellectual force

---

THE TRAGEDY OF THE COMMONS

The tragedy of the commons develops in this way. Picture a pasture open to all. It is to be expected that each herdsman will try to keep as many cattle as possible on the commons. Such an arrangement may work reasonably satisfactorily for centuries, because tribal wars, poaching, and disease keep the numbers of both man and beast below the carrying capacity of the land. Finally, however, comes the day of reckoning, that is, the day when the long-desired goal of social stability becomes a reality. At this point, the inherent logic of the commons remorselessly generates tragedy.

As a rational being, each herdsman seeks to maximize his gain. . . . The rational herdsman concludes that the only sensible course for him to pursue is to add another animal to his herd. And another, and another. . . . But this is the conclusion reached by each and every rational herdsman sharing a commons. Therein is the tragedy. Each man is locked into a system that compels him to increase his herd without limit—in a world that is limited. Ruin is the destination toward which all men rush, each pursuing his own best interest in a society that believes in the freedom of the commons. Freedom in a commons brings ruin to all.

Source: Garrett Hardin, "The Tragedy of the Commons," *Science*, December 13, 1968.

advocating libertarianism was Ayn Rand (1905–1982), the novelist and objectivist philosopher who attacked welfare-state notions of selflessness and sacrifice for a common good in best-selling fiction such as *The Fountainhead* (1943) and *Atlas Shrugged* (1957). In *Capitalism: The Unknown Ideal* (1966), she wrote: "The only proper function of the government of a free country is to act as an agency which protects the individual's rights, i.e., which protects the individual from physical violence."

HOW HAYEK TURNED OUT THE LIGHTS IN CALIFORNIA

From the Regan era onward, Hayek-inspired public-choice solutions were installed by reducing the staffing levels and budgets of the regulatory agencies, placing as regulators Republican Party stalwarts who were philosophically hostile to the government regulation of business to begin with, and abolishing regulations whenever possible.

The Hayekian trust in free markets gained increasing ascendancy as the Republican Party surged in membership (especially in state legislatures) in the wake of the 1980s Reagan Revolution. This movement toward less government regulation took hold of the electric utility industry. Following this national trend, both houses of the California state legislature in 1996 voted unanimously to lower its citizens' electric bills by creating a free market for wholesale electricity. The utility companies, which had previously both generated and distributed electricity to consumers, would now have to sell off their power stations and reorganize themselves as electricity distribution—not producing—companies. They would then buy wholesale electricity on the spot market and sell it retail to consumers. This was fine so long as there was plenty of power to buy.

However, California's expanding population demanded more and more electricity, while California's environmental movement made sure that no new power plants were built. The result was a collision between supply and demand. By the end of 2000, the wholesalers, in response to rising demand for power and no new producers of power, raised their prices up to ten times what they had been a year earlier. After all, this was the free market in action. The utilities could not pass on these costs to their customers because the retail prices of electricity were still regulated by the state. In effect, the utilities were forced to buy electricity for as much as one dollar but to sell it for as little as ten cents.

Pleas to the state regulators brought only modest relief in terms of price hikes that could be passed on to consumers. As a result, the wholesalers, sensing bankruptcy in the future, refused to sell electricity to the utilities on credit; they feared, quite rationally, that they might never be paid. By early 2001 the utilities were literally billions of dollars in debt as a result of buying electricity high and selling it low; and their looming bankruptcies would not even allow them to buy enough electricity for all their customers. So they started occasional rolling blackouts to conserve power and share the pain. During January 2001 the lights went out for several hours at a time over many parts of California. The state then passed legislation that had the effect of re-regulating the industry—exactly the opposite of what had been originally intended.

So, did Hayek turn the lights out in California from beyond the grave? The answer must be yes, because his intellectual footprints are all over the deregulation movement. However, the California legislature only half-heard what he had to say. If they had listened to him more thoroughly, listened to what he had to say about free markets for both buyers and sellers, the electricity would have continued to flow—albeit more expensively. California wanted to get electric utility deregulation in the worst way—and that is exactly how California got it.

AYN RAND'S REVENGE

Hayek was a strong intellectual advocate of free-market classical liberalism, but there were others who also espoused the same core ideas, albeit from different platforms. If Hayek sang like a canary from his academic perch, Ayn Rand roared the same unfettered-market song in her novels, polemics, and screenplays. Hayek wrote for professional economists and public policy wonks, whereas Rand, who came to the United States in 1926 as a refugee from Communist Russia, was a free-market zealot who sought a mass audience. Hayek was a cloistered scholar; Rand was the charismatic leader of a movement.

As befits a spell-binding innovator, she had disciples who seem to have preached her philosophy with the same intensity as those original disciples in the *New Testament*. Foremost among them in reknown, achievement, and position in the U.S. political economy was Alan Greenspan, chairman of the Federal Reserve Board from 1987 to 2006. More than any single individual in government, he deserves the credit—the blame, actually—for the near-meltdown of the U.S. economy in 2008.

Greenspan, a professional economist, was well aware of Hayek and his voluminous academic works, but he was an intimate friend of Ayn Rand. How intimate we shall never know. What is certain is that Greenspan was part of a small coterie of young intellectuals who were closely associated with Rand in New York in the 1950s. They were close enough that she trusted him to read and comment on chapter drafts of her greatest novel, *Atlas Shrugged* (1954). Incidentally, Rand seems to have been a "cougar" long before that term was fashionable for an older woman who preys sexually on younger men. It is well documented that her appetites led to the divorce of at least one of her coterie. The embittered wife, Barbara Branden, wrote a book about the affair that destroyed her marriage, *The Passion of Ayn Rand* (1986). This in turn was later made into an Emmy-award-winning TV film starring Helen Mirren as Rand.

We can only assume that the Rand–Greenspan relationship was purely intellectual. What is certain is that they continued a close association that ended only with her death in 1982. The photographic proof of this is a picture of Greenspan in 1974 at the White House being sworn in as the tenth chair of the Council of Economic Advisors. Standing next to him is President Gerald Ford and Ayn Rand. Anybody who did not recognize one of the world's best selling novelists would have assumed that she was Greenspan's mother.

Was Alan Greenspan Ayn Rand's revenge? Rand, Hayek's populist counterpart, had only one disciple who rose to the top of the U.S. economic policy-making mountain and stayed there for two decades. When the economy was doing fine, he was considered a genius. But when it crashed in 2008, analysts looked back at the causes and saw Greenspan driving the economy into a ditch by implementing the Hayek/Rand/Reagan ideology of the less regulation, especially of banking, the better.

After all, the ideology held that the free markets would take care of themselves; they were in effect self-regulatory. Tell that to Senator John McCain, the Republican Party presidential nominee who lost the election of 2008 to Barack Obama (when the economy stalled as he approached the campaign home stretch) because of the Greenspan-engineered subprime mortgage crisis.

Greenspan is not a bad man personally. He did not knowingly cause the greatest economic crisis since the Great Depression of the 1930s. What he did, beginning in the early 2000s, was to pump up the economy by drastically lowering interest rates while forestalling any efforts to regulate the financial markets.

The combination of less and less regulation and more and more cheap money (available from the Greenspan-led Federal Reserve for as little as 1 percent) allowed the traditional savings-and-loan institutions to go from a conservative mortgage strategy in which loans were long-term propositions to essentially gambling on subprime mortgages, in that these once-conservative banks would loan money via a mortgage to virtually anyone on any property without any real concern about whether the loan could ever be paid back. The concern for payback was gone because the subprime loan would almost immediately be securitized, aggregated into derivative securities. These, in turn, would be given, hastily and irresponsibly, a high credit rating by highly respected but ultimately irresponsible credit rating agencies and then sold off to mutual funds, pension funds, and the gullible public in general.

Then all those subprime mortgage holders started behaving as you might expect borrowers with incomes so low that they clearly could not afford to make their monthly payments: They defaulted. By the millions, they defaulted. Suddenly those AAA-rated securitized mortgages were suspect and could not be traded. However, all the major financial institutions had invested in them so heavily that the financial markets were frozen until the government stepped in with a massive bailout. Unemployment shot up, and the economy went into the deepest recession since the Great Depression of the 1930s. The point here is that probably none of this would have happened if the New Deal regulatory regime had been allowed to stay in place, and to expand to reflect new kinds of securities on the market.

The irony of all this is that part of the problem to begin with was that Greenspan turned out to be a Hayek heretic. Hayek, a believer in free markets, opposed having government agencies, such as the Federal Reserve Bank, set interest rates. And it was just the Fed's artificially low rates that fueled the subprime crises. Classically liberal economists such as Hayek believed that government intervention in the economy is always the wrong policy, because it only makes things worse. Modern liberals believe just the opposite, which is why the government, in responding to the 2008 crisis, became more involved than ever. Hayek would be dismayed.

FOR DISCUSSION

Is it fair to assign blame for the economic crisis that began in 2008 to Hayek because his policies were adopted by others? How has Hayek's defense of free-market solutions to social problems influenced public policy making and public administration in the contemporary world?

BIBLIOGRAPHY

Anderson, Martin. *Revolution*. New York: Harcourt Brace Jovanovich, 1988.

Basler, Roy P., ed. *The Collected Works of Abraham Lincoln*, vol. 2. New Brunswick, NJ: Rutgers University Press, 1953.

Boettke, Peter J. "Friedrich A. Hayek (1899–1992)." *The Freeman*, August 1992.

Branden, Barbara. *The Passion of Ayn Rand*. Garden City, NY: Doubleday, 1986.

Buchanan, James M., and Gordon Tullock. *The Calculus of Consent*. Ann Arbor: University of Michigan Press, 1962.

Burns, Jennifer. *Goddess of the Market: Ayn Rand and the American Right*. New York: Oxford University Press, 2009.

Cannon, Lou. *President Reagan: The Role of a Lifetime*. New York: Simon & Schuster, 1991.

Cassidy, John. "The Price Prophet." *New Yorker*, February 7, 2000.

Downs, Anthony. *An Economic Theory of Democracy*. New York: Harper & Row, 1957.

Ebenstein, Alan. *Friedrich Hayek: A Biography*. New York: St. Martin's, 2001.

Friedman, Milton. *Capitalism and Freedom*. Chicago: University of Chicago Press, 1962.

Galbraith, John Kenneth. *A Life in Our Times*. Boston: Houghton Mifflin, 1981.

Goldberg, Robert Alan. *Barry Goldwater*. New Haven, CT: Yale University Press, 1997.

Goldwater, Barry. *The Conscience of a Conservativ.e* Shepherdsville, KY: Victor Publishing, 1960.

Greenspan, Alan. *The Age of Turbulence*. New York: Penguin, 2009.

Hayek, Friedrich A. *The Constitution of Liberty*. Chicago: University of Chicago Press, 1960.

———. *The Road to Serfdom*. Chicago: University of Chicago Press, 1944.

Heller, Anne C. *Ayn Rand and the World She Made*. New York: Doubleday, 2009.

Keynes, John Maynard. *The General Theory of Employment, Interest and Money*. London: Macmillan, 1936.

Niskanen, William A. *Bureaucracy and Public Economics*. Brookfield, VT: E. Elgar, 1994.

———. *Bureaucracy and Representative Government*. Chicago: Aldine-Atherton, 1971.

Olson, Mancur. *The Logic of Collective Action: Public Goods and the Theory of Groups*. Cambridge, MA: Harvard University Press, 1965.

Perlstein, Rick. *Before the Storm: Barry Goldwater and the Unmaking of the American Consensus*. New York: Hill & Wang, 2001.

Rand, Ayn. *Capitalism: The Unknown Ideal*. New York: New American Library, 1966.

Ranelagh, John. *Thatcher's People: An Insider's Account of the Politics, the Power, and the Personalities*. London: HarperCollins, 1991.

Thatcher, Margaret. *The Path to Power*. New York: HarperCollins, 1995.

Will, George F. *The New Season*. New York: Simon & Schuster, 1987.

Woods, Thomas E., Jr. *Meltdown*. New York: Regnery, 2009.

CHAPTER SIX

From German Chancellor Otto von Bismarck to U.S. President Bill Clinton

HOW POLITICAL LEADERS CREATED THE MODERN WELFARE STATE USING SOCIAL INSURANCE AS AN ALTERNATIVE TO SOCIALISM

PREVIEW

People continue to believe many legends of public policy despite no evidence to support them. Thus we frequently hear that the Social Security Act of 1935 set 65 as the normal retirement age, because that is the age German Chancellor Otto von Bismarck (1815–1898) deemed appropriate for Germany's workers to begin receiving government pensions. False!

What is true is that in 1889 Germany became the first state to adopt an old-age social insurance program. The idea was first put forward, at Bismarck's behest, in 1881 by Germany's Kaiser William I, in a letter to the German Parliament stating that "those who are disabled from work by age and invalidity have a well-grounded claim to care from the state." Many thought that Germany adopted age 65 as the standard retirement age because that was Bismarck's age. In fact, Germany initially set age 70 as the retirement age (and Bismarck himself was 74 at the time). It was not until twenty-seven years later (in 1916) that the age was lowered to 65. By that time, Bismarck had been dead for eighteen years.

According to the U.S. Social Security Administration, the German system was not the major influence on the Committee on Economic Security (CES), the committee created in 1934 by President Franklin D. Roosevelt to make recommendations for Social Security legislation, when it proposed age 65 as the retirement age. The decision was in fact not based on any European precedent. It was primarily pragmatic and stemmed from two sources. One was a general observation about the retirement ages of the few private pension systems in existence at the time; the second, and more important, was the thirty state old-age pension systems then in operation. Roughly half of the state pension systems set age 65 as the retirement age; half set seventy as the retirement age. The new federal Railroad Retirement System created by Congress earlier in 1934 had also set 65 as its retirement age.

Taking all this into account, the CES planners made a rough judgment that age 65 was probably more reasonable than age 70. This judgment was then confirmed by actuarial studies, which showed that age 65 could be self-sustaining with only modest levels of payroll taxation. So, these two factors, a pragmatic judgment about prevailing retirement standards and the favorable actuarial outcome of using 65, were the real reasons that age 65 was chosen. Bismarck had nothing to do with it.

DON'T BLAME BISMARCK FOR RETIREMENT AT AGE 65

The assumption that Bismarck was behind the age-65 decision persists for another reason as well. Bismarck, the "Iron Chancellor," who created modern Germany in 1871 by a series of wars and cynical political manipulations, had a decidedly nasty reputation. It was comforting to blame a man of his character for setting a retirement age that, taking into account life expectancies, few workers would ever see.

According to the U.S. Social Security Administration, if we look at life expectancy statistics from the 1930s, we might naturally come to the conclusion that the Social Security program was designed in such a way that most people would work for many years paying in taxes, but would not live long enough to collect benefits. Life expectancy at birth in 1930 was only 58 for men and 62 for women. However, life expectancy at birth in the early decades of the twentieth century was low because of high infant mortality. And someone who died as a child would never work and pay into Social Security. A more appropriate measure is life expectancy after reaching adulthood.

When Social Security pensions started, the majority of Americans who made it to adulthood (age 21) could expect to live to age 65 and then could look forward to collecting benefits for many years. For example, almost 54 percent of men could expect to live to age 65 if they first survived to age 21. Men who attained age 65 could expect to collect Social Security benefits for almost thirteen years, women for almost fifteen years.

There were already 7.8 million Americans age 65 or older in 1935, so there was a large and growing population of people who could receive Social Security. Indeed, the actuarial estimates used by the Committee on Economic Security in designing the Social Security program projected that there would be 8.3 million Americans age 65 or older by 1940 (when monthly benefits started). Social Security was thus never designed so that few people would collect benefits, although people thinking in terms of life expectancies from birth were reasonable in thinking so. And Bismarck, whose reputation only got worse with all the then-recent anti-German propaganda of World War I, was just the kind of cynical, manipulative, and alien politician to blame it on.

KEEPING IT DOWN!

German Chancellor Otto von Bismarck tries to keep down the "Socialist Jack in the Box" in this 1878 *Punch* cartoon. Bismarck's plan to keep the socialists down included legislation for compulsory sickness insurance in 1883 and compulsory old-age insurance (state pensions), paid for jointly by workers and employers. Germany was simply the first Western state to seek to steal the thunder of the radical socialists by adopting elements of their political agenda as their own. This was why, Norman Thomas (1884–1968), the six-time (1928 to 1948) candidate for president of the United States of the Socialist Party, complained that "The American people will never knowingly adopt socialism. But, under the name of 'liberalism,' they will adopt every fragment of the socialist program." He was largely correct. It is often said that President Franklin D. Roosevelt saved the U.S. capitalistic system during the Great Depression of the 1930s. To the extent that he did, he did it by adopting many of the policies advocated by Thomas's Socialist Party. Bismarck's tactics easily crossed the Atlantic and kept the American "Socialist Jack" in its box. *Source:* © Bettmann/CORBIS. All Rights Reserved.

THE EVOLUTION OF WELFARE

Some Biblical scholars contend that the commandment, "Thou shalt not kill," contained the essence of a welfare program. After all, if a wandering desert tribe did not help those members in need (the ill, the old, the widowed and orphaned), they would surely die. Thus we can conclude that the social provision of welfare services has always been mandated from above—sometimes far above. Nevertheless, history reveals that divine intervention cannot be depended on for regular meals and rain-proof shelters. Consequently, when the problem of what to do with displaced workers and their families grew too much for traditional charity to handle, the state stepped in. Our story is just how the U.S. state stepped in; how government-sponsored welfare programs evolved politically and developed administratively through social insurance.

Throughout history, economic security has often been elusive. Only comparatively recently have people in industrial states been pretty sure where their next meal was coming from. The refrigerator? It is easy to joke about this now, when obesity is the number-one health problem in the United States. But just go back a few hundred years before the refrigerator, before the ice box, to a time when food preservation was inherently chancy and life was precarious. Then only an elite felt any sense of economic security. Nevertheless, many others aspired to have it as well.

For example, during the Middle Ages, merchants and craft workers—any group with common business interests—might form guilds or mutual-aid societies to enhance their personal economic security. Although these associations were created primarily to fix prices and dictate employment standards, they also offered what we now call welfare benefits to their members to ward off poverty in hard times and to compensate for illness. Beginning in the sixteenth century, friendly societies, the forerunners of fraternal organizations, emerged. These would grow rapidly during the Industrial Revolution that began in the mid-eighteenth century, often evolving into the modern craft unions of today. These organizations allowed members to provide for their own welfare by paying into funds for life insurance, burial expenses, and other forms of assistance in time of need. Many of these societies still thrive in the United States and are well known—for example, the Free Masons, the Odd Fellows, the Benevolent and Protective Order of Elks, and the Royal Order of Moose.

By the latter half of the nineteenth century, work was inexorably moving from an agricultural base to one that was increasingly industrial and urban. Away from the traditional farm and their extended farm families, these new city workers were increasingly threatened with destitution and starvation. Mass production, coupled with the use of machines, reduced the skill level necessary for factory work. Workplaces became increasingly impersonal. Workers were viewed less and less as human beings, and more and more as factors of production.

The laborer was increasingly a specialized cog in the manufacturing process. Workers also felt threatened by massive immigration from Europe, which assured an ever-replenishing supply of unskilled "green hands," who suppressed industrial wages and were ready, willing, and eager to supplant native workers if they complained. Finally, increasing urbanization made workers almost completely dependent on their wages. Discharged factory workers capable of retreating or returning to a family farm continuously dwindled in number. More often than not, there simply was no family farm to which a worker could return. The problem, in essence, was that by the beginning of the twentieth century, the archetypical industrial worker had no social safety net whatsoever. No job meant no food, no shelter, and no hope. This was a classic recipe for potential political unrest.

GOVERNMENT'S TRADITIONAL APPROACH TO WELFARE

The English Poor Law of 1601 was the first systematic codification of English ideas about the responsibility of the state to provide for the welfare of its citizens. It provided public funds to pay for relief (public assistance programs for the poor). It distinguished between the "deserving" (such as a widow with children) and the "undeserving" (an able-bodied man who was just lazy) poor. Relief was local and community controlled. Almshouses and poor farms were also established. This essential structure was the tradition the English settlers brought with them when they colonized North America.

The first colonial poor laws required local taxation to support the destitute, distinguished between the "worthy" and the "unworthy" poor, and mandated relief as a local responsibility. This tradition continued until well after the U.S. Civil War. Local officials decided who was worthy of support and how that support would be provided. Relief was made as unpleasant as possible in order to "discourage" dependency. Those receiving relief could lose their personal property as well as the right to vote. Figure 6.1 illustrates this traditional approach.

Four important demographic changes beginning in the mid-1880s rendered the traditional (usually county-based) systems of welfare increasingly unworkable. First, the Industrial Revolution had transformed the majority of working people from self-employed independent farmers into wage earners toiling for large, impersonal corporations. In an agricultural society, personal prosperity is linked to individual labor. Everyone willing to work hard enough can usually provide at least a bare subsistence for themselves and their family. However, when one's income is primarily from wages, one's economic security can be threatened by factors outside one's control—such as recessions, layoffs, and business failures.

Second, urbanization increased along with the shift from an agricultural to an industrial society. Americans moved from farms and small rural communities to large cities—where the industrial jobs were. In 1890, only 28 percent of the population lived in cities; by 1930, this percentage had doubled, to 56 percent.

Third, this trend toward urbanization contributed to the disappearance of the extended family and the concomitant rise of the nuclear family. Today, we tend to assume

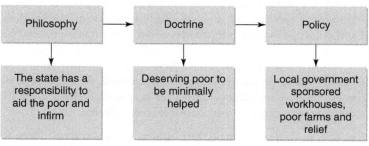

Figure 6.1 The Traditional Approach to Welfare

that "the family" consists of parents and children—the so-called nuclear family. For most of human history, we lived in "extended families" that included children, parents, grandparents, and other relatives. The advantage of the extended family was that when a family member became too old or infirm to work, the other family members assumed responsibility for his or her support. No longer.

Finally, thanks primarily to better health care, modern sanitation, and effective public health programs, Americans began to live significantly longer. In the three decades from 1900 to 1930, average life spans increased by ten years. The result was a rapid growth in the number of older citizens, from 3 million in 1900 to 7.8 million by 1935.

The net result of this complex set of demographic and social changes was that Americans became older, more urban, more industrial, and less likely to live on farms in extended families. Consequently, the traditional strategies for the provision of economic security (such as relying on the extended family and family farm) became increasingly fragile—and during the Great Depression, they proved to be overwhelmingly inadequate.

THE GREAT DEPRESSION AS A CHANGE AGENT

There were, generally speaking, three basic approaches to the Great Depression that began in 1929.

1. Do nothing, because nothing needed to be done. The problem was just another dip in the inevitable "boom-and-bust" economic cycle. Prosperity would eventually be just around the corner. It always had been. Right? Nevertheless, the problem remained that prosperity was taking too long to turn the corner.

2. Rely on individual or organized private charity. Traditional charitable good works were well established in a nation with a large church-going population. However, the problem was simply too huge. The nation lost half its total wealth by the end of the first three years of the Depression. Six years after the Depression began, President Franklin D. Roosevelt said in his second inaugural address: "I see one third of a nation ill-housed, ill-clad, ill-nourished." The nation was simply too ill for the "pill" of charity to make it better.

3. Expand welfare programs. Even before the Depression, many states had been forced to deal with the problems of economic distress in a wage-based, industrial economy. Once the Depression hit, all levels of government responded with expanded relief and public works (government-sponsored construction projects) programs. The main state-level strategy for providing assistance to the increased number of distressed elderly was to create various forms of old-age "pensions." These were means-tested welfare programs based on financial need. By 1934, most states had such programs. However, these pension plans were so restrictive in eligibility and so limited in payments that they were only minimally effective.

The essential problem with these three approaches was that the Depression just continued. President Franklin D. Roosevelt sought to change the debate on how to deal with economic insecurity. His goal was to have a long-term, permanent program of social insurance, already widespread in Europe, which would become the alternative to the current patchwork of ad-hoc solutions.

SOCIAL INSURANCE TO THE RESCUE

Social insurance, as conceived by President Franklin Roosevelt and a Democratic-controlled Congress, would address the permanent problem of economic security for the elderly by creating a work-related, contributory system in which workers would provide for future pensions through taxes paid while they were employed. Thus it was an alternative both to reliance on welfare and to radical changes in our capitalist system. In the context of its time, it can be seen as a conservative, yet activist, response to the challenges of the Depression.

By 1935, almost all of the European states had some form of social insurance. These state-sponsored efforts to provide for economic security would come to be seen as the practical alternative to the siren calls of those who preached socialism. "Socialism" is one of the most loaded words in U.S. politics. To the political right, it represents the beginnings of communist encroachment on traditional American values and institutions. To the political left, it represents the practical manifestation of America's pragmatic and generous spirit.

All social insurance programs include these two basic features: (1) an insurance principle, by which a defined group of citizens are "insured" in some way against predetermined risks; and (2) a social element, meaning that the program has broader social objectives than simply the self-interest of the individual participants. This means that to some extent, the richer participants in the programs get less out of it compared to what they put into it than the poor. This enforced charitable element is why all such programs are correctly labeled socialistic.

Social insurance is not a Ponzi scheme; it is not a fraudulent investment. Charles Ponzi (1882–1949) was a scam artist who, in the 1920s, sold bogus investments that paid returns to early investors from the investments of those who invested later. After being exposed, he spent more than a decade in prison. Ponzi's scheme was hardly unique—it had even been described by novelist Charles Dickens in *Little Dorrit* (1857). Ponzi's trial generated so much publicity that his name has stuck to the scam. It is essentially the same type of investment fraud as was carried out by Bernard Madoff (1938–), who was sentenced to 150 years in federal prison in 2009 for stealing billions through his own Ponzi scheme.

Nevertheless, social insurance is inherently similar to a Ponzi scheme in that funds from today's investors are used to pay yesterday's investors. When the government does it, however, this "Ponzi scheme" becomes a perfectly legal intergenerational transfer of wealth—an intergeneration social insurance plan—with today's workers paying into the system to support their parents in the expectation that their children will be equally generous in supporting them. Social insurance is not based on a pension fund. There is no fund. Money just comes in from one generation and goes out to another.

Social insurance has been the pragmatic answer to a wide variety of widespread problems, from disability and death to old age or unemployment. These are problems that can be ameliorated by a pooling of risk. Social insurance seeks to solve the eternal problem of economic security by pooling the assets (the insurance contributions)

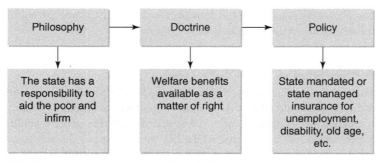

Figure 6.2 The Social Insurance Approach to Welfare

from a large social group and providing income to those members whose economic security is being immediately threatened. Figure 6.2 illustrates the social insurance approach to welfare.

THE CRITICAL ROLE OF THE SOCIAL SECURITY ACT OF 1935

As President Franklin D. Roosevelt signed into law the Social Security Act on August 14, 1935, he stated: "We can never insure one hundred percent of the population against one hundred percent of the hazards and vicissitudes of life, but we have tried to frame a law which will give some measure of protection to the average citizen and to his family against the loss of a job and against poverty-ridden old age."

Nevertheless, the Social Security Act did not quite achieve all the aspirations its supporters had hoped by way of providing a "comprehensive package of protection" against the "hazards and vicissitudes of life." Certain features of that package, notably disability coverage and medical benefits for the elderly, would have to wait until 1954 and 1965, respectively. However, it did provide a wide range of programs. In addition to the old-age pensions that we immediately think of as Social Security, it included unemployment insurance as well as aid to dependent children. And this was just the beginning. The act would be amended time and again, becoming the foundation of the U.S. welfare state.

OLD-AGE PENSIONS

Social Security is the popular name for the Old Age, Survivors, and Disability Insurance (OASDI) system established by the Social Security Act of 1935. At first, Social Security covered only retired private-sector employees. In 1939, the law was changed to cover survivors when the worker died and to cover certain dependents when the worker retired. In the 1950s, coverage was extended to include most self-employed persons, most state and local employees, household and farm employees, members of the Armed Forces, and members of the clergy. Today, almost all jobs are covered by Social Security.

Disability insurance was added in 1954 to give workers protection against loss of earnings due to total disability. The Social Security program was expanded again in 1965 with the enactment of Medicare, which assured hospital and medical insurance protection to people 65 years of age and over. Since 1973, Medicare coverage has been available to people under 65 who have been entitled to disability checks for two or more consecutive years and to people with permanent kidney failure who need dialysis treatment or kidney transplants. Amendments enacted in 1972 provided an automatic cost-of-living adjustment (an increase in compensation in response to increasing inflation).

The biggest problem with Social Security is demographics. In 1950 the ratio of taxpaying workers to pensioners was 120 to 1. In the year 2030 it will be 2 to 1. This is why, Social Security payroll taxes have risen from 1 percent in 1940 to 7.65 percent in 2010 (6.2 of the 7.65 percent is for traditional Social Security pensions; the remainder goes to fund Medicare). And that percentage is for both employees and employers—so it is double if you are self-employed.

Brookings Institution analyst Paul C. Light (1985) contends that if you want to understand U.S. politics you must first study Social Security. "Those who care about budget deficits must know something about the single largest program on the domestic ledger; those who care about electoral politics must know something about the central concern of older voters; those who care about trust in government must know something about the lack of confidence in Social Security among young and old Americans alike." Nevertheless, as Light (1994) asserts, even with all its problems and deficiencies, Social Security remains "the most important program for helping elderly women and minorities."

The critical importance of Social Security as an antipoverty program can be summarized with a few statistics. According to the Social Security Administration, in 2007, nearly 87 percent of all citizens over age 65 received benefits. For 53 percent of couples and 73 percent of singles, Social Security represented 50 percent or more of their income. Social Security income payments in September 2009 averaged $1,160 a month for retired workers. More than 52 million citizens currently rely on monthly Social Security payments of one kind or another (old age insurance, disability insurance, etc.). Table 6.1 shows average Social Security benefits for various classes of recipients as of January 2009.

Table 6.1 Average January 2009 Social Security Benefits

All retired workers	$1,153
Aged couple, both receiving benefits	$1,876
Widowed mother and two children	$2,399
Aged widow(er) alone	$1,112
Disabled worker, spouse and children	$1,793
All disabled workers	$1,064

Source: Social Security Administration.

SOCIAL SECURITY REFORM

Social Security is not a static program. Discussions to expand and contract it have been going on since its inception. For its first four decades it kept expanding, with additional classes of workers being covered and new benefits added. The high-water mark of this expansion occurred in 1972, when benefits started being automatically adjusted for inflation. By the 1980s, it had become obvious that something had to be done if the system was to retain its long-term viability. So, in 1981 President Ronald Reagan appointed the bi-partisan National Commission on Social Security Reform (known as the Greenspan Commission for its chair, Alan Greenspan). The commission's recommendations, which were signed into law in 1983, sought to make the system fiscally solvent by raising Social Security taxes from 5.4 percent to its present rate of 7.65 percent, taxing the benefits themselves to recover a portion of benefits paid out to higher-income recipients, and gradually raising the age at which one could receive full benefits from 65 to 67.

In 2001 President George W. Bush appointed the President's Commission to Strengthen Social Security, a bi-partisan sixteen-member group "to study and report recommendations to preserve Social Security for seniors while building wealth for younger Americans." Then-Governor Bush had campaigned for president in 2000 pledging to take Social Security to its "logical conclusion" by allowing Americans to use part of their Social Security contribution to create "personal retirement accounts." These accounts—unlike the current Social Security program, which provides benefits only for recipients, their spouses, and dependent minor children—would facilitate wealth creation. Similar in concept to Individual Retirement Accounts and 401(k) accounts, the accumulated assets could be inherited, as they would be personally owned and not subject to the vagaries of politics.

Although there was considerable national debate on the merits of such accounts and how they might be gradually implemented, the commission issued its report at a most unfortunate time—at the end of 2001, when the United States was deep in a recession and the stock market's decline was being compared to that of the Great Depression. Consequently, the whole matter of reform and the creation of personal accounts to be invested in the stock market was quietly dropped off the national agenda.

The only certainty with Social Security reform is that reform efforts will continue. The current system is simply not sustainable. Now that the "baby boomers" have started to retire, the system will suffer from a significant decline in the number of workers paying into the system, with a corresponding significant number of new retirees demanding benefits. Obviously, something must be done, but it is hard to muster the political will to deal with a problem that is still decades away. Only two things are certain: (1) Reform must come; and (2) the sooner it comes, the less painful it will be. One common suggestion is to gradually raise the retirement age to 70, but don't raise it for all those baby boomers who are about to retire. Raise it for the generations behind them. If no one feels any immediate pain, this fix for the system becomes much more palatable.

UNEMPLOYMENT INSURANCE

The first unemployment insurance law in the United States was passed by Wisconsin in 1932 and served as a forerunner for the unemployment insurance provisions of the Social Security Act of 1935. Unlike the old-age provisions of the Social Security legislation, which are administered by the federal government alone, the unemployment insurance system was made federal–state in character.

The Social Security Act provided an inducement to the states to enact unemployment insurance laws by means of a tax offset. A uniform national tax was imposed on the payrolls of employers who had eight workers or more during twenty weeks or more in a calendar year. Employers who paid a tax to a state with an approved unemployment insurance law could credit (offset) the state tax against the national tax (up to 90 percent of the federal levy). Thus, employers in states without an unemployment insurance law would not have an advantage in competing with similar businesses in states with such a law, because they would still be subject to the federal payroll tax. Furthermore, their employees would not be eligible for benefits. In addition, the Social Security Act authorized grants to states to meet the full costs of administering the state systems.

Unemployment benefits are available to workers from the various state unemployment insurance programs. Unemployment benefits are available as a matter of right to unemployed workers who have demonstrated their attachment to the labor force by a specified amount of recent work or earnings in covered employment. To be eligible for benefits, the worker must be ready, able, and willing to work and must be registered for work at a public employment office. A worker who meets these eligibility conditions may still be denied benefits if he or she is disqualified for an act that would indicate the worker is responsible for his or her own unemployment. This means that a worker who quits a job is ineligible for benefits. Some examples of maximum state weekly unemployment benefits in 2009 are listed in Table 6.2.

Table 6.2 Selected Maximum State Weekly Unemployment Benefits in 2009

Alabama	$208
Arizona	221
California	319
Florida	239
Michigan	290
Mississippi	195
New York	319
Pennsylvania	355
Texas	330
Virginia	323

Source: U.S. Department of Labor.

AID TO FAMILIES WITH DEPENDENT CHILDREN

When the Social Security Act was passed in 1935, it included a small program to help widows and orphans. This was the origin of Aid to Families with Dependent Children (AFDC), the program by which the federal government matched state spending on welfare. AFDC provided federal funds, administered by the states, for children living with a parent or a relative who met state standards of need. The program became controversial because of charges that it not only promoted illegitimacy but also encouraged fathers to abandon their families so they could become eligible for AFDC. In 1994 more than 14 million people were receiving AFDC, up from just over 2 million in 1955.

Claiming that the system had produced "welfare queens," women conceiving children out of wedlock to qualify for AFDC benefits, and a cycle of generational poverty encouraged by the welfare system, the Republican-controlled Congress in 1995 decided to act. It would change the system by giving the problem back to the states. After all, welfare was a local problem to begin with. The money spent on AFDC would be converted to block grants with which the states in their fifty varieties of wisdom would decide who was worthy of the new-style welfare and under what conditions. In essence, most of the federal strings would be removed, and the states would overall get less than before, but they would have far greater discretion on how to spend it. Thus a comprehensive welfare reform bill was passed by the Congress in 1996. This repealed the entitlement aspect of AFDC and was signed into law by President Bill Clinton. The states—with the encouragement of the federal government—are now busy simultaneously reinventing welfare programs while they seek to discourage the expansion of the welfare rolls by holding fathers more responsible for supporting their children. Simply put, the problem has proved so difficult that the Congress gave up on it and dumped it back on the states.

CHANGING WELFARE DOCTRINE

The welfare reform law of 1996 was hailed as a great success. States reported dramatic declines in their welfare rolls. One reason was the booming economy. Even without reform, we would expect welfare rolls to decrease when jobs are plentiful. However, other, more lasting factors are at work as well—factors that determined that the rolls did not "automatically" go up significantly when the economy went into recession, as it did in 2001. Devolution means that welfare is not what it used to be; most important, it is no longer an entitlement. According to Barbara Vobejda and Judith Havemann (1998), in at least three dozen states, welfare managers actively seek to prevent applicants from getting welfare. "Welfare offices are urging applicants to ask for help from relatives instead of signing up for government assistance, writing onetime emergency checks in place of monthly benefits, or requiring applicants to spend weeks searching for work before they receive their first welfare payment." This raises questions "of whether they have found jobs on their own, never truly needed them in the first place, or have been scared off or intimidated from applying for help that their children genuinely require."

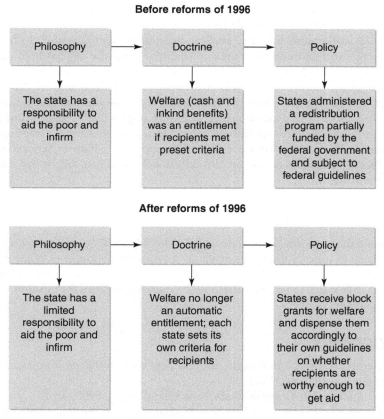

Figure 6.3 Welfare Reform Before and After

This change in welfare doctrine is illustrated in Figure 6.3. Notice how we have come full circle: Those who are deemed unworthy or undeserving of aid, because they refuse to accept work or educational opportunities, may now be cut off completely. And even if they are highly deserving, they may be cut off if they reach a preset time limit such as two years. The theory is that if welfare recipients know that funds for them will run out at a certain date, they will be more energetic about finding work or obtaining job training beforehand. The new act was entitled the "Personal Responsibility and Work Opportunity Reconciliation Act," specifically because welfare recipients were generally expected to take more "personal responsibility" for their situation in life by seeking an appropriate "work opportunity."

Such diversion tactics are now commonplace. California, Kansas, Florida, Oregon, and New York, among other states, all seek to direct applicants into jobs or one-time cash payments (they cannot then reapply for a prescribed period). This leads to the second major new factor. The traditional welfare office is evolving into a new administrative animal. According to Rachel L. Swarns (1998), in New York City, "job centers are replacing welfare offices. Financial planners are replacing caseworkers. And the entire bureaucracy is morphing into the Family Independence Administration. In truth the same workers still do business in the same buildings, but the city has been infected by a name-changing frenzy that has been sweeping the country. Massachusetts' Department of Public Welfare is now the Department of Transitional Assistance. Florida's welfare program is now the Work and Gain Economic Self-Sufficiency Program." Indicative of this major change in terminology is the 1998 decision of the American Public Welfare Association (which represents social service agencies) to change its name after sixty-six years to the American Public Human Services Association. Welfare reform may not yet have killed welfare in fact, but it has certainly killed it in name.

FOR DISCUSSION

Should the age at which citizens are eligible for full Social Secuity retirement benefits remain static or change gradually in response to the longevity of the population? Are you concerned about whether the Social Security system will remain financially viable to pay the current level of benefits, adjusted for inflation, to your generation?

BIBLIOGRAPHY

Blank, Rebecca M., and Ron Haskins, eds. *The New World of Welfare.* Washington, DC: Brookings Institution, 2002.

Carnegie, Andrew. *The Gospel of Wealth.* New York: Century, 1900.

Cook, Gareth G. "Devolution Chic: Why Sending Power to the States Could Make a Monkey Out of Uncle Sam." *Washington Monthly,* April1995.

Diamond, Peter A. *Social Security Reform.* New York: Oxford University Press, 2003.

Diamond, Peter A., ed. *Issues in Privatizing Social Security.* Cambridge, MA: MIT Press, 1999.

Donahue, John M. *The Privatization Decision.* New York: Basic Books, 1989.

Light, Paul C. *Artful Work: The Politics of Social Security Reform.* New York: Random House, 1985.

———. *Still Artful Work: The Continuing Politics of Social Security Reform,* 2nd ed. New York: McGraw-Hill, 1994.

Morgan, D. R., and R. E. England. "The Two Faces of Privatization." *Public Administration Review* 48 (1988).

Moynihan, Daniel Patrick. "The Devolution Revolution." *New York Times,* August 6, 1995.

Savas, E. S. *Privatizing the Public Sector: How to Shrink Government.* Chatham, NJ: Chatham House, 1982.

Strop, Leigh. "Report: Social Security Deficit to Boom." *Washington Times,* July 29, 2003.

Swarns, Rachel L. "A New Broom Needs a New Handle: Welfare as We Know It Goes Incognito." *New York Times,* July 5, 1998.

Vobejda, Barbara. "Will There Be a Race to the Bottom on Welfare?" *Washington Post National Weekly,* September 18–24, 1995.

Vobejda, Barbara, and Judith Havemann. "States' Welfare Shift: Stop It Before It Starts." *Washington Post,* August 12, 1998.

Weaver R. Kent. *Ending Welfare As We Know It.* Washington, DC: Brookings Institution, 2000.

CHAPTER SEVEN

Gun Shows, Gun Laws, and Gun Totin'

SECOND AMENDMENT FANATICS VERSUS ALL LEVELS OF GOVERNMENT

PREVIEW

In August 2009, a man with an assault rifle slung over his shoulder walked just outside the gates of a Phoenix, Arizona, convention hall where President Barack Obama was holding a discussion about health care reform in the United States. Given a history that includes the assassination of four U.S. presidents by gunfire, it would seem reasonable that the police officers outside the convention hall would use all powers at their disposal to subdue the armed man before he got any closer to the arena where the president was speaking. However, as the man moved around the perimeter of the hall, the Phoenix police officers standing guard quietly watched him without taking any actions to either disarm or restrain the rifle-toting Arizonan.

Were the police officers in Phoenix being derelict in their duties? Were they failing to recognize the threat that an assault rifle–bearing man may pose to the president of the United States? The answer to these questions is no. The officers could not do anything to the rifle-carrying citizen because he was not breaking any law. This was a gun show; the man was showing off his gun to prove that he had one, to reassert his right to do so, and to allow his testosterone levels to have a public airing. In the state of Arizona, people can carry unconcealed guns. So long as no physical or verbal threats were made toward a citizen, including the president, the man was acting within the legal limits that governed him.

Of course, the man carrying the weapon was well aware of the Arizona statute that protected his right to walk in public with a rifle slung over his shoulder. He, along with a number of other men, brought their weapons to the area outside the convention hall to assert their right to bear arms, and their actions were indeed within the letter of the law in Arizona. Even President

Obama's press secretary, Robert Gibbs, seemed to recognize the legality of the situation when he noted: "There are laws that govern firearms that are done state or locally and those laws don't change when the president comes to your state or locality."

GUNS AND PRESIDENTS

The events in Arizona in 2009 provide a good example of the complexities of firearm regulation in the United States. Within the confines of U.S. federalism, the national, state, and local governments have constructed a complicated web of laws and regulations that govern the possession and use of guns in the United States. The Second Amendment of the U.S. Constitution provides that "the right of the people to keep and bear arms, shall not be infringed," but the details on when and where Americans can hold and use their guns have been formed through a baroque array of laws and court cases that have developed over two centuries. In this chapter we examine firearm regulations through the perspective of the travels of the president of the United States. From the moment he steps outside the grounds of the White House on to the Streets of Washington, D.C., to the time *Air Force One* touches down in places like Phoenix, Arizona, the president moves through jurisdictions with vastly varying rules on what is and is not permissible in terms of firearms.

When one thinks of the most dangerous job in the United States, there are certain jobs that most likely come to mind. Thanks to popular television shows such as *The Deadliest Catch* and *Ax Men,* the public has become well aware that commercial fishing and logging pose great risks to the individuals who work in those fields. More specifically, one of every 1,000 loggers dies each year as a result of a logging accident. Those numbers may look pretty risky, but when they are compared to the fatality statistics for another U.S. profession, they look positively safe. Is that other dangerous profession something like trapeze artist, fireworks specialist, or deep-sea diver? No, the job is president of the United States. Among the forty-four men who have served as president of the United States, four have been killed while doing there job as the nation's chief executive. Put in ratio terms, one in ten presidents has been assassinated while serving in office. Whereas loggers and fishermen are killed by a variety of means (e.g., drowning, blunt force), presidents who are killed in office have all died by the same means: bullet wounds.

Beginning with the assassination of Abraham Lincoln in 1865 and ending with John Kennedy's murder in 1963, the residents of the United States have seen four chief executives killed by an array of firearms. Along with the four successful assassinations of U.S. presidents by gunfire, numerous other men and women have attempted to shoot presidents. Ronald Reagan was hit by gunfire shortly after taking office in 1981. Both Harry Truman and Gerald Ford were subjected to near-misses. Additionally, Theodore Roosevelt was shot after he left office (saved only by the metal eyeglass case in his pocket), and Franklin D. Roosevelt was shot at as president-elect (the gunman just missed him and killed the man next to him, the mayor of Chicago).

In each of these four cases, it was only a matter of inches. If you consider these four failed assassinations, then the job is twice as dangerous, with close to a 20 percent chance of being shot at. George Washington wrote, after his first combat experience in 1754 during the French and Indian War, that "I heard bullets whistle and believe me there was something charming in the sound." Subsequent presidents have not found the sound so "charming."

With such a long and horrific history of gun violence against the nation's highest elected officials, it seems reasonable to expect that both the president and Congress would have aggressively attempted to control gun violence in the United States. Such expectations may be reasonable, but they are not very accurate. Despite occasional efforts to restrict gun use at the national level, the federal government has had a fairly limited role in regulating gun use. Of course, much of the limited federal action on gun control may be traced to the Second Amendment of the Constitution, which established that "the right of the people to keep and bear arms, shall not be infringed." With this right established by the Constitution, the ability of the Congress and president to regulate guns has always been fairly constrained by the recognition that the courts may not allow any restrictions to stand.

Perhaps the most significant attempt by the federal government to get tough on guns was inspired by the assassination of President John F. Kennedy in 1963. Coupled with the 1968 murders of his brother, Senator Robert F. Kennedy, and of Dr. Martin Luther King, Jr., the killing of the president helped fuel public sentiments for a crackdown on gun violence. Congress responded to this public opinion with the passage of the Gun Control Act of 1968. This act tightened license requirements for gun dealers and restricted the sale of guns to convicted felons. The act also banned the mail-order purchase of rifles and shotguns. This element of the bill was both practically and symbolically important, because President Kennedy's assassin, Lee Harvey Oswald, had purchased the weapon he used to kill the president through a mail-order company.

The assassination attempt on Ronald Reagan also played a role in expanding federal firearm restrictions. When John Hinkley, Jr., fired his handgun toward President Reagan on a chilly March day in 1981, he hit not only the president but also a Washington, D.C., police officer and Reagan's press secretary, James Brady. Brady suffered a serious head wound, spent months in a hospital, and became permanently paraplegic. Despite his ongoing health problems, Brady and his wife Sarah committed themselves to tightening national restrictions on handguns in the United States. With the support of Reagan after the president left office, Congress passed the Brady Handgun Violence Prevention Act in 1993. The Brady Act required a new National Instant Criminal Background Check System to be used to determine if an individual meets the eligibility guidelines to purchase a firearm.

The Gun Control Act of 1968 and the Brady Act of 1993 placed some national restrictions on gun ownership, but the reality is that it is the states and local governments that set most of the rules that govern firearms in the nation. When the commander in chief leaves the safety of the White House and travels through the nation, he passes through a complex mix of state and local gun laws that range from incredibly open to fairly restrictive. To demonstrate this variety we will examine the gun control laws in the three places where U.S. presidents have been killed by guns. These three places, Washington, D.C., Texas, and New York, display the variety of approaches that states take when dealing with the issue of guns.

GUN CONTROL IN THE NATION'S CAPITAL

Two sitting U.S. presidents have been killed by guns in their adopted home city of Washington, D.C. In April 1865, President Abraham Lincoln traveled only blocks from the White House to watch a play called *Our American Cousin* at Ford's Theater. In a time when security around the president was very scant, a classically trained actor and Southern sympathizer named John Wilkes Booth snuck into the president's box and shot the sixteenth president in the back of the head at point-blank range. Lincoln died the following morning in a residence across the street from the theater, becoming the first U.S. president to be assassinated.

Only sixteen years after Lincoln's murder, another president, James A. Garfield, was cut down by an assassin's bullet. Garfield was shot by Charles Guiteau because Guiteau had been denied a patronage appointment. Guiteau had stalked the president, eventually shooting him at short range at the Baltimore and Potomac Railroad Station in Washington, D.C. After suffering for months, Garfield died in September 1881, becoming the second president to be murdered in office. There is no doubt that civil service reform would have eventually come about without the assassination of Garfield; there is also no doubt that the assassination helped by creating a political climate more susceptible to reform—reform of the civil service, not reform of laws governing gun ownership.

Garfield was the last president to be killed in Washington, D.C., but the city's experience with gun violence only grew during the following century. For many years, the official capital of the United States was unofficially known as America's murder capital. With murder rates among the highest in the nation, Washington, D.C., had earned a reputation for having some of the most dangerous streets in the country. The presence of exceptional numbers of murders just blocks away from Congress and the White House posed a great embarrassment to both the city and the nation as a whole. By the 1970s the city that had witnessed two presidents killed by gunfire and hundreds of its citizens killed by guns each year had decided that it was time to act.

In 1976, the District of Columbia City Council passed the Firearms Control and Regulation Act (FCRA), thus enacting the nation's strictest firearms control law. The FCRA banned residents of the city from owning most types of firearms, including handguns, automatic weapons, and many semiautomatic guns. The law also required residents who owned permitted weapons such as hunting rifles to register those weapons with the city. Going even further in its efforts to limit gun violence, the FCRA required permitted firearms kept in the home to be unloaded, disassembled, or bound by a trigger lock.

Washington, D.C., had established the benchmark for stringent gun control laws, but the effectiveness and constitutionality of those efforts was regularly called into question. Decades after the enactment of the FCRA, the numbers of gun-related murders in the District were still among the highest in the United States. Fueled by the crack cocaine epidemic of the late 1980s, gun violence reached record levels by the early 1990s. As skepticism about the effectiveness of the District of Columbia gun laws grew with each additional firearm-related murder, challenges of the legality of the restrictions also mounted. With the Second Amendment limiting the government's ability to infringe on a citizen's right to bear arms, there were many who believed that Washington's gun law had gone too far. Eventually these questions about the constitutionality of the firearm restrictions made it into the judicial system.

In 2003, six residents of the nation's capital filed a lawsuit in the Federal District Court for the District of Columbia, directly challenging Washington, D.C.'s gun laws. For years, gun right advocates had searched for just the right case to sue as the challenge to the District's gun law. Through the efforts of the conservative Cato Institute, six city residents from diverse backgrounds came together as plaintiffs in the case. However, the D.C. District Court, which is generally considered one of the more liberal federal courts in the nation, dismissed the lawsuit, thus preserving the gun control restrictions.

The plaintiffs and their legal advisors anticipated dismissal in the District Court and proceeded to appeal the decision at the federal appellate level. In 2007, The U.S. Court of Appeals for the District of Columbia reversed the decision of the District Court, finding that Washington, D.C.'s handgun ban violates the Second Amendment provisions regarding the right to bear arms. In *Parker v. District of Columbia*, the Court of Appeals also found that the District of Columbia's rules requiring firearms to be unloaded and disassembled "amounts to a complete prohibition on the lawful use for self-defense" and, therefore, also violates the Second Amendment.

Only a year after the *Parker* decision in the Court of Appeals, the U.S. Supreme Court heard an appeal of that case, ultimately deciding the constitutionality of the Washington gun law. In the landmark decision of *District of Columbia v. Heller* (2008), the Supreme Court affirmed the *Parker* ruling in a five-to-four decision, thus determining that Washington, D.C.'s efforts to control guns had violated the intent of the Constitution. Importantly, the decision in this case was the first in U.S. history to address directly whether the right to bear arms is a right of individuals in addition to a collective right that applies to state-regulated militias.

The majority in the *Heller* case emphasized that Second Amendment rights were not unlimited, and that a person does not have the right to carry "any weapon whatsoever in any manner whatsoever and for whatever purpose." In the Court's opinion, Washington, D.C.'s gun laws had simply gone too far. As will be seen in the overview of the next jurisdiction's firearm laws, no one has ever claimed that Texas has gone too far in restricting guns.

DON'T MESS WITH TEXANS AND THEIR GUNS

On a cool, clear November day in 1963, President John F. Kennedy's motorcade wound through the streets of Dallas, Texas. Kennedy had gone to Texas in hopes of helping his chances of winning reelection in the 1964 election. As his car made its way around a bend into Dealey Plaza, the President and his wife Jacqueline waved to the Texans lining the streets. Seconds later, shots rang out in the Dallas sky. Kennedy was struck by a number of shots from the rifle of a troubled loner named Lee Harvey Oswald. By the time the president's motorcade had made it to Parkland Hospital, his life had ended. The nation's thirty-fifth President had become its fourth assassinated chief executive.

Like the nation's capital, Texas has seen a president gunned down in its streets and has been among the national leaders in gun-related deaths. In 2008, nearly 1,400 individuals were killed by gunfire in Texas. But if Washington, D.C., set the standard for the most aggressive gun control legislation in the nation, Texas has established itself as a national leader in permissive gun rules. In the Lone Star State, owning and carrying a gun is about as easy as you will find anywhere in the nation, with the state often restricting its municipal and county governments from putting limits on the right of a Texan to keep and bear arms. Unless convicted of a felony, a resident of Texas who is 18 years or older has no restrictions on his or her right to own a rifle or shotgun. Texas also has no laws regarding possession of handguns for residents over the age of 21. And as long as the weapon is not banned by the federal government, a Texan can own such weapons and firearm accoutrements as automatic weapons, sawed-off shotguns, and silencers.

One of the defining features of gun laws in Texas is the state's protection of the right to carry a gun in public. In a state where the Wild West tradition of pistol-packing pioneers is tightly embraced, it is not surprising that the right to carry firearms remains very much alive. If you like to strap your rifle or shotgun over your shoulder and wander down the street, Texas is the place for you. The state has no restrictions on openly carrying a rifle or shotgun. And although Texans are generally no longer able to carry a revolver (or other handgun) openly, as they once did, the state generously hands out concealed-weapons permits to its residents.

Texas firearm laws are so permissive that it is hard to see how they could be made even more accommodating to state residents seeking to arm themselves. Nevertheless, Texas Governor Rick Perry has made increasing gun rights one of the key initiatives during his time in office. Since becoming the Lone Star State's chief executive in December 2000, Perry has worked hard to protect and expand the rights of gun owners in his state.

In 2005 Perry signed into effect House Bill 1815, allowing any Texas resident to carry a concealed handgun in the resident's motor vehicle even if the resident does not have a concealed-weapons permit. Thus, if you own one, you can carry a loaded and concealed weapon in your car anywhere in Texas. No permit is required. And while protecting the rights of Texans to drive with their guns was a nice accomplishment for Perry, protecting their right to use those weapons was an even bigger victory for the man who replaced George Bush as the state's governor.

On March 27, 2007, Perry signed Senate Bill 378 into law, making Texas a "castle doctrine" state. Under the castle doctrine, Texans lawfully occupying a dwelling may shoot a person who unlawfully, and forcefully, enters or attempts to enter the dwelling. In addition, a gun owner who is on his own property has no responsibility to try and "retreat" from a trespasser before using a gun on that person. Thus, in Texas, if someone enters your "castle" without being invited, you can shoot her on sight, without even trying to avoid the invader.

Finally, Perry set his sights on expanding the places that Texans could take their guns. One place in the Lone Star State where guns were not welcome was college campuses. Public universities such as the University of Texas prohibit guns within the confines of the campus. However, in the wake of the killings at Virginia Tech University in 2007, Perry pushed for Texas to allow students over the age of 21 to carry concealed handguns along with their calculators and IPods.

No matter what the results of Governor Perry's efforts to expand guns onto campus, he need not fear his gun rights accomplishments being overturned by a future court decision. Unlike the restrictive gun control efforts in Washington, D.C., that were struck down in 2008, there are no state constitutional limits on gun ownership that could be used to constrain the rights of Texans to keep and use their firearms.

THE GUNS OF NEW YORK

In September 1901, President William McKinley was enjoying his time at the Pan America Exposition in Buffalo, New York. At the Exposition's Temple of Music, McKinley held a public reception during which fairgoers could stop and shake hands with the president. After about ten minutes at the reception, a man with a bandaged hand approached the president and fired two shots into McKinley's chest and abdomen. The shooter was an unemployed factory worker from Detroit named Leon Czolgosz, who believed that McKinley was hurting the working people of the nation. Although he appeared initially to survive the wounds inflicted by Czolgosz, McKinley died eight days later of infection and gangrene.

The assassination of President McKinley and the shooting of New York City Mayor William Jay Gaynor in 1910 increased public calls for regulation of handguns. As gun violence intensified in places like New York City, efforts to create gun controls grew even stronger. Following the public sentiment to limit access to guns, the State of New York passed the first major gun control regulations in U.S. history. On May 29, 1911, the Sullivan Act was signed into law, requiring New Yorkers to obtain licenses to possess firearms small enough to be concealed. If a resident of the Empire State is found possessing a firearm without a permit, he can be charged with a misdemeanor offense, but if he is caught carrying a handgun without having a permit, the offense is a felony.

As with everything in New York, the workings of the Sullivan Act differ considerably between New York City and the rest of the state. Outside of Gotham, the licensing of handguns is usually taken care of by the counties where the weapons request is being made. In New York City, however, the licensing authority is the city's police department. Over the years, the New York Police Department has been very stingy in handing out licenses. If you are not a retired police officer, a well-known movie star, or a high-profile elected official, your chances of getting a license to carry a firearm are fairly low. Ever since its adoption, the Sullivan Act has been criticized as being discriminatory to the poor because it requires individuals to pay a fee to get a permit. So, while ordinary New Yorkers have sometimes struggled to get gun permits, famous individuals such as Don Imus, Harvey Keitel, Robert DeNiro, Howard Stern, Joan Rivers, and Donald Trump were readily issued licenses to carry handguns.

Although it is almost a century old, the Sullivan Act remains very relevant and controversial today. Just ask former New York Giants football player Plaxico Burress. For years, Burress was among the best wide receivers in the National Football League, catching the winning touchdown for the Giants in their Super Bowl victory in 2008. During the season after his Super Bowl heroics, Burress decided to spend a Friday evening partying at Manhattan night clubs. As part of his wardrobe that evening, Burress decided to take along his loaded Glock pistol, tucking the handgun into the waistband of his pants. When the gun accidently slid down his pants leg, Burress reached for the weapon, inadvertently pulling the trigger and shooting himself in the thigh. The football star's wound was not life-threatening, but his troubles with the law were quite serious.

When Plaxico Burress crossed the Hudson River from his New Jersey home and entered Manhattan with his loaded handgun, he committed a felony offense. Burress had broken the Sullivan Act's provision requiring owners of handguns to be licensed. Burress did have an expired permit to carry a handgun in Florida, but he had no permit to carry a gun in New York City. Worse, he was carrying his gun in the worst possible place—in the waistband of his sweatpants. Had he been from Texas, he would have known to tuck his gun into his waist only if he was wearing a thick belt, as all cowboys do. So, because of his poor fashion sense, among other reasons, Burress turned himself into the police and was charged with criminal possession of a handgun. This offense carries a three-year jail sentence.

Given Burress's high profile, gun control and gun rights advocates attempted to make his case part of their broader political efforts. New York City Mayor Michael Bloomberg advocated strongly that Burress be prosecuted to the fullest extent of the law, and that anything short of the three years in jail would be a mockery of the law. Clearly, Bloomberg hoped that the prosecution of a football hero would send a message that New York took its gun laws seriously. Rather than go to trial, Burress in September 2009 accepted a plea bargain for two years in prison to be followed by two years of probation. Meanwhile, gun rights advocates used the Burress incident to demonstrate that the gun control laws in New York were focused more on punishing gun owners than on punishing criminals who use guns to commit crimes.

FROM MY COLD DEAD HANDS

The United States remains one of the most heavily armed and most violent countries in the developed world. On average, more than 30,000 Americans die each year from gunshot wounds, of whom about 12,000 are murdered with a firearm. As these numbers suggest, most deaths by gunfire are accidents or suicides.

Most gun owners are responsible, law-abiding people who feel fervently about their Second Amendment rights. Even those who have concealed-weapon permits seldom carry out crimes and very often prevent them. Legal gun owners tend to be as responsible in their handling of their guns as they are fanatical about their rights to possess them.

This fanaticism, which we mean in a positive sense, was best summarized by Charlton Heston, the actor who portrayed Moses in the 1955 film, *The Ten Commandments*.

As president of the National Rifle Association (NRA) from 1998 to 2003, he popularized the NRA's informal slogan: "From my cold dead hands." Thus the iconic voice of the biblical Moses would end his speeches to the NRA faithful by raising a rifle (often a Revolutionary War replica) over his head and shouting, presumably to the government in Washington, "I'll give you my gun when you take it from my cold dead hands." Tens of millions of others, even millions who are not members of the NRA, feel exactly the same way. Their attitude is that gun ownership is not just for hunting and personal defense; it is the first line of defense against an incipient tyrannical government.

Four of the nation's presidents have been cut down by assassins' bullets. Despite their reputation as the most powerful men in the world, U.S. presidents have been extremely vulnerable to the dangers posed by guns. In their capacity as commander in chief of the nation's Armed Forces, presidents can unleash unprecedented fire power on the country's enemies, but their ability to control and manage guns within the United States remains extremely limited. The Second Amendment has and will always leave the federal government in a limited position of power in the area of gun control.

As has been the case since New York passed the Sullivan Act in 1911, the states will continue to play the most active role in determining the rules that govern firearm ownership and use. The Supreme Court's decision in *District of Columbia v. Heller* appears to have placed some limits on what states and cities can do to restrict firearms; but the majority opinion in that case made it clear that governments maintain the power to regulate guns in a manner that does not violate the Constitution. So, as U.S. presidents continue to travel about the nation they serve, they will pass though places such as Texas, where the residents' credo is "from my cold dead hands;" and where all citizens can pack weapons on their bodies and in their cars without ever asking government permission. Compare this to New York City, where even carrying an unlicensed weapon can make you a felon. Such is the reality of U.S. federalism.

FOR DISCUSSION

How does the nature of U.S. federalism make it difficult, to the point of being almost impossible, to have any kind of comprehensive gun control? Openly carrying loaded weapons near a U.S. president may be a constitutionally protected right, but is it also bad manners or poor common sense?

BIBLIOGRAPHY

Barnes, Robert. "Justices Reject D.C. Ban on Handgun Ownership." *Washington Post,* June 27, 2008.

Doherty, Brian. *Gun Control on Trial: Inside the Supreme Court Battle over the Second Amendment.* Washington, DC: Cato Institute, 2009.

Kleck, Gary. *Targeting Guns: Firearms and Their Control.* Piscataway, NJ: Aldine Transaction, 1997.

Liptak, Adam. "Carefully Plotted Course Propels Gun Case to Top." *New York Times,* December 3, 2007.

Maske, Mark. "Burress to Face Weapons Charge." *Washington Post,* November 30, 2008.

Myers, Amanda Lee, and Terry Tang. "Man Carrying Assault Weapon Attends Obama Protest." *The Associated Press,* August 17, 2009.

Poe, Richard. *The Seven Myths of Gun Control: Reclaiming the Truth About Guns, Crime, and the Second Amendment.* New York: Three Rivers Press, 2003.

Spitzer, Robert. *The Politics of Gun Control,* 4th ed. Washington, DC: CQ Press, 2007.

Weir, William. *A Well-Regulated Militia: The Battle over Gun Control.* North Haven, CT: Archon Books, 1997.

Whiteley, Glenna. "Texas Concealed Gun Laws Loosen." *Dallas Observer,* October 24, 2007.

CHAPTER EIGHT

The Politics–Administration Dichotomy Negated Again

HOW THE ROVE DOCTRINE SUBORDINATED STATE, LOCAL, AND NATIONAL ENVIRONMENTAL POLICY TO THE SERVICE OF THE REPUBLICAN PARTY

PREVIEW

There has always been considerable tension between politics and the administration of public policy. In theory, there is a wall that separates those who make the laws and those who carry them out. A public administrator is charged with taking the decisions of elected officials and translating them into reality without consideration for the political implications of the actions. Neutrality on the part of civil servants has long been held as the standard that guides government workers in their duties. Although these principles of neutrality and the maintenance of a divide between those who make the laws and those who implement the laws remain today, the reality is that all administrations at all levels of government implement their programs with an eye toward political considerations.

Historically, in academic public administration this separation became known as the politics–administration dichotomy. This dichotomy, which grew out of the progressive and civil service reform movements, asserted that the spoils system and political interference in administration eroded the opportunities for administrative efficiency. Consequently, the policy-making activities of government ought to be wholly separated from the administrative functions; administrators need an explicit assignment of objectives before they can begin to develop an efficient administrative system. Public administration theorists in the early part of the twentieth century argued that politics and administration could be distinguished, in the words of Frank J. Goodnow (1859–1929), the first president of the American Political Science Association, as "the expression of the will of the state and the execution of that will" (1900).

Paul Appleby (1891–1963), a New Deal administrator and one-time dean of the Maxwell School at Syracuse University, became the leading critic of this theoretical insistence on apolitical government processes when he asserted that it went against the grain of the American experience. Appleby, in *Big Democracy* (1945), held that it was a myth that politics was separate and could somehow be taken out of administration. Political involvement was good—not evil, as many of the progressive reformers had claimed—because political involvement in administration acted as a check on the arbitrary exercise of bureaucratic power. In the future, those who would describe the political ramifications and issues of administration would not begin by contesting the politics–administration dichotomy as incorrect or irrelevant; rather, they would begin from the premise, so succinctly put by Appleby, that "government is different because government is politics." Today, most public administration theorists accept the notion that politics and administration are inherently and inevitably intertwined.

THE POLITICIAN–ADMINISTRATOR NEXUS

Bureaucrats depend on elected officials for many things, including their budgets, equipment, duties, and, in many cases, their jobs. With such high stakes resting on the decisions of elected officials, public administrators cannot afford to ignore the political world in which they operate. To do so would be irrational. Instead, administrators are keenly aware of the political figures that decide so much about their professional lives. And while bureaucrats may keep an eye on politicians, those same politicians are well aware that public administrators are often well positioned to help them reach their political aspirations. Because public administrators maintain a great deal of discretion in carrying out public policies, in implementing the public interests, their decisions can directly affect the standing of elected officials with various interests and the public at large.

The public interest is the universal label in which political actors wrap the policies and programs that they advocate. Would any lobby, public manager, legislator, or chief executive ever propose a program that was not "in the public interest"? Hardly! Because the public interest is generally taken to mean a commonly accepted good, the phrase is used both to further policies that are indeed for the common good and to obscure policies that may not be so commonly accepted as good. A considerable body of literature has developed about this phrase, because it represents an important philosophic point that, if defined successfully, could provide considerable guidance for politicians and public administrators alike. Walter Lippmann (1889–1974), the journalist and political philoopher, wrote that "the public interest may be presumed to be what men would choose if they saw clearly, thought rationally, acted disinterestedly and benevolently" (1955). Clear eyes and rational minds are common enough. Finding leaders who are disinterested and benevolent is the hard part.

In the early twentieth century, E. Pendleton Herring (1903–2004) examined the problems posed by the dramatic increase in the scope of the administrative discretion of government. He accepted that laws passed by legislatures are necessarily the products of legislative compromise; thus they are often so vague that they need further definition. The bureaucrat, by default, then has the task of giving definitional detail to the general principles embodied in a statute by issuing supplemental rules and regulations. "Upon the shoulders of the bureaucrat has been placed in large part the burden of reconciling group differences and making effective and workable the economic and social compromises arrived at through the legislative process" (1936). In effect, it becomes the job of anonymous administrators to define the public interest. Sometimes they just need a little help from a high-level political appointee—someone like Carl Rove.

Elected officials at all levels of government have attempted to influence public administrators to make them perform their duties in a manner that will be beneficial to their needs. However, one man stands above all others in recognizing the electoral advantages that can be gleaned from the manipulation of bureaucrats. That man is Republican Party political guru Carl Rove. During his tenure as President George W. Bush's chief political consultant, Rove established a new standard for merging politics with public administration.

THE ARCHITECT ARRIVES

Since the beginning of this new century, no individual had a greater impact on the way U.S. politics is practiced than Carl Rove. The man that President George W. Bush affectionately called the "architect" shaped the strategies that helped Republicans gain control of both the White House and Congress between 2000 and 2006. But while Rove received tremendous credit for his ability to win elections, his effect on public policy was less obvious to the U.S. public. Nevertheless, Rove established a doctrine that intertwined politics and policy in a manner that directly affected the way public policies are conducted in the United States.

To be sure, elected officials have always used their control over government policies to advantage their fortunes at the ballot box. From patronage appointments to the signing of legislation, politicians have concentrated their powers in ways that increase their likelihood of maintaining their positions as elected officials. However, when Carl Rove arrived in Washington in 2001, he set off to redefine how politics and policy can be intertwined. Under Rove, the Bush administration introduced the electoral well-being of the Republican Party into all aspects of the policy-making process. This heavy integration of electoral politics into policy decisions was identified as the "Rove Doctrine" by authors Tom Hamburger and Peter Wallsten in their 2006 book, *One Party Country*. According to these authors, the Rove Doctrine established a political lens under which all policy decisions were examined. Under Rove's direction, not even the smallest localized policy decisions were immune from being evaluated in terms of their impact on maintaining Republican control of the federal government. Such focus required integrating political strategists and policy administrators in ways that had not been seen before the advent of the Bush administration. This doctrine's effect were most observable within the realm of environmental and natural resource policy in the United States.

THE BLUEPRINT

Almost immediately upon arriving in Washington and setting up his operation in Hillary Clinton's old office in the West Wing, Rove began plotting his strategy for the mid-term elections of 2002. Foremost among Rove's objectives for 2002 was regaining Republican control of the Senate. This meant that the Republican Party had to win a number of tight races throughout the nation. For Rove, securing these wins would involve harnessing the powers of the federal government to advantage Republicans.

In the case of Oregon Senator Gordon Smith's reelection bid, Rove saw the opportunity to use natural resource policy to pave Smith's return to Capital Hill. During the election year, a bitter dispute regarding the use of water from the Kalmath River was taking place in Oregon. The conflict arose over a plan to divert water from the river to the state's agricultural industry. While farmers supported the plan, the state's environmental community opposed the proposal because of the effect the water diversion would have on Oregon's salmon population. At the center of the controversy was the U.S. Department of Interior, which had jurisdiction over the water decision. With high political stakes in place, the Kalmath situation posed a clear test of the Rove Doctrine.

In January 2002, Rove went to meet with fifty Interior Department managers at a department retreat in West Virginia. At that conference, the president's key political advisor informed them of the administration's support of the water diversion, and reminded the managers of the importance of supporting the GOP base. Rove also sent polling data to the Interior Department administrators that linked their work to electoral politics. According to Hamburger and Wallsten, a high-ranking Department of Interior official was quoted as saying, "We were constantly being reminded about how our decisions could effect electoral results." In the end, Interior Secretary Gale Norton joined Senator Smith in Oregon to open the floodgates that brought irrigation to farms, death to tens of thousands of salmon, and an assist to Smith's eventual victory in the mid-term election.

While the Rove Doctrine's focus on political gain came at the expense of lots of salmon in the Kalmath River case, environmental preservation was also seen as a political tool in the 2002 Florida governor's race. In that campaign President Bush's younger brother, Jeb, was being challenged in his reelection bid. The issue of off-shore drilling was a major policy question in the election. With an economy heavily dependent on tourism, Florida residents were strongly opposed to oil and natural gas drilling near their pristine beaches. However, the federal government had granted leases to Chevron and other oil companies to drill in the areas just off the coast of the Florida panhandle.

Enter the Rove Doctrine. Sensing the opportunity to help Jeb Bush's reelection bid, Rove stressed the electoral ramifications of oil leasing policy in Florida to the managers at the Department of Interior. Not surprisingly, Interior officials announced that leasing of drilling rights off the coast of the Sunshine State would be halted, giving a boost to the younger Bush's campaign. And then, to cover all the bases, the president himself announced a $115 million payment to oil companies to reduce the financial losses entailed by the drilling moratorium. These payments assured that the appeasement of voters would not alienate the oil and gas industry, which had always been an ardent Bush ally.

The Rove Doctrine also affected federal government employees researching the issue of global warming. In an attempt to have more control over the dissemination of climate change research from federal agencies, the Bush administration was extremely active in establishing protocols for vetting findings from government agencies. This drive to control federal research was consistent with the Rove Doctrine's convergence of politics and policy, but it caused considerable controversy.

Since 1988, NASA climatologist James Hansen had been warning the public of the implications of human activity on the earth's climate. In 2006 Hansen went public with claims that Bush administration officials were attempting to censor his agency's findings on global warming. Hansen claimed that political appointees in both NASA and the National Oceanographic and Aeronautics Administration (NOAA) were restricting full disclosure of scientific research in order to protect the White House positions on climate change. Administration officials claimed that their efforts to manage the release of findings were to protect the scientists, yet the political aspects of the policy were hard to deny.

The Rove Doctrine went beyond mere policy; it extended to personnel as well. Although patronage hirings often draw the most public attention and criticism, patronage firings can also raise concern about public personnel management. Such was the case in 2007, when a major uproar followed the dismissal of eight United States attorneys by the Bush administration. The eight attorneys were serving as federal prosecutors in the Justice Department when, on December 7, 2006, they were notified that they would not be retained in their positions. Importantly, their dismissal was completely within the legal purview of President Bush, for prosecutors serve at the pleasure of the chief executive. Sometimes, however, legal protection of patronage decisions does not equate to political protection from patronage practices.

In this case, at least six of the eight fired lawyers had recently received positive reviews by the Justice Department, but they were fired by Attorney General Alberto Gonzalez anyway. Although there is no legal protection of a prosecutor's job even if he or she is doing it well, the dismissals placed the Bush administration in a very awkward position. It became clear that the firings were based on the desire of the White House to have more loyal Republicans serving as federal prosecutors, and that, in this case, loyalty was more important than competence. And it seemed that the Bush administration's idea of loyalty could only be demonstrated by prosecuting Democrats. Such highly publicized priorities for the Bush administration did not jive very well with the popular, if naïve, notion that the law should be above politics. Bush and Gonzalez held the legal powers to make these personnel decisions in the prosecutors' case, but the court of public opinion got to render the verdict on the acceptability of the practice.

Ironically, as the firings and Rove's role in them were being investigated by Congress and the attorney general was defending his decision to replace the prosecutors, it was discovered that Gonzalez had made contradictory statements about his role in the dismissal of the attorneys. These inconsistencies led to even greater scrutiny by members of the Senate Judiciary Committee, and the calls for Gonzalez's resignation or firing became louder throughout the summer of 2007. Of course, attorney generals serve at the pleasure of the president as well. Thus Gonzalez's fate came down to yet another patronage decision for President Bush. So Gonzalez "voluntarily" resigned.

ROVE'S LEGACY

In the world of electoral politics, Carl Rove's reputation took some hard hits with the Republican Party's poor performance in the 2006 elections and disasterous performance in 2008. The magical touch that he displayed in the elections between 2000 and 2004 seemed to disappear under Democratic Party landslides later in the decade. Rove left office on August 31, 2007, under the shadow of a number of scandels and investigations that had followed him during much of the time since the beginning of George Bush's second term as chief executive. A short stint as an informal advisor to the ill-fated Republican presidential campaign of 2008 only contributed to his tarnished reputation as a political genius.

When the book on the administration of George W. Bush is closed, Carl Rove is sure to be remembered as the central figure in the political victories of the forty-third president. However, a closer look at Rove's work may show that he should be equally remembered for his impact on the way policies are made and implemented by the federal government. Note that there is nothing new or illegal about the Rove doctrine. All administrations at all levels of government implement their programs with an eye toward political considerations. The essential difference here—what elevates these common practices to a doctrine—is how consistently the Bush administration made this a priority, how often it allowed ideological or purely political considerations to trump science, and how well Rove functioned as a sheepdog doing his master's bidding by keeping the always-fretful bureaucrats in line.

However, while Rove's reputation in the political world became tarnished, the strategies he emphasized regarding the use of public administrators to help deliver electoral victories remain very much in fashion. Ironically, it was the individual who most empitomized the end of the "Rove era" who seemed to take Rove's lessons to heart. Then-Senator Barack Obama, like Rove, recognized that attention to the actions of bureaucrats could help electoral aspirations. Since coming into office in January 2009, President Barack Obama uniquely employed his former campaign organization to be vigilant in helping him get his policy agenda enacted. Organizing for America, founded just after the inauguration of Obama as the forty-fourth President, seeks to mobilize support for the president's goals. Organizing for America focused much of its attention on influencing members of Congress, but it also paid attention to the federal bureaucracy to make sure it was functioning in a way that benefited the president's interests. President Obama may not be as direct as Rove, but his use of his nongovernment organization to keep an eye on public administartors follows in the Rovian tradition of political oversight and the continous campaign.

FOR DISCUSSION

Are the practices implicit in the Rove Doctrine any different from what other presidential administrations have done to achieve political advantages? Just as war is too important a matter to be left to the generals alone, is not environmental policy too important to be left to technical experts—and thus rightly subject to political influences?

BIBLIOGRAPHY

Appleby, Paul. *Big Democracy.* New York: Knopf, 1945.

Goodnow, Frank J. *Politics and Administration.* New York: Russell and Russell, 1900.

Hamburger, Tom, and Peter Wellsten. *One Party Country: The Republican Plan for Dominance in the 21st Century.* Hoboken, NJ: Wiley, 2006.

Herring, E. Pendleton. *Public Administration and the Public Interest.* New York: McGraw-Hill, 1936.

Kettl, Donald F. *Environmental Governance, A Report on the Next Generation of Environmental Policy.* Washington, DC: Brookings Institution, 2002.

Kraft, Michael. *Environmental Policy and Politics.* New York: Pearson Longman, 2004.

Lippmann, Walter. *The Public Philosophy.* Boston: Little, Brown, 1955.

Moore, James, and Wayne Slater. *Bush's Brain: How Karl Rove Made George W. Bush Presidential.* New York: Wiley, 2004.

———. *The Architect: Karl Rove and the Dream of Absolute Power.* New York: Three Rivers Press, 2007.

Rabe, Barry G. *Statehouse and Greenhouse: The Emerging Politics of American Climate Change Policy.* Washington, DC: Brookings Institution, 2004.

Wilson, James Q. *Bureaucracy: What Government Agencies Do and Why They Do It.* New York: Basic Books, 1991.

CHAPTER NINE

The Gas Chamber of Philadelphia

HOW A 1977 INCIDENT AT INDEPENDENCE MALL ILLUSTRATES THE "BANALITY OF EVIL" CONCEPT FIRST APPLIED TO ADOLF EICHMANN, THE NAZI HOLOCAUST ADMINISTRATOR

PREVIEW

It was a dark and stormy night somewhere, but it was mainly dark on the night of May 11, 1960, in Argentina. Three men in a car were waiting for a bus bringing commuters home from jobs in the city to a distant working-class suburb of Buenos Aires. As the bus pulled away from its stop, a middle-aged balding man with glasses began walking in their direction. As he approached the car, two of the men jumped out, overpowered the astonished commuter, and shoved him into the back seat. The car then drove away as fast as it could without attracting attention. This was a kidnapping. The man taken was Adolf Eichmann, one of the leading public administrators behind one of history's greatest crimes, the murder of more than 6 million European Jews. His kidnappers were Israeli agents. This quest for vengeance had a surprising result. The kidnappee, who was thought to be the personification of evil, turned out to be so ordinary that subsequent events caused people to question the nature of evil itself—and where it comes from.

FROM ARGENTINA TO ISRAEL

Adolf Eichmann was surprised; and surprisingly talkative. As soon as he realized that his captors were not planning to kill him, he confessed to his part in the systematic round-up, deportation, and murder of millions of innocent civilians. From his point of view, he was merely a high-level clerk, rising only to the rank of lieutenant colonel, never even a full colonel. He was just another cog in a vast murdering machine, a cog that was only following orders from above.

After a few weeks of interrogation in a safe house, his Israeli captors smuggled Eichmann out of Argentina by sedating him and passing him off as a sleepy crew member of an El Al civilian aircraft. Once he was safely locked up in a Jewish jail, the Prime Minister of Israel, David Ben Gurion, announced to the world that his country had captured one of the prime movers in the World War II German effort to exterminate the Jews.

The Argentine government was appropriately indignant. Its corrupt rulers had been making substantial money by allowing Nazi war criminals on the run to hide out in their country under assumed names. This snatching of one of their "customers" was bad for business. However, the Israelis were adamant that despite Argentinean complaints of an illegal kidnapping and violations of international law, Eichmann would go on trial in Israel.

The fourteen-week-long courtroom drama that followed in 1961 was an international sensation. The Israeli state used the trial to educate the world through the media about the nature, mechanics, and duration of the Holocaust. A special bullet-proof glass box was built for Eichmann to sit in during the court sessions, so he would be protected from the extremely angry and aggrieved relatives of his victims. The mild-mannered, bespectacled man sitting in the glass booth became the iconic image of the proceedings.

Eichmann was charged most famously with "crimes against humanity." This was the post–World War II phrase for the murder and ill treatment of civilians. According to the 1945 charter of the International Military Tribunal (the legal framework for the postwar Nuremberg Trials in Germany), crimes against humanity consisted of: "murder, extermination, enslavement, deportation and other inhumane acts against any civilian population before or during war; or persecution on political, racial or religious grounds in execution of or in connection with any crime within the jurisdiction of the domestic law of the country where perpetrated."

Ironically, Eichmann was equally guilty of murder under German military law in existence at the time, as if the Nazis paid any attention to the subtleties and niceties of the law. Nevertheless, Article 47 of the German Military Penal Code of 1872, which, according to U.S. Nuremberg prosecutor Telford Taylor (1971), remained in effect throughout World War II, read that "If execution of an order given in line of duty violates a statute of the penal code, the superior giving the order is alone responsible. However, the subordinate obeying the order is liable to punishment as an accomplice if . . . he knew that the order involved an act the commission of which constituted a civil or military crime or offense."

Consequently, Eichmann's basic defense that he was "only following orders" would not have been acceptable, in theory, even in a contemporary German court. It has long been and remains a maxim in the military services of major industrial states that clearly illegal orders are not to be obeyed. Thus, Eichmann had no viable courtroom defense under German or international law.

In the end, he was found guilty. Everyone knew he would be. After all, he was no anonymous concentration camp guard, but the well-known and highly visible administrative head of a massive operation to deport Jews to extermination camps in Eastern Europe. However, the Germans in general, and Eichmann in particular, were never as efficient as they thought they were. That's why, there were survivors: those few who survived the round-ups, and those few who survived the camps. And many of these survivors were now Israelis, locally available and ready to offer their testimony to the court and to history. Ninety of these survivors testified against Eichmann at the trial.

Eichmann was so guilty of so many crimes that at the time of his sentencing, Israel, for the only time in its history, set aside its policy of not using capital punishment and sentenced him to die. Thus, in 1962, after his verdict had been appealed and reviewed, he was hanged. His body was then cremated (how ironic!). His ashes were then taken by boat to international waters (so they would not remain in Israeli territory) and unceremoniously dumped into the Mediterranean Sea; food for indiscriminate fishes.

Adolf Eichmann sitting in his clear bullet-proof courtroom cage on trial in Jerusalem, Israel, July 4, 1961. As "the man in the glass booth," Eichmann became the living personification of Nazi evil; he thus inspired plays, films, and countless editorial cartoons. He, as a true-life character, often pops up as a supporting player in dramas about the Holocaust. Sometimes he gets to star. In the best film about his capture, *The Man Who Captured Eichmann* (1996), he is depicted by Robert Duvall. In the best film about the planning of the Holocaust, *Conspiracy* (2001), he is played by Stanley Tucci. And beyond historical representations of Eichmann, there have been a wealth of Eichmann-like fictional characters in literature and drama who exemplify evil while on the surface appear to be perfectly normal—to the point of blandness, and mediocre to boot. From being the despised real-life murderer of millions, Eichmann as a *persona* has degenerated into a stock character in cheap fiction as well.
Source: © Bettmann/CORBIS. All Rights Reserved.

THE BANALITY OF EVIL

Eichmann's trial, one of the first to be broadcast on live television, generated a lot of journalism and one very important book. In the provocative *Eichmann in Jerusalem: A Report on the Banality of Evil* (1963), based on a series of *New Yorker* magazine articles on the trial, Hannah Arendt (1906–1975), herself a Jewish refugee from Nazi persecution, looked at the murderer of millions of innocent civilians and found him to be merely a banal bureaucrat, a functionary who might otherwise have been perfectly harmless and led a normal life. This highly controversial analysis implied that too many other "normal" people might have done the same under the circumstances; that too many otherwise normal people were just waiting to do the same when circumstances permitted.

Arendt was both a serious academic political theorist with major books already to her credit and a public intellectual much like her contemporaries Arthur Schlesinger, Jr., and John Kenneth Galbraith. While solidly engaged in the academic world, they also wrote popular works and used the media to popularize their ideas and themselves. The *New Yorker* articles and the ensuing book made Arendt not just popular but notorious. Here was this Jewish intellectual, forced out of Europe by the Nazis, seemingly defending this mass murderer by saying that he was just a guy with a job that just happened to involve the large-scale murder of men, women, and children. However, Arendt never defended Eichmann. She merely offered an explanation of how he, or anyone, could do what he did. She fully agreed that he deserved the death penalty for his crimes.

Nevertheless, outrage followed. For example, in a stinging rebuttal to Arendt's contention, historian Barbara W. Tuchman wrote in the *New York Review of Books* (May 29, 1966) that "Eichmann was an extraordinary, not an ordinary man, whose record is hardly one of the 'banality' of evil. For the author of that ineffable phrase—as applied to the murder of six million—to have been so taken in by Eichmann's version of himself as just a routine civil servant obeying orders is one of the puzzles of modern journalism. From a presumed historian it is inexplicable."

This was nasty stuff. Tuchman, the author of *The Guns of August,* the classic analysis of the origins of World War I, was then America's best-selling nonacademic historian and a Pulitzer Prize winner. To call Arendt, whose academic credentials were impeccable, a "presumed historian" was insult indeed. And this is just one example of the blitz of criticism that stormed over Arendt.

Arendt's concept of the "banality of evil" was heavily criticized at the time because it seemed to offer justification for horrendous crimes. However, subsequent social science research, historical analysis, and recent events have supported her analysis. She has been completely vindicated. The initial criticism of her has been effectively forgotten.

THE MILGRAM EXPERIMENTS

The best-known controlled experiments of Arendt's concept were conducted by Yale University psychologist Stanley Milgram (1933–1984) just a few months after the start of the Eichmann trial. After reading of Arendt's "banality of evil" thesis in the *New*

Yorker articles on the Eichmann trial, Milgram sought to discover if ordinary people would harm otherwise innocent subjects if told to do so by an authority figure. In his now classic *Obedience to Authority* (1974), he reported that almost all (37 out of 40) of the ordinary citizens agreed to inflict pain by electric shock on subjects when told to do so by a phony authority figure. And they did inflict pain, so they thought. Of course, the pain was also phony. When a button was pressed, actors pretended to be hurt by electric shocks. However, Milgram proved his point—and Arendt's too. In the contest of morality versus authority, authority won. The banality thesis seemed to be confirmed; and this has also been the case in subsequent experimental research.

THE DEATH TRAINS OF THE *REICHSBAHN*

The Holocaust as a major field of modern history has come into its own since the Eichmann trial. This has presented ever-increasing support for Arendt. One of the most apt analyses is provided by Raul Hilberg, a Holocaust historian who has paid particular attention to the German railroads. Remember that it was Eichmann who was responsible for rounding up and transporting the Jews by train to the extermination camps in Poland. He set the schedules, arranged for the trains, and had soldiers gather and force the unlucky passengers onto the overcrowded wagons. To prevent panic, they were deviously told they were to be resettled in Eastern Europe.

For obvious reasons, these death camps were built in isolated areas that were easily accessible only by rail. In the three-year period between October 1941 and October 1944, the *Reichsbahn* (German railroad) transported about half of the doomed to their final destination. According to Raul Hilberg (1976), "throughout that time, despite difficulties and delays, no Jew was left alive for lack of transport."

This story poses in a gruesomely direct manner a central issue of modern bureaucracy. In 1942 the German railroad network employed roughly 1.8 million people, about 500,000 of whom were German civil servants. Aside from moving the condemned, the system transported military as well as civilian personnel and freight. Despite bombings and occasional breakdowns, the system operated thousands of trains a day over a system that encompassed almost all of Europe. The technical skills required to compose timetables, assemble trains, and retain knowledge of what trains were going where represented a considerable managerial accomplishment. Moreover, since the *Reichsbahn* had to be paid for its services, whether performed for the military or other users, rates and accounting procedures had to be established and maintained. While the Holocaust was large-scale mass murder, it was also a large-scale administrative endeavor, and Adolf Eichmann was in charge of the complicated arrangements to move the condemned to their final destination.

There is no doubt that those associated with Jewish transports were aware of both the conditions under which their passengers were shipped and the fate that awaited them at their destinations. But were the railroad workers themselves trapped by the system, or did they share in its objectives and strive to make it more effective? One common view is that because dictatorial regimes rule through terror, those under their control had no choice but to do the bidding of the ruling group. As Hilberg (1976) explains, in this view,

THE FINAL DESTINATION: AUSCHWITZ IN ACTION

Prisoners, selected for gassing straight from the trains on the railway line, and others selected in the camp, were driven to the crematoria on foot, those who were unable to walk were taken in motor trucks. . . . In the middle of the road lorries were continually fetching the weak, old, sick, and children, from the railway. In the ditches at the road-sides lay SS men with machine guns ready to fire. And SS men addressed the crowd huddled in the yard telling them that they were going to the baths for disinfection as they were dirty and lousy, and in such a state they could not be admitted into the camp. The gassing was carried on under the personal supervision of the doctor SS-Hauptsturmführer Mengele. The prisoners who arrived in the yard of the crematorium were driven to the dressing-room over the door of which was the inscription "Wasch und Desinfektionsraum." In the dressing room . . . there were clothing pegs with numbers. The SS men advised the victims huddled in the cloak-room each of them to remember the number of the peg on which he had hung his clothes so that he might find them again easily afterwards. After undressing they were driven through a corridor to the actual gas chamber which had previously been heated with the aid of portable coke braziers. This heating was necessary for the better evaporation of the hydrogen cyanide. By beating them with rods and setting dogs on them about 2000 victims were packed into a space of 210 sq. meters.

From the ceiling of this chamber, the better to deceive the victims, hung imitation shower-baths, from which water never poured. After the gas-tight doors had been closed the air was pumped out and through four special openings in the ceiling the contents of cans of cyclon, producing cyanide hydrogen gas, were poured in.

Source: Central Commission for Investigation of German Crimes in Poland, *German Crimes in Poland* (1947).

"the soldiery, functionaries, and small entrepreneurs are all considered members of a broad mass that is held down, silenced, and oppressed."

Yet this view may be too unrealistic, too easy. Hilberg argues that to say that the railroads were merely "a means to an end" is too simplistic; for many of the rail workers, "these means *were* the end. As bureaucrats and technocrats they worked ceaselessly to increase the capacity of the network for all the transports projected in the German Reich, and to the very end they found purpose in that endeavor." In short, "no matter whether the purpose was preservation of life or infliction of death, the *Reichsbahn* made use of the same rules, the same channels, the same forms." There were no resignations or protests within the ranks of the organization; only a few requested transfer.

Does the nature of bureaucracy necessarily subsume the human element? Is there something about the nature of bureaucracy that differentiates it from other forms of social organization? Yes. A bureaucracy's elaborate system of rules and procedures as well as its hierarchical structure makes it easier for individual bureaucrats to accomplish their functions while at the same time providing a ready rationalization for disrupting and even destroying the lives of innocent people. To the extent that the administrators of the *Reichsbahn* worked on the basis of "orders from above," it is clear that those making decisions were pretty much isolated from the human consequences of their choices. There is a considerable difference between scheduling and assembling trains on the one hand, and pulling some passengers' corpses out of the overcrowded freight cars at the final destination, on the other. This, of course, is not to suggest that bureaucrats—even those of the *Reichsbahn*—do not also bring great happiness to many people, but simply to state that the many advantages of bureaucratic impersonality frequently hide an ethical flaw.

Studies such as Hilberg's examination of the *Reichsbahn's* operations during World War II support Arendt's banality thesis. Eichmann, for purposes of the Holocaust, was effectively the head of the *Reichsbahn's* efforts. What about the thousands of railroad employees who worked under his orders? They saw people so forced into cattle cars that there was only room to stand; even the dead were not allowed to lie down. They, too, had to stand until the end of the line, which was often days away. The railroad workers knew of and, just as Eichmann, participated in the horrors. Yet after the war, feeling innocent of any war crimes themselves ("Ve vas just vorking on the railroad!"), they returned to transporting ordinary freight and were never again associated with mass murder. A job is a job.

ADDITIONAL SUPPORT OF THE BANALITY THESIS

The Holocaust has been a word now uniquely associated with the German effort to kill off the Jews. Subsequent but loosely parallel efforts to murder an entire religious or social group is now referred to as "ethnic cleansing"—such an antiseptic and hygienic phrase for the mass murder of innocent civilians. Since World War II, major instances of such "cleansing" have occurred in Cambodia in southeast Asia, in Rwanda in the middle of tropical Africa, in the Sudan in central Africa, in Bosnia and Croatia in southeast Europe, and, most recently, in Iraq. In each instance, the murderers were so numerous, for the most part such ordinary people, that it has been virtually impossible to bring even a small fraction of them to justice. Instead, as the violence died down because of changing circumstances, the "evildoers" just went back to their regular jobs. Some high-profile killers were prosecuted, but the banal ones just got on with their banal existence—not knowing that, in so doing, they were reinforcing the thesis of a refugee professor from the Holocaust now best known for explaining the banality of their evil acts to the world.

THE GAS CHAMBER OF PHILADELPHIA

Historians have often written of the civilian bureaucrats in Nazi Germany who cooperated to murder millions of victims in concentration camps. However, you probably have not heard of the few U.S. bureaucrats, just ordinary workers, who nearly gassed to death hundreds of innocent people because, like the Germans, they were only following orders. It happened in Philadelphia's Independence Mall, a several-block landscaped area in front of Independence Hall, the building in which the Declaration of Independence was signed in 1776. Under this mall a three-level, 650-car parking garage was built to accommodate all the visitors to the historic sites. Normally, people come and go at odd times, and the cashiers at the underground garage exits are not overburdened.

On the night of July 4, 1977, Independence Day, there was a big celebration with fireworks and music, as might be expected. After it was over, the crowd went to their cars in the underground garage, started their engines, and sought to drive home. However, because of stalled and illegally parked cars, there were not sufficient exit lanes open. The ventilation system of any underground garage cannot cope with the exhaust fumes of hundreds of automobile engines running at once. Still, the cashiers' duty was clear: Collect payment from every car before it leaves. Because this was a slow process, the fumes built up. Some people began to get sick. The cashiers, in best bureaucratic fashion, kept methodically collecting their tolls. The backup was made only worse by the refusal of the cashiers to allow vehicles to leave the garage until their drivers had stopped to pay the parking fee—even though many people were obviously passing out from the exhaust fumes.

For only a few dollars you could exit this impromptu municipal gas chamber. The problem was that you had to still be alive when it came your turn to pay. These minimum-wage cashiers were about to inadvertently kill hundreds of innocent civilians because they had to follow orders and policies. They felt that they had no discretion. It may have been your life, but it was their job! Were they any different from those railroad workers in Germany? Tragedy was only averted when firefighters wearing gas masks ordered the motorists to turn off their engines and walk out—if they could. Then the police ordered the cashier to just open the gates and let everyone who still could drive out—without paying. This certainly goes far in proving 1930s Chicago gangster Al Capone's famous remark that "You can go a lot further with a kind word and a gun than just with a kind word alone." In the end, more than sixty people were taken to area hospitals.

No one died, but it was close. Had the police and firefighters arrived only a few minutes later, there would have been a "holocaust": hundreds dead, and only a few sad, overwhelmed minimum-wage cashiers to blame—the "banality of evil" in action yet again.

ADMINISTRATIVE EVIL

Thirty-five years after Hannah Arendt's "banality of evil" first shocked the world, a team of public administration academics took the concept to its logical conclusion. In *Unmasking Administrative Evil* (1998), Guy B. Adams and Danny L. Balfour bemoan the fact that public administration as an activity has no clear values, no ethical standards adequate enough to prevent administrative evil, the using of existing bureaucratic organizations following specific, preset rules and procedures to achieve reprehensible public policies. All the advantages of bureaucratic impersonality so praised by sociologist Max Weber in his classic analysis of bureaucracy (1946) suddenly seems far less advantageous when it is realized that such impersonality can be used for evil as well as good. And the individuals themselves within the bureaucratic structures, such as the German railway workers during World War II, may not even realize or admit to themselves that they are participating in an evil enterprise. Thus, the evil is "masked," as the title of their book suggests.

According to Adams and Balfour, "The significance of the connections between the Holocaust and the civil service in Germany is such that responsibility for the event shifts to include not only those who planned and committed overt acts of killing innocent human beings but also routine and seemingly neutral acts of state." Furthermore, "without the full complicity of professional civil servants (and myriad other professionals), it is virtually inconceivable that the mass murder of Europe's Jews could have been accomplished." They concluded, as we must also, that the history of the Holocaust and state-sponsored evils in the decades since World War II "seriously call into question the adequacy of the ethical foundations of modern public administration."

The problem is that public administration merely reflects the cultural norms, beliefs, and power realities of its society. Local laws may sanction innocuous acts of administration by otherwise well-meaning bureaucrats that yield evil results. What about ethics? Ethics are for philosophers and academics. In the real world, there is only power and law tinged by compassionate corruption—violating the organizational rules or the law of the state to prevent administrative evil. Fortunately, there are always some bureaucratic heroes who see such a higher duty. Still, there is often a thin line between a thwarter of evil for the greater good and a disloyal subordinate who takes it upon himself to subvert government policy.

It is just through such compassionate corruption that Hannah Arendt was able to escape death at the hands of the Nazis and come to the United States in 1941. Hiram Bingham IV (1903–1988), the U.S. vice-consul in Marseille, France, helped over 2,500 Jews escape the death camps by issuing them entry visas to the United States in direct defiance of U.S. State Department policy. When his superiors discovered what he was doing, he was abruptly transferred to Portugal and passed over for promotion. Only after his death in 1988, when his family discovered a vast trove of letters and documents from his time in France, was his heroic role publicized. Consequently, in 2002, U.S. Secretary of State Colin Powell gave a "courageous dissent" award to his children, and in 2006, the U.S. Postal Service issued a commemorative stamp bearing his likeness. The Bingham case illustrates the central problem with being such a bureaucratic hero: All too often, your career is ruined and you only get praised posthumously, if at all. However, Bingham remains an exemplar to us all. This was the man who saved the life of the woman (and her husband and mother) who first suffered from and then conceptualized the "banality of evil" as she stared at the personification of evil in his glass booth in an Israeli courtroom. They were both made world-famous by the trial. She became one of the best-known and most controversial public intellectuals on both sides of the Atlantic Ocean. He, in contrast, was converted into toasty bits of burnt calcium for the creatures of the sea.

FOR DISCUSSION

Can you think of any historical instances in which the "banality of evil" could have been observed in the workings of government bureaucracies in the United States? What would you do if you found yourself in a bureaucratic position performing perfectly legal duties that ultimately resulted in an evil end?

BIBLIOGRAPHY

Adams, Guy B., and Danny L. Balfour. *Unmasking Administrative Evil.* Thousand Oaks, CA: Sage, 1998.

Arendt, Hannah. *Eichmann in Jerusalem: A Report on the Banality of Evil.* New York: Penguin, 1963.

Bingham, Robert Kim. *Courageous Dissent: How Hiram Bingham Defied His Government to Save Lives.* Moores Hill, IN: Triune, 2007.

Blass, Thomas. *The Man Who Shocked the World: The Life and Legacy of Stanley Milgram.* New York: Basic Books, 2004.

Cesarani, David. *Eichmann: His Life and Crimes.* London: Heinemann, 2004.

Cooper, Dick, and Edgar William. "Unfortunate Chain of Events Led to Fumes." *Philadelphia Inquirer,* July 6, 1977.

Eisner, Peter. "Saving the Jews of Nazi France." *Smithsonian Magazine,* March 2009.

Harel, Isser. *The House on Garibaldi Street: The First Full Account of the Capture of Adolf Eichmann.* New York: Viking, 1975.

Hilberg, Raul. "German Railroads/Jewish Souls." *Society* 14, November–December 1976.

Milgram, S. *Obedience to Authority; An Experimental View.* New York: Harper Collins, 1974.

Miller, Arthur G. *The Obedience Experiments: A Case Study of Controversy in Social Science.* New York: Praeger, 1986.

Taylor, Telford. *Nuremberg and Vietnam.* New York: Quadrangle, 1971.

Weber, Max. *From Max Weber.* Edited by H. H. Gerth and C. Wright Mills. New York: Oxford University Press, 1946.

Yablonka, Hanna. *The State of Israel vs. Adolf Eichmann.* New York: Schocken, 2004.

CHAPTER TEN

The Red Ink of Orange County

WHEN IS IT ETHICAL FOR PUBLIC TREASURERS TO GAMBLE WITH PUBLIC MONEY? ONLY WHEN YOU WIN!

PREVIEW

Imagine the following scenario. Revenues plummeted and interest require-ments mounted. Many claimed that default was inevitable. The precarious situation existed for nearly two years. Attempts were made to refinance the government's bonds in an effort to relieve the financial strain. However, it became increasingly difficult to convince new creditors to buy the new bonds. No assistance was forthcoming from the federal government. Finally, on March 1, the first of the major defaults on bond obligations occurred when the government could not make its regular interest payment.

Many analysts claimed that the situation had been untenable from the start, given the demographics of the area. Others assessed it as a miscalcu-lation of revenue capacities balanced against an impulsive borrowing spree. Critics observed that the jurisdiction's financial policy was foolishly designed to not have enough revenue from taxes to cover expenses.

The legislative body was called into session and a Refunding Act was passed that reduced the bond interest rates by nearly 35 percent and ex-tended their maturation dates. At the same time, new constitutional amend-ments were passed that prohibited any increase in tax rates or future bond issues except by voter approval. Irate bondholders lost little time in filing a host of suits against the government. Several asked for receiverships of toll bridges so that their revenues could be used exclusively to pay off their bonds. The State Supreme Court rejected such requests. Undaunted, the bondholders appealed to the federal courts and began winning appeals. A receiver was actually appointed for one toll bridge.

The issue became even more acute when several state governments that held the jurisdiction's bonds for trust funds filed suit in federal court to com-pel the government to raise its taxes in oder to pay off its obligations. When confronted with this pressure, a special session of the legislature agreed to pay off, in full, all interest on bonds held by state governments only. In the meantime, the private bondholders continued their suits, and by November 1 had obtained a federal injunction against disbursement of government funds for certain purposes. Finally, a federal court produced a landmark ruling; the refunding law was deemed unconstituional. Furthermore, the court forbade the jurisdiction's treasurer from paying out funds to service the new bonds. The court held that if officials invade contractual rights guaranteed by the federal Constitution, they are bound by federal court remedies available to the injured parties.

Now the government was in total chaos. Its funds were tied up, the refunding law was void, and it could not even service bonds at the new 35 percent lower interest rate. Another legislative session was called. A second refunding law was passed. This time the bonds were given their old, higher interest rates and a ten-year extension of their maturation dates. Almost needless to say, the government's credit rating was a shambles.

The events recounted above actually happened to the state of Arkansas in 1933, when it went "bankrupt" by excessive borrowing to finance highways and the pensions of Confederate Civil War veterans and their dependents. Caught up in the depths of the Depression, its falling revenues resulted in default of its debt.

Unlike the private sector, where a corporate default may result in the end of the corporation and division of all remaining assets, the fiscal organizations of government inevitably live on. There is life after default—but it is a hell of litigation.

THE ORANGE COUNTY DEFAULT

A default is a failure to pay a debt when it is due. Unlike the private sector, where a corporate default can result in a forced bankruptcy, the end of the corporation and the division of all remaining assets, governmental organizations almost invariably survive to borrow another day.

However, it is one thing for a government to default on its debts and be forced into bankruptcy because of a depressed economy and/or a failure to curtail spending, as in the case of Arkasas; it is quite another thing altogether for a government to go bankrupt because one of its most prominent elected officials was literally gambling with the funds in the public treasury. Depressions and recessions happen. But why were the Confederate Civil War pensions still such a financial burden in 1933, when the war had ended in 1865? Because, the pensions were paid to the veterans and their widows. Thus family members saw to it that no veteran died unmarried. Well, hardly any. Thus many an elderly veteran hooked up with a teenage cousin to keep the pension in the family long after the veteran was in the grave.

Yes, life after default can be a hell of litigation even if the deault was caused in large measure by a bunch of nice old Confederate widows. Just how hellish this can be was illustrated when the specter of default was upon Orange County, California.

Adjacent to Los Angeles, Orange County, as its name implies, had long been known for its orange groves and in more recent decades as the home of Disneyland. Among the largest and richest counties in the nation, Orange County was hit hard by the tax revolt, a nationwide grass-roots movement heralded by California's 1978 Proposition 13, which decreased or limited the rate of increase possible on property taxes. In a sense, this was a revolt by the middle class against the rising cost of government services.

The nationwide tax revolt, it is important to note, was not over the unfairness of the tax burden but over the levels of taxation, especially on real estate, which were increasing dramatically in a period of double-digit inflation. By 1980, the tax revolt movement forced thirty-eight states to reduce or at least stabilize tax rates. In 1990, when California passed Proposition III, which, among other things, doubled the state gasoline tax over five years to pay for new highways, many analysts hailed this as the end of the "tax revolt." However, the damage had already been done. What with new state mandates and rising costs for education, health care, law enforcement, and immigrants (both legal and otherwise), local governments all over California were being fiscally squeezed.

To help out the localities financially, the state of California relaxed restrictions on the kinds of investments that local treasurers could make with public funds. This is when Robert L. Citron, the elected Orange County treasurer since 1972, started his remarkably lucky run of effectively gambling with county funds by making extremely risky investments. The problem with gambling is that when your luck runs out, you lose. And Citron, after seven consecutive elections for, and a quarter-century as, the county treasurer, ran out of luck in 1994.

Ironically, in that year his last opponent in his last election for Orange County treasurer was John M. Moorlach, who made a campaign issue of the risks that Citron was taking with the public's money. After the finanical debacle, Citron was forced to resign in disgrace, and his foresightful opponent was appointed to fill the vacant office and clean up the fiscal mess. Moorlach, as the "boy who cried wolf," finally came to the rescue when the wolf was at the door. He would later be twice elected as treasurer and serve a total of twelve years, leaving the county in far better fiscal shape than it had been in when he arrived in office. He also became one of the nation's leading experts on municipal bankruptcy—not that he ever wanted to be.

Citron lost more than one-and-a-half billion dollars (yes, billion!) of public money. This was initially hard to believe by the citizens of a county that was so rich. The average household income in Orange County in1994 was $57,302, compared to a national average of $38,453. The problem was that the swaggering, free-wheeling aggressive business culture of the county—aptly symbolized by the larger-than-life statue of John Wayne in full cowboy regalia that greets visitors to the county's John Wayne Airport—had infected its public finances.

GUILTY OF SIX FELONY COUNTS

In 1995, Citron pleaded guilty to six felony counts. He was not embezzling or stealing the missing money. He was just managing an investment pool (valued at about $7.5 billion before its decline) for the county and 241 other localities and agencies.

His investors in this mutual fund hybrid were pleased when he gave them returns several percentage points above what treasurers were earning in other counties. He did this by borrowing to buy interest-rate-sensitive derivative securities—essentially "bets" that interest rates would remain stable or go lower. Alas, interest rates rose, and he lost $1.7 billion, about 20 percent of the fund's total value. The loss was so great, and the pool of invested funds was so large to begin with, because it was not just Orange County money. However, Orange County, being the largest member of the pool, suffered the most. It was forced to cut its budget by more than 40 percent, reduce its workforce by 10 percent (which amounted to 1,500 jobs), and put the John Wayne Airport and its statue of John Wayne himself ready to draw his six-gun, up for sale. There was an explosion of litigation. The other pool members wanted their money back. The bondholders wanted their interest. The county even sued its former auditor, Peat Marwick, for over $1 billion, claiming it should have been warned about the treasurer's now obviously ill-advised investment policies. The county supervisors figured that with the cuts in jobs and programs and a modest tax increase (which would raise $130 million in new revenue each year), they could cope and eventually repay everybody. So a half-a-percentage-point increase in the county sales tax (from 7.75 to 8.25 percent) was submitted to the voters. In most states a county can raise taxes on its own, but since the 1978 passage of Proposition 13, California localities can raise taxes only after a referendum vote of the people.

Unfortunately, the people were not willing to cooperate. In June 1994, the citizens rejected the tax increase by a margin of more than 3 to 2. Shortly after the election, the Standard and Poor's Credit Rating Service declared Orange County to be in default. On December 6, 1994, the county filed for Chapter 9 bankruptcy protection. The irony here is that the additional interest costs demanded by suspicious creditors exceeded by far the tiny tax increase. The citizens were penny-wise and pound-foolish. After all, when rating agencies examine a municipality's ability to repay debt, they look at both ability to pay and willingness to pay. Orange County will get low marks for "willingness" for years to come. And these low marks will mean higher interest rates.

During the Great Depression of the 1930s, Chapter 9 was added to the federal bankruptcy code. Its purpose was to help municipalities fight off paralyzing lawsuits by aggrieved creditors. According to John Peterson (1991), "Up until now, Chapter 9 has remained a curiosity; there had been only about 70 filings since 1980, and they involved very small governments, usually limited-purpose districts, that were hit by some fiscal meteor." Orange County used Chapter 9 to give itself enough of a respite from litigation to make deals with its creditors. According to *New York Times* reporter Joe Mysak (1995), "By filing for Chapter 9 bankruptcy last fall, Orange County did what no other city, town or county—not even New York City in the 1970s—has ever done. It told the holders of its general obligation notes to get in line with the rest of its creditors." When Bruce Bennett, the bankruptcy lawyer representing the county, was asked if he intended to make a specialty of Chapter 9 municipal bankruptcy cases, he said, "What the hell are you talking about? These cases aren't supposed to happen."

THE DIAGNOSIS OF, AND CURE FOR, THE ORANGE COUNTY SCANDAL

In recent years it has become generally accepted, in both politics and public administration, that local governments should be run like businesses. California has been a leader in the belief that the "entreprenurial spirit" will transform local government. Both elected politicians and appointed executives, such as city and county managers, have bought the notion that government should be market-oriented. Local governments should be so enterprising, it is believed, that they must earn money. Like firms in the market, local governments should compete. Local officials should be more enterprising and should take more risks. Red tape and regulations are bad. . . . And finally, taxpayers are to be thought of as customers. . . .

So, the primary diagnosis is this: The Orange County investment disaster was caused by the widespread acceptance of the belief that the market model is broadly applicable to the public sector and that certain business practices should be applied to public and governmental jurisdictions.

If this diagnosis is correct, what is the cure? First, that democratically adopted laws and regulations must be followed. Second, that making money is not one of the purposes of government. Third, that public funds should never be put at risk. Fourth, that while it might be acceptable in business for the customer to beware, the citizens of local government should not have to beware. Finally, that the primary responsibility of public officials is to vouchsafe the legitimacy of democratic government in the eyes of the citizens.

When Orange County stops trying to act like a business (and not a very good one at that) and starts acting like a government again, it will get well.

Source: H. George Frederickson, "Misdiagnosing the Orange County Scandal," *Governing,* April 1995.

Finally, in September 1995, the California state legislature helped complete the Orange County bailout. It authorized the county to use hundreds of millions of dollars in earmarked funds to pay creditors. This meant that those millions that were earmarked for highways and mass transit, parks, flood control, beaches, and harbors would not be available for those original purposes. However, untended parks and polluted beaches are just a small part of the price Orange County citizens will pay for fiscal peace.

The pain of Orange County, like an infectious disease, will be shared with its neighbors. Because investors shy away from the fiscally unstable, all California localities—like it or not stained by Orange—will be paying higher interest rates than municipal bond issuers in other states. The entire Golden State became more Orange than it ever wanted to be.

So what happened to Robert Citron, the man who caused all this trouble? It turns out that what he did was unethical, if you consider it unethical to gamble with public funds for which you have a fiduciary responsibility. But unethical is not necessarily illegal. Most of his gambling turned out to be legal in that it was not strictly forbidden. It turned out that Orange County did not have strict investment policy guidelines, investment risk controls, regular reporting requirements, or independent oversight of its invested assets.

To his credit, Citron was not engaging in this risky business for his personl advantage. He never stole or embezzeled any money. In his perverted way, he was acting in what he thought was the county's best interest. And almost everyone agreed—for years—until the day came that his house of cards collapsed. It was not as if people couldn't have seen what was coming; but the public officials of Orange County and the 241 other jurisdictions in the investment pool run by Citron were blinded by its success. Besides, what Citron was doing was so complicated, with the leveraging of risk and reverse repurchase agreements, that no one but an expert could even understand what he was doing.

In the end, the investors in the pool, the 241 local governments, got back 77 cents on the dollar in 1995. The following year Citron, having pled guilty to six felony counts, was sentenced to a year in jail and assessed a $100,000 fine. The sentence was so short becase he was not out to enrich himself in any direct way. Ultimately, he never even went to jail but was able to serve his time under house arrest. Many residents of Orange County, especially those laid-off workers and those denied previously available public services, were furious.

The county, with new financial leadership, proceded to sue everyone in sight, meaning the securities firms, law firms, and accounting firms that abetted and benefited from Citron's dealings as treasurer. In 1998 Merrill Lynch settled for $400 million while maintaining that it acted "properly and professionally in our relationship with Orange County." To Merrill Lynch this was a nuisance suit better settled than litigated. Thirty other firms also settled, so that by the year 2000, about $864 million in total had been recovered and proportionately distributed to the local governments that had losses from the pool. There were no trials. None of the firms involved admitted any criminal wrongdoing. Only Citron was threatened with jail, and even he avoided it in the end.

The core problem with Citron's gambling with public funds is not the legality of his acts. What he did would have been perfectly legal if he had been using his own money. And what he did in the main was not clearly illegal under the vague guidelines given to the treasurer by the county at that time. The felonies he pled to were technicalities that did not address the core issue. And that issue was the neglect of his fiduciary responsibility. A fiduciary is a trustee, one who acts on behalf of another in his or her best interests. Citron betrayed the trust placed in him by the voters of Orange County because his fiduciary sense was perverted. Instead of making prudent, conservative investments with modest returns, he chose high-risk investments that offered more than modest returns. Taking this additional risk, no matter how great the potential return, was clearly unethical from the beginning. However, it was only widely considered to be unethical years later, when Citron's winning streak ran out. Citron did not steal, but he did cheat. He cheated on his fiduciary responsibility.

FOR DISCUSSION

Should Citron have been allowed to continue with his risky investment strategy so long as he continued to achieve high returns for Orange County? Is it ever possible to codify every aspect of a fiduciary responsibility into law?

BIBLIOGRAPHY

Baldassare, Mark. *When Government Fails: The Orange County Bankruptcy.* Berkeley, CA: Public Policy Institute of California and the University of California Press, 1998.

Frederickson, H. George. "Misdiagnosing the Orange County Scandal." *Governing,* April 1995.

Jorion, Phillippe, and Robert Roper. *Big Bets Gone Bad: Derivatives and Bankruptcy in Orange County.* New York: Academic Press, 1995.

Lemov, Penelope. "Managing Cash in a Post-Orange County World." *Governing,* May 1995.

Mydans, Seth. "Taxes a Hard Sell in Orange County." *New York Times,* May 8, 1995.

Mysak, Joe. "Winking at Debt." *New York Times,* June 23, 1995.

Peterson, John E. "Is Municipal Bankruptcy an Alternative?" *Governing,* September 1991.

Ratchford, B. U. *American State Debts.* Durham, NC: Duke University Press, 1941.

CHAPTER ELEVEN

Using Systems Theory to Understand How Sun Tzu Predictably Turned Concubines into Soldiers in Ancient China; and How Chaos Theory Explains Why Systems Are Ultimately Unpredictable Even When They Are Otherwise Understood

PREVIEW

In every country and in every jurisdiction within that country, the public policy-making and administrative systems are different. There are always different leaders, different laws, different customs, and differing levels of corruption influencing the system. At the same time as they are different, however, they are also the same in that all policy-making systems share common elements. The first of which is that they are systems.

The newest thing about systems thinking is theorizing about it as if it were new. However, ancients such as Aristotle and poets such as Shakespeare understood systems instinctively. Perhaps the best description of the human social system is that of the English poet John Donne (1572–1631). When he wrote that: "No man is an island, entire of itself; every man is a piece of the continent, a part of the main," he provided the preamble for modern social science. And when he concluded that "any man's death diminishes me, because I am involved in mankind; and therefore, never send to know for whom the bell tolls [announcing a death]; it tolls for thee," he explained why everyone has to understand the doctrines of systems theory. When Donne wrote that "any man's death" diminished him, it was because he was "involved in mankind"—meaning part of the same system. You are too! That is why, the following story from ancient China will help explain your place in the myriad systems in which we all live.

SUN TZU'S SYSTEM FOR TRAINING CHINESE CONCUBINES

Sun Tzu (fourth century BCE) was the ancient Chinese writer whose essays, traditionally published as *The Art of War*, have influenced all Western military analysts since they were first available in European editions in the late eighteenth century. Sun Tzu was the first writer to formulate a rational basis for the conduct and planning of military operations. He believed that skillful strategists should be able to beat an adversary without engaging him, to take cities without destroying them, and to overthrow states without bloodshed. He advocated the use of secret agents—spies and intelligence—to keep leaders informed and to make them able to plan better. His essays emphasize how to conduct a war of maneuver. According to James Coates and Michael Kilian's *Heavy Losses* (1985), in World War II a military aide of Nationalist General Chiang Kai-shek stated that "in Chiang's army, Sun Tzu's *The Art of War* was considered a classic but out of date. A few years later Chiang fell to Sun Tzu's tactics—employed at the hands of Mao [the leader of the Chinese Communists]."

Sun Tzu has never been more relevant than today. The whole concept of asymmetrical warfare (in which large conventional forces fight small nonconventional forces) can be found in his writings. This is the kind of war the United States lost in Vietnam and is now fighting in Iraq and Afghanistan. All this is just to assert that Sun Tzu is not an obscure figure known only to historians. Indeed, it is fair to say that he is bigger today in terms of the influence of his ideas than he ever was in real life. Now to our story.

There was a time when Sun Tzu was a general without an army; he needed a job. So, like many a high-level political appointee out of power—even today—he wrote a book, *The Art of War*, to demonstrate his usefulness to potential employers. According to Samuel B. Griffith's biographical account of Sun Tzu in Griffith's translation of *The Art of War* (1963), this book earned Sun Tzu an employment interview with the King of Wu in central China.

The king, wondering how to determine Sun Tzu's merit as a general, asked him if he could "conduct a minor experiment in the control of the movement of troops. . . . And can you conduct this test using women?" After Sun Tzu agreed to the employment test, the king sent for 180 women. Many of them were the king's concubines. Concubines were quite common in the ancient world; for example, in the Bible (1 Kings 11:1–3) it is reported that King Solomon had 700 wives and 300 concubines.

Sun Tzu organized this group of women into two companies, each of which was commanded by an especially favored concubine of the king. Thus we see the advantages of political patronage.

Sun Tzu then instructed them on how to march while holding a halberd (a long pole with an axlike blade at the top). After the procedures were explained, attention was drawn to the fact that executioners were standing by. There is nothing like a few executioners hanging about to instill a sense of discipline in a crowd of young women.

Then Sun Tzu gave his "orders three times and explained them five times." A drum was sounded for them to start, but "the women all roared with laughter." This was not very military of them.

Sun Tzu now found himself responsible for an organization, a system, that was not working as intended. He had to modify the situation, adjust the system—and fast. His hoped-for job, not to mention his reputation, was at stake. So, after waiting for the laughter to die down, he sternly announced, "If instructions are not clear and commands not explicit, it is the commander's fault. But when they have been made clear, and are not carried out in accordance with military law, it is a crime on the part of the officers."

Then he immediately ordered that the errant officers, the king's two favorite concubines, be beheaded. The executioners would be put to good use. This was how Sun Tzu sought to create and maintain discipline. This was how to create and maintain his system of military drill using women who laughed at his efforts instead of taking the drill seriously. This same essential technique, the same system, is used in basic training today; only instead of being executed, recruits who do not take the drill seriously enough are ordered to do fifty push-ups.

The king, who was watching from a distance, sent a message to Sun Tzu: "Without these two concubines my food will not taste sweet. It is my desire that they not be executed." Obviously, the king was thinking about more than military maneuvers.

The king got this reply from Sun Tzu: "Your servant has already received your appointment as commander and when the commander is at the head of the army he need not accept all the sovereign's orders."

The two favored concubines were then promptly beheaded as an example to the others. Thus, we see the disadvantages of political patronage. Thereupon, there was no more laughter. The drum was sounded and the women went through the drill exactly as explained. Sun Tzu's system for training raw recruits worked. He then sent this message to the king: "The troops are now in good order . . . even to the extent of going through fire and water."

The king was initially quite put out by Sun Tzu's system for inculcating concubines with the discipline for military maneuvers. However, upon reflection, the king realized that it was not so difficult for a king to find other concubines that would make his food "taste sweet," but that finding an excellent military commander was a happy rarity.

So Sun Tzu got the job as general because of his ability to take inexperienced recruits, men or women, and train them to drill as soldiers. The king, thanks to his sophisticated personnel test, enjoyed many victories in the future because he employed the struggling author of *The Art of War*. Two dead concubines were a small price to pay.

Sun Tzu, through his determination and daring (after all, he risked being killed himself by beheading the king's favorites), had created a social system—a group (the women) able to accomplish a task (formal drill). Since ancient times the world has been ruled by such systems and the generals, managers, and politicians who had the fortitude to invent and dominate them. The true masters of the universe are those who at first instinctively, and later by study, understand the doctrine behind the development and management of such social systems.

Our story of Sun Tzu and the concubines is certainly an extreme example—purposely so to make it memorable. But this story can be retold countless times in other, less lethal contexts. Are there not systems to train lab technicians, police officers, and building inspectors? Processing insurance claims, auditing income taxes, and developing government budgets are all examples of activities with an underlying systemic base. Quite simply, employees must follow the systems—the procedures—laid out for them by their "generals." And if they do not, they know that they will be executed—meaning fired, not killed as in the olden days. Sun Tzu, if he were alive today, would have no trouble understanding and fitting in with systems of modern organizations.

SYSTEMS THEORY

A system is any organized collection of parts that are united by prescribed interactions; it is designed for the accomplishment of a special goal or a general purpose. A systems approach is any analytical framework that views situations as systems. The ancient "big three" of the Greek philosophers (Socrates, Plato, and Aristotle) were fully aware of the utility of how a systems approach, though they did not use the phrase, could enhance understanding. For example, according to an account by Xenophon (430–355 BCE), Socrates understood the universality of management systems—that the same skills are needed whether you are managing a business, a government, or an army. Plato, in his *Republic,* presented a complete political system. And Aristotle, in his *Politics,* systematically explained all of the elements of a political community: that it is best when "formed by citizens of the middle class" and "exists for the sake of noble actions, not of mere companionship."

The systems approach became self-conscious only after Ludwig von Bertalanffy (1901–1972) sought to organize scientific knowledge into a unified system in the mid-twentieth century. This, in turn, influenced David Easton (1917–), who first applied the approach to modern political analysis. Any review of a policy that seeks to put it in the context of a larger system is using a systems approach.

All social (really, social-biological) systems start with individual cells. Once they combine and grow to be embryos and then people, they prove Aristotle's contention that "the whole is more than the sum of its parts." Once these "whole systems," as individuals, combine, they create families, clans, and tribes. Now they are part of an organization or social system that focuses on the attainment of specific goals and contributes, in turn, to the goals of a more comprehensive system, such as a larger organization or society itself. With the immense number of systems in the world, this can get very complicated very fast.

To help sort out and better understand how all these social systems interact, sociologists developed the structural-functional approach by which societies, communities, and organizations are viewed as systems. Their particular features are then explained in terms

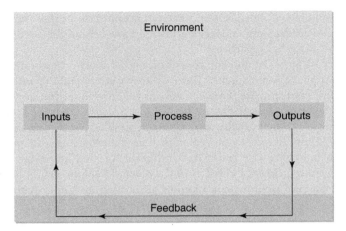

Figure 11.1 Norbert Weiner's Model of an Organization as an Adaptive System

of their contributions (their functions) in maintaining the system. Structural–functional analysis, pioneered by sociologist Talcott Parsons (1902–1979), emphasizes the social system at the expense of, or as opposed to, the system's recognized political organizations, actors, and institutions.

Since World War II, the social sciences have increasingly used systems theory to examine their assertions about human behavior. Systems theory views social organizations—whether they are as small as a family or as large as a state—as a complex set of dynamically intertwined and interconnected elements. Every system includes inputs, processes, outputs, feedback loops, and the environment in which it operates and with which it continuously interacts (see Figure 11.1). Any change in any element of the system causes changes in other elements. The interconnections tend to be complex, dynamic (constantly changing), and often unknown. For example, consider a beehive. If the drone worker bees ventured forth one day and most of them never came back (because they inadvertently flew into a mist of insecticide), the whole hive would have to change. Honey production would have to be curtailed so that more drones could be raised until the hive—the system—was back in a state of equilibrium. Similarly, when policy makers make decisions involving one element of the system, unanticipated effects may occur throughout the system. Systems theorists study these interconnections in order to anticipate what was once unanticipated.

OPEN SYSTEMS THEORY

An open system is any organism or organization that interacts with its environment, as opposed to a closed system, which does not. A closed system is mainly a theoretical concept, because even the most isolated mechanical system will eventually be affected by its environment. So, for all practical purposes, all systems theory—especially in the social sciences—is open systems theory.

Because all social organizations are adaptive (and open) systems that are integral parts of their environments, they must adjust to changes in their environment if they are to survive. In turn, virtually all of their decisions and actions affect their environment. Norbert Wiener's model of an organization as an adaptive system, from his 1948 book, *Cybernetics,* epitomizes the basic theoretical perspectives of the systems perspective. Cybernetics, from a Greek word meaning "steersman," was used by Wiener to mean the multidisciplinary study of the structures and functions of control and information-processing systems in both animals and machines.

The basic concept behind cybernetics is self-regulation: biological, social, or technological systems that can identify problems, do something about them, and then receive feedback to adjust themselves automatically. For example, humans must maintain a relatively stable body temperature. When the environment gets too hot, our bodies adjust by sweating to expel excess heat. When it gets too cold, our skin contracts to retain heat. These are automatic—cybernetic—body adjustments because they are done spontaneously, without thinking. A thermostat that regulates heating and/or air conditioning performs this same function for a house.

The search for order among complex variables has led to an extensive reliance on quantitative analytical methods and models. The systems approach is strongly cause-and-effect oriented in its philosophy and methods. In these respects, systems theories have close ties to Frederick W. Taylor's scientific management approach. Whereas Taylor used quantitative methods (such as time study, measurement techniques for determining the time it should take a worker to perform a specified task) to find "the one best way" to undertake a production task, the systems theorist uses quantitative methods to identify cause-and-effect relationships and to find optimal solutions. In this sense, the conceptual approaches and purposes between the two perspectives are strikingly similar. Thus, systems approaches are often called management science or operations research. Be careful, though, never to make the unpardonable error of calling them scientific management!

SYSTEMS ANALYSIS

Systems theory is a doctrine. Systems analysis is a set of techniques derived from it: the methodologically rigorous collection, manipulation, and evaluation of data on social units (as small as an organization or as large as a polity) to determine the best way to improve their functioning and to aid a decision maker in selecting a preferred choice among alternatives.

Systems analysis is also used to describe the development and use of mathematical models as an aid in decision making. However, this can be dangerous if nonquantifiable factors are not also taken into account. The classic example of this is the U.S. experience in Vietnam, but our example begins in World War II, when the U.S. Army Air Corps (the U.S. Air Force was not created until 1947) used statistical control with great effectiveness. By developing techniques to count almost everything, they were able to offer the kind of policy advice that saved millions of dollars and thousands of lives. For example, the B-17 bomber was to be gradually replaced by the newer B-24, which would carry 50 percent more bombs. However, statistics proved that the B-24 had so many defects that the overall performance of the B-17 was better. Result: Production of the B-24s was scaled down, and more air crews survived the war because the B-17 could take far more combat damage and return to base. Once a B-24 was hit, the crew's chances of survival were far lower. Number crunching pays off—sometimes in lives!

After the war, the head of the Air Corps' statistical control unit, Colonel Charles "Tex" Thornton, and nine of his best analysts "sold" themselves to the Ford Motor Company as a team. Using the techniques they had pioneered during the war, now renamed management control, they turned around Ford, which was on the verge of being run out of the auto business by competition from General Motors. They were known as the "whiz kids" because of their high-powered intellects and obvious youth. According to management historian John A. Byrne (1993), they "built a mystique for the methods of rational management they invented during the war—a system of tight financial controls that made quantitative analysis of every business problem essential." Because of their enormous influence, "a postwar generation of managers became slaves to numbers, taught to squeeze out costs in every part and every product while building looming hierarchies of white-collar staffs that centralized authority and decision-making."

And just who was the number-one "whiz kid," the so called human computer who was the first of the group to rise to be president of Ford in 1960? None other than Robert S. McNamara, who, as Secretary of Defense under Presidents Kennedy and Johnson, used this same kind of quantitatively based decision making to fight and lose the Vietnam War. So the military, which helped to create modern management control of far-flung operations, was influenced by a corporate version of it that put control over the more traditional values of morale and culture. By seeking to solve problems just by using numbers, it lost sight of too many other factors. By viewing the war as an exchange of firepower, McNamara ignored the morale and motivation of the enemy. He should have read Sun Tzu.

BEWARE THE SYSTEM

Napoleon, in his *Military Maxims* (1827), said: "Unhappy the general who comes on the field of battle with a system." McNamara's system of pure numbers allowed him to outsmart himself. This is why, the story is often told that a frustrated general in the Pentagon of 1968 fed into a computer all of the known data about the Vietnam War; then asked when the United States would win. The computer answered: "You won in 1964."

McNamara's whole Vietnam strategy of piecemeal escalation at indecisive points was in gross violation of the principles of war. His managerial approach to problem solving undermined the effectiveness of the military down to the smallest units. For example, to give more officers combat experience, they were given only six-month tours of duty with front-line troops. The enlisted troops, however, served one-year tours. It has been known since ancient times that unit cohesion is the glue that holds armies together. This necessitates a belief among soldiers that their officers will fight and, if necessary, die with them. According to military historians Richard Gabriel and Paul Savage (1978), "In Vietnam the record is absolutely clear on this point: the officer corps simply did not die in sufficient numbers or in the presence of their men often enough. . . . The troops began to perceive that their officers simply were not prepared to share the risk of the ultimate sacrifice—and they came to despise them for it."

Overall, McNamara's number-crunching approach to military leaderships was a disaster at all levels, strategic and tactical. Numbers alone are never the whole story. This is why, the notorious body-count statistics were so misleading—leaving aside the fact that they were also notoriously inaccurate. Such policies destroyed the effectiveness of the U.S. Army for a generation. Fortunately, organizations can renew themselves, but it was not until the Persian Gulf War in 1991 that the Army was able to demonstrate its full recovery from the trauma of Vietnam and McNamara.

However, neither war nor the real world always responds rationally to superior resources or good intentions. Military strategist Edward N. Luttwak (1979) examined this problem and found that: "Even though the historical record of war shows quite conclusively that superior firepower is often associated with defeat, and that winners more often than not were actually inferior in firepower, these mathematical models continue to be devastatingly influential because they capture all that is conveniently measurable about warfare. Thus bookkeepers may fancy themselves strategists."

The first question that must be asked in systems analysis is "What level?" After all, looking at things cosmically, the whole world is a single system. So what subsystem do you examine? Do you want your level of analysis to be the individual citizen, a small group such as Sun Tzu's concubines, or the state itself? Regardless of your level of analysis, you will be looking at a system in action, because systems by definition are dynamic and constantly changing. So what you must look at is not a frozen, static snapshot of a system, but a system in constant motion.

The public policy-making system involves so many aspects, so many players, and so many issues that it is difficult to grasp it as one single thing. Of course, it is not a tangible thing; it is a never-ending intangible process. It is a process because it is constantly changing. Social systems need maintenance even more than mechanical ones do. The wind blows in from the north and the people in a group feel cold. Suddenly the goal of the group changes from whatever their task was to getting warm, by finding clothing or shelter. Good managers or officers of such small systems anticipate and plan for such contingencies. Sun Tzu anticipated that the concubines might not take him seriously. Being a good manager, he had the executioners ready—and willing!

Systems come in every conceivable size. Sun Tzu's little parade and drill group is hardly a microcosm of the U.S. political process. Nevertheless, it contained all of the elements of Weiner's model of an organization as an adaptive system. Note that the outputs from Sun Tzu's process of giving orders were inadequate until feedback (heads chopped off) encouraged the members of the system to adapt. Larger systems work and adapt in essentially the same way. Heads may not be chopped off; but firings, transfers, and lost elections may have the same effect: a more responsive system in the future.

CHAOS THEORY

Systems thinking is critically important because the whole world, in essence, is a collection of interrelated systems. Nothing happens in isolation. Your reading this page is made possible by your visual system. Your turning to the next page is a function of your nervous system and muscular system—which is also related to your visual system. How else would you know when to turn the page? The systems of the world seem so infinite that another theory—chaos theory—has evolved to explain why they are often unexplainable. This theory postulates that the tiniest change in the smallest part of a system can eventually produce enormous effects.

Chaos theory was formally discovered by Edward Lorenz (1917–2008), a meteorologist who, in 1961, was trying to use a computer to help predict the weather and accidentally stumbled on his now-famous theory. Lorenz was seeking to repeat a computer weather simulation for a shorter period of time than the initial simulation. His second simulation should have been identical except for the time, but there was a vast divergence. It turned out that the first simulation used numbers that went to six decimal places (for example, 0.123456); but for the second simulation, Lorenz used numbers only to three decimal places (for example, 0.123). This miniscule difference led to vast changes in the two weather trajectories. This discovery, in turn, led to a new theory on why the weather is so inherently unpredictable.

In weather forecasting, this discovery of Lorenz became known as the "butterfly effect." According to James Gleick (1987), this is "the notion that a butterfly stirring the air today in Peking can transform storm systems next month in New York." The origin of this phrase seems to have been a paper that Lorenz presented at a 1972 meeting of the American Association for the Advancement of Science, entitled "Predictablity: Does the Flap of a Buterfly's Wings in Brazil Set off a Tornado in Texas?" However, Lorenz may have been influenced in choosing his title by a 1952 short story by science fiction author Ray Bradbury, "Sound Like Thunder," in which time travelers from the present kill a butterfly in the far past and thus alter the future.

Chaos theory seeks to explain how the smallest elements of a system, whether weather or organizational, can have the biggest consequences. All this was summed up by Benjamin Franklin in a 1758 issue of *Poor Richard's Almanac:*

> For the want of a nail the shoe was lost,
> For the want of a shoe the horse was lost,
> For the want of a horse the rider was lost,
> For the want of a rider the battle was lost,
> For the want of a battle the kingdom was lost,
> And all for want of a horseshoe-nail.

FOR DISCUSSION

Can you take Sun Tzu's basic system for acculturating new organization members and apply it to contemporary training and management development programs? Can systems analysis still be useful if all of the elements of a system cannot be reduced to numbers for quantitative analysis?

BIBLIOGRAPHY

Byrne, John A. *The Whiz Kids: The Founding Fathers of American Business—And the Legacy They Left Us.* New York: Doubleday, 1993.

Donne, John. "Meditation 17." *Devotions upon Emergent Occasions,* 1624.

Easton, David. *A Systems Analysis of Political Life.* New York: Atherton, 1963.

Gabriel, Richard A., and Paul L. Savage. *Crisis in Command: Mismanagement in the Army.* New York: Hill and Wang, 1978.

Gleick, James. *Chaos: The Making of a New Science.* New York: Viking, 1987.

Handel, Michael I. *Masters of War: Sun-Tzu, Clausewitz, and Jomini.* London: Frank Cass, 1992.

Jomini, Antoine-Henri. *The Art of War.* Philadelphia: Lippincott, 1862.

————. *Treatise on Great Military Operations.* New York: Van Nostrand, 1805.

Luttwak, Edward N. "The American Style of Warfare." *Survival,* March/April 1979.

Parsons, Talcott. *The Social System.* New York: Free Press, 1951.

Rivlin, Alice. *Systematic Thinking for Social Action.* Washington, DC: Brookings Institution, 1971.

Shapley, Deborah. *Promise and Power: The Life and Times of Robert McNamara.* Boston: Little, Brown, 1993.

Steinbruner, John. *The Cybernetic Theory of Decision.* Princeton, NJ: Princeton University Press, 1974.

Sun Tzu. *The Art of War.* Translated by Samuel B. Griffith. London: Oxford University Press, 1963.

Wiener, Norbert. *Cybernetics.* Cambridge, MA: MIT Press, 1948.

CHAPTER TWELVE

Using William Shakespeare's Plays to Prove That He Was an Instinctive and Early Organization Theorist

WHETHER IN A BEEHIVE OR THE COURT OF ELIZABETH I, HE KNEW HOW HONEY (OR MONEY) GOT THINGS DONE

PREVIEW

William Shakespeare's contributions to literature and the development of the English language have long been acknowledged and thoroughly documented, but his insights into modern management and administration have been all but ignored until now. This is a surprising oversight when you consider that many of his plays deal with issues of personnel management and organizational behavior.

Remember *Hamlet,* the poignant case study of a too sensitive young executive who fails to move up in the organizational hierarchy because of his inability to make decisions. What is *Julius Caesar* if not a very hostile takeover attempt by disgruntled stockholders? The tragedy of *Macbeth* was that the title character was a ruthless workaholic who allowed his overly ambitious wife to egg him on to the top, only to find that he couldn't hack it in the end. Who has not felt compassion when seeing *Othello,* the tale of a minority manager who incurs resentment because of his personnel policies and then finds that jealousy at the office leads to murder. And is not *King Lear* a warning to all executives of family businesses on the perils of divestiture and early retirement?

Modern management has its gurus such as Peter Drucker and Tom Peters. William Shakespeare is certainly, if not chronologically, their peer. He just needs a bit of interpretation. Remember the character in Moliere's 1670 play, *The Would-Be Gentleman*, who suddenly says to himself one day, "Good Heavens! For more than forty years I have been speaking prose without knowing it." It is the same with Shakespeare. Most managers have read or seen at least some of his plays, but have yet to realize that they have been reading organization lore. The interpretive commentary that follows merely seeks to bring out the management concepts that were always there.

BUREAUCRACY AND HIERARCHY

Shakespeare surely anticipated the bureaucracy of modern organizations. What else could Hamlet have meant when, in Act III, scene i, he refers to "the insolence of office"? Obviously this is one of the earliest instances of "bureaucrat bashing."

In two longer passages from two other plays, Shakespeare provides portraits of bureaucratized societies using the metaphor of a beehive. In *Troilus and Cressida* he has Ulysses (Act I, scene iii) use the image of the hive to describe the hierarchical structure of Greek military society:

When that the general [society] is not like the hive
To whom the foragers shall all repair,
What honey is expected? Degree being vizarded [hidden],
The unworthiest shows as fairly in the mask.
The heavens themselves, the plants, and this centre [earth]
Observe degree, priority, and place,
Insisture [regularity], course, proportion, season, form,
Office, and custom, in all line of order.

Shakespeare, a political conservative, was greatly concerned that established government and organizational hierarchies be maintained. Thus, he has Ulysses explain later in this same scene what happens when the elements of a system fall out of their "line of order":

But when the planets
In evil mixture to disorder wander,
What plagues, and what portents, what mutiny.

In *Henry V*, Shakespeare has the Archbishop of Canterbury explain (Act I, scene ii) how Heaven has ordained a hierarchically ordered universe in which each person is assigned an occupational specialization, a social rank, and formal obligations:

Therefore doth heaven divide
The state of man in divers functions,
Setting endeavor in continual motion,
To which is fixed, as an aim or butt,
Obedience; for so work the honey-bees,
Creatures that by a rule in nature teach
The act of order to a peopled kingdom.

They have a king and officers of sorts,
Where some, like magistrates, correct at home,
Others, like merchants, venture trade abroad,
Others, like soldiers, armed in their stings,
Make boot upon the summer's velvet buds,
Which pillage they with merry march bring home
To the tent-royal of their emperor; . . .

Note how Shakespeare uses the concept of division of labor: "heaven divide . . . man in divers functions." Later in this same long speech, the Archbishop of Canterbury further develops this concept:

As many fresh streams meet in one salt sea;
As many lives close in the dial's centre;
So many a thousand actions, once afoot,
End in one purpose. . . .

Books on the history of organization theory generally credit Adam Smith, in his *Wealth of Nations* (1776), with pioneering this concept, but few seem to realize that Smith, the "father of economics," must have been a disciple of Shakespeare, the father of organization theory.

MOTIVATING EMPLOYEES

Virtually every student in every introductory course on management learns of the Hawthorne experiments made by the Harvard Business School at the Hawthorne Works of the Western Electric Company during the late 1920s and early 1930s. The researchers stumbled on a finding that today seems obvious: Factories and other work situations are, first of all, social situations. Thus managers, if they are to be optimally effective, have to be aware of both the formal as well as the informal organization. Of course, Shakespeare had already shown that those managers who rely only on formal authority are at a disadvantage compared to those competitors who can also mobilize the informal strength of their organizations. Shakespeare demonstrated this when, in *Macbeth* (Act V, scene ii), he has Angus describe Macbeth's waning ability to command the loyalty of his troops:

Those he commands move only in command,
Nothing in love: now does he feel his title
Hang loose about him, like a giant's robe
Upon a dwarfish thief.

Any manager whose title hangs "loose about him" does not command the full potential of his organization; he or she cannot inspire motivation—only order movement. The same loss of an organization's full potential occurs if managers allow discipline to become too lax. In *Measure for Measure,* the Duke (Act I, scene iii) offers this lamenting description of a society in which the informal norms that developed over time made "biting laws" things to be "more mock'd than fear'd":

> We have strict statutes and most biting laws,
> The needful bits and curbs to headstrong steeds,
> Which for this nineteen years we have let slip;
> Even like an o'ergrown lion in a cave,
> That goes not out to prey. Now, as fond fathers,
> Having bound up the threatening twigs of birch,
> Only to stick it in their children's sight
> For terror, not to use, in time the rod
> Becomes more mock'd than fear'd; so our decrees,
> Dead to infliction, to themselves are dead;
> And liberty [license] plucks justice by the nose;
> The baby beats the nurse, and quite athwart
> Goes all decorum.

Shakespeare's most famous acknowledgment of the importance of informal norms occurs in *Hamlet* (Act I, scene iv), when the Danish Royal Court noisily drinks toasts to the accompaniment of drums and trumpets. Horatio, startled by this unusually noisy practice, asks Hamlet if this is "a custom." Hamlet replies:

> But to my mind, though I am native here
> And to the manner born, it is a custom
> More honour'd in the breach than the observance.

Thus, Shakespeare has illustrated that while formal procedures are in place, the organization usually ignores them. Often this is for the good. Western literature is full of examples of servants not obeying stupid or ill-advised orders of their masters. As Posthumus asserts in *Cymbeline* (Act V, scene i):

> Every good servant does not all commands;
> No bond but to do just ones.

Shakespeare anticipated many of the findings about human behavior in organizations that were first brought to the formal attention of management in the twentieth century. For example, in the 1940s, psychologist Abraham Maslow first put forth his "needs hierarchy," by which individuals progressively reach self-fulfillment and become "all that they are capable of becoming." This theory of human motivation holds that it is all right that many individuals may never reach their goals, because it is the striving—the ambition—that is paramount. Yet Shakespeare sums this all up in a single line, when he has Cressida in *Troilus and Cressida* (Act I, scene ii) say: "Men prize the thing ungained more than it is."

Then there is J. Sterling Livingston's 1969 *Harvard Business Review* study of "Pygmalion in Management," in which he reports that management expectations of employee performance tend to become self-fulfilling prophecies. Yet Shakespeare had summed the essence of this scholarly analysis in two lines from *The Merchant of Venice* (Act III, scene iii), when Shylock says to Antonio:

> Thou call'dst me dog before thou hadst a cause,
> But since I am a dog, beware my fangs.

Shakespeare even anticipated the work of Frederick Taylor, the "father of scientific management." Early in the twentieth century, Taylor published his pioneering analyses of the best way to organize work. He wrote that jobs should be designed so that employees do not wear out too early in the day. Physical work should be structured so that it can be continued all day—steady, persistent effort was better than exhausting spurts. Yet John of Gaunt, in *Richard II* (Act II, scene i), explained this very concept and thought himself "a prophet" for it:

> Methinks I am a prophet new inspired
> And thus expiring do foretell of him:
> His rash fierce blaze of riot cannot last,
> For violent fires soon burn out themselves;
> Small showers last long, but sudden storms are short;
> He tires betimes [quickly] that spurs too fast betimes [early].

Many a management meeting offers a demonstration of Miles's law (first formulated by Rufus E. Miles, Jr., in the late 1940s, when he was an analyst in the Bureau of the Budget): "Where you stand depends on where you sit." Thus, managers may be expected to argue for the policy position of the organizational unit they represent. Yet the essence of Miles's law is clearly anticipated by Philip the Bastard in *King John* (Act II, scene i):

> Well, whiles I am a beggar, I will rail
> And say there is no sin but to be rich;
> And being rich, my virtue then shall be
> To say there is no vice but beggary.
> Since Kings break faith upon Commodity [expediency],
> Gain, be my Lord, for I will worship thee.

As for people who work only for "gain," the Fool has a song about them in *King Lear* (Act II, scene iv):

> That sir which serves and seeks for gain,
> And follows but for form,
> Will pack when it begins to rain,
> And leave thee in the storm.

SYSTEMS ANALYSIS

Although he never used the term, Shakespeare understood the basics of systems analysis: the methodologically vigorous collection, manipulation, and evaluation of organizational data. He knew that any analysis has to start with the present situation. As Lady

Macbeth says in *Macbeth* (Act III, scene ii): "Things without all remedy should be without regard: what's done is done."

Shakespeare would also have been quite comfortable with the scientific method of today. After all, he has Fluellen in *Henry V* (Act V, scene i) exclaim: "There is occasions and causes why and wherefore in all things."

The main reason to examine systems, whether organizational or mechanical, is to solve actual problems. In *The Merchant of Venice* (Act I, scene i), Shakespeare has Bassanio offer this basic trouble-shooting technique:

> In my schooldays, when I had lost one shaft,
> I shot his fellow of the self-same flight
> The self-same way with more advised watch,
> To find the other forth; and by adventuring both,
> I oft found both.

Sometimes a "more advised watch" is all it takes—even today.

LEADERSHIP

A transformational leader is one with the ability to change an imbedded organizational culture by creating a new vision for the organization and marshalling the appropriate support to make that vision the new reality. Perhaps the best-known transformational leader is General George S. Patton, Jr., who, during World War II, took charge of a defeated and demoralized U.S. army in North Africa and transformed it into a winning team. The task was different but arguably no less difficult for Lee Iacocca when he took charge of a Chrysler corporation on the verge of bankruptcy and disintegration and brought it back into profit. Similar challenges faced the leadership of AT&T when it went from a monopoly public utility to a company that had to change its corporate culture to compete in the open market.

Shakespeare, in *Henry V* (Act V, scene ii), has King Henry, while courting his future wife, Katherine, explain how they will be transformational leaders: When Katherine, the daughter of the King of France, explains in response to King Henry's demand for a kiss to seal their engagement, that "it is not the fashion for the maids in France to kiss before they are married," King Henry assures her

> O Kate, nice customs curtsy to great kings. Dear Kate, you and I cannot be confined within the weak list [boundary] of a country's fashion: we are the makers of manners, Kate; and the liberty that follows our places stops the mouth of all find-faults.

The one thing that all transformational leaders have in common is that they, as Shakespeare said, "are the makers of manners" and because of "the liberty that follows" from the positions that they hold, they have the power to "stop the mouth(s)" of those who would find fault with their reforms. Thus, Shakespeare uses a request for a kiss as the basis for an analysis of why those who don't support organizational reforms can kiss off.

Since we are talking about Henry V and Katherine, note that she was the original "trophy wife"—not the modern kind (the young second wife of a much older, status-conscious executive), but the literal kind; Henry conquered France and brought her back as a "trophy."

Only in the twentieth century did the long-known concept of unity of command, that the entire organization should be responsible to only one person, become firmly established as one of the most basic principles of management. Yet Shakespeare wrote of it in *King Lear* (Act II, scene iv), when he had Regan (one of Lear's daughters) say:

> How, in one house,
> Should many people, under two commands,
> Hold amity? 'Tis hard; almost impossible.

Shakespeare knew that joint command, which was practiced in ancient Rome, all too often led to indecision and defeat. Thus, unity of command became conventional wisdom long ago. Niccolo Machiavelli, the greatest political analyst of the Italian Renaissance, wrote in 1517 that "it is better to confide any expedition to a single man of ordinary ability rather than to two even though they are men of the highest merit." Military analysts since, from Napoleon to Eisenhower, have agreed. When the modern corporation was created in the nineteenth century, it was structured on the military model of hierarchical command. Although there are occasional deviations from this structure, they are the exception to the rule. Shakespeare, and all organizational analysts since, knew that it was "almost impossible" for "two commands" to "hold amity." Why? Because, as Shakespeare explains in *Coriolanus* (Act III, scene i):

> when two authorities are up,
> Neither supreme, how soon confusion
> May enter 'twixt the gap of both, and take
> The one by th' other.

PERSONNEL MANAGEMENT

Shakespeare knew that it was best to place people in jobs they enjoyed. Modern job design experts seek to create positions that employees find intrinsically self-fulfilling. It is, as Antony said in *Antony and Cleopatra* (Act IV, scene iv):

> To business that we love we rise betime,
> And go to 't with delight.

Even Iago, in *Othello* (Act II, scene iii), knew that: "Pleasure and action make the hours seem short." The essence of modern job design philosophy is perhaps best summed up by Tranio in *The Taming of the Shrew* (Act I, scene i):

> No profit grows where is no pleasure ta'en.
> In brief, sir, study what you most affect.

Very often the personnel policies of large organizations are dysfunctional: Their rigid rules often defeat their own purposes. Talented employees are often inadequately rewarded and quit as a result. Only then is it realized how valuable they were—because it proves so difficult to replace them. In *Much Ado About Nothing* (Act IV, scene i), Shakespeare has Friar Francis observe this same problem:

> It so falls out
> That what we have we prize not to the worth
> Whiles we enjoy it, but being lack'd and lost,
> Why, then we rack the value, then we find
> The virtue that possession would not show us
> Whiles it was ours.

One of the most difficult aspects of personnel management is firing people. It is even worse if you are the one losing the job. Being fired in an organizational context may be compared to being killed in a battle. Similar considerations often apply. One takes risk to achieve gain. If you are defeated in battle, you lose your life; if you are defeated in an organizational war, you often lose your job. Those who constantly worry about such losses tend to be less effective in battle or business than those who are like Caesar in *Julius Caesar* (Act II, scene ii) and can philosophically accept their eventual death (or firing):

> Cowards die many times before their deaths;
> The valiant never taste of death but once.
> Of all the wonders that I yet have heard,
> It seems to me most strange that men should fear:
> Seeing that death, a necessary end,
> Will come when it will come.

Top executives often tend to make it as hard as possible for others to follow their paths to success, perhaps because they fear possible rivals. Shakespeare knew that those who succeed in rising to the heights of their organization's pyramid often spend an inordinate amount of time worrying about being supplanted by those with more youthful ambitions. In *Julius Caesar* (Act II, scene i), Shakespeare has Brutus observe this all-too-common phenomenon:

> But 'tis a common proof,
> That lowliness is young ambition's ladder,
> Whereto the climber-upward turns his face;
> But when he once attains the upmost rung
> He then unto the ladder turns his back,
> Looks in the clouds, scorning the base degrees
> By which he did ascend.

Tom Peters, the best-selling author of *In Search of Excellence* (1982) and *Thriving on Chaos* (1987), is a strong advocate of "management by wandering around." This calls for an executive to test the accuracy of reporting systems by making random visits to employee worksites to gain information about what is really happening—as opposed to what the various levels of middle management say is happening. As Peters puts it: "You must visit and chat with these knowledgeable people where and when the action is—at 3 a.m. on the loading dock," for example. This is exactly what Shakespeare has King Henry do on the eve of the Battle of Agincourt in 1415. In *Henry V* (Act IV, scene i), the king, knowing that his outnumbered army must fight the French in the morning, borrows a cloak to disguise himself so that he may randomly roam about the campfires of his troops and take their measure. The Chorus (the narrator) calls this "A little touch of Harry in the night."

The information he gains by wandering around, mainly that the men are fearful that they are massively outnumbered, he uses in his famous "St. Crispin's Day" speech (Act IV, scene iii) to his troops on the morning of the battle. He begins by addressing the fact that they are outnumbered three to one:

> If we are mark'd to die, we are enow [enough]
> To do our country loss; and if to live,
> The fewer men, the greater share of honor.

Then he turns their numerical inferiority to advantage with one of the best-known motivational speeches in all of English literature, made all the more memorable by the fact that it celebrates one of England's greatest victories:

> This day is call'd the feast of Crispian:
> He that outlives this day, and comes safe home,
> Will stand a tip-toe when this day is named,
> And rouse him at the name of Crispian.
> He that shall live this day, and see old age,
> Will yearly on the vigil feast his neighbours,
> And say 'To-morrow is Saint Crispian:'
> Then will he strip his sleeve and show his scars,
> And say 'These wounds I had on Crispin's day.'
> Old men forget; yet all shall be forgot,
> But he'll remember with advantages
> What feats he did that day: then shall our names,
> Familiar in his mouth as household words,
> Harry the king, Bedford and Exeter,
> Warwick and Talbot, Salisbury and Gloucester,
> Be in their flowing [brimming] cups freshly remember'd.
> This story shall the good man teach his son;
> And Crispin Crispian shall ne'er go by,
> From this day to the ending of the world,
> But we in it shall be remembered:
> We few, we happy few, we band of brothers;
> For he to-day that sheds his blood with me
> Shall be my brother; be he ne'er so vile [lower class],
> This day shall gentle his condition:

And gentlemen in England now a-bed
Shall think themselves accursed they were not here,
And hold their manhoods cheap whiles any speaks
That fought with us upon Saint Crispin's day.

It is interesting to compare Henry's offer of perpetual glory to General George S. Patton's parallel statement to U.S. troops just before D-Day in 1944:

There's one great thing you men can say when it's all over and you're home once more. You can thank God that twenty years from now, when you're sitting around the fireside with your grandson on your knee and he asks you what you did in the war, you won't have to shift him to the other knee, cough, and say, "I shovelled shit in Louisiana."

Shakespeare, the managerial psychologist par excellence, knew that leaders had to offer the positive reinforcement of glory (or wealth) as opposed to the negative reinforcement of merely not having been a Louisiana shoveller; that the manager who wanders around has to discover what reinforcements are needed—and provide them.

FOR DISCUSSION

Which of these plays by Shakespeare would be most useful as part of a leadership training program and why: *Henry V, Macbeth, Julius Caesar,* or *Hamlet?* Why is a knowledge of Shakespeare or literature in general a great advantage in understanding organizational behavior, motivating subordinates, and leading public, private, and nonprofit organizations?

BIBLIOGRAPHY

Augustine, Norman, and Kenneth Adelman. *Shakespeare in Charge: The Bard's Guide to Leading and Succeeding in Business.* New York: Hyperion, 2001.
Corrigan, Paul. *Shakespeare on Management: Leadership Lessons for Today's Managers.* London: Kogan Page, 1999.
Shafritz, Jay M. *Shakespeare on Management: Wise Business Counsel from the Bard.* New York: HarperCollins, 1992.
Whitney, John O. and Tina Packer. *Power Plays: Shakespeare's Lessons in Leadership and Management.* New York: Simon & Schuster, 2000.

CHAPTER THIRTEEN

The Case of the Ubiquitous Chief of Staff

HOW A JOB INVENTED BY AND ONCE CONFINED TO THE MILITARY ESCAPED ITS UNIFORMED EXISTENCE AND IS NOW COMMONLY FOUND IN GOVERNMENT AND CORPORATE OFFICES

PREVIEW

On January 20, 1953, Dwight D. Eisenhower, the five-star general who led the Western Allies to victory against Nazi Germany in World War II, took the oath of office as president of the United States. A few hours later, he was handed a sealed envelope. According to Eisenhower biographer Geoffrey Perret (1999), "Eisenhower was annoyed." He told the man who gave him the envelope, "Never bring me a sealed envelope again." Perret wrote that this sealed envelope was "concrete proof of something he already believed—that this place [the White House] was badly organized, badly run. Hundreds of letters addressed to him arrived each day. Just opening them would have been a chore. More than that, though, they had to be screened so that only those that he had to read, whether to conduct government business or to keep old friendships in good repair, were placed before him." To deal with the problem that was symbolized by the sealed envelope, Eisenhower adopted a variant of the system—the general staff system—that was pioneered and perfected by the Germans whose army he had so recently defeated. (To be completely honest, Eisenhower's forces only confronted about a quarter of the German Army; the rest were defeated by the Red Army of the Soviet Union.) President Eisenhower's variant of a German invention is the beginning of the widespread use of the civilian chief-of-staff system that has since been so widely copied by governments at all levels.

THE STAFF CONCEPT

The traditional hierarchical organization with its pyramid structure allowed leaders at the top to extend their reach, but the organization was still dependent on the necessarily limited intellectual energy at the highest levels. Even the greatest mind with the best advisors has limits—as Napoleon found out at Waterloo. The staff concept evolved to overcome the inherent limitations of a single mind and ever fleeting time.

Staff refers to two mutually supporting ideas that gradually evolved in both military and civilian contexts. As the management function became increasingly complex and differentiated, managers started using assistants; secretaries, and clerks at first, and later, personnel and purchasing specialists. This traditional use of staff was followed by the staff principle (or staff concept), which created a specific unit in the larger organization whose primary responsibility was to think and plan, to ponder over innovations and plan for their implementation.

Under the factory system that emerged from the Industrial Revolution, business success resulted from well-organized production systems that kept machines busy and costs under control. Industrial and mechanical engineers—and their machines—were the keys to production. Organizational structures and production systems needed constant tinkering and refining to take best advantage of ever-evolving technology. Organizations, it was thought, should work like machines, using people as their parts. Just as industrial engineers sought to design "the best" machines to keep factories productive, industrial and mechanical engineering-type thinking dominated theories about "the one best way" to organize people for their role as part of the overall industrial machine. In the civilian context, this was called scientific management.

THE PRUSSIAN GENERAL STAFF DEFEATS NAPOLEON

As an organizational model to be copied and adapted to local conditions, the German general staff has no peer in the history of administration and policy making. Large military organizations as far back as the armies of Alexander the Great (336–323 BCE) had staff elements for logistics and intelligence, but the birth of the modern staff system can be traced to a specific time and place: eastern Germany, October 14, 1806. In a single day, a smaller French army led by Napoleon destroyed (killed, wounded, or captured) virtually the entire Prussian army at the battles of Jena and Auerstadt.

At that time, Prussia was the large German-speaking state occupying most of what is now eastern Germany and western Poland. In 1871, under the leadership of its famous chancellor, Otto von Bismarck, it united all of the other German-speaking states (except Austria) into modern Germany. Thereupon, the Prussian general staff became the German general staff. This 1871 consolidation was the second *Reich*. *Reich* is the name for the union of German states first applied by historians to the Holy Roman Empire that began in 962 and was abolished by Napoleon after he conquered and occupied Prussia in 1806. The second or Prussian *Reich,* created in 1871 under the Hohenzollern dynasty, lasted until the last Kaiser was overthrown in 1918. In 1933, when the Nazis came to power, they proclaimed a Third *Reich,* which they boasted would last a thousand years—but under Hitler's poor management it actually lasted for only twelve. No fourth *Reich* has followed, because "Reich" now implies the kind of aggressive militarism that is no longer internationally acceptable—at least in a rhetorical sense.

Now, back to the Napoleonic wars. In the wake of the 1806 defeats and occupation of their country by the French, two of Prussia's brighter officers, Gerhard Scharnhorst (1755–1813) and August Gneisenau (1760–1831), convinced their king that there was a way to eventually defeat Napoleon. But to do it the Prussians had to copy some of the French military reforms and come up with a few new ones of their own. The Prussian army then began to imitate the French by selecting officers on the basis of merit as opposed to social rank, in a new emphasis on field maneuvers instead of parade-ground drill, and in the creation of a citizens' as opposed to a mercenary army. Then they bettered the French by inventing the general staff—a think tank for the army.

Napoleon had plenty of staff but no real general staff because he, being a military genius, didn't need one. True geniuses, though, are rare. Thus a general staff, which brings together the brightest officers to plan future operations, is in effect a collective substitute for individual genius. In 1806 the Prussian army was so incompetently organized and led that it deserved to lose to Napoleon. By 1813 the Prussians had so reformed their army, thanks to recommendations developed and installed by the new cadre of general staff officers, that they defeated Napoleon and helped force his initial abdication and exile to the Mediterranean island of Elba. When Napoleon escaped from Elba and assumed power again in 1815, it was the Prussians who joined the British under the Duke of Wellington at Waterloo in Belgium to defeat Napoleon again. Two of the most famous German battleships of the 1930s were named in honor of the dual creators of the general staff, Scharnhorst and Gneisenau; both, fortunately, were destroyed by the British during World War II.

COPYING THE GERMAN MODEL

By the beginning of the twentieth century, all of the major military powers had adopted a variant of the German general staff system. Of course, it sometimes took a large-scale demonstration of incompetence for the military to see the wisdom in reform. For example, both the United States and Great Britain created general staffs only after the demonstrably poor management of major wars: the Spanish–American War of 1898 and the Boer War of 1899–1902, respectively.

Inspired by—really dismayed by—the performance of the U.S. Army during the Spanish–American War, Elihu Root (1845–1937), the New York lawyer who became the U.S. Secretary of War in 1899, just after the war, was determined on reform. This is why, he wrote in his *Annual Report* for 1902 that "the most important thing to be done now for the Regular Army is the creation of a general staff." He did not have to remind his readers that this was necessary because of the poor management of the last war: Soldiers sent to fight in the heat of Cuba had only wool shirts to wear; the famous charge up San Juan Hill by cavalry troops led by Colonel (later President) Theodore Roosevelt was made on foot because no horses were sent with them; and U.S. soldiers gave away their positions to the enemy every time they fired their smoky black-powder weapons, while the enemy stayed hidden using smokeless powder. The most telling number was that only 300 of the 3,000 U.S. soldiers who died in the war were killed in combat. It was obvious that the lack of planning—the lack of professional staff work—cost lives. Richard Harding Davis (1898), the most famous war correspondent of his era, wrote of the Cuban campaign: "Someone has said that 'God takes care of drunken men, sailors, and the United States.' This expedition apparently relied on the probability that that axiom would prove true."

Elihu Root's 1902 *Annual Report* complained that:

> Our system makes no adequate provision for the directing brain which every army must have to work successfully. Common experience has shown that this cannot be furnished by any single man without assistants, and that it requires a body of officers working together under the direction of a chief and entirely separate from and independent of the administrative staff of an army. . . . This body of officers, in distinction from the administrative staff, has come to be called a general staff.

The following year, the U.S. Army was ordered by an act of Congress to create a general staff. The president who signed the bill into law was Theodore Roosevelt, the same colonel whose men, because of poor staff work, lacked horses when they had to charge up San Juan Hill. Root's description of the duties of the general staff, while written in English in his *Report*, was figuratively a translation from the German:

> Such a body of men doing general staff duty is just as necessary in time of peace as it is in time of war. It is not an executive body; it is not an administrative body; it acts only through the authority of others. It makes intelligent command possible by procuring and arranging information and working out plans in detail, and it makes intelligent and effective execution of commands possible by keeping all separate agents advised of the parts they are to play in the general scheme.

It took a while for the general staff concept to be widely understood. For example, D. Clayton James (1970) tells of the time in 1914 when President Woodrow Wilson read in the *Baltimore Sun* that the general staff of the U.S. Army was working on plans for a war with Germany. World War I had just started in Europe, and Wilson was determined at that time to keep the United States out of it. So he directed the secretary of war to launch "an immediate investigation, and if it proved true, to relieve at once every officer of the general staff." Once it was explained to Wilson that preparation of theoretical war plans is a continuing and primary function of the staff, the president quietly allowed the matter to drop.

What Wilson did not understand was that the essence of general staff work was planning. The classic analyst of nineteenth-century warfare, French General Antoine Henri Jomini (1779–1869), made this perfectly clear when he wrote in his 1838 *Summary of the Art of War* that "In times of peace the general staff should plan for all contingencies of war. Its archives should contain the historical details of the past, and all statistical, geographical, topographical, and strategic treatises and papers for the present and future."

Jomini's thinking on strategy, tactics, and staff work was so influential that it was commonly said that American Civil War officers went off to war carrying two books if any at all: The *Bible* and Jomini. Of course, the winning general of that war, Ulysses S.

Grant, denied he had ever read it; but it was taught at West Point when he was a student, and his professed ignorance of it may account for his graduating 21st out of 39 cadets.

The military staff, led by its chief, is an essential part of modern defense structures, but it is not universally admired. The soldiers who have to implement staff plans, and who may have to pay with their lives or limbs for a staff's poor judgment, tend to be severely critical judges of staff performance. This is perhaps best summed up by one of the most famous bits of poetry from World War I, from Siegfried Sassoon's (1886–1967) *The General* (1918):

> "Good morning; good morning!" the general said
> When we met him last week on our way to the line.
> Now the soldiers he smiled at are most of 'em dead,
> And we're cursing his staff for incompetent swine.

Despite his name, Sassoon was an English officer, and despite his contempt for the staff, he fought with great distinction. The general theme of front-line soldiers being contemptuous of the back-of-the-line staff officers is universal, in that it applies to armies of all nations and is equally applicable in civilian operations, where assembly-line, as opposed to battle-line, workers often have a parallel contempt for their bosses.

THE SPOKE-AND-WHEEL VERSUS HIERARCHICAL STRUCTURE

When President Eisenhower was inaugurated in 1953, the White House had plenty of both personal and professional staff for the president. Steve Neal (2001) reports that outgoing President Harry Truman told President-Elect Eisenhower "that any member of the cabinet and any secretary or administrative assistant is at liberty to see the President at any time on any subject." This described a spoke-and-wheel administrative structure that allowed all senior staff to have direct access to the president. Eisenhower immediately supplanted this with a hierarchical structure under which all staff reported to a chief of staff, who became the gatekeeper to the president. This protected the president's time and ensured that all proposals were adequately "staffed out" before being presented to him.

Eisenhower was comfortable working with a hierarchical staff system. After all, he was the West Pointer who rose to become the commanding general of perhaps the largest military staff ever assembled: the staff that organized the June 6, 1944, D-Day invasion of Europe and the conquest of Nazi Germany from the West. Not only had he graduated first in his class at the Army's Command and General Staff School in 1925, he went on to defeat the German general staff that inspired the school in the first place. So Eisenhower was quite comfortable—indeed, insistent—in giving the White House its first true staff system.

Both Presidents Kennedy and Johnson, who followed Eisenhower, reverted to the spoke-and-wheel approach, but the White House staff gradually became increasingly involved with departmental policy reviews and independent policy development.

Richard M. Nixon was vice president under Eisenhower. For eight years he watched and learned from Eisenhower's staff system. So when Nixon became president in 1969, he immediately appointed a chief of staff for the White House, as has every president since. Despite the fact that Nixon's first chief of staff, H. R. Haldeman, and several dozen of his henchmen, went to jail for Watergate-related crimes, the White House staff remains the *de facto* national think tank whose job, in addition to helping the president oversee the federal bureaucracy, is to develop national policy and the president's legislative agenda.

When Gerald R. Ford assumed the presidency in 1974 in the wake of Richard M. Nixon's resignation, he sought to avoid having a chief of staff. The job title had been given a bad odor by Nixon's first chief, H. R. Haldeman, who was forced to resign (and later go to jail) because of his heavy involvement in the Watergate scandal. Haldeman was succeeded by Alexander Haig, an Army general who came from the National Security Council staff. This made many people uncomfortable because it called into question the tradition of civilian control of the military. The U.S. Constitution (Article II, Section 2), by making the president "commander in chief of the army and the navy," mandates civilian control in the United States. Even though some generals have become president, they were elected as civilians. Of course, as Richard J. Walton (1972) warned: "Civilian control versus military control is a distinction without a difference if the civilians think the same way the military does." President John F. Kennedy, in a West Point Commencement Address (June 7, 1962), called for continued civilian control: "I wish all of you the greatest success. While I say that, I am not unmindful of the fact that two graduates of this Academy [Grant and Eisenhower] have reached the White House and neither was a member of my party. Until I'm more certain that this trend will be broken, I wish that all of you may be generals and not commanders in chief."

President Ford opted for the old spoke-and-wheel model for his White House staff. However, recognizing that the structure he had created was not serving him well, Ford then asked Donald Rumsfeld, at that time the U.S. ambassador to NATO, to become his chief of staff. Rumsfeld, who was a friend of Ford's dating from the time they served together in the U.S. House of Representatives, flatly refused to accept the position until Ford agreed to reform the spoke-and-wheel system, which gave every cabinet member direct access to the president. In his memoir (1979), Ford recounts Rumsfeld's blunt analysis: "It won't work. You don't have the time to run the administrative machinery at the White House yourself. I know you don't want a Haldeman-type chief of staff, but someone has to fill that role, and unless I have that authority, I won't be able to serve you effectively."

Ford finally agreed that Rumsfeld was right: that his "accessibility was making [the President] fair game for ridiculous requests and the spokes and wheel structure wasn't working well." Rumsfeld got the job on his terms. This was the last time any president sought to avoid the chief-of-staff model. However, Rumsfeld did not keep the coveted job for long. After a few months, Ford appointed him Secretary of Defense and promoted Rumsfeld's deputy, 33-year-old Richard B. Cheney, to be the youngest chief of staff ever. Yes, this is the same Cheney who reappeared in the White House as President George W. Bush's vice president beginning in 2001; the same Cheney who successfully lobbied Bush to reinstate his old mentor Rumsfeld as Secretary of Defense, for all the good and ill that followed from that appointment.

As Rumsfeld told Ford, the chief of staff's primary job is to protect the president's time. Subsequently, Andrew Card, President George W. Bush's chief of staff, told G. Robert Hillman (2001): "There are probably 150 people—and that's not an exaggeration—working in the White House—just in the White House—that say, 'Gee, if I could just get five minutes with the president, I could solve some problem.'" Card regrets that: "There's not enough time in a year to do that." After all, he added: "the president is a human being. He still has to eat, sleep and be merry."

A chief of staff was once a rarity and strictly military. This is no longer the case. Fashion is a factor here. The White House sets trends. When Mrs. John F. Kennedy, as the president's wife, wore a pillbox hat, that became a national fashion trend. There is fashion in administration, too. If the president has a chief of staff, lesser officials seeking to emulate the highest office also start appointing chiefs of staff. The trend continues and expands to all levels of government and to many levels within those levels.

The influence of the German general staff model is now so pervasive that you can hardly walk into a government office without bumping into a chief of staff. Most governors and mayors and county administrators have them. So do major department heads from police chiefs (yes, the chief has a chief!) to school superintendents. Increasingly, even individual legislators have them. The point is that you as a public manager are not very important unless you have one—even if your chief of staff is really not much more than a chief of a few clerks.

Even first ladies now have chiefs of staff. First lady Michelle Obama seems particularly pleased that she has one. According to an Associated Press report of May 8, 2009, she told a meeting of the nonprofit Corporate Voices for Working Families: "Everyone should have a chief of staff and a set of personal assistants." Well! That's easy enough for her to say.

Just as the chief-of-staff concept has developed many variations, so too has the notion of a think tank. The phrase itself, while used here to describe the core function of the traditional general staff, is really just a colloquial term for an organization, or organizational segment, whose sole function is research. The purpose of civilian think tanks is to identify options, assess policies, and generally contribute to the debate over public policies. Although they began, at least on a large scale, after World War II as a particularly American phenomenon, other countries have emulated the U.S. experience. Now think tanks are pervasive throughout the world. Many are associated with universities, others with government. More recently, there has been a trend toward partisan think tanks. The U.S. tax code encourages any eccentric with enough money to establish a foundation to fund research on virtually anything. So, what was once solely the tool of nations to deal with the great issues of war and peace is now also a vehicle for social reformers and crackpot millionaires. Blame Napoleon!

FOR DISCUSSION

What are the pros and cons of having civilian organizations adopt a military-inspired chief-of-staff system? Why is it that the job title of chief of staff, which once meant something quite specific, is now so broadly assigned that there is no way to tell what it means without extensive investigation?

BIBLIOGRAPHY

Dale, Ernst, and Lyndall F. Urwick. *Staff in Organization*. New York: McGraw-Hill, 1960.

Davis, Richard Harding. *The Cuban and Puerto Rican Campaigns*. New York: Scribner's Sons, 1898.

Dupuy, Trevor Nevit. *A Genius for War: The German Army and the General Staff, 1807–1945*. Englewood Cliffs, NJ: Prentice-Hall, 1977.

Ford, Gerald R. *A Time to Heal*. New York: Harper & Row, 1979.

Hart, John. "No Passion for Brownlow: Models of Staffing the Presidency." *Politics* 17, no. 2 (1982).

Hess, Stephen. *Organizing the Presidency*. Washington, DC: Brookings Institution, 1976.

Hillman, G. Robert. "Texans Settle into Staff Roles." *Dallas Morning News*, March 18, 2001.

James, D. Clayton. *The Years of MacArthur*. Vol. I. Boston: Houghton Mifflin, 1970.

———. *The Years of MacArthur*. Vol. II. Boston: Houghton Mifflin, 1975.

Jomini, Antoine Henri. *Summary of the Art of War*. New York: Putnam, 1854.

Keegan, John. *A History of Warfare*. New York: Knopf, 1993.

Krames, Jeffrey A. *The Rumsfeld Way*. New York: McGraw-Hill, 2002.

Neal, Steve. *Harry and Ike: The Partnership That Remade the Postwar World*. New York: Scribner, 2001.

Perret, Geoffrey. *Eisenhower*. New York: Random House, 1999.

Walton, Richard J. *Cold War and Counterrevolution*. New York: Viking, 1972.

Warshaw, Shirley Anne. *The Keys to Power: Managing the Presidency*. New York: Longman, 2000.

Weigley, Russell F. *History of the United States Army*. Enlarged edition. Bloomington, IN: Indiana University Press, 1984.

Weisband, Edward, and Thomas M. Frank. *Resignation in Protest*. New York: Grossman, 1975.

CHAPTER FOURTEEN

Organization Development in Hollywood War Movies

FROM JOHN WAYNE IN *THE SANDS OF IWO JIMA* TO *G.I. JANE* AND BEYOND

PREVIEW

Since prehistory, the building blocks of armies has been the squad, an eight- to twelve-man unit that eats, sleeps, and fights together. Forging this small group into an effective force has always been the most basic task of military training. Only after World War II, with the explosion of growth in behavioral science research, did this long-standing forging of effectiveness get a name: organization development. However, as this case shows, Hollywood, in its war movies, was way ahead of the behavioral scientists in illustrating just how this process works.

THE SQUAD

Demi Moore and John Wayne may not appear to have much in common. However, they have both played roles in feature films that illustrate small-scale organization development. In the 1997 film *G.I. Jane,* Moore takes a disparate group of would-be Navy SEALs (sea-air-land teams) and forges them into a competent combat team—just in time to see "real" action on a fictional mission off the coast of Libya.

What Demi Moore did in her performance was not much different from what John Wayne did in two films set during World War II: *The Sands of Iwo Jima* (1949) and *Flying Leathernecks* (1951). In the former, Wayne is the sergeant of a Marine infantry squad; in the latter, he is the commanding officer of a Marine fighter squadron. In both cases, he forges his unruly and high-spirited young charges into an effective, highly disciplined fighting force. He, as an older, more mature character, teaches them by example and instruction. And when someone inevitably dies because one of his men failed the group, Wayne is ready (in *The Sands*) with the kind of after-action fatherly consolation that makes his charges determined not to screw up again. "A lot of guys make mistakes, I guess, but every one we make, a whole stack of chips goes with it. We make a mistake, and some guy don't walk away—forevermore, he don't walk away." He says this with his eyes welling up with moisture and his voice choking to give it greater poignancy. Wayne was always most effective as here, when he gets almost to the point of crying but manfully holds it in.

Taking a cue from the John Wayne school of acting, Demi Moore also "manfully" holds in her tears throughout much of *G.I. Jane*—especially during a brutal mock prisoner-of-war interrogation. She is finally accepted by the SEALs as one of the guys when she, hands tied behind her back, attacks her sadistic interrogator with a brutal kick to the groin (thus denying him—at least temporarily—his masculine advantage) and lets forth with a blue streak of verbal abuse that shows once and for all that she can use the foul language of the barracks like the toughest of the guys. After this, the men she commands are ready to follow her anywhere. The point is that her actions—her example—like Wayne's, forge them into an effective team, whereas previously they lacked group cohesion. *G.I. Jane* and many other war movies, such as those of John Wayne, demonstrate how organization development is, and always has been, an inherent part of military training.

Of course, Moore, even with her hair in a crew cut, is not *really* the new John Wayne. After all, she has not made a career of war movies and become the symbol of an aggressive U.S. military. Wayne, despite having appeared in a dozen previous war films, first became that symbol in a major way in 1949 when he played Sergeant Stryker in *The Sands*. Wayne earned his first Academy Award nomination with his portrayal of a tough disciplinarian whose men hated him for his rigorous training methods until the end of the film, when they realize that his toughness saved many of their lives by making them an effective combat team. According to Lawrence Suid, in *Guts and Glory: Great American War Movies* (1978), Wayne himself described the plot of *The Sands* as "the story of Mr. Chips [a benevolent English boarding school teacher] put in the military. A man takes eight boys and has to make men out of them." But Randy Roberts and James Olson, in *John Wayne: American* (1995), add: "If one can imagine Mr. Chips cracking the jaw of one of his students with the butt of a rifle, the comparison is an apt one."

SQUAD LEADERSHIP

This film, *The Sands of Iwo Jima,* made with the complete cooperation of the U.S. Marine Corps (the "cast of thousands" are mostly real Marines), has often been derided by "serious" critics but has nevertheless become one of the more influential films of the twentieth century. It taught a whole generation of Americans what it meant to be a leader—especially of small groups. Stryker's hallmark shouts of impending action—"saddle up" and "lock and load"—are still commonly heard in both military and civilian contexts. For example, journalist Pat Buchanan, who never served in the military, often used those phrases during his ill-fated political campaign for the 1996 Republican presidential nomination. The former speaker of the House of Representatives, Newt Gingrich of Georgia, told Elizabeth Drew in *Showdown* (1996) that *The Sands* was "the formative movie of my life." Stryker's style of leadership—make them tough and effective even if they hate you for it—was Gingrich's self-confessed tactic for shaping up his Republican insurgents for their successful 1994 assault on the House of Representatives.

Wayne played similar roles, outwardly tough but inwardly caring older leaders of younger men, in *Flying Leathernecks* (1951) and director John Ford's U.S. Cavalry trilogy: *Fort Apache* (1948), *She Wore a Yellow Ribbon* (1949), and *Rio Grande* (1950). However, only his character in *The Cowboys* (1971) was a reprise of his role as Sergeant Stryker in a different guise. In *The Cowboys* he is a Texas rancher who must use untrained boys to drive his cattle herd to the railhead many hundreds of miles away, but the plot—the organization development effort—is essentially the same: Make these boys men enough for the job at hand. In both movies, the boys dislike him at first but then learn to love him because they realize his way will see them through. In both movies, Wayne is killed—by a Japanese sniper as the U.S. flag is raised on Iwo Jima in *The Sands* and by a despicable cattle rustler played by Bruce Dern in *The Cowboys*. In both movies, the team can now carry on without him because he has trained, nurtured, and developed them so well. In *The Sands* the squad goes on to secure the island as the Marine Corps hymn reminds us that this same kind of thing has been going on "from the halls of Montezuma to the shores of Tripoli." In *The Cowboys* the group realizes that they—because of the John Wayne character—are now strong enough to go it alone, to take back the herd from the rustlers and to kill the villains for good measure. In both movies, Wayne, much like Moses in the Old Testament, gets his people close to the "promised land" but then dies before reaching the goal. They must go on without him, and they can do it because of what they learned from him. It is just this patriarchal aspect of Wayne that makes him, his characters, and his movies so sublimely moving and ultimately lasting.

THE REAL JOHN WAYNE

Alas, the real John Wayne was no "John Wayne." The archetypal hero of so many movies and of America's popular imagination, far from being a hero, was quite the opposite. As a warrior he was a complete phony. Unlike many of his contemporary film stars, such as Clark Gable, Robert Taylor, James Stewart, Tyrone Power, Henry Fonda, Glenn Ford, and Sterling Hayden, to name a few, who gave up established Hollywood careers to serve with distinction in World War II, Wayne made every effort to avoid military service during the war. He was, more than any other major public figure, an active, artful, and successful draft dodger many times over. He simply arranged for the movie studios to say he was in a job that was essential to the war effort. However, by 1943 Wayne decided he would serve his country if he could get the assignment he wanted: working for director (now Navy officer) John Ford's naval photography unit. Ford, however, was not able to get him in, because all such billets were frozen at that time. According to Ford's grandson, Dan Ford (1979), "Wayne tried other avenues but couldn't get a commission. The only way he could get in the service was to enlist in the army as a private." Wayne explained, "I felt that it would be a waste of time to spend two years picking up cigarette butts. I thought I could do more for the war effort if I stayed in Hollywood."

Wayne's career thrived during the war when so many other leading men were in uniform facing the enemy while he faced the cameras. Many in the film industry never forgave Wayne for refusing to serve. Political analyst Garry Wills (1977) wrote: "A few even claim that Wayne did not forgive himself—that the compensatory superpatriotism of later years, when he urged the country on to wars in Korea and Vietnam, was a form of expiation. If so, it was not enough. This is a man who called on other generations to sacrifice their lives, and called them 'soft' if they refused."

Wayne's personal honor and patriotism notwithstanding, in the postwar era he became—and remains—the national icon of organization development. Wayne's performance in *The Sands of Iwo Jima,* while excellent in its own right, was a movie cliché even then. The stern fatherly taskmaster who takes error-prone "boys" under his wing and makes men out of them is a dramatic device that can be found as far back as the works of Homer in ancient Greece. It became the standard plot device for so many war movies because it lent itself so well to a story line needing a neat beginning, middle, and end. *The Sands* is simply the leading example of this genre. Other films with almost identical plot structures include *Gung Ho!* (1943), starring Randolph Scott; *Battle Cry* (1954), starring Van Heflin; *Cockleshell Heroes* (1956), starring José Ferrer; *Darby's Rangers* (1958), starring James Garner; *The Dirty Dozen* (1967), starring Lee Marvin; *The Devil's Brigade* (1968), starring William Holden; *Gallipoli* (1981), starring Mel Gibson; *Heartbreak Ridge* (1986), starring Clint Eastwood; and *The Last Samurai* (2003), starring Tom Cruise.

THE THREE ACTS OF GROUP DEVELOPMENT

The formula used by these films has three acts. In the first, the disparate group is assembled and seen as a bunch of individualists not capable of functioning as a team. Almost always, the group is ethnically diverse, to represent the tensions and composition of the larger society. Thus there is often the college boy, the lumberjack, the "dead-end" kid, the farmer, and the urban ethnics (characters that are obviously meant to be Polish, Italian, or Jewish). Historians agree. According to Steven E. Ambrose (1997):

> Unlike the Civil war, when army units were recruited from a single state, in World War II men, in most cases, were thrown together willy-nilly—so much so that a war-spawned cliché of film and fiction is the squad made up of the hillbilly from Arkansas, the Jew from Brooklyn, the coal miner from Pennsylvania, the farmer from Ohio, the lumberman from Oregon, the Italian from Chicago, the Pole from Milwaukee, and the Cajun from Louisiana. At first they hate each other; training draws them together; combat welds them into a band of brothers; they emerge by the final scene as just plain Americans with a strong sense of nationalism. And the truth is that this happened in life before it happened in art.

Later, as U.S. society became more inclusive, Hispanic, Asian, and African Americans appeared. The first "act" always has the various types gradually lose their "street" identities and, under the harsh but benevolent guidance of the father-figure drill instructor, mold themselves into a team whose motto might well be that of Alexander Dumas's *Three Musketeers* (1844): "All for one, one for all."

The second act has the group performing as a team in training exercises and, often equally important, while on leave. For the purposes of the plot, it is equally valid for the group to realize they are a team in a barroom brawl or on field maneuvers. It's the group adventure, the sharing of mutual stress and danger, that finally cements the individuals into a team. (For the same reason, retreats and outdoor adventures are still popular means of developing civilian groups. The team that drinks together and climbs mountains together will perform the mundane duties of their everyday work in a more cooperative manner.) Once team status is achieved and the young soldiers realize how good the tough training they initially hated has been for them, they are ready for the third act: combat.

The third act validates the first two. It "proves" that the training works. Some lives are inevitably lost, but discipline and teamwork are shown to save lives and save the day. The father figure—whether John Wayne or Randolph Scott—is never more fatherly than when he leads them into danger and helps them fulfill their destiny as soldiers or cannon fodder.

One of the reasons films that follow this three-act formula have been so popular is that they ring true. Although they have been decidedly sanitized for the mass public, they are true in that this *is* how the military—of all countries for seemingly all times—has indoctrinated and readied new soldiers for service. Thus the genre represents a time-tested method of organization development. The problem, of course, is that this particularly brutal method cannot be universally applied. First-line supervisors (the industrial equivalent of sergeants) cannot demand an instant fifty push-ups from an errant worker. In the industrial world the punishments must be more psychological than physical.

AT THE COMMAND LEVEL

So far we have discussed the low end of war movie organization development. Although such small unit plots offer the greatest opportunity for character development and audience identification, there is also a high end: organization development at the command level. This is best illustrated by films such as *Patton* (1970), starring George C. Scott, and *Twelve O'Clock High* (1949), starring Gregory Peck. In both movies, new generals take charge of large units whose performance has been deficient. They may be generals, not sergeants, but they use the same techniques as John Wayne's Sergeant Stryker to change the dysfunctional organizational culture that has led to failed operations and the sacking of the previous commanders. When Scott and Peck use their general's stars to impose a harsh disciplinary regime on their errant outfits, they are simply following Stryker's example and techniques on a higher organizational level. And they get the same results: an effective team that has high morale and carries out successful operations.

This same phenomenon can be seen at sea. Films of wartime naval action often demonstrate how organization development works on a single ship. *In Which We Serve* (1942) has Noel Coward commanding a Royal Navy destroyer with a green crew that he molds into an efficient ship's company. In *The Cruel Sea* (1953), Jack Hawkins has the same task as the commander of a convoy-escorting corvette. However, by far the best Navy organization development film is *Away All Boats* (1956), starring Jeff Chandler as the captain of a Pacific Theater troop transport. This film shows organization development at two levels: The captain develops his staff of officers while the chiefs develop the sailors in a parallel manner. In each of these films the plot is a pure organization development play in that the captain is taking command of a brand-new ship; then he has the opportunity to instill the organizational culture he thinks will be the most effective.

War movies offer seemingly countless examples of effective organization development, but they also provide some excellent examples of the most ineffectual kind of organization development efforts: those that make an organization far worse than it should be. The most famous example is probably *The Caine Mutiny* (1954), in which destroyer captain Humphrey Bogart gradually loses control of his ship to mutinous officers. In *Attack!* (1956), Jack Palance stars as an infantry platoon leader who has to "carry" his inept commanding officer, until Palance, for excellent reasons, finally shoots his cowardly commander. Because it graphically demonstrates that sometimes the best way to save the organization is to kill the boss, this is one of the few U.S. war movies of the 1950s to be made without the cooperation of the U.S. Department of Defense.

In *Paths of Glory* (1957), Kirk Douglas, as a French infantry colonel during World War I, suffers from the criminal incompetence of the French general staff. For showing the deadly consequences that can come from dysfunctional organizations, this film was banned in France for many years. Nevertheless, it remains the classic film of dishonor at the top and how not to do strategic planning.

The essence of this case study has been to demonstrate that the military throughout the ages—and U.S. war movies in particular—evidenced a sophisticated understanding of organization development long before it became a formal element of modern management education. Wayne's Sergeant Stryker may not have been anyone's ideal of a friendly organization development facilitator or consultant, but he—quite literally—knew the drill. Even without an advanced degree in applied behavioral science or public administration, he and his brothers-in-arms, going back to the legions of ancient Rome and beyond, knew how to instill planned organizational change. Higher education is a wonderful thing, but sometimes you can learn just as much by staying home and watching a bunch of old war movies.

Hollywood continues the tradition of using war films to illustrate the utility and methods of organization development by employing variants of the formula described above. In *Master and Commander* (2003), Russell Crowe as a British Navy captain, spends less time fighting than teaching his crew of disparate characters to develop their skills as team players. The proof of his success as an organization developer is that his small ship (meaning small team) defeats a ship and a team twice as large in the end. Crowe is confident that his team will follow him as he jumps aboard an enemy ship. He—meaning his character—is literally betting his life on his team development efforts.

Similarly, in *The Last Samurai* (2003), Tom Cruise is part of a group of nineteenth-century U.S. Army officers hired by the Japanese government to change a traditional hand weapon–wielding army into a modern one using firearms. After the usual developmental problems, the newly developed higher-tech organization triumphs. This is a trend that will never end—because social improvements, whether military or civilian, are almost always premised upon successful organization development interventions. This is even more true in real life than in the movies. Unfortunately, in real life, the process inevitably takes longer than two hours.

FOR DISCUSSION

Why are each of the "three acts" of organization development so essential to under-standing how the process works in both a military and a civilian context? Is organization development limited to war movies, or can examples of it be found in other types of films as well?

BIBLIOGRAPHY

Ambrose, Stephen E. *Americans at War.* Jackson, MI: University Press of Mississippi, 1997.

Drew, Elizabeth. *Showdown.* New York: Simon and Schuster, 1996.

Ford, Dan. *Pappy: The Life of John Ford.* Englewood Cliffs, NJ: Prentice Hall, 1979.

Roberts, Rand, and James S. Olson. *John Wayne: American.* New York: Free Press, 1995.

Suid, Lawrence. *Guts and Glory: Great American War Movies.* Reading, MA: Addison-Wesley, 1978.

Wills, Garry. *John Wayne's America.* New York: Simon and Schuster, 1977.

CHAPTER FIFTEEN

George Orwell's Big Brother Is Bigger and Better than Ever

NOT ONLY IS HE WATCHING YOU, HE IS COUNTING THE NUMBER OF TIMES YOU VISIT HIS WEBSITE, TAKING YOUR PICTURE, CONVERTING IT TO A SERIES OF NUMBERS, AND DESTROYING YOUR ANONYMITY!

PREVIEW

When he was a soldier during the Spanish Civil War, George Orwell ran away—not from the enemy who shot him in the neck, but from ostensible friends on his own side. The war began in 1936, when the Spanish drove out their king and elected a government of centrists and leftists. However, right-wing fascists led by General Francisco Franco refused to accept the results of the election and rebelled. The three-year war that followed has been called a "rehearsal for World War II" because it pitted elected republican forces aided by communists (especially the Soviet Union) against a fascist army aided by the dictatorships of Benito Mussolini of Italy and Adolf Hitler of Germany. Most notably, the Germans sent the Condor Legion to fight on the side of their Spanish fascist brothers. The Legion totaled less than 10,000 men at any one time, but because of rotation policies it gave over 16,000 German soldiers combat experience in this live-action "rehearsal" for World War II. The Legion, which included air elements, was notorious for the 1937 killing of civilians in the northern Spanish town of Guernica. One of Pablo Picasso's most famous paintings, *Guernica,* commemorates the destruction of this Basque town.

To counter the foreign fascist troops, many citizens of countries such as the United States, Great Britain, France, and Poland formed international brigades—units of volunteers often recruited by local communist parties. Orwell, an idealistic young man with some military experience (he had been a British police officer in colonial Burma), volunteered and fought bravely on the republican side until he was wounded.

Unfortunately for the Spanish people, the communists who came to dominate the republican side were as dictatorial and undemocratic as the fascists were on the other side. When Orwell pointed this out, the communists, always reluctant to accept constructive criticism graciously, decided that they would be better off if he were dead. So Orwell decamped back to England.

The Spanish Civil War ended in 1937 with the victory of the fascists under Franco, who would continue to rule as a dictator until his death in 1975. Orwell fought two wars in Spain: (1) the hot war against the Fascists and (2) the cold war against the communists. He lost both his wars, wounded in the first and forced to flee home by the second. Nevertheless, the wars were a pivotal influence on Orwell. As he wrote in his essay, "Why I Write" (1946), "The Spanish war and other events of 1936–37 turned the scale and thereafter I knew where I stood. Every line of serious work that I have written since 1936 has been written, directly or indirectly, against totalitarianism and for democratic socialism, as I understand it." Thus it was Orwell's participation in the Spanish Civil War that inspired the two most devastating and influential critiques of rule under totalitarian governments, *Animal Farm* (1945) and *Nineteen Eighty-Four* (1949)—proof positive that if you don't kill critical writers, they will likely continue to puncture you with their pen.

ALL-INTRUSIVE GOVERNMENT

George Orwell's 1949 novel, *Nineteen Eighty-Four,* is perhaps the world's best-known account of an all-intrusive government. Twice made into major films (in 1956 starring Edmund O'Brien and in 1984 starring Richard Burton), its core concepts have crept into the consciousness of all those concerned about civil liberties and democratic institutions. Even though it was written as a warning about the then-looming threat of totalitarian communism, its concerns still resonate today. Evolving technologies have made its science fictional account of a government that literally oversees and regulates every aspect of life more science than fiction. As Orwell warned in *Nineteen Eighty-Four,* "If you want a picture of the future, imagine a boot stamping on a human face—forever."

Orwell loathed oppressive totalitarian governments such as those of Hitler's Germany and Stalin's Soviet Union because they denied citizens the right to think freely for themselves. Under totalitarianism, a dominating elite holds all power, controls all aspects of society, allows no opposition, and maintains itself by internal terror and secret police. In *Inside the Whale and Other Essays* (1940), Orwell wrote that "From the totalitarian point of view, history is something to be created rather than learned. A totalitarian state is in effect a theocracy, and its ruling caste, in order to keep its position, has to be thought of as infallible. But since, in practice, no one is infallible, it is frequently necessary to rearrange past events in order to show that this or that mistake was not made. . . ." Therefore, "every major change in policy demands a corresponding change of doctrine and a revaluation of prominent historical figures. This kind of thing happens everywhere, but is clearly likelier to lead to outright falsification in societies where only one opinion is permissible at any given moment." Consequently, "totalitarianism demands, in fact, the continuous alteration of the past, and in the long run probably demands a disbelief in the very existence of objective truth."

Orwell wrote in essay form the political essence of *Nineteen Eighty-Four* many times over. As is demonstrated by the above quotations, the novel that has become the world's most famous literary indictment of totalitarianism just provides fictional characters and situations to literally play out the points of his essays as if they were a staged drama.

Animal Farm, his 1945 satirical short novel of Soviet communism, was his first real financial success as a writer. Finally, he had an audience, a readership that would be receptive to his message—his warning—if he could frame it in a readily digestible forum. He wrote *Nineteen Eighty-Four* as he was dying from tuberculosis. He knew he didn't have much time left. He saw the Soviet Union take over Eastern Europe. He saw the Chinese Communists consolidate their power in China. He feared for the future of the Western democracies and put his fears in the form of one last novel.

BIG BROTHER

In the 1950s, the globe-trotting comedian Bob Hope returned home to the United States from a visit to the Soviet Union and told a television audience: "Sure they have television in Russia; only it watches you." This, though Hope did not intend it so, was an excellent summation of the Orwellian future depicted in *Nineteen Eighty-Four*. The novel's most famous catch phrase, "Big Brother is watching you," referred to the "reality" that people were constantly under surveillance. As the actual year 1984 came and went, there was considerable analysis of the status of Orwell's predictions. It was generally concluded that the novel, at least in the Western world, was still political science fiction. In the subsequent quarter-century, however, so much has changed in the realm of technology that Orwell's conception of a constantly watchful "Big Brother" must be reexamined.

Consider how far we have gone down the road toward Orwell's "1984." With the widespread use of personal computers and the advent of the Internet, many millions of e-mail messages are sent every day. And on any given day, government and corporate computers access and read large numbers of those messages in order to forestall illegal and terrorist operations, to gather marketing information, and to monitor employees.

Many Internet websites are programmed to extract information about users; so that their buying habits, reading habits, and viewing habits—even music tastes—are available to those who might use that information to sell you products, to sell you politicians, or, ultimately, perhaps to sell you out. For example, someone who buys a book from Amazon.com will thereafter receive e-mail advertisements for new books or used books on related topics. This same technology allows a power—a government, a corporation, a religious group, etc.—to divine what books you read and, by implication, what you believe. And if you are against "them" in your reading habits, they know who you are and where you live. This gives a whole new meaning to the ancient adage, "Let the buyer beware!"

But wait; there's more. In this age of the electronic book such as Kindle, which can hold hundreds of individual titles, a "Big Brother" government or corporation can know not only what you are reading, but can take those books away from you electronically. This is not speculation: It really happened in 2009, when, because of copyright issues, Amazon.com deleted the books of George Orwell from the Kindles of thousands of its customers. This caused massive outrage and concomitant bad publicity for the company. Jeff Bezos, Amazon.com's chief executive officer, was forced to issue a formal apology. How ironic that the "Big Brother" corporation had to apologize for deleting the book that introduced the term "Big Brother" to the world. This is a fact that could bring out the paranoia that lurks deep within all of us.

DAILY SURVEILLANCE

Now that video cameras are so small and relatively inexpensive, they have popped up in an enormous number of places—banks, offices, grocery stores, busy intersections, etc.—for routine surveillance, just in case a crime is committed. Increasingly, such devices are being used in apartment buildings and gated communities. Thus, in seeking to protect ourselves, we willingly put ourselves under surveillance—surveillance that might be highly objectionable if it were undertaken by government. Such surveillance is now so commonplace that almost the first thing police do when they arrive at a crime scene is to check whether video surveillance tapes are available. Even a camera from blocks away may have captured the license plate of a getaway car. You can learn stuff like this just by watching detective shows on television.

The nexus of television and computer surveillance has become so sophisticated that police departments can use video cameras to instantly scan the faces of thousands of people—on a public street or at a sporting event such as the Superbowl—and in a fraction of a second compare each face to those of known criminals or terrorists. Faceprints, much like fingerprints, use measurable features such as the distances between the corners of the mouth, nostrils, and eyes to create a unique biometric portrait that can be compared to a database of such portraits. According to Peter Slevin (2001), "Casinos use face-recognition technology to identify card counters and other patrons considered undesirable."

Biometric facial recognition technologies are neither invasive, inconvenient, nor even much known to the public. John D. Woodward, Jr. (2001), writes: "The technological impartiality of facial recognition also offers significant benefits for society. While humans are adept at recognizing facial features we are also susceptible to prejudices and preconceptions. The controversy surrounding racial profiling illustrates the problems that can result." However, "facial recognition systems . . . do not focus on a person's skin color, hairstyle or manner of dress, and they do not recognize racial stereotypes." Of course there is always the possibility of an incorrect match—but no more so than with long-standing methods of identification such as mug shots or line-ups.

New technologies are being developed that go beyond just looking at or photographing you. According to Anne Kadet (2009), the Transportation Security Administration, those wonderful folks at the airport who love to sniff your empty shoes and finger the finger food in your carry-on bag, are presently employing 2,400 "behavioral detection officers," who look for travelers acting scared, stressed, or suspicious. However, this job may soon be turned over to a machine. Kadet reports that "new devices being tested would remotely monitor your pulse, temperature, respiration and expressions to reveal signs of 'harmful intent.' Yes, you could literally be stopped for breathing wrong."

Perhaps you think such surveillance is fine if it is used to catch thieves. Many a thief has been caught because cell phone calls can be instantly traced, or stolen cars with secretly planted transponders can be instantly located. Modern surveillance in the new age of Big Brother has become so pervasive and sophisticated that it is changing the nature of policing. Police agencies at all levels of government not only have to train their officers to use these new technologies, but also have to teach them when it is constitutional to use them. After all, there is no point in using high-tech surveillance if the results won't hold up in court. Only in totalitarian states can Big Brother ignore the constitutionally guaranteed civil liberties of the citizens. However, it is not just the bad guys who are being watched; it is all of us—all the time. Do we want this level of intrusion in our lives?

LARGER IMPLICATIONS

The implications of widespread electronic surveillance go far beyond the political and legal issues of civil liberties. It is one thing to be watched in public—on the street and in stores. What about the stress of being watched at work throughout the day? Not just cameras in the office or on the factory floor, but computer programs that monitor every keystroke, and that can tell the boss exactly, to the nanosecond, how fast (or slow) you are working.

Companies and governments monitor employee computer activities for many reasons: to ensure adequate productivity, to see whether e-mail is being used appropriately (for work-related messages) and not inappropriately (to send jokes to friends and/or co-workers), and to ensure that Internet surfing is work- and not porno-related. And they have every legal right to do this, because it is the company's time, the company's computer, and the company's policies on their usage that must be followed.

Every day, employees are fired or disciplined for "cyber-loafing" or sending inappropriate e-mail messages during office hours. Organizations, both public and private, can do this because of the easy availability of "snoopware" programs. According to Sheryll Poe (2001), such programs take a series of "snapshots of whatever is on the screen every few seconds while the user is online. It records all keystrokes, even if the person immediately deletes them. Since the recorded files are stored in a special area of the hard disk, the program doesn't show up in any directory." In consequence, "only the person who installed the software knows it is there." Citing an American Management Association study, Poe reports that two-thirds of all large corporations "now perform some type of in-house electronics surveillance."

After a hard day of being watched and snooped on at work, you head home on a train or bus that also has cameras watching in case you pick your nose. If you drive, you are likely to find cameras at busy intersections, at the convenience store where you stop for milk, and at your gated community. You finally arrive home thinking you are finally alone, but as soon as you turn on your personal computer to access your e-mail or the Internet, you are once again under surveillance.

Finally, we do it to ourselves. Social networking sites provide information about ourselves not only to our friends but also to anyone else who may be curious. Your twitter account is a version of personal broadcasting. A tweet may not be so sweet if the police discover that an invitation to a party suggests underage drinking or illegal drug use.

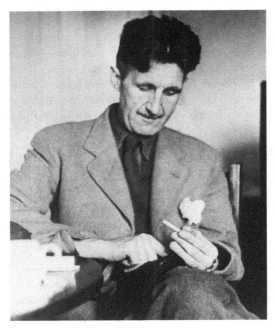

George Orwell (1903–1950), the "father" of Big Brother. Born Eric Blair in India, the son of a British official in the Indian Civil Service, Orwell followed the family tradition and became a colonial police officer in Burma. As his political consciousness grew, however, he was repelled by his role as a cog in the imperial machine. He resigned and lived among the poor of Europe as a hobo and occasional dishwasher. This gave him the material for his first book, *Down and Out in Paris and London* (1933). Further novels during the 1930s were marginally successful and kept him well acquainted with poverty. His developing socialist consciousness led him to join the republican militia during the Spanish Civil War. After being seriously wounded he fled Spain, not because of his wound, but because the communists on whose side he had been fighting (they led the republican faction) were trying to kill him. It seems that Orwell was critical of how the commies treated their political opponents. This experience inspired his two most famous books. *Animal Farm*, his 1945 novella, has become the classic satire on Soviet communism and a warning that all revolutions eventually betray their revolutionary ideals. The revolutionary ideal was that "all animals were equal." After the pigs took over, however, they decided that "some animals [pigs] were more equal than others." Orwell's last and most influential novel, *Nineteen Eighty-Four*, was written between periods of hospitalization for tuberculosis, from which he died early in 1950. He lived to see his last novel published but died before anyone knew how immensely successful it would become.
Source: © CORBIS. All Rights Reserved.

Facebook and similar sites should be considered as permanent records that future prospective employers will check. Do you really think you will be eligible for a government job requiring security clearance once investigators find out about some of your dubious friends or party exploits? So many people are so thoughtless about their future or such exhibitionists in the present that they are more than willing to do Big Brother's job for him. Perhaps a greater sense of privacy, decency, and modesty is best advised here.

Orwell wrote that every floor of every apartment building had a poster in the hall from which an "enormous face gazed from the wall. It was one of those pictures which are so contrived that the eyes follow you about when you move. BIG BROTHER IS WATCHING YOU, the caption beneath it ran." Has Orwell's "1984" finally arrived? Is Big Brother watching *YOU?*

FOR DISCUSSION

Does the massive use of Big Brother surveillance technologies make you feel safer because it can protect you from crime, or less safe because of possible violations of your civil liberties? Will you be more careful now using communication technologies, knowing that anything you type or send electronically could be reconstructed and used to judge your lawfulness or your character?

BIBLIOGRAPHY

Agathocleous, Tanya. *George Orwell: Battling Big Brother.* New York: Oxford University Press, 2000.

Becker, Ted. "Rating the Impact of New Technologies on Democracy." *Communications of the ACM* 44, no. 1 (2001).

Crick, Bernard R. *George Orwell, A Life.* Boston: Little, Brown, 1980.

Garfinkel, Simson. *Database Nation: The Death of Privacy in the 21st Century.* Sebastopol, CA: O'Reilly, 2002.

Hitchens, Christopher. *Why Orwell Matters.* New York: Basic Books, 2002.

Kadet, Anne. "My Airport Massage." *Smart Money,* September 2009.

Poe, Sheryll. "I Spy." *American Statesman,* Austin, TX, January 12, 2001.

Sheldon, Michael. *Orwell: The Authorized Biography.* New York: HarperCollins, 1991.

Slevin, Peter. "At Tampa's Turnstiles, Crowd Wasn't Faceless." *Washington Post,* February 1, 2001.

Sykes, Charles J. *The End of Privacy.* New York: St. Martin's, 1999.

Ulin, David L. "Amazon's 'Deletes' Show Big Brother Can Arrive in Another Form." *Las Vegas Review Journal,* August 2, 2009.

Woodward, John D., Jr. "And Now, the Good Side of Facial Profiling." *Washington Post,* February 4, 2001.

CHAPTER SIXTEEN

Did Al Gore Really Invent the Internet? And Did Gore Lose the 2000 Presidential Election to George W. Bush by Threatening to Take Away the Internet?

PREVIEW

The Internet has changed the way people get their information, becoming more popular for news purposes than any other single element of the mass media, including television. Far more than half of the adult population of the United States are online regularly, and that number continues to grow. It has significantly changed the way people get political and policy information. Even twenty-four-hour news programs such as MSNBC, Fox News, and CNN refer constantly to their Internet sites for additional coverage of a topic. The variety of news sources available online, with virtually every newspaper having an online edition and every browser having a list of up-to-date headlines, is massive.

The Internet is also changing the way policy gets made—no longer behind closed doors or in tedious public hearings that no one but the policy makers, lobbyists, and obscure professors attend. Policy makers, for better or worse, have immediate access to millions of voters and vast amounts of information that was not previously available in a timely fashion. Practically every major government agency, every executive, and every legislator now has a website on which they continuously present information, often distort information, and obtain feedback from the public.

Most users of the Internet appreciate what it is now and not what it was. Those with a limited understanding of its early beginnings may not be aware that early policy decisions about "the Net" made it what it is today.

And as with most policy decisions, it was not something that happened in a straight line. No policy maker said, as President John F. Kennedy did in 1961, "I believe that this nation should commit itself to achieving the goal, before this decade is out, of landing a man on the moon and returning him safely to the earth." There was no policy decision, as with the moon landing, to create the modern Internet. It just evolved from a series of "smaller" decisions that were inspired by the necessities of the Cold War.

THE CHAIN OF CIRCUMSTANCE

The history of the Internet is a neat little case study on how public policy evolves along with what British diplomat Harold Nicolson (1886–1968) called the "chain of circumstance." Nicolson wrote in his 1946 history, *The Congress of Vienna,* that "Nobody who has not watched 'policy' expressing itself in day-to-day action can realize how seldom is the course of events determined by deliberately planned purpose, or how often what in retrospect appears to have been a fully conscious intention was at the time governed and directed by that most potent of all factors—'the chain of circumstance.'" Nicolson concluded that it was only on rare "occasions on which any statesman sees his objective clearly before him and marches towards it with undeviating stride; numerous indeed are the occasions when a decision or an event, which at the time seemed wholly unimportant, leads almost fortuitously to another decision which is no less incidental, until, little link by link, the chain of circumstance is forged."

Unfortunately, the links in the chain, so critical to a full understanding of an issue, are often lost as facts are distorted during debate, experts on the subject disappear (by resigning, dying of natural causes, or being murdered), and the underlying basis for a policy or decision matter less than the fact that the current policy simply exists. Thus, as in Shakespeare's *Romeo and Juliet,* the fact that the Montagues hate the Capulets is more important than the underlying, effectively forgotten, reasons for the initial hatred. Similarly, the fact that the Internet exists is more important than how it came about. Still, its evolution is an inherently valuable example of how a public policy is built one "little link" at a time. Nicolson, though he died before the birth of the Internet, described in a totally different context the accidental nature of that birth.

A CHILD OF THE COLD WAR

Given the freewheeling nature of the Internet, it is somewhat amusing that the first efforts in its development were as a result of the deadly serious Cold War between the United States and the Soviet Union. According to Moschovitis and others in their *History of the Internet* (1999), the first step occurred soon after the Soviet Union launched *Sputnik* (the first artificial earth satellite) in 1957. Fearing that the Soviets would gain the lead in the arms race with their move into space, the U.S. Congress passed the National Defense Education Act in 1958 in an effort to increase scientific research and train future scientists. At the same time, President Dwight D. Eisenhower created, within the Department of Defense, the Advanced Research Project Agency (ARPA) to stimulate defense-related research. ARPA's ample funding for new research attracted ample numbers of scientists from major universities. Computers, critically needed by these scientists, were still relatively new, and memory was extremely expensive.

In order to share scarce computer resources and increase the sense of community among research sites, Bob Taylor, an ARPA manager, had a vision of computers connected to research sites, usually universities, around the country. What then occurred is an example of how important policy decisions involving significant money can be made in a flash, with no memos, meetings, new committees, or formal policy analyses. Taylor simply went to see his boss, Charles Herzfeld, the head of ARPA, and explained the situation. According to Hafner and Lyon (1996), Taylor made his case by complaining that the ARPA contractors (their researchers) "were beginning to request more and more computer resources. Every principal investigator, it seemed, wanted his own computer. Not only was there an obvious duplication of effort across the research community, but it was getting damned expensive." Taylor then suggested "building a system of electronic links between machines, researchers doing similar work in different parts of the country could share resources and results more easily. Instead of spreading a half dozen expensive mainframes across the country devoted to supporting advanced graphics research, ARPA could concentrate resources in one or two places and build a way for everyone to get at them." Taylor wanted ARPA to fund "a small test network, starting with say, four nodes and building up to a dozen or so."

Herzfeld thought it was a great idea and told Taylor, "Get it going. You've got a million dollars more in your budget right now. Go." The presentation and the momentous decision that followed "only took twenty minutes." Thus, "ARPAnet," the first multiple-computer network and the baby that was to grow into the Internet, was born in 1969 when four universities (the University of California at Los Angeles, the University of California at Santa Barbara, the University of Utah, and Stanford Research Institute) were connected together. Twenty more universities were added two years later.

FROM ARPAnet TO INTERNET

The second major step was the result of efforts in the late 1950s to develop a "survivable communications" system for military command and control purposes in case of a nuclear attack. In 1959 Paul Baran of the RAND Corporation began to explore possible alternatives for survivable communications. Because most communications at that time were hierarchical and concentrated and could be easily disrupted (such as a telephone system), Baran developed what he called "distributed communications (see Figure 16.1)." In these systems there were numerous links to each node and many switching nodes with much redundancy. Knocking out a few nodes would still allow information to get to other nodes. To move data through this network, Baran developed a message-switching system that allowed some messages to be stored at nodes until a line was available to send the message to another node. This was not a particularly new idea—the telegraph companies of that period had used something similar for some time—but it was then a cumbersome process. Baran argued that the systems were cumbersome because the speeds at which the messages moved were much too slow. He wanted to increase the speed and reduce the size of the message centers at each node.

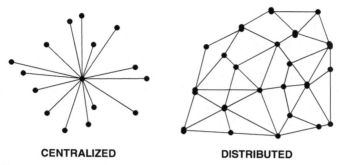

CENTRALIZED   **DISTRIBUTED**

Figure 16.1 Centralized Versus Distributed Networks
Note how the distributed network resembles a fishing net or spider web.

Although Baran's idea of distributed communications was not new, his idea of how messages were routed was. He had the idea of bundling messages and sending a block of messages through at one time, with the control for routing the messages at each node. If one node was disrupted, other nodes would simply reroute the messages. Such a concept required nodes to machine-generate routes; consequently, each node had to have some intelligence—as opposed to all of the intelligence being at a centralized switch. Computerized switches at each node would be required, a very different concept from the then-current mechanical switches, which depended on a centralized switching center. Baran's ideas never made it into an actual system, but Janet Abbate, in *Inventing the Internet* (1999), asserts that his ideas helped to lay the foundation for ARPAnet.

By 1982, ARPAnet's users had been allowed to make changes to the system to make it more user-friendly. More and more universities were using it, not only to communicate with other research centers, but to communicate within the university as well. Considerable flexibility was allowed in terms of what was transmitted. On January 1, 1983, one networking protocol was officially adopted and every site had to adapt to that protocol. ARPAnet formally became known as the "Internet." The Defense Communications Agency, responsible for the network, divided it into two sectors: one for defense sites (MILNET) and the Internet, for all others.

IS IT THE "NET" OR THE "WEB"?

The Internet is the physical linking of computers and their connecting cables. The World Wide Web is the totality of information (document, sounds, videos, etc.) that travels along the Internet. So when you want to refer to the physical infrastructure, you say "Net." When you want to refer to the information that travels on this "information superhighway," you say "Web."

The Web exists because of programs that allow computers to communicate with each other. It is the Web that has made the Net useful. It is just like with television. Few people know or care how their televisions work. They just want to be able to watch their favorite shows. And few people care about the Net so long as they can get information from the Web.

Efforts to make the system more flexible and faster continued. In 1992 the World Wide Web with its URLs (Universal Resource Locator) and HTML (Hypertext Markup Language) debuted. Browsers, designed to locate particular documents, were not far behind. In 1993 the first graphical-user-interface browser, Mosaic, which combined text and graphics on the same page, was released. By the end of 1993, there were 1 million users of this browser for both Macintosh and Windows computers. Mosaic was succeeded by Netscape Navigator in 1994 and by Microsoft Explorer in 1996. By 2000 more than 56 percent of Americans over the age of eighteen were regular users of the Internet.

DID AL GORE REALLY INVENT THE INTERNET?

Al Gore was President Bill Clinton's vice president for two terms, from 1993 to 2001. In 2000, Gore was the Democratic Party's presidential nominee, who ran against Texas Governor George W. Bush. Gore actually got the most votes, but because Bush won the vote for the Electoral College, with the intervention of the U.S. Supreme Court, Bush became president. It was during this presidential campaign between Gore and Bush that Gore's "invention" of the Internet became an issue.

The simple truth is that Gore did not invent the Internet, nor did he ever say he did except as an occasional joke toward the end of his ill-fated 2000 presidential campaign. What started this controversy was a March 9, 1999, Cable News Network interview with Wolf Blitzer during the primary election season. Blitzer threw then-Vice President Gore a softball question: "Why should Democrats, looking at the Democratic process, support you instead of Bill Bradley, a friend of yours, a former colleague in the Senate?" Gore responded with a rambling answer that included this: "During my service in the United States Congress, I took the initiative in creating the Internet."

It was a particularly poor choice of words on Gore's part—and he would pay dearly for it. Blitzer didn't pick up on Gore's "creating" assertion during the interview, but the rest of the political world did so soon afterward. Because the assertion seemed so bold and ridiculous on the surface, opposition politicians chose to ridicule it with similar hyperbole. The Republican Senate majority leader, Trent Lott of Mississippi, announced that he had "invented the paper clip." Former vice president Dan Quayle, who was often publicly challenged by spelling while in office, asserted: "If Gore invented the Internet, then I invented Spell-Check." Soon Jay Leno and David Letterman were doing jokes on their late-night comedy shows based on the notion that Gore was a guy who commonly told whoppers. On December 3, 1999, Gore was the subject of a Letterman "Top Ten" list of his additional achievements, which included giving mankind fire and accidentally inventing the orgasm while riding his bicycle one day. Even the president got in on the act. At the 1999 Gridiron Club Press Corps dinner, President Clinton joked, "Al Gore invented the Internet. For the record, I, too, am an inventor. I invented George Stephanopoulos."

Gore was never able to explain the "creating" assertion adequately, and was never able to get out from under the shadow of the ridicule he brought down on himself by poor phraseology. It could be argued that this element of his public persona may have cost him a very close election. Ironically, Gore was essentially telling the truth, in that he did take "the initiative in creating the Internet." However, the initiative he took involved his support in the U.S. Senate for funding the basic research that helped lead to the modern Internet.

As early as 1986, Gore was supporting funding for the National Science Foundation, in part because he recognized the need for a "telecommunications highway" to "transport data and ideas." In 1988 Gore supported the National High-Performance Computer Technology Act because it would, in part, "build an information infrastructure composed of data bases and knowledge banks."

By the late 1980s, Gore had made the phrase "information superhighway" his own and took every opportunity to advance his vision of it. For example, in a 1989 floor debate, he told the Senate that "the creation of this nationwide network and the broader installation of lower capacity fiber optic cables to all parts of this country, will create an environment where work stations are common in homes and even small businesses." Gore's legislative efforts on behalf of the infant Internet led to the High-Performance Computing Act of 1991 (known as the Gore Act), which supported the spread of the Internet beyond computer science.

It is without doubt that for two decades, throughout his career in the Congress and as vice president, Gore was at the forefront in support of federal programs and funding for the development of the Internet. What a pity it is that, in seeming to take too much credit, Gore effectively negated his very real and vital contributions. Still, he never lost his sense of humor about the awkward position in which he found himself. Less than two months before the 2000 election, on September 15, he appeared on David Letterman's show and menacingly said, "Remember, America: I gave you the Internet, and I can take it away. Think about it." Yes, think about it. His opponent, George W. Bush, never threatened to take away the Internet. Gore's creation assertion, followed by his flippant threat to take away the Internet, may have cost Gore the election.

FOR DISCUSSION

What were the major links in the chain of circumstances that brought the Internet into existence? How much credit does Al Gore really deserve for "inventing" the Internet?

BIBLIOGRAPHY

Abbate, Janet. *Inventing the Internet,* Cambridge, MA: MIT Press, 1999.
Armas, Genaro C. "U.S.: Over Half of Americans Use Web." *Washington Post,* February 5, 2002.
Baran, Paul. "On Distributed Communication Networks." *Rand Memoranda,* vols. 1–11. Santa Monica, CA: Rand Corporation, 1964.

Cailliau, Robert, and James Gillies. *How the Web Was Born: The Story of the World Wide Web.* New York: Oxford University Press, 2000.

Goff, Leslie. "What's It like to Work in IT on a Presidential Campaign." *Computerworld,* November 6, 2000.

Hafner, Katie, and Matthew Lyon. *Where Wizards Stay Up Late: The Origins of the Internet.* New York: Simon & Schuster, 1996.

Moschovitis, Christos J. P., Hilary Poole, Tami Schuyler, and Theresa M. Senft. *History of the Internet: A Chronology, 1843 to the Present.* Santa Barbara, CA: ABC-CLIO, 1999.

Nicolson, Harold. *The Congress of Vienna.* New York: Harcourt, 1946.

Wiggins, Richard. "Al Gore and the Creation of the Internet." *First Monday* 5, no. 10 (2000).

CHAPTER SEVENTEEN

How the U.S. Strategic Policy of Containment (of Communism in General and the Soviet Union in Particular) Gradually Evolved Just After World War II to Win the Cold War in 1989

PREVIEW

A cold war is a war with no traditional combat (in contrast to a "hot war") that emphasizes ideological conflict, brinksmanship, and consistently high international tension. This is not new. Thomas Hobbes (1588–1679), the English social contract theorist so famous for observing that in a state of nature without a strong government, human life was "solitary, poor, nasty, brutish and short," also had much to say about war. In *Leviathan* (1651), he wrote: "War consisteth not in battle only, or the act of fighting; but in a tract of time, wherein the will to contend by battle is sufficiently known." Then he compared this "not in battle" war to bad weather. "For as the nature of foul weather, lyeth not in a shower or two of rain; but in an inclination thereto of many days together; so the nature of war, consists not in actual fighting; but in the known disposition thereto, during all the time there is no assurance to the contrary. All other time is peace."

In the twentieth century, "the" Cold War was the hostile but (in the Hobbesian tradition) nonlethal relations between the United States and the Soviet Union that began in 1945 after World War II and ended in 1989 with the dismantling of the Berlin Wall that divided East from West Germany and was the symbol for the Soviet domination of Eastern and Central Europe. By 1991 the Soviet Union itself was dismantled and replaced by constituent republics formed into a loose confederation known as the Commonwealth of Independent States. Credit for the modern use of "cold war," for the revival of Hobbes's concept, goes to journalist Herbert Bayard Swope (1882–1958), who first used it in speeches he wrote for financier Bernard Baruch (1870–1965). After Baruch told the Senate War Investigating Committee on October 24, 1948, "Let us not be deceived—today we are in the midst of a Cold War," the press picked up the phrase, and it became part of everyday speech.

Cold wars, like hot ones, have strategies and tactics by which they are fought. The case that follows tells how the United States developed and implemented the strategy of containment to fight and win the worldwide Cold War with the Soviet Union.

STRATEGIC MANAGEMENT

Strategic management, efforts to achieve long-term organizational goals, is a sloppy business. It is not that managers do not want to be neat; it's just that the managerial environment is inherently and notoriously lacking in neatness. It is not just as Scottish poet Robert Burns asserts, that the "best laid schemes of mice and men" often go awry; it is also that these plans are seldom comprehensive documents, if they exist at all. Often the overall strategy exists only as a vague document or ambiguous statement of overall philosophy. The full implementation of a strategic plan usually takes many years—sometimes decades or even more. The usefulness of a strategic plan is that it provides the long-term doctrine—the overall guidance—so essential for short-term, or tactical, management decisions.

Ancient Rome was into strategic management in a big way. Of course, there was no one single document entitled "The Strategic Plan for the Roman Empire," but all of its elements lay scattered about in various laws, policies, and proclamations. It was much like the British Constitution of today, unwritten but nevertheless thoroughly understood by all those with the responsibility for its implementation. Indeed, strategic planning has always been done, especially in a military context, where it began. However, the Romans of old were among the first to apply strategic concepts to the large-scale nonmilitary aspects of government as well.

Julius Caesar espoused a strategic doctrine that so enraged the Roman aristocracy, they assassinated him in 44 BCE. Nevertheless, his nephew Augustus, who succeeded him after a nasty civil war that led to the deaths of Mark Antony, Cleopatra, and a cast of thousands, implemented the plan that became known as the Pax Romana. This established relatively stable borders and coopted possible opposition to Roman governance by expanding Roman citizenship. The several centuries of mostly peace that followed were made possible by a relatively small military establishment, which was so well trained and managed that disturbances within the Empire could be suppressed with the utmost efficiency and ruthlessness. Josephus, a contemporary analyst of the Roman military, wrote: "their peace maneuvers are no less strenuous than veritable warfare; each soldier daily throws all his energy into his drill, as though he were in action. . . . Indeed, it would not be wrong to describe their maneuvers as bloodless combats and their combats as sanguinary maneuvers." This unremitting management discipline was the critical element in the tactical doctrine that provided for the peace and prosperity envisioned by the strategic plan.

Two millennia later, U.S. President John F. Kennedy had plans for civil rights and other domestic programs that he could not get implemented by a Congress controlled by Southern conservatives. However, after his assassination in 1963, his successor, Lyndon B. Johnson, got much of this legislation passed as part of the Great Society program. The point here is not that assassinations further strategic plans, although clearly they sometimes do, but that strategic planning and implementation often goes far beyond the goals of one leader or one administration.

THE TRUMAN DOCTRINE

Arguably the most significant single strategic plan of the second half of the twentieth century was the Truman Doctrine, the policy of President Harry S Truman's administration of extending military and economic aid to those countries (originally Greece and Turkey) seeking to resist "totalitarian aggression." President Truman presented this doctrine in 1947 in his address to a joint session of the Congress in support of the "Act to Provide Assistance to Greece and Turkey." The Soviet Union was putting pressure on Turkey for free passage through the straits from the Black Sea to the Mediterranean Sea, and on Greece through support of a guerrilla war. The development of the Truman Doctrine was precipitated by Great Britain's reluctant decision that it could no longer afford military and economic aid for Greece and Turkey. If the United States did not assume this burden, both Greece and Turkey would surely fall into the communist camp.

The Truman Doctrine, as outlined in Figure 17.1, provided the vision, which was the overall direction for all of these efforts. Its strategic vision guided all of the details of the Cold War that followed—from the Marshall Plan to the Korean and Vietnam wars. President Truman made this statement to a joint session of Congress, on March 12, 1947:

> At the present moment in world history nearly every nation must choose between alternative ways of life. The choice is too often not a free one.
>
> One way of life is based upon the will of the majority, and is distinguished by free institutions, representative government, free elections, guarantees of individual liberty, freedom of speech and religion, and freedom from political oppression.

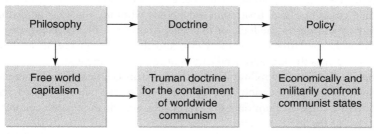

Figure 17.1 The Truman Doctrine

The second way of life is based upon the will of a minority forcibly imposed upon the majority. It relies upon terror and oppression, a controlled press and radio, fixed elections, and the suppression of personal freedoms.

I believe that it must be the policy of the United States to support free peoples who are resisting attempted subjugation by armed minorities or by outside pressures.

I believe that we must assist free peoples to work out their own destinies in their own way.

I believe that our help should be primarily through economic and financial aid which is essential to economic stability and orderly political processes.

KENNAN AND CONTAINMENT

The Truman Doctrine became the cornerstone of the U.S. policy of containment, the underlying basis of U.S. foreign, military, and much of domestic policy since World War II. After the war ended in 1945 and the Cold War with the Soviet Union began, an overall strategy of how a war-weary United States could deal with this new threat was needed. In 1946 George F. Kennan (1904–2005), a foreign service officer stationed at the U.S. embassy in Moscow, outlined in a long telegram what he regarded as Soviet objectives as well as the need for a U.S. response. The ideas in the telegram subsequently provided the basis for Kennan's article, "The Sources of Soviet Conduct" (1947), which appeared the next year under the pseudonym "X" in *Foreign Affairs,* still the most prestigious journal of international relations. (The official author of this article was "X" because Kennan wrote it while serving as a Foreign Service officer, but it was never a secret who the actual author was.) Kennan asserted that "Soviet pressure against the free institutions of the Western World is something that can be contained by the adroit and vigilant application of counterforce."

Importantly, Kennan noted that the source of Russian behavior was not a feeling of recent injustice by others but a long-term push to expand, dating back centuries. As he put it in the *X* article, ". . . the United States has it in its power to increase enormously the strains under which Soviet policy must operate, to force upon the Kremlin a far greater degree of moderation and circumspection than it has had to observe in recent years, and in this way to promote tendencies which must eventually find their outlet in either the break-up or the gradual mellowing of Soviet power." After all, he predicted, the Kremlin could not "face frustration indefinitely without eventually adjusting itself in one way or another to the logic of that state of affairs." The developments in the Soviet Union in the latter half of the 1980s and the demise of the Soviet Union in 1991 can be seen as the ultimate vindication of the containment strategy.

Although Kennan used military analogies in this article, he saw containment as essentially political in character and believed that it was crucial that the United States rebuild Western Europe economically so that it could provide indigenous countervailing power to that of the Soviet Union.

After retiring from government service, Kennan became an esteemed scholar of diplomacy and Russian history as well as one of the major critics of the way containment

PRESIDENT JOHN F. KENNEDY ON THE ORIGINS OF THE COLD WAR

You may remember that in 1851, the New York Herald Tribune, under the sponsorship of Horace Greeley, included as its London correspondent an obscure journalist by the name of Karl Marx. We are told that. . . Marx, stone broke and with a family ill and undernourished, constantly appealed to Greeley. . . for an increase in his munificent salary of $5 per installment. . . .

But when all his financial appeals were refused, Marx looked around for other means of livelihood and fame, and eventually terminated his relationship with the Tribune and devoted his talents full time to the cause that would bequeath to the world the seeds of Leninism, Stalinism, revolution and the Cold War.

If only this capitalistic New York newspaper had treated him more kindly, if only Marx had remained a foreign correspondent history might have been different, and I hope all publishers will bear this lesson in mind the next time they receive a poverty-stricken appeal for a small increase in the expense account from an obscure newspaperman.

Source: President John F. Kennedy, Speech to American Newspaper Publishers Association, April 27, 1961.

was implemented. Much of Kennan's subsequent career as a scholar consisted of successive critiques of U.S. policy and recommendations for moving beyond the military stalemate into which the Cold War had degenerated by the early 1950s. This was evident in his proposals for military disengagement in Europe, which first appeared in the mid-1950s, and his subsequent criticisms of U.S. military strategy, especially its reliance on the first use of nuclear weapons to forestall a Soviet invasion of Western Europe. In a sense, the divergences between Kennan and subsequent U.S. administrations over the nature of the Soviet threat and the appropriate U.S. response defined the main parameters of the debate in the United States about foreign and security policy throughout the Cold War. Kennan was always scrupulous both in his efforts to understand the Soviet Union and in his willingness to criticize the United States. However, it is for his contribution to creating the policy of containment that Kennan will be most remembered—and in particular, for his prediction of the breakup of the Soviet Union.

ECONOMIC CONTAINMENT

A few weeks after President Truman's doctrine called for aiding Greece and Turkey, an economic aid program for post–World War II Europe was proposed by Secretary of State George C. Marshall, Jr. During a graduation speech at Harvard University on June 5, 1947, Marshall announced the European Recovery Program, a massive aid program that became known as the Marshall Plan: "Our policy is directed not against any country or doctrine but against hunger, poverty, desperation and chaos. Its purpose should be the revival of a working economy in the world so as to permit the emergence of political and social conditions in which free institutions can exist."

The Marshall Plan directly addressed the policy of containment by attempting to end postwar financial problems in Western Europe and thus reduce vulnerability to communism while limiting U.S. involvement in Europe. The Marshall Plan was the first large-scale foreign assistance program of the post–World War II period. Between 1947 and 1950, it supplied grants and credits of $13.2 billion, as Western European industrial production rose 45 percent and reached a level 25 percent over that of 1938, the last prewar year. Such an increase originally had a target date of 1952–1953. Most of the funds went to Great Britain ($3.2 billion), France ($2.7 billion), Italy ($1.5 billion), and West Germany $1.4 billion). Funds were also offered to the states of Eastern Europe, but Stalin, the dictator of the Soviet Union, refused to allow these states to participate.

The Marshall Plan worked so well and became so well known that the term entered the language to mean any massive use of federal funds to solve a major social problem. President Harry S Truman wrote in his *Memoirs*, II (1956), "I had referred to the idea [European Recovery Program] as the 'Marshall Plan' when it was discussed in staff meetings, because I wanted General Marshall to get full credit for his brilliant contributions. . . . He had perceived the inspirational as well as the economic value of the proposal. History, rightly, will always associate his name with this program, which helped save Europe from economic disaster and lifted it from the shadow of enslavement by Russian communism." Marshall's plan, far more than his superlative service as head of the U.S. Army during World War II, earned him the 1953 Nobel Peace Prize. Truman's credit gambit worked!

The Marshall Plan was significant historically as a major step on the road to a U.S. security commitment to Western Europe. The North Atlantic Treaty Organization was created in large part to provide a security shield behind which the Economic Recovery Program could prosper. This is somewhat ironic given that the plan as initially conceived was intended to limit U.S. involvement in European security issues by reinvigorating the states of Western Europe in the hope that they would then be able to contain Soviet power by themselves.

Ironically, in the aftermath of the collapse of the Soviet Union, there was much discussion of the need for a new Marshall Plan for Russia. That did not materialize. There was no desire in the United States to give billions in aid to a country that had already cost the United States billions in aid to other countries—not to mention the additional billions it cost to fight the Cold War and its hot flare-ups in Korea and Vietnam. The economic victories of the Cold War were difficult to see directly; they slowly accumulated in government statistics on personal income, calories consumed, and automobile ownership. As for the military aspects, they were to be found almost every day in front-page newspaper headlines all over the world. Though we cannot replay forty years of hot and cold war containment, a few highlights follow.

CONTAINMENT IN BERLIN

The Berlin blockade was the first of the many Berlin crises during the Cold War. With Berlin located 110 miles inside the Soviet occupation zone, the Soviets believed it vulnerable and exerted pressure to force the Americans out. The blockade occurred from June

1948 to May 1949, when the Soviet authorities stopped all overland travel (by highway and railroad) to Berlin. After World War II, Berlin had been divided into four zones of occupation, with sectors administered by France, Britain, the United States, and the Soviet Union. The western sectors of Berlin had 2.4 million inhabitants. With few food stocks, Berliners faced starvation. The Soviets erected the blockade in retaliation to the introduction of a strong currency in the western zones, but wanted to forestall the emergence of a West German state and, if possible, force the United States out of Europe altogether.

The United States and its allies responded to this ten-month blockade with a massive airlift of food, fuel, and other basic supplies to the city. With the blockade increasingly counterproductive, the Soviets announced that railroads and roads closed for nearly a year "for repairs" would be reopened to western traffic. West Berlin had food for only a month and coal for ten days when the blockade started. The "Berlin Airlift" consisted of over a quarter-million individual flights, which supplied the city with 2,300,000 tons of food and fuel. The crisis was also important because of the care taken by the superpowers to prevent it from resulting in war. Although both made coercive moves, neither crossed the line between coercion and violence. This was important to the development of crisis management as a key element in keeping the Cold War from becoming a hot war.

NATO: THE MILITARY FACE OF CONTAINMENT

The North Atlantic Treaty Organization (NATO) was established in 1949 through the Atlantic Treaty and tied the United States and Western Europe together with a pledge, through Article V, that an attack on one of the signatories would be regarded as an attack on all and that all such action as was deemed necessary, including the use of armed force, would be taken in response. Initially there were twelve signatories: the United States, Canada, Britain, France, Belgium, Luxembourg, the Netherlands, Italy, Portugal, Iceland, Norway, and Denmark. Greece and Turkey joined in 1952, and the Federal Republic of Germany joined in 1955. Spain joined after the death of Francisco Franco, its World War II–era dictator, and its transition to democracy, bringing the Cold War membership to sixteen nations. NATO expanded significantly after the end of Cold War, when many of the Cold War "allies" of the former Soviet Union sought to join to protect themselves from the new Russia.

When the Atlantic Alliance was created in 1949, it was widely seen in the U.S. Senate (which ratified the treaty in July 1949) as a political guarantee pact. The organization was not really established until 1950, when the Korean War led to a more alarmist threat assessment and prompted the United States to send troops to Europe, initiate the process of West German rearmament (even though Germany was not yet a member and other European nations were unhappy about this), and appoint General Dwight D. Eisenhower as the first Supreme Allied Commander Europe (SACEUR). In a sense, Korea put the "O" in NATO and changed it from a political guarantee into a collective defense organization.

The history of NATO has been a rather turbulent one. There have been arguments over strategy and burden sharing, with the United States demanding that the

THE NATO GUARANTEE

The Parties agree than an armed attack against one or more of them in Europe or North America shall be considered an attack against them all; and consequently they agree that, if such an armed attack occurs, each of them, in exercise of the right of individual or collective self-defense recognized by Article 51 of the Charter of the United Nations, will assist the Party or Parties so attacked by taking forthwith, individually and in concert with the other Parties, such action as it deems necessary, including the use of armed force, to restore and maintain the security of the North Atlantic area.

Source: Article 5 of the North Atlantic Treaty of April 4, 1949.

Europeans increase conventional forces and the Europeans preferring to rely instead on the protection of the U.S. nuclear guarantee, something that became increasingly uncertain as the Soviet Union developed nuclear forces capable of retaliating against the United States. There have also been arguments about whether NATO as a body should respond to contingencies outside the formal area of its responsibility as defined in Article Six, which restricts the obligations to contingencies involving armed attacks on the territory of any of the parties in Europe or North America, and attacks on their vessels or aircraft north of the Tropic of Cancer. In other words, it excluded areas such as the Persian Gulf and the Indian Ocean, which the United States in the 1980s argued were vital for NATO. There is considerable uncertainty about the future of the Alliance in post–Cold War Europe. Critics argue that NATO was a creation of the Cold War and that with the end of the Cold War, it is moribund. Proponents argue that although there is no longer a Soviet threat or even a Soviet Union, there is so much potential for instability in Europe that NATO is an important hedge against this. At the very least, though, it is clear NATO no longer has a monopoly on dealing with security problems in Europe.

Despite its uncertain future, NATO's past was a critical element in containing the Soviet Union. During the Cold War the Soviet Union periodically sent its Red Army troops to suppress revolutionary movements in Poland, Hungary, and Czechoslovakia, but it never crossed the line into a NATO state. Containment military style worked, at least in Europe.

CONTAINMENT IN KOREA

The Korean War was a fight for containment. This war between communist North Korea and noncommunist South Korea began on June 25, 1950, when the North invaded the South. In 1945, at the end of World War II, the Soviet Union accepted the Japanese surrender north of the 38th degree of latitude in Korea and established a communist state, while the United States accepted the Japanese surrender south of that line and established a pro-Western state. Negotiations to unify the two states failed, and the issue was turned over to the United Nations. By 1949 both the United

States and the Soviet Union had withdrawn the majority of their troops from the Korean Peninsula.

The decision on the part of President Harry S Truman and his advisors to promote intervention once the war had started was a reversal of a policy previously announced by Secretary of State Dean Acheson, that Korea lay outside the defense perimeter of the United States. The decision was based on the belief that the actions of North Korea reflected larger policy interests promoted by the Soviet Union and communist China and, therefore, required a strong U.S. response. The U.S. intervention was a symbolic signal to the Soviets that the United States was determined to halt—to contain—the spread of communism. With the encouragement of the United States, the United Nations Security Council (with the Soviet Union temporarily absent) asked member nations to aid South Korea in resisting the invasion.

Thus the war, called a "police action," was fought under the flag of the United Nations by U.S. forces with small contingents from over a dozen other nations. The war initially went very badly for the South Korean and U.N. forces, but with the landing of U.S. forces at Inchon, the North Koreans were forced to retreat. In spite of reassurances that the United States was interested only in restoring the *status quo ante,* General Douglas MacArthur continued to advance into North Korea. Assurances were given to communist China that the United States was not interested in going beyond the Yalu River, the border between North Korea and China. MacArthur, however, made threatening statements. The Chinese attempted to make clear to Washington how seriously it viewed the attempt to unify Korea under U.N. auspices, but this concern was not fully appreciated in Washington and MacArthur was allowed to continue to advance toward the Yalu. When MacArthur's actions finally provoked Chinese intervention, the United States was taken by surprise both politically and operationally.

The U.N. forces were compelled to retreat in the face of the North Korean and Chinese "volunteer" offensive. Fighting eventually stabilized along the 38th parallel, but the war continued until 1953, when newly elected President Dwight D. Eisenhower let it be known that unless there was a cessation of hostilities, the United States was prepared to use nuclear weapons. Secretary of State John Foster Dulles said at the time: "The principal reason we were able to obtain the armistice was because we were prepared for a much more intensive scale of warfare. . . . [We] had already sent the means to the theater for delivering atomic weapons. This became known to the Chinese communists through their good intelligence sources and in fact we were not unwilling that they should find out." (quoted in McGeorge Bundy, *Danger and Survival* [1988]). After three years, an armistice was signed on July 27, 1953, which maintained the division of the Koreas almost exactly where it had been before the war started. No peace treaty has ever been signed, but the communists were contained.

CONTAINMENT IN VIETNAM

The Vietnam War of 1956–1975 was a conflict between the noncommunist Republic of Vietnam (South Vietnam) and the communist Democratic Republic of Vietnam (North Vietnam), which resulted in the victory of the North over the South and the unification of the two countries into the communist Socialist Republic of Vietnam on July 2, 1976. The United States first offered financial support to South Vietnam during the Eisenhower administration. Military assistance began with President John F. Kennedy's administration in 1961. By 1963, the United States had 16,000 military "advisors" in South Vietnam.

In 1964, the Gulf of Tonkin Resolution allowed the administration of President Lyndon B. Johnson to expand U.S. involvement in spite of the fact that Johnson had promised, notably in a campaign speech in Akron, Ohio, on October 21, 1964, that: "We are not about to send American boys nine or ten thousand miles away from home to do what Asian boys ought to be doing for themselves." Johnson lied, but he had reasons. He told his biographer, Doris Kearns, in 1970: "I knew that Harry Truman and Dean Acheson had lost their effectiveness from the day that the communists took over in China. I believed that the loss of China had played a large role in the rise of Joe McCarthy. And I knew that all these problems, taken together, were chickenshit compared with what might happen if we lost Vietnam" (*Lyndon Johnson and the American Dream* [1976]).

By 1968, the United States had over half a million men engaged in the most unpopular foreign war in U.S. history. As a direct result, the Democrats lost control of the White House to Republican Richard M. Nixon. The Nixon administration's policy of Vietnamization called for the South Vietnamese to gradually take over all the fighting from the Americans. The Americans continued to pull out, and the South held off the North for a while. As the U.S. forces dwindled, the North became more aggressive and more successful. Finally, the North's January 1975 offensive led to the South's unconditional surrender by April. More than 58,000 Americans died in the Vietnam War; another 150,000 were wounded.

Views of the war in the United States still diverge very considerably. There are those who believe that if the war had been fought without being "micromanaged" from Washington, then U.S. forces would have been much more successful. This view was represented by President Ronald Reagan when he said on February 24, 1981, that U.S. soldiers "came home without a victory not because they had been defeated but because they had been denied permission to win." A similar view was evident in the comment of Graham A. Martin, the last U.S. Ambassador to South Vietnam, who was quoted in the *New York Times* (April 30, 1985) as saying: "In the end, we simply cut and ran. The American national will had collapsed."

On the other side are those who believe that the war was a profound strategic and moral blunder, that the United States extended containment to a region in which it was far less applicable, attempted to frustrate genuine nationalist aspirations of the Vietnamese, backed a succession of governments that lacked real legitimacy, and essentially fought an illegitimate and unwinnable war. President George H. W. Bush, in his Inaugural Address, January 20, 1989, observed: "That war cleaves us still. But, friends, that war began in earnest a quarter of a century ago; and surely the statute of limitations has been reached. This is a fact: The final lesson of Vietnam is that no great nation can long afford to be sundered by a memory."

Yet memories of Vietnam had a major impact on U.S. policy in the confrontation with Iraq in 1990 and 1991. The U.S. military, represented most articulately by the chairman of the Joint Chiefs of Staff, Colin Powell, were anxious to avoid the mistakes of Vietnam and made clear that if force was to be used, it should be done massively and decisively. In the event, this is what occurred, and the first war against Iraq was fought without political interference in day-to-day operations.

THE OBJECTIVES OF CONTAINMENT

Although there was broad agreement on the objective of containment at least until the reaction against U.S. involvement in Vietnam in the late 1960s, different strategies have been used to implement this objective. From 1947 until 1950, the emphasis was on military deterrence through NATO and rebuilding allies in Western Europe, both economically and militarily. During the Korean War, the emphasis moved to actual fighting on the borders of the Free World to prevent the spread of communism. The Eisenhower administration emphasized the possibility of massive retaliation, a euphemism for using nuclear weapons, to contain communism in Korea and elsewhere. Then the Kennedy and Johnson administrations used containment as its rationale for massively escalating what had been a limited war in Vietnam. The Nixon administration did not abandon containment but tried instead to uphold it through greater reliance on allies and détente with the Soviet Union. The Carter administration initially tried to ignore containment, but embraced it after the 1979 Soviet invasion of Afghanistan. The Reagan administration not only pursued a highly military containment policy but tried to go beyond it and roll back some of the Soviet gains of the 1970s in the Third World through support for anticommunist revolutionary movements.

The Bush administration saw containment come to an end in 1991 with the demise of the Soviet Union, a development that vindicated the logic of the initial architects of containment. According to President George H. W. Bush in a May 12, 1989, speech at Texas A & M University: "Wise men . . . crafted the strategy of containment. They believed that the Soviet Union, denied the easy course of expansion, would turn inward and address the contradictions of its inefficient, repressive and inhumane system. And they were right. The Soviet Union is now publicly facing this hard reality. Containment worked."

THE SYMBOL OF VICTORY

Certainly the great symbol of the overall validity and eventual victory of containment was the dismantling of the Berlin Wall. This was a concrete-and-barbed wire wall built by East Germany in 1961 to divide East and West Berlin. It was designed to prevent the flight to the West of East Germans through this last escape hatch. Just prior to the construction of the wall, the exodus had reached 2,000 per day.

The United States accepted the wall because it recognized that the exodus of refugees was undermining the East German state and that this in turn could challenge the Soviet position in Eastern Europe. In other words, vital interests were at stake for the Soviet Union in the way that they were not for the United States. In fact, it has been argued by Michael R. Beschloss in *The Crisis Years* (1991) that Kennedy encouraged the

Soviets to erect the wall, at least tacitly, by not taking advantage of several advance opportunities they presented for him to warn against it.

At the same time, Kennedy did reaffirm the commitment to protect West Berlin and responded vigorously to Soviet probes challenging Western rights in the city. Indeed, the wall became the occasion for one of the most dramatic speeches ever given by U.S. president. To bolster the morale of the West Berliners, President John F. Kennedy visited the city on June 26, 1963, and before a crowd of cheering thousands said: "All free men, wherever they may live, are citizens of Berlin. And therefore, as a free man, I take pride in the words, '*Ich bin ein Berliner!*'" This literally translates to "I am a jelly doughnut," but everyone knew what he meant.

The Wall became the symbol of the division of Eastern and Western Europe. It was a sign of improving relations between the two Germanys when in 1987, East Germany told its guards along the wall *not* to shoot their own citizens attempting to escape to the West. Finally, when the collapse of communism in Eastern and Central Europe, especially East Germany, allowed the wall to be dismantled in October 1989, George F. Will wrote that in 1989, "Voyager 2 discovered 1,500-mph winds on Neptune, but even more impressive winds blew down the Berlin wall" (*Newsweek,* January 1, 1990).

There were massive celebrations throughout Europe, but the U.S. government, while it did not discourage such joyous demonstrations, made no effort to encourage them. It was the informal policy of the George H. W. Bush administration not to gloat over the discomfiture of the failing Soviet Union. No lofty victorious rhetoric was forthcoming from the administration. Containment won. That was enough.

A few weeks before the end of the U.S. Civil War in 1865, when it became obvious that the Union was on the verge of victory, President Abraham Lincoln was asked by his generals how the defeated confederates should be treated. He told them to "let them down easy." His goal was reconciliation, not retribution. This is why General Ulysses S. Grant offered such generous surrender terms to General Robert E. Lee and his Army of Northern Virginia. Although nobody quoted Lincoln, it was clearly the policy of President George H. W. Bush to "let them down easy." The Cold War did not end with a formal surrender. It ended because one side started to self-destruct, just as George F. Kennan had predicted half a century earlier. The strategy of containment, messy and contentious as it was, ultimately worked. No more proof was needed than the dissolution of the Soviet Union in 1991.

DOMESTIC IMPLICATIONS

The domestic implications of the strategy of containing communist expansion are equally important for understanding why the Cold War was such a dominant influence on American national life. The looming menace of international communism, always secretly led by those devious Russians, affected many seemingly non–military-related domestic programs. For example, the communist threat justified the Federal Aid Highway Act of 1956 (which built the U.S. Interstate road network—the National Defense Highway System), the National Defense Education Act of 1958 (which provided loans and fellowships for students and grants to schools and colleges), and the National Aeronautics and Space Administration Act of 1958 (for the peaceful exploration of space). Yes, the space race was all part of containing Soviet expansionism, to ensure that the Soviets did not expand to the moon. President John F. Kennedy, in 1961, made it a national goal that the United States would get there first, and U.S. astronauts did just that in 1969, when, following in the tradition of Christopher Columbus, they planted the flag of their nation in a new world.

Of course, Truman never envisioned his doctrine eventually supporting local road construction or graduate student education, but the Cold War goal of defeating communism meant that anything that could be presented as part of this international struggle would get a more sympathetic legislative reception. Thus, graduate student fellowships and academic research in almost every field were justified as aiding the national defense effort. As more and more people accepted the plan, it turned out that

Elvis Presley, Cold Warrior. During the Cold War with the Soviet Union, the United States marshaled all of its resources to deter the Soviets from marching into Western Europe. This maximum effort included drafting "rock and roll" idol Elvis Presley. The conscription of young men into the army was a major aspect of the Cold War at least until 1973, when Congress ended the draft because of the unpopularity of the Vietnam War. For eighteen months, Presley, and tens of thousands of his fellow draftees, guarded the borders of the Free World in West Germany, until March 1960, when he returned home. This photo shows Elvis on his last day of active duty. At the Fort Dix (New Jersey) Separation Center, he has just been given his separation papers (in his right hand) and his final pay (in his left hand). The Soviets were much relived to hear of this. So were his fans.
Source: © CORBIS. All Rights Reserved.

there was hardly any worthwhile government project that could not be designed, however farfetched, to defeat communism. It turned out that every single member of Congress was willing—indeed, eager—to fight the worldwide communist menace by bringing pork barrel projects home to his or her district.

This combination of limited wars on the perimeter, interstate highways, and fellowships for graduate students was more than the Soviet Union could bear. When the great communist experiment finally failed, credit was given to the containment policies of the Truman administration and its successors and more recently to the Reagan administration's massive arms buildup, which the Soviets could not match. However, no direct credit was given to the overall strategic plan, because there was no plan as such. There was the Truman Doctrine of containment and all that followed. Thousands of programs and millions of people each played their part in an effort to achieve a goal that often seemed impossible. It was messy. Only retrospectively can we behold all the oars in the water rowing to the same philosophy. All the warriors, diplomats, highway builders, and scholars rowed out of faith, out of self-interest, or out of the simple desire to have a job. In the end, however, and because of the overall doctrine, they rowed in the same direction. What more could you ask?

FOR DISCUSSION

How can the doctrine of containment be considered a success when it involved multiyear wars in Korea and Vietnam that cost more than 100,000 American lives? Has the United States been using a new version of the policy of containment against modern adversaries such as Iran and North Korea?

BIBLIOGRAPHY

Beschloss, Michael. *At the Highest Levels: The Inside Story of the End of the Cold War.* Boston: Little, Brown, 1993.

Gaddis, John Lewis. *The Cold War: A New History.* New York: Penguin, 2005.

Hughes-Wilson, John. *A Brief History of the Cold War.* New York: Carroll & Graf, 2006.

Isaacson, Walter, and Evan Thomas. *The Wise Men: Six Friends and the World They Made.* New York: Simon & Schuster, 1997.

Smith, Jean Edward. *Lucius D. Clay: An American Life.* New York: Henry Holt, 1990.

Josephus, Flavius. *Josephus: The Complete Works.* Nashville, TN: Thomas Nelson, 1998.

Kennan, George F. *At a Century's Ending: Reflections, 1982–1995.* New York: W. W. Norton, 1996.

———. *Memoirs, 1925–1950.* Boston: Little, Brown, 1967.

Lukacs, John. *George Kennan: A Study of Character.* New Haven, CT: Yale University Press, 2007.

McCullough, David. *Truman.* New York: Simon & Schuster, 1993.

CHAPTER EIGHTEEN

The RAND Corporation as an Exemplar

THE ORIGINS OF AND INCREASINGLY IMPORTANT ROLE OF STRATEGIC THINK TANKS

PREVIEW

The Wright brothers, Orville (1871–1948) and Wilbur (1867–1912), tested the first fixed-wing, motor-powered, heavier-than-air flying machine in 1903 on the beaches of Kitty Hawk, North Carolina. By 1911 they had improved their machines to such an extent that they were able to sell them to the U.S. Army. This also involved teaching some officers how to fly. This is why, the Wright Brothers taught First Lieutenant Henry "Hap" Arnold (1886–1950) how to pilot an airplane. Arnold, a 1907 graduate of West Point, over the next four decades, would rise to be the chief of the U.S. Army Air Corps throughout World War II, obtain the rank of a five-star General of the Army, then, as the founding head of the U.S. Air Force, in 1947 become the five-star General of the Air Force—the only person to hold such exalted rank in two services. In 1946 Arnold initiated Project RAND to create a civilian organization that, under contract to the military, would undertake studies on the future role and capabilities of air power. Thus we have a direct line of continuity from the Wright brothers teaching Arnold the basics of aviation to Arnold contracting for an organization of intellectuals to continuously think about the prospects of aviation in the future. It is universally acknowledged that Arnold is the "father" of the RAND Corporation; what is less widely known is that the Wright brothers are the "grandfathers."

THE RAND PROJECT BEGINS

On March 2, 1946, General Arnold, as the commander (and the creator) of the U.S. Army Air Force, authorized a letter of contract to the Douglas Aircraft Company of Santa Monica, California, which said: "The Contractor will perform a program of study and research on the broad subject of intercontinental warfare, other than surface, with the object of recommending to the Army Air Forces preferred techniques and instrumentalities for this purpose."

RAND produced its first research report two months later. In *Preliminary Design of an Experimental World-Circling Spaceship* (May 2, 1946), RAND warned that "Technology and experience have now reached the point where it is possible to design and construct craft which can penetrate the atmosphere and achieve sufficient velocity to become satellites of the earth." Therefore, "it is not inappropriate to view our present situation as similar to that in airplanes prior to the flight of the Wright brothers." Then the report predicted two things:

1. A satellite vehicle with appropriate instrumentation can be expected to be one of the most potent scientific tools of the Twentieth Century.

2. The achievement of a satellite craft by the United States would inflame the imagination of mankind.

The report was correct on both predictions, except that it was a Russian satellite, *Sputnik,* that "would inflame the imagination" when it was launched in 1957. However, RAND later predicted, within two weeks, exactly when this would happen.

The RAND approach of having civilians do military-related research proved so useful to the Air Force that Project RAND within Douglas Aircraft was reincarnated as the RAND Corporation, separate from Douglas, in 1948. It was located in Santa Monica partly on the grounds that it was better to have a think tank of this kind away from the political pressures of Washington, but mainly because the staff, which by then had grown to 200, was already there. Besides, Santa Monica, right on the Pacific Ocean just north of Los Angeles, was a delightful place from which to recruit deep thinkers who liked deep-sea fishing.

RAND was initially concerned with the application of scientific and social scientific methods to the problems of strategy and security in the nuclear age. It became the

---

WHAT DOES "RAND" MEAN?

[During World War II] a corps of civilians—mostly scientists and engineers—was mobilized to fight on the technological front. . . . At the end of the war, when this corps was starting to break up, the military decided it wanted to retain some of the gifted personnel permanently to develop military technology in the years ahead, and, more specifically, it wanted to continue to nurture operations research. With this end in mind, in late 1945 General H. H. "Hap" Arnold . . . got approval for an arrangement between the Douglas Aircraft Company and the Air Force that would create a unique experimental institution to be called Project RAND. The acronym was for Research And Development originally, but as things got moving, it became apparent that it was almost entirely a research outfit, so it has been suggested, not altogether puckishly, that it more aptly stood for Research And No Development.

Source: Paul Dickson, *Think Tanks.* New York: Atheneum, 1971.

key institution in the development of civilian expertise on nuclear strategy and functioned as the incubator for the work of many civilian strategists, including such figures as Thomas Schelling, Herman Kahn, and Bernard Brodie. The civilian strategists were crucial in the effort to understand the impact of nuclear weapons on international politics, but in the process produced many highly controversial ideas such as limited nuclear options (a wide array of targeting plans for the limited use of strategic nuclear forces). Another controversial concept to come out of RAND about this time was the idea of "brushfire" wars (local wars that do not involve outside powers), a term apparently inspired by the kind of fires that often occur near Santa Monica.

RAND's research in strategic analysis was often extremely controversial within the military. RAND's civilian analysts became world-famous for their examination of the various uses of nuclear weapons. This is one of the major areas of military policy in which civilians have always played a major role. Indeed, in the West, all of the major writers in this area have been civilians. This has always caused a certain amount of friction with military leaders. Admiral Carlisle A. H. Trost, then Chief of Naval Operations, offered a typical attack: "Much of the criticism concerning today's Navy stems from career-academic strategists and so-called 'defense analysts' who have never set foot on a Navy deckplate. It is folly for these individuals, who have the responsibility neither to deploy a military force nor face the threat, to attempt to determine military requirements" (*Philadelphia Inquirer,* August 22, 1987). In response to just this kind of criticism, Alain Enthoven, a top civilian systems analyst in the Pentagon, is quoted by Fred Kaplan, in *The Wizards of Armageddon* (1983), as offering a typical response: "General, I have fought just as many nuclear wars as you have."

THE BIRTH OF NUCLEAR THEORY

Nuclear theory—systems thinking about how to use nuclear weapons militarily and diplomatically—was born at RAND. Indeed, it is one of the core reasons that RAND was created: to figure out—to strategize—how best to use "the bomb" now that the United States had it.

Staffers at RAND in the 1950s and 1960s were the architects of U.S. strategy in the nuclear age, the intellectual fathers of nuclear weapons as a deterrent, as a weapon that could keep the peace. RAND, as might be anticipated from its southern California location near Hollywood, created its own version of the movie studio system in that it manufactured intellectual stars: scholars capable of thinking up nuclear strategy, selling it to the powers that be, and then selling it again in nonfiction books and articles available to the general public and opinion leaders.

Bernard Brodie (1910–1978), at RAND from 1951 to 1966, was the first major academic theorist of nuclear warfare. His 1946 book, *The Absolute Weapon,* contained all the fundamental ideas of nuclear strategy that others would refine and expand upon. According to Brodie, the atomic bomb placed the United States in a dilemma: It could either preemptively strike an enemy before that enemy could develop its own atomic weapons, or it could accept deterrence and its implications as the only sane strategy. Brodie was the first analyst to recognize that nuclear weapons bring us "a long way from the subtleties of a Clausewitz, a Jomini, or a Mahan. . . . It brings us, in short, to the end of strategy as we have known it" (*Harper's*, October 1955).

Brodie was exactly right. The nuclear age did end traditional thinking about strategy. A new approach to strategy was needed, and RAND would provide it. Its foundation was provided by Brodie, who asserted that "the only sane strategy" was that of deterrence. Consequently, all subsequent strategies sought and still seek to deter. That the United States has been able to do that successfully since World War II is a tribute to RAND.

Albert Wohlstetter (1913–1997), a physicist associated with RAND from 1951 to 1963, provided the critical analysis on basing policy for nuclear weapons. While he was at RAND, he was asked to do a study of overseas basing for the Strategic Air Command. The Air Force just assumed that the best places to base its most powerful bombers would be overseas, as close as practical to possible targets in Eastern Europe and the Soviet Union. Wohlstetter, however, took his analysis far beyond a focus on overseas bases to deal with the whole question of the vulnerability of U.S. strategic forces. Wohlstetter's essential argument, certainly influenced by the 1941 Japanese surprise attack on Pearl Harbor, which brought the United States into World War II, was that deterrent forces could also be a tempting target, especially in the nuclear age. Consequently, it was essential that strategic forces be invulnerable, capable of riding out a surprise attack by the enemy and still being able to strike back afterwards.

This necessity for invulnerability is why he recommended that the Strategic Air Command, the heavy bomber force, be based not overseas but in the heartland of the United States. This not only provided the sheer distance that created more warning time in case of an attack but the financial advantage of being on home ground. Because the key concept was invulnerability, a certain number of bombers could be kept in the air at all times, ready to retaliate even if their bases were destroyed. What made all this possible was the relatively recent development of in-flight refueling, which allowed bombers to reach any place on earth from the middle of the United States.

Although Wohlstetter had some difficulty persuading Strategic Air Command to accept the need for invulnerability, this idea, and the concomitant distinction between first- and second-strike forces, gradually became the strategic orthodoxy. Consequently, throughout the Cold War, the Strategic Air Command (SAC) was headquartered in Omaha, Nebraska, right in the middle of the United States and not in Europe. In 1991, after decades of always having nuclear armed bombers in the air and ready to strike on a moment's notice, President George H. W. Bush decided that the danger of a surprise attack from the Soviet Union had so subsided that he ordered SAC to stand down from its alert status. They had completed their mission of deterrence.

RAND'S SUPERSTAR

RAND had many analysts who were esteemed scholars and authors, but during its history it has had only one superstar, whose name and work broke out of the confines of defense policy analysis and academia: Herman Kahn (1922–1983). Kahn, a RAND staffer from 1949 to 1961, helped the United States move away from its 1950s policy of massive retaliation to the present one of flexible response. Kahn argued that it was necessary to think about ways of fighting limited as opposed to unlimited or "spasm" nuclear wars. Indeed, if there was to be any chance of imposing some kind of restraint in warfare, then it would only be possible if there had been prior thinking as to how this might be achieved. Kahn distinguished among different kinds of nuclear deterrence but saw it as operating even at very high levels of violence, as both the United States and the Soviet Union would be deterred from inflicting the ultimate strikes against each other's cities.

In bestselling works such as *On Thermonuclear War* (1960), *Thinking About the Unthinkable* (1962), and *On Escalation: Metaphors and Scenarios* (1965), Kahn not only wrote about millions of deaths from nuclear war and suggested that the survivors might envy the dead, but did so in a way that seemed detached and totally amoral. As John Garnett wrote in a chapter on Kahn in *Makers of Nuclear Strategy* (1991), "Kahn, quite uncompromisingly, stared right down the throat of thermonuclear war without flinching. What is more he was the first person to do it, and when a totally unprepared public was suddenly confronted by his findings they reacted with a mixture of fear, horror and amazement."

Critical opinion, too, was often unfavorable. James Newman, for example, writing in a book review in *Scientific American* (March 1961), described *On Thermonuclear War* as "an insane, pornographic book, a moral tract of mass murder: how to plan it, how to commit it, how to get away with it, how to justify it." Kahn's willingness to think through some of the "what if" questions, however, helped to highlight some of the dangers involved in deterrence. Moreover, it was clear that although Kahn focused in large part on surviving nuclear war, his main concern was how to avoid it. And this was something he believed could best be discerned through analysis rather than emotion.

KAHN ON NUCLEAR WAR

When one examines the possible effects of thermonuclear war carefully, one notices that there are indeed many postwar states that should be distinguished. If most people do not or cannot distinguish among these states it is because the gradations occur as a result of a totally bizarre circumstance—a thermonuclear war. The mind recoils from thinking hard about that; one prefers to believe it will never happen. If asked, " How does a country look on the day of the war?" the only answer a reasonable person can give is " awful." It takes an act of iron will or an unpleasant degree of detachment or callousness to go about the task of distinguishing among the possible degrees of awfulness.

Source: Herman Kahn, *On Thermonuclear War.* Princeton, NJ: Princeton University Press, 1960.

THE DOOMSDAY MACHINE

The doomsday machine, though it was not the most influential single idea to come out of RAND in its nuclear theory heyday, was certainly the most famous. The doomsday machine was Herman Kahn's concept in *On Thermonuclear War* (1960) of a theoretical device that would automatically set off enough hydrogen bombs to destroy the entire world if the state that built it suffered severe damage from an aggressor's nuclear weapons. Thus the doomsday machine, with its ability to kill virtually everyone on earth, would function as a deterrent. The crucial element of this concept was that, once the machine was activated, even its creators could not deactivate it. It was just this automatic nature of the device that was supposed to provide credibility.

Kahn's theory took the logic of the U.S. Air Force's war plans to their ultimate conclusions to illustrate their absurdity. In the event of an attack from the Soviet Union, the Strategic Air Command planned to unleash all its nuclear weapons against the Soviets. Kahn used the doomsday theory to argue for a more flexible range of responses to a nuclear attack. According to Gregg Herken, in *Counsels of War* (1987), Kahn "had actually borrowed the idea from physicist Leo Szilard in order to burlesque the concept of deterrence. Critics, however, mistook Kahn's subtle satire for advocacy." Fred Kaplan, in *The Wizards of Armageddon* (1983), recounts: "As Kahn half expected, not a single military officer liked the idea. Yet the Doomsday Machine was only a slightly absurd extension of existing American and NATO policy: the Soviets do something provocative, and we blow up most of their citizens, which provokes them to blow up most of ours."

According to Fred Kaplan, Kahn's main purpose in writing *On Thermonuclear War* was "to create a vocabulary" so that strategic issues could be "comfortably and easily" analyzed, "a vocabulary that reduces the emotions surrounding nuclear war to the dispassionate cool of scientific thought." Consequently, "to the extent that many people today talk about nuclear war in such a nonchalant, would-be scientific manner, their language is rooted in the work of Herman Kahn. And to the extent that people have an image of defense analysts as mad-scientist Dr. Strangelove who almost glorify the challenge of nuclear war, that image, too, comes from Herman Kahn."

RAND EXPANDS

Although RAND was initially concerned with strategic issues, it quickly expanded into new areas. For example, in 1954, David Novick, a RAND economist, proposed "program budgeting," a form of budgeting that would permit global understanding of expenditure purposes, which consolidated spending into "programs", and which, therefore, laid foundations for a focus on effectiveness, because the total resources directed to any purpose should now be more readily apparent. Novick defined a program as "the sum of the steps or interdependent activities which enter into the attainment of a specified objective."

If a budget were to comprise large slabs of spending, called programs, directed toward particular objectives, the disaggregation problem common to line-item and performance budgeting would be overcome. Compliance could still be monitored, but the monitoring of efficiency and effectiveness would also be facilitated. And instead of being primarily an instrument of control and management information, the budget would become a planning document, and a document supporting the comparison of alternative expenditures at some meaningful level of aggregation. These were important conceptual breakthroughs.

The team that fashioned program budgeting at the RAND Corporation had an ambitious program, for they proposed not merely a rewrite of budget structure, but a new framework for the analysis of policy and the review of accomplishment. According to David Novack (1968), they proposed not just program budgeting but planning–programming–budgeting, a linked system that had elements of forward planning, what they termed "the analytical comparison of alternatives," the allocation of resources in the framework of a multiyear cycle, and budgeting related to broad program groups rather than individual items. The "package" was named PPBS, for Planning Programming Budgeting Systems; it was intended "to create a new environment of choice." The budget document was now no longer about "where we are," but about "where do we want to go?" It seemed that the theorists were at last making a contribution that had the potential to reshape government budgeting, planning, and resource allocation in a fundamental way.

Budgeting during the 1960s was dominated by PPBS. It was first installed in the Defense Department during the Kennedy administration, and it seemed to represent the height of rationality for the budget process. According to the historian of budgeting, Allen Schick (1966), the stages of budget reform went from the development of budgetary theory with its concerns for accountability and control, which were the hallmark of the line-item budget; to performance budgeting, with its emphasis on managerial efficiency; to PPBS, which stressed objectives, planning, and program effectiveness.

In 1965 President Lyndon Johnson mandated the use of PPBS for all federal agencies. Implemented hastily, with insufficient time for understanding, training, and development, the across-the-board implementation of PPBS failed quickly, leaving a platform for cynics and incrementalists to lambaste national initiatives and planning indiscriminately for many years. What was once mandatory for all federal agencies and widely adopted by state and local jurisdictions, by the end of the decade was officially "un" adopted by the federal government and was widely considered to be unusable in its original format. Nevertheless, the influence of PPBS as a major budgeting process remains. Where it is still in use, however, it tends to exist in a hybrid rather than a pure form.

The point here is that ideas generated by RAND were able to dominate thinking on the subjects RAND took up. Its prestige was enormous, its name magical. A RAND study eked competence and demanded attention. What happened next is reminiscent of the motto of the French Foreign Legion: "March or Die." Momentum had to be maintained. So RAND became imperialistic, as bureaucratic organizations tend to do. It hired more staff (720 professional researchers in 2005, 80 percent with advanced degrees), expanded to six major locations (two overseas), and diversified into almost every conceivable research area from child policy to elder care. Anthony Downs, a one-time

RAND researcher, considers such organizational expansion an illustration of his "law of progress through imperialism," which holds that "the desire to aggrandize breeds innovation." And Downs wrote his classic book on bureaucracy, with its many laws, *Inside Bureaucracy* (1967), while he was on the staff at RAND watching what was going on about him.

THINK TANK PROLIFERATION

Just as the chief-of-staff concept has developed many variations (see Chapter 13), so, too, has the notion of a think tank. The term itself, while used here to describe the function of a true general staff, is really just a colloquial term for an organization or organizational segment whose primary function is research. The purpose of civilian think tanks is to identify options, assess policies, and generally contribute to the debate about public policies in ways that improve the quality of those policies.

Although think tanks began, at least on a large scale, as a particularly American phenomenon, other countries have emulated the U.S. experience. In 2009, *Foreign Policy* published its "Think Tank Index," a reputational study of the 5,465 think tanks worldwide. The editors sought to do for think tanks what *U.S. News & World Report* did for college rankings in its annual surveys of academic programs. According to *Foreign Policy,* there are 1,872 think tanks in North America (1,777 in the United States), 1,208 in Western Europe, 653 in Asia, 538 in Latin America and the Caribbean, 514 in Eastern Europe, 424 in sub-Saharan Africa, and 218 in the Middle East and North Africa. They even found 38 in Oceania. About 170 countries were represented. As you might have expected, the world's single greatest concentration of think tanks is to be found in the Washington, D.C., metropolitan area, with 350 to its credit.

Because this was a reputational study in which think tank scholars and executives, among others, ranked the tanks, who won? Table 18.1 lists the top ten U.S. and non-U.S. think tanks.

Be aware that the index of 5,465 worldwide think tanks assembled by *Foreign Policy* is incomplete. It sought to assess and rank all of the legitimate think tanks, but there is another category, illegitimate think tanks, which it ignores except for some passing references to "phantom" think tanks created by authoritarian governments. Consequently, organizations such as the Institute for Democracy and Cooperation in Russia and the Center for Political Studies in Uzbekistan may function less as proper think tanks and more as propaganda arms of the government. However, when it comes to disseminating propaganda through organizations that appear to be and that seek to borrow the prestige and credibility of well-known think tanks, the corporate world has no peers. There is a long tradition in corporate advertising and public relations of creating phony institutions that seem like traditional think tanks but whose real purpose is to publicize biased research to influence consumers or policy makers. Both the tobacco and health insurance industries have been notorious for this. So always remember that some think tank research may be no more valid than that $5 Rolex wristwatch you bought from a street vendor.

Table 18.1 *Foreign Policy*'s 2009 Ranking of the Top Ten U.S. and Non-U.S.
Think Tanks

U.S. Think Tanks	*Non-U.S. Think Tanks*
Brookings Institution Washington, D.C.	Chatham House London
Council on Foreign Relations New York	International Institute for Strategic Studies London
Carnegie Endowment for International Peace Washington, D.C.	Stockholm International Peace Research Institute Solna, Sweden
Rand Corporation Santa Monica, Calif.	Overseas Development Institute London
Heritage Foundation Washington, D.C.	Centre for European Policy Studies Brussels
Woodrow Wilson International Center for Scholars Washington, D.C.	Transparency International Berlin
Center for Strategic & International Studies Washington, D.C.	German Council on Foreign Relations Berlin
American Enterprise Institute Washington, D.C.	German Institute for International and Security Affairs Berlin
Cato Institute Washington, D.C.	French Institute of International Relations Paris
Hoover Institution, Stanford, Calif.	Adam Smith Institute London

Source: Foreign Policy, January/February 2009.

NONACADEMIC THINK TANKS

University faculty are notoriously independent—especially those that are tenured. Their
research agendas are often idiosyncratic and personal. Although there are always excep-
tions, faculty tend to operate as individual research entrepreneurs. Consequently, organizations that want to sponsor policy research often turn to nonacademic, or loosely
academic, institutions. There, researchers can be assigned projects and can be expected to
deliver their work on a deadline. Such organizations, of which there are vast varieties,
tend to focus on the policy and behavioral sciences. Similar research efforts in the natural
sciences take place in organizational units known colloquially as "skunk works" because

of the often-smelly nature of their experiments. Policy research doesn't smell, but critics have often complained that the conclusions stink.

Of course, universities often have centers or institutes independent of the traditional departments that function as think tanks. However, these efforts tend to be both budgetarily and physically separate from the normal faculty departments. So, while they are part of the university, they are at the same time independent of the regular faculty. And to the extent that they are financially successful in "selling" their research (by obtaining grants and contracts), they are increasingly independent of their university's administration. The universities tolerate this situation (having quasi-independent entities as part of their structure) because of the immense riches that they receive from the overhead costs attached to grants and contracts. What distinguishes a think tank from any other organizational unit with similar responsibilities is its structural independence. It is this independence that allows think tank researchers to advocate policy positions free of hierarchical intimidation. This is why the Germans created a general staff that was independent of the line commanders, why the urban reform movement of the Progressive Era got its impetus from independent municipal research bureaus, and why the U.S. Air Force created the archetypical think tank, the RAND corporation, as a civilian organization outside the military chain of command.

GOVERNMENTAL THINK TANKS

All large governmental entities have think tank operations of one kind of another, although they are often difficult to spot because they don't wear "think tank" labels. However, if you delve behind title phrases such as strategic planning, audit and evaluation, or management and budget, you will often find thinking going on. The Office of Policy Development is the president's primary advisory group on domestic issues. It assists the president in the formulation, coordination, and implementation of economic and domestic policy. In 1970, President Richard M. Nixon established the Domestic Council, a nineteen-member body, "as a domestic counterpart to the National Security Council." In 1977, President Jimmy Carter supplanted it with the Domestic Policy Staff. In 1981, President Ronald Reagan changed it to the Office of Policy Development. President Bill Clinton created the Domestic Policy Council and the National Economic Council within the overarching Office of Policy Development. The primary changes have been in title.

Note that whenever you have a large governmental entity such as a national, state, or big-city government, there will exist a hierarchy of think tanks. Those at the bottom percolate ideas up to the next level in the hope that attention will be paid. So a federal agency evaluation unit may come up with a new idea for improving program effectiveness, but the idea has to be sold to all the levels above until it reaches the level that can approve it. Legislative staff perform a similar function, except that the idea must only be sold to a legislator with enough influence over an agency to get that agency's attention. This often happens during appropriation hearings, when agencies are especially attentive to legislative thinking.

THINK TANKS FOR PROFIT OR NOT

RAND remains the exemplar among nonprofit policy research organizations. Although its genre was once rare, now it has, quite literally, thousands of cousins seeking to imitate its financial success and professional prestige. The difference between for-profit and nonprofit think tanks is mainly a matter of classification for Internal Revenue Service purposes.

A nonprofit organization is in many respects a concept rather than a specific entity, and it can be defined in many different ways. The primary essence of a nonprofit organization, however, is that it is organized and operated for public or societal purposes (such as public policy research) rather than for private purposes (such as return on shareholders' investments). Despite common misconceptions to the contrary, nonprofit organizations can make profits from their activities and engage in commercial-type enterprises. However, such profits must be returned to the organization; not paid out to individuals. Nevertheless, individuals who work for nonprofit organizations can be paid extremely large salaries—just don't call them dividends. Examples of nonprofit think tanks, besides RAND, include the Urban Institute in Washington, D.C.; the Carter Center in Atlanta, Georgia; the Hoover Institution in Palo Alto, California; and the thousands of centers and institutes associated with universities.

For-profit think tanks are structured as traditional corporations and are commonly known as consulting firms. Modern management and policy consulting originated early in the twentieth century with Frederick W. Taylor, Harrington Emerson, and the other pioneers of scientific management. The giant worldwide management consulting firms of today have their intellectual origins in the scientific management movement. And that movement, because it essentially offered "staff research for sale" is the intellectual child of the military general staff model pioneered by the Germans. So, the German General Staff, despite plotting two world wars and causing untold misery and death for tens of millions in the twentieth century, actually did the world some good, too. However, doing good by creating a better policy-making mechanism for humanity was hardly their intention. Still, they deserve the credit—even though it is not enough to wash the blood off their hands.

FOR DISCUSSION

What is the better institutional home for incubating research in the social sciences in general and public policy and administration in particular, a traditional university or the modern U.S. think tank? What is the role of the contemporary partisan think tank in U.S. politics and policy formulation today?

BIBLIOGRAPHY

Brodie, Bernard. *Escalation and the Nuclear Option.* Princeton NJ: Princeton University Press, 1966.

———. *Strategy in the Missile Age.* Princeton, NJ: Princeton University Press, 1959.

———. *War and Politics.* New York: Macmillan, 1973.

Dickson, Paul. *Think Tanks.* New York: Atheneum, 1971.

Downs, Anthony. *Inside Bureaucracy.* Boston: Litle, Brown, 1967.

Garnett, John. "Herman Kahn." In *Makers of Nuclear Strategy,* edited by John Baylis and John Garnett. New York: St. Martin's, 1991.

Herken, Gregg. *Counsels of War.* New York: Oxford University Press, 1987.

Holden, Matthew, Jr. "Imperialism in Bureaucracy." *American Political Science Review* LX (December 1966).

Kahn, Herman. *On Escalation: Metaphors and Scenarios.* Princeton, NJ: Princeton University Press, 1965.

———. *On Thermonuclear War.* Princeton, NJ: Princeton University Press, 1960.

———. *Thinking About the Unthinkable.* Princeton, NJ: Princeton University Press, 1962.

———. *Thinking About the Unthinkable in the 1980s.* New York: Touchstone, 1983.

Kaplan, Fred. *The Wizards of Armageddon.* New York: Simon & Schuster, 1983.

McGann, James. "The Think Tank Index." *Foreign Policy,* January–February, 2009.

Novick, David. "The Origin and History of Programming Budgeting." *California Management Review* 11 (Fall 1968).

Schick, Allen. "A Death in the Bureaucracy: The Demise of Federal PPB." *Public Administration Review* 33 (March–April 1973).

———. "The Road to PPB: The Stages of Budget Reform." *Public Administration Review* 26 (December 1966).

Smith, Bruce L. R. *The RAND Corporation.* Cambridge, MA: Harvard University Press, 1968.

Smith, James A. *The Idea Brokers: Think Tanks and the Rise of the New Policy Elite.* New York: Free Press, 1993.

Stone, Diane, Andrew Denham, and Mark Garnett, eds. *Think Tanks Across Nations: A Comparative Approach.* Manchester, UK: Manchester University Press, 1998.

Taylor, Frederick W. *The Principles of Scientific Management.* New York: Harper Bros., 1911.

Wohlstetter, Albert. "The Delicate Balance of Terror." *Foreign Affairs,* January 1959.

CHAPTER NINETEEN

Implementing Strategy Through the Levels of Leadership and Strategic Optimism

HOW STRATEGIC LEADERSHIP INVARIABLY DEVOLVES INTO TACTICAL OPERATIONS

PREVIEW

All political decisions are made at one level of government or another, sometimes even by several at the same time. Consequently, the level of analysis is one of the classic issues in the study of politics because it poses an eternal question: Should the focus of political analysis be the individual political actor (a lone citizen or organization), a local government (a municipality, county, or special district), a national government, or the international political system as a whole? The forces at play and the links within and between these levels make single-level analysis problematic at best. So there is really no point in undertaking a political analysis of a political actor in isolation—because that actor is never in isolation. He or she is always a citizen of a state and/or a member of other large groups, and there are always a large number of links and interactions among the various levels of government and other social groupings.

Doctrine as organizational policies presents a similar level-of-analysis problem. It is inherently hierarchical with a seemingly sacrosanct chain of command. The most general notions come down from the top to be implemented at various stages leading to the bottom. When the president orders "justice" for America's enemies, that order travels down the chain of command until a soldier pulls the trigger on his rifle and administers a full measure of such justice to a deserving person.

Doctrine sets into action the ways and means by which people are ultimately shot, or given food stamps, or provided health care. Whether the end result is bullets or bedpans, the doctrine involved travels a similar route toward implementation: from the grand strategic (the national policy-making) level to the strategic (the highest organizational level) to the operational (the planning or administrative) level to the tactical (the service-delivery) level. Each level accepts doctrine from above but uses discretion to create subdoctrine or level-specific doctrine that facilitates implementation.

The whole history of public administration since antiquity is, in essence, just tinkering with this core concept. It explains how societies as large as a state and as small as an office work to do their assigned tasks. Consequently, what follows is absolutely essential for an understanding of how to succeed in a world of organizations.

THE GRAND STRATEGIC LEVEL

The grand strategic level is the highest level of a state's leadership, at which decisions are made to marshal all the resources of a nation to achieve a goal. Sometimes the leadership turns out to be insufficient to the task, as when President Bill Clinton, during his first term (1993–1997) sought but failed to obtain health insurance for all Americans. Sometimes the goal is only partially achieved, as when President Lyndon B. Johnson, in his 1964 State of the Union message, stated: "This administration today, here and now, declares unconditional war on poverty in America." And sometimes the goal is fully achieved, as when, in the wake of the Japanese surprise attack on Pearl Harbor in Hawaii, President Franklin D. Roosevelt, on December 8, 1941, stated: "No matter how long it may take us . . . , the American people, in their righteous might, will win through to absolute victory."

In each of the above cases, the decisions were made at the highest possible level, the grand strategic level. This is the level at which President George W. Bush operated after the September 11, 2001, terrorist attack. He made the essential decision for war and then, after soliciting their advice, gave specific "marching orders" to his various lieutenants. Thereafter, the Department of Defense, the Department of State, the Department of Justice, the Central Intelligence Agency, and the Federal Bureau of Investigation, among others, all went about developing and implementing their strategic plans, which, in their totality, would seek to achieve the overall grand strategy of winning what Bush called the "war on terror."

THE STRATEGIC LEVEL

Strategy, the overall conduct of a war or other major enterprise, is derived from a Greek word (*strategia*) meaning the art of the general. Until recent decades the word was confined mainly to its military context. In the mid-1960s, however, H. Igor Ansoff (1918–2002), a mathematician-turned-business school professor, started producing works advocating strategic planning for better business success. Later, Ansoff discovered that planning was not comprehensive enough. A broader concept was needed that would subsume strategic planning and go on to encompass implementation as well. This was strategic management.

What Ansoff did was revolutionary. It was not that strategic leadership was new, but its self-conscious application to business policy was. Ansoff's revolution was confirmed when, over the next two decades, strategic management almost completely supplanted business policy as a core subject of MBA (and eventually MPA) programs. Strategic management has thus become the modern application of this ancient art to contemporary business and public administration.

Strategic management can be formally defined as the conscious selection of policies, development of capability, and interpretation of the environment by managers in order to focus organizational efforts toward the achievement of preset objectives. These objectives necessarily vary. In the private sector, it might be the doubling of annual dividends to stockholders within so many years. In the nonprofit sector, it might be the creation of a repertory theater or a significant increase in attendance at symphony orchestra concerts. In the public sector, it might be a reduction in the crime rate, an increase in the high school graduation rate, or the defeat of a worldwide terrorist network.

All strategic management efforts take an essentially similar approach to planning where an organization wants to be by a future target date. These are the features that identify a strategic as opposed to a nonstrategic management approach:

1. The identification of objectives to be achieved in the future (these are often announced in a vision statement)

2. The adoption of a time frame (or "planning horizon") in which these objectives are to be achieved

3. A systematic analysis of the current circumstances of an organization, especially its capabilities

4. An assessment of the environment surrounding the organization, both now and within the planning horizon

5. The selection of a strategy for the achievement of desired objectives by a future date, often by comparing various alternatives

6. The integration of organizational efforts around this strategy

The strategic management process is often conducted by a strategic planning unit within the organization. For a nation's military forces, this is typically the general staff. Civilian planning efforts may be undertaken in a budget office, in the chief executive's office, or in any of a variety of other units. Eventually, the findings are presented in a detailed document known as the strategic plan. Military plans—except for their objectives—are normally kept secret from the public, for obvious reasons, and are distributed within the military and its government on a need-to-know basis.

The inherently political nature of public policy and administration can place a premium on short-term, as opposed to strategic, thinking. As British Prime Minister Harold Wilson (1916–1995) said, "A week is a long time in politics." By this he was drawing attention to the fickle nature of the public's attention, to the fact that an issue of premier

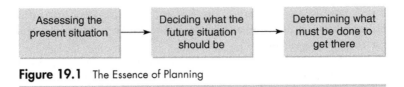

Figure 19.1   The Essence of Planning

significance one week may be forgotten the next. Political leaders may lose power unexpectedly. "Today a rooster, tomorrow a feather duster" sums up the uncertain job prospects of those who would lead the political barnyard. Thus the reigning administrations in developed democracies feel they must be very sensitive to the results of very short-term opinion polling. These factors and all others bring a short-term focus to bear on public policy making and work—work very hard—against strategic planning efforts. Public budgeting procedures, because of their annual nature, only reinforce this tendency. Planning, which always starts with an assessment of the present situation (see Figure 19.1), is all the more difficult in the public sector because the present situation is so often in flux.

Strategic management has been described, most notably by H. Igor Ansoff (1979), as "a matching process" in which the variables of strategy, capability, and environment are matched as the organization seeks to manage change through strategy. As the environment moves from stable to turbulent, Ansoff argues that the required capability moves from "custodial" toward "entrepreneurial." In a stable environment, a custodial, unchanging capability may suffice, but as the environment becomes surprising and turbulent, a more entrepreneurial and risk-taking capability is needed. This is never more obvious than in wartime.

THE OPERATIONAL LEVEL

The strategic level decides that something should happen, and the operational level decides how it should happen: how the big ideas at the top will eventually be implemented at the bottom. The military calls this level *operations,* meaning a command or planning center; it is middle management in the civilian sector.

The essential job of this level is to make things happen. Whether the undertaking is an individual operation in the military or the creation of a long-lasting social program, those assigned the task are expected to use their utmost creativity. During World War II, General George S. Patton, Jr., was famous for saying: "Never tell people *how* to do things. Tell them *what* to do and they will surprise you with their ingenuity."

Management refers both to the people responsible for running an organization and to the running process itself: the use of numerous resources (such as employees and machines) to accomplish an organizational goal. Top managers make the big policy decisions and are responsible for the overall success of the organization. In government, the top managers are always the political leaders, whether they gain power by election, appointment, or assassination. When a new president comes into office in the United States, he or she will appoint loyalists to approximately 3,000 jobs, to be the top managers who will be responsible for implementing policy derived from their political party's doctrine. These appointees, while functioning as top policy makers and having significant management responsibilities, are seldom professional managers and rarely think of themselves as management experts.

Consequently, the public administrators of a jurisdiction (the actual management specialists) are to be found in the vast area of middle management: the group responsible for the execution and interpretation of top management policies and for the day-to-day operation of the various organizational units. These individuals often have advanced degrees in general fields such as public administration or business administration or in technical fields such as public health or social work. These are the people who have made the management of government programs their life's work. They typically have reporting to them supervisory or first-level managers, who are in turn responsible for the final implementation of policies by rank-and-file employees. These middle managers, despite their disparity in functions and technical backgrounds, largely constitute the management specialty of public administration. They spend their working lives fighting as officers in the administrative wars started by their political leaders.

THE TACTICAL LEVEL

The tactical level gets the job done and actually does what has been conceptualized at the top and planned for in the middle. Traditionally, *tactics* refers to the art and science of maneuvering troops in the face of the enemy. Those who control grand strategy decide to pursue war. The nation's generals decide when and where to campaign. The operational planners place the colonel on the battlefield. And what that colonel does once there is tactical.

It is at this point that strategy and tactics are often mixed up, at least semantically. It is perfectly reasonable to talk of a general's strategy for winning a battle. This simply means that tactical considerations are being confined to a much lower level of decision making: to the division, company, battalion, or squad level. Every leader of a tactical unit can consider the level of decision making above him or her to be strategic, even though the level may be tactical to those even further above them. Nevertheless, the essence of tactics is to achieve the objectives set by the level above you—no matter whether that level is called strategic by you or tactical by those above you. Figure 19.2

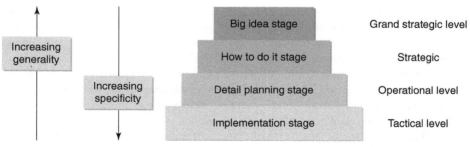

Figure 19.2 The Hierarchy of Doctrine

illustrates the hierarchy of doctrine by which plans and orders are increasingly specific the closer they are to the bottom of the organization. Thus a big city mayor may demand a crackdown on crime, which results in a cop on the beat arresting a prostitute. Or, on a larger scale, a president may order an invasion, and thousands of soldiers put their boots on the ground to do the implementation.

EMBRACING STRATEGIC MANAGEMENT

The public sector was slower than the private sector to embrace strategic management notions, probably because, traditionally, public administrators were expected to focus not on their objectives—what they were trying to achieve—but on their functions and responsibilities—that is, the duties assigned to them by law. Indeed, public administration was traditionally defined as the enforcement or implementation of public policy—that is, the law.

A world in which public administrators take responsibility for unchanging functions still exists in some corners of the public sector in most countries, but it is increasingly being replaced by a focus on objectives, which is an inherently tactical concept. No longer do we begin by asking a public administrator, "What do you do?" (i.e., "What is your function?"). Today the question more likely to be asked is, "What are you trying to achieve?" (i.e., "What are your objectives?"). There are many reasons for this change in perspective, but three are paramount.

The first reason is the popularization of the concept of management by objectives (MBO) by Peter Drucker (1909–2005), generally considered the intellectual father of modern management, through his pioneering 1954 work, *The Practice of Management*. MBO, as espoused by Drucker and now by countless others, is an approach to managing whose hallmark is the mutual—by both organizational subordinate and superior—establishment of measurable goals to be accomplished by an individual or team over a set period of time. The widespread adoption of the MBO concept around the world has aided in the distinction between a function and an objective. It is now widely understood that an emphasis on the latter can stimulate a focus on performance and effort as opposed to the more traditional custodial focus toward one's organizational obligations.

Second, the ever more rapid pace of change in the communities served by the public sector is such that there are now few functions that can go on unchanged from year to year. The public organizations of today must generally fight and compete in a less sheltered environment, where the luxury of just "administering" timeless functions rarely exists. The objectives of public-sector organizations have become moving targets, and public sector managers must move with them.

Third, the ideas of strategic management and the use of objectives are now pervasive in the private sector. There is no Berlin Wall dividing the sectors and managers move increasingly in and out of each sector, so there is an ever-increasing unification of language, concepts, and standards among the sectors.

Tactical operations, however well done, are inherently small elements of a larger strategic plan. Thus a tactical success can often be a false indicator of what may come. Tactical success is gratifying, but one should be aware that it will not always lead to a comparable strategic success. The best-known example of such a Pyrrhic victory is the Japanese attack on Pearl Harbor on December 7, 1941. The attack was a great tactical victory, but it so incensed the people of the United States that it led eventually to Japan's strategic defeat.

OPTIMISM AS A STRATEGIC FACTOR

Finally, we should consider one element of strategic leadership that is not usually considered in discussions of strategic implementation: optimism. Optimism has been used as a tool by great leaders throughout the ages. For example, in December 1944, at the beginning of the World War II Battle of the Bulge, U.S. forces were reeling from a German counterattack and things seemed quite desperate. As matters went from bad to worse, General Dwight D. Eisenhower called a meeting of his leading commanders and announced: "The present situation is to be regarded as one of opportunity for us and not of disaster. There will only be cheerful faces at this conference table." His newly "cheerful" commanders went on to win the battle.

Historian Stephen E. Ambrose (1994) wrote that Eisenhower felt it was critical that he maintain an air of absolute confidence, no matter what his personal feelings at the time. He knew that confidence, or "cheerleading," at the top would permeate down through every level of his immense organization. Eisenhower knew instinctively, as social science has now proved, that a confident organization is far more likely to succeed than a doubtful one—even if its leader actually has doubts. Optimism, or positive thinking, works—even when the leader has to fake it.

Throughout history, the most successful leaders—whether generals, managers, or football coaches—have been those who were the most optimistic. Was there ever a more optimistic politician than President Franklin D. Roosevelt, who, in the depths of the Great Depression, told his nation in his 1933 Inaugural Address that "the only thing we have to fear is fear itself." Here was a man who in his prime was crippled by polio, yet he succumbed only to physical paralysis. He did not let his affliction prevent him from becoming governor of New York and then president of the United States. His optimism was infectious. People around him caught it. This was a communicable "disease" that was good for the country.

Effective leaders have long known the importance of instilling a winning optimism in their followers. Even though it may not be warranted by circumstances, it is a far more potent force in leading than logic would dictate. What is certain is that the opposite of optimism, pessimism, depression, or what social psychologist Martin E. P. Seligman (1992) has called "learned helplessness," tends to lead to failure both of the mission at hand and eventually of health. When people find themselves in situations where they feel that they have no control and that their best efforts are futile, they "learn" from this repeated experience that they are "helpless" and thus become pessimistic and depressed. Seligman uses the example of U.S. prisoners of war in Korea. Those who retained an optimistic outlook were far more likely to survive their ordeal. Those who felt helpless and consequently depressed were far more likely to die in captivity, even though they got the same food and the same treatment as the others.

Optimistic attitudes on the part of leaders often become self-fulfilling prophecies. This is known as the Pygmalion effect. Pygmalion was a legendary sculptor in ancient Greece who so loved a statue of a woman he had created that his prayers gave it life so that he could then marry her. This theme of willing something into existence that you then learn to love was explored by George Bernard Shaw in his play, *Pygmalion* (1913), which was later made into the musical, *My Fair Lady* (1956).

This effect of causing something to happen by believing it will has been often demonstrated in both teacher/student and manager/worker relationships. If the teacher or manager believes his or her student or workers are capable (or not capable), they will tend to live up (or down) to expectations. This helps to explain why optimistic leaders are more likely to have successful followers—and why pessimistic leaders tend to wind up with a bunch of losers.

Social psychologists have now documented the utility of optimism, but leaders through the ages have known it instinctively. History is replete with tales of leaders getting their followers to do extraordinary deeds by installing optimism and forestalling pessimism. The latter task is every bit as important as the former. As British Field Marshall Bernard L. Montgomery wrote in his memoirs: "Generals who become depressed when things are not going well, who lack the 'drive' to get things done, and who lack the resolution . . . to see their plan through to the end—are useless. They are, in fact, worse than useless—they are a menace—since any sign of wavering or hesitation has immediate repercussions down the scale." Defeatism, depression, and failure are every bit as infectious as optimism.

During the presidential campaign of 1932, then–New York Governor Franklin D. Roosevelt spoke for all political executives when he said, "the Presidency is not merely an administrative office. That's the least of it. It is more than an engineering job, efficient or inefficient. It is pre-eminently a place of moral leadership." *Moral* here means both clarifying right from wrong but also teaching correct attitudes. This gets to the original meaning of *doctrine* as a teaching.

Presidents have traditionally used what President Theodore Roosevelt (Franklin's cousin) called their "bully pulpit" for just such teaching. For example, on April 10, 1899, Theodore Roosevelt said in a speech: "I wish to preach, not the doctrine of ignoble ease, but the doctrine of the strenuous life." Then he went on to explain what we can call his doctrine of optimism: "Far better it is to dare mighty things, to win glorious triumphs, even though checkered by failure, than to take rank with those poor spirits who neither enjoy much nor suffer much, because they live in the gray twilight that knows not victory nor defeat."

This is the credo of all optimistic leaders. This is how they live and sometimes die. Remember the advice traditionally given to actors: Always be sincere: Once you can fake that, you've got it made. It is the same with leadership. Always be optimistic; fake it if you don't feel it. New York City Mayor Rudy Giuliani admitted as much when discussing his inspiring leadership after the terrorist attacks that destroyed the twin towers of the World Trade Center on September 11, 2001: "I wonder how much of it [his leadership] was bluff. A lot of it had to be bluff. . . . Look, in a crisis you have to be optimistic. When I said the spirit of the city would be stronger, I didn't know that. I just hoped that" (*Time,* December 31, 2001). And do

Winston Churchill (1874–1965), Prime Minister of Great Britain during most of World War II, addressing a joint session of Parliament in 1954. Churchill, generally considered the greatest European leader of the twentieth century, first became Prime Minister as the Germans overran Western Europe and Great Britain stood alone against a seemingly unstoppable German military. Then, as U.S. President John F. Kennedy would say in an April 9, 1963, speech conferring honorary U.S. citizenship on Churchill: "In the dark days and darker nights when England stood alone—and most men save Englishmen despaired of England's life—he mobilized the English language and sent it into battle. The incandescent quality of his words illuminated the courage of his countrymen." Churchill and the British Empire alone led the world's resistance to Nazi tyranny until the United States entered the war eighteen months later. At the beginning of this ordeal, Churchill told the British people: "Let us therefore brace ourselves to our duties, and so bear ourselves that, if the British Empire and its Commonwealth last for a thousand years, men will say, 'This was their finest hour.'" Novelist George Orwell would later write: "Whether or not 1940 was anyone else's finest hour, it was certainly Churchill's" (*New Leader*, May 14, 1949). Churchill remained optimistic and preached optimism while too many others despaired and talked of surrender.

This photo shows Churchill speaking at the end of a parliamentary tribute to him on his 80th birthday. He said: "Mr. Attlee described my speeches in the war as expressing the will not only of Parliament but of the whole nation. It fell to me to express it, and if I found the right words you must remember that I have always earned my living by my pen and by my tongue. It was a nation and race dwelling all around the globe that had the lion's heart. I had the luck to be called upon to give the roar. I also hope that I sometimes suggested to the lion the right place to use his claws." The life-size portrait behind Churchill was his parliamentary birthday gift. Both Churchill and his wife, Clementine, hated the likeness. So when he died, she had him buried and the portrait cremated.
Source: © Bettmann/CORBIS. All Rights Reserved.

THE CONFIDENT LEADER

Anyone who accomplishes anything of significance has more confidence than the facts would justify. It is something that outstanding executives have in common with gifted military commanders, brilliant political leaders, and great artists. It is true of societies as well as of individuals. Every great civilization has been characterized by confidence in itself.

Lacking such confidence, too many leaders add ingenious new twists to the modern art which I call "How to reach a decision without really deciding." They require that the question he put through a series of clearances within the organization and let the clearance process settle it. Or take a public opinion poll and let the poll settle it. Or devise elaborate statistical systems, cost-accounting systems, and information-processing systems, hoping that out of them will come unassailable support for one course of action rather than another.

This is not to say that leadership cannot profit enormously from good information. If the modern leader doesn't know the facts he is in grave trouble, but rarely do the facts provide unqualified guidance. After the facts are in, the leader must in some measure emulate the little girl who told the teacher she was going to draw a picture of god. The teacher said, "But Mary, no on knows what God looks like;" and Mary said, "They will when I get through."

Source: John W. Gardner, "Some Maladies of Leadership." Annual Report 1965, Carnegie Corporation of New York.

---

you think President Franklin D. Roosevelt really thought that the only thing we had "to fear was fear itself"? All who knew him agree that he was a great actor. Of course, all politicians are actors. Some just get better reviews than others.

FOR DISCUSSION

Why is leadership that provides direction from the top to the bottom, from the highest strategic level to the lowest tactical level, an inherent aspect of all large military and civilian organizations? Why is optimism, sometimes called morale, often as important a strategic factor in organizational success as ample supplies of both human and all other resources?

BIBLIOGRAPHY

Ambrose, Stephen E. *D-Day*. New York: Simon & Schuster, 1994.

Ansoff, H. Igor. *Corporate Strategy*. New York: McGraw-Hill, 1965.

———. *Strategic Management*. New York: Macmillan, 1979.

Barnard, Chester I. *The Functions of the Executive*. Cambridge, MA: Harvard University Press, 1938.

Bryman, Alan. *Charisma and Leadership in Organizations*. Newbury, CA: Sage, 1992.

Burns, James McGregor. *Leadership*. New York: Harper & Row, 1978.

Drucker, Peter. *The Practice of Management.* New York: Harper & Row, 1954.

Giuliani, Rudolph. *Leadership.* New York: Miramax Books, 2002.

Livingston, J. Sterling. "Pygmalion in Management." *Harvard Business Review,* July–August 1969.

Montgomery, Bernard Law. *Memoirs.* Cleveland, OH: World Publishing, 1958.

Peterson, Christopher. *Learned Helplessness: A Theory for the Age of Personal Control.* New York: Oxford University Press, 1993.

Pfeffer, Jeffrey. *Power in Organizations.* Marshfield, MA: Pitman, 1981.

Rosenthal, Robert, and Lenore Jacobson, *Pygmalion in the Classroom.* New York: Holt, Rinehart & Winston, 1968.

Seligman, Martin E. P. *Helplessness: On Depression, Development, and Death.* New York: W. H. Freeman, 1992.

———. *Learned Optimism.* New York: Knopf, 1991.

Wills, Garry. "What Makes a Good Leader?" *Atlantic Monthly,* April 1994.

CHAPTER TWENTY

Was It Good Leadership for General Douglas Macarthur to Take His Staff with Him When He Abandoned His Army in the Philippines and Ran Away to Australia at the Beginning of World War II?

PREVIEW

At the beginning of World War II, General Douglas MacArthur (1880–1964) decided to kill himself. In February 1942, MacArthur, commander of all the U.S. and Filipino troops fighting the Japanese invaders of the Philippines, knew the enemy would eventually starve out his besieged forces on the Bataan peninsula and the island fortress of Corregidor. Surrender would be too shameful for the 62-year-old son of a Medal of Honor winner, for a man who himself won the Silver Star for valor seven times over in World War I. Besides, it would be too great a victory for the enemy. He knew how obsessed the Japanese were with honor, and that this was one honor he had the power to deny them. So, eschewing the standard Army-issue .45-caliber pistol, he carried a lightweight, palm-size, double-barreled derringer. As he loaded two bullets into the barrels, he stared into the eyes of Lt. Col. Sidney Huff of his staff and said: "They will never take me alive, Sid."

EARLY LIFE

The U.S. Army was Douglas MacArthur's whole life. He was born into it in 1880, lived on frontier outposts as a child, and then graduated first in the West Point class of 1903. After a shaky start in junior officer assignments, he found his true niche in 1916 as the

Army's first press relations officer. He was so effective in this role that he was promoted to colonel and made chief of staff of one of the first infantry divisions sent to France when the United States entered World War I. There, he excelled in every possible way. He ended the war as a famous general with a chestful of medals and an honestly earned reputation for absolute fearlessness under fire. This was made possible by his faith—not religious faith, but faith in himself, in his stars, in his destiny. Much like Napoleon, he really believed that he was a man of destiny, one of the anointed few for whom glory and renown are objective goals. Consequently, he was never afraid of being killed or wounded in combat. His destiny would not allow it. He even boasted: "All of Germany cannot fabricate the shell that will kill me."

After the war he was appointed superintendent of West Point, where he became famous as a reformer and as a publicizer of his reforms. Prophetically, he even lectured to some cadets about how "war with Japan is inevitable." By 1930 he had risen to the top of his profession, Chief of Staff of the U.S. Army. In 1937 he retired from the Army and became the Field Marshal of the Philippines, a U.S. protectorate that in 1934 had been promised independence in 1944. When war with Japan began to be more than a theoretical possibility in early 1941, MacArthur was recalled to active duty as the U.S. Far East commander.

When the Japanese attacked the Philippines on the day after they bombed Pearl Harbor, MacArthur had spent years preparing the Filipino soldiers for just such an eventuality and a whole career leading the U.S. Army. No more experienced, more qualified, or more famous officer could have been chosen to lead the combined force of U.S. and Filipino troops. Yet this obvious choice had performed so poorly as a commander that he was preparing to kill himself rather than face ignominious defeat.

MacArthur's seeming willingness, even eagerness, to die with his troops has been amply documented during two world wars. In the Philippines he constantly and unnecessarily exposed himself to enemy fire. During countless air raids, while others were cowering in shelters, he stood out in the open with not so much as a steel helmet for protection, almost defying the enemy to strike him down. He even asserted that "the Japs haven't yet fabricated the bomb with my name on it." This boast has a familiar ring. Here was a man whose suicidal tendencies were seemingly counterbalanced by the most extraordinary good luck. Once, after narrowly avoiding death from strafing fighter planes, he philosophically explained: "It was close, but that's the way it is in war. You win or lose, live or die—and the difference is just an eyelash." Two of MacArthur's major biographers, William Manchester and Geoffrey Perret, reported that MacArthur was exhilarated by his close brushes with death—on always being on just the right side of the "eyelash." After all, it was his destiny at work.

Charles Willoughby, who was with MacArthur as a staff officer on Corregidor, was only one of many observers of his general's frequent coolness under fire. According to Willoughby and co-author John Chamberlain (1956), "His quixotic defiance of the enemy was not an exhibition of Renaissance Italian bravado, but the subtle application of psychology. It was intended as a deliberate act of leadership." There is no doubt that it was manfully deliberate, but was it appropriate leadership? "To dare the bombs in a sally to the open is a commander's bitter privilege." True, but it is equally applicable to say that a general who dares too much may be setting a poor example and demonstrating a longing for a quick way out of a hopeless situation.

ORDERED TO DIE

MacArthur prepared for death. In the very submarine that smuggled the civilian leaders of the Philippines away to safety, he sent a footlocker to be delivered to the Riggs National Bank in Washington, D.C. It contained his will, medals, and financial papers among miscellaneous family photographs and personal documents. The bank was instructed to hold it for his legal heirs.

Courtney Whitney (1955), who was an officer on MacArthur's staff, later reported that in a formal message to President Franklin D. Roosevelt the general vowed he and his troops would fight "to complete destruction." Brave words, yes, but these were also MacArthur's explicit orders. The president of the United States had publicly demanded that as long as the flag of the United States flew on Filipino soil, "it will be defended by our own men to the death." Roosevelt forbade any thought of surrender "so long as there is any possibility of resistance." He explained that "it is mandatory that there be established once and for all in the minds of all peoples complete evidence that the American determination and indomitable will to win carries on down to the last unit. I, therefore, give you this most difficult mission in full understanding of the desperate situation to which you may shortly be reduced."

MacArthur's commander in chief had told him in no uncertain terms that, like Leonidas and his 300 Spartans in ancient Thermopylae, he and his men were expected to fight and die to uphold the honor of the people they represented. And the honor of not just the people of the United States was at stake. The Pacific-wide conflict was a race war, and MacArthur represented the "whites" on the chessboard of war. This was a major reason why Roosevelt gave MacArthur his stand-and-die orders. Roosevelt reasoned that if he ordered MacArthur out to a safe area: "It would mean that whites would absolutely lose all face in the Far East. White men can go down fighting, but they can't run away."

MacArthur had his orders, but these orders did not apply to his family. It is understandable that a defeated general would, much like a captain going down with his ship, prefer death to dishonor. However, it is inexplicable why MacArthur would allow his wife and son to share his fate—especially when he had the power to send them out of harm's way. They could have easily been sent home in one of the submarines that periodically slipped by the Japanese naval blockade. Incredibly, he said: "My family, with whom I have consulted, wish to remain with me to such end and I will not interfere with their decision."

During this period, submarines brought in more than 100 tons of supplies and ferried more than 200 people to safety, including the 75-man U.S. Navy code-breaking unit that would be so critical to future victories over the Japanese. Passage home for MacArthur's wife and son was specifically offered by Roosevelt, but Mrs. MacArthur, using the florid diction so typical of her husband, said: "We have drunk from the same cup. We three shall stay together." MacArthur then responded to the president's offer to evacuate his family by saying that "I have decided that they will share the fate of this garrison" (James, 1970).

Long afterward, Sidney Huff wrote that MacArthur said: "I fully expected to be killed. I would never have surrendered. If necessary, I would have sought the end in some final charge. . . . And Jean [his wife] and the boy might have been destroyed in some final general debacle." There is no doubt that he was devoted to his wife and doted on his son, but he accepted "their decision" is as if this were a proper matter for a family consultation. MacArthur proudly told an aide: "Jean is my finest soldier." When another aide questioned his son's poor prospects for the future, MacArthur coldly replied: "He is a soldier's son." True, but he was only five years old! In response to MacArthur's brave stand against an overwhelming enemy, the National Father's Day Committee of Alvin, Texas, named him "Father of the Year" for 1942. Of course, they did not know that he was making his little boy stand with him.

In the end, however, there was no "MacArthur's Last Stand." The general would die without his boots on at the Walter Reed Army Hospital in 1964. Cause of death: old age. The 90,000 soldiers he abandoned would surrender to the Japanese and be sent off to prisoner-of-war camps. They would die of Japanese bayonets on the Bataan Death March and the brutality of their imprisonment. Barely half of them would survive the war. Commanders who desert their troops seldom come to a good end. Napoleon Bonaparte did it twice— in Egypt in 1799 and in Russia in 1813—but eventually even many of his own officers turned on him, and he died a prisoner of the British on a barren island in the South Atlantic. Erwin Rommel did it in North Africa on explicit orders from Adolf Hitler in 1943. But then, the following year Rommel was murdered (forced to commit suicide) on Hitler's orders. MacArthur did it and became a big hero, getting bigger commands and every honor his nation could bestow on a soldier.

Was MacArthur a greater general than Napoleon or Rommel? The context of the three careers varied so much that such a question is pointless. What is indisputable is that MacArthur was superb at the politics of being a general. If he was not always the master of the battlefield, he was master of the back-room maneuvering that got troops to the battlefield. It was MacArthur's public relations and political skills, not his generalship, that made him a hero in those first months after Pearl Harbor. It was those skills, first honed as the U.S. Army's first press relations officer in 1916, that made it desirable for his president finally to order MacArthur to safety. It was those skills that made an inherently cowardly act seem noble and heroic.

A GENERAL SUPREME IN RHETORIC

MacArthur often said that a general's most important technical skill had to be a sophisticated command of the English language. Of all of the U.S. generals of the twentieth century, MacArthur was the one who was supreme in rhetoric. No one could write or deliver a more stirring speech. MacArthur had two advantages here that all of the others lacked: He had a natural facility with words, and he was not inhibited by the truth. Thus, during his ineptly managed and ultimately losing battle to defend the Philippines, MacArthur's most important weapon was the signals equipment, which allowed him to tell both his superiors in Washington and the world at large his version of events. He reported battles that were never fought, victories that were never his—even the death of the enemy commander. These falsehoods cannot be blamed on underlings, because MacArthur wrote, edited, or approved every communiqué that was sent from his headquarters. Because MacArthur seldom gave credit to anyone else in his reports, it seemed as if he were winning the war single-handed.

Both President Franklin D. Roosevelt and General MacArthur knew that the situation in the Philippines had implications far beyond the fate of the besieged U.S. garrison. Ever since December 7, 1941, that "day which will live in infamy," when they attacked Pearl Harbor, the Japanese seemed invincible in their advance across the Asian Pacific. As the only allied leader continuously fighting the Japanese during the first months of the war, MacArthur became a hero of mythic proportions.

Roosevelt did not believe the myth because he knew the truth. He knew that, despite ample warning, MacArthur had allowed the Japanese to destroy his air force—then the largest concentration of U.S. air power in the world—on the ground. Roosevelt knew that when MacArthur retreated to Bataan and Corregidor, he neglected to ensure that there were adequate food supplies—despite the fact that these supplies were readily available. Without air power and without food, both Roosevelt and MacArthur knew it was only a matter of time before the Japanese had complete control of the Philippines. MacArthur was not so much a hero to Roosevelt rather as a "criminal" who would have been subject to removal and court martial under other conditions. However, MacArthur became so enormously popular with the public as the only "aggressive" U.S. general that it was politically impossible to remove him. Better to just let him die in the mess he had done so much to create. Or was it?

EISENHOWER'S RECOMMENDATION

MacArthur's former top aide in the Philippines, Dwight D. Eisenhower, recently made a brigadier general, had been assigned to the Pentagon's War Plans Division specifically because of his expertise on the Philippines and on MacArthur. George C. Marshall, the Chief of Staff of the U.S. Army throughout World War II, knew MacArthur to be a "prima donna." Marshall wanted Eisenhower as an aide specifically because of his perceived skill in handling MacArthur. Eisenhower, who had been MacArthur's chief speech writer for years, would now draft Marshall's messages to his old boss. Marshall knew that what he had to say would be received bitterly and resentfully. Consequently, he wanted them drafted with the utmost sensitivity. Eisenhower, who would later say that he "studied dramatics" for twelve years under MacArthur, was the one officer in the entire Army with the most experience in studying both the Philippines and MacArthur.

On the first day of his new job, December 14, 1941, Eisenhower was asked how the United States should respond to MacArthur's plight. Within a few hours Eisenhower made two recommendations to Marshall. First, he recommended that major reinforcements be denied to MacArthur, because the Philippines garrison would be overrun before any significant aid could reach them. This was contrary to the long-standing plans for defending the Philippines, which called for MacArthur to retreat to Bataan and Corregidor and, quite literally, wait for the U.S. Cavalry to come to the rescue. However, there were now two insurmountable problems with the plan: The Pearl

Harbor attack left the Pacific fleet in such disarray that it would be many months before it could transport a counterattacking force; and MacArthur had neglected to transfer adequate ammunition and especially food to his defensive positions.

The plan never envisioned that much of the Pacific fleet would be sunk by a Japanese surprise attack or that the U.S. commander in the Philippines—whoever he was— would not adequately stockpile food for an anticipated long siege. If the saying is true that amateur strategists talk tactics while professionals talk logistics, then MacArthur acted very much the amateur in the face of the Japanese invasion. And he was on the verge of paying for it with his life. Weeks later, when the Allied garrison finally surrendered to the Japanese, it was not because they were overrun. Their positions, as planned, were impregnable. They surrendered because they had run out of food, ammunition, and medical supplies.

Taking the long view, Eisenhower told Marshall that: "Our base must be in Australia, and we must start at once to expand it and to secure our communications to it." Marshall agreed. Eisenhower's second recommendation was that MacArthur's garrison, including their commander, go down fighting. This was an excruciatingly difficult recommendation to make. Eisenhower had spent almost a decade working directly for MacArthur, the last four years of that time with him in the Philippines. He was intimately acquainted with the officers and men under MacArthur—and with their wives and children. However, there was nothing the United States could do at that time to save them. When the Secretary of War, Henry L. Stimson, was given this appraisal, he wrote in his diary that night: "There are times when men must die."

AUSTRALIA RESCUES MACARTHUR

MacArthur only escaped his fated deadly end in the Philippines because of John Curtin, the Prime Minister of Australia. Curtin wanted to save Australia from the fast-encroaching Japanese. Fearing that the British, who could barely defend themselves against Germany, would not be able to honor their pledge to defend Australia, Curtin looked to the United States. And all he saw was MacArthur.

By the time of Pearl Harbor, all of Australia's best-trained and most experienced divisions were stationed far from home. This became more and more difficult for the Australians to tolerate as the Japanese got closer and closer. According to Curtin biographer Norman E. Lee (1983), Churchill "did not think it would be such a calamity if parts of Australia should fall for a time to the Japanese; they could be won back later when Hitler had been beaten." The Australians saw things differently. The Japanese, those people who make such nice cars today, were in the rape, murder, and pillage business in the early 1940s. The Australians, with the recent example of Hong Kong before them (where the Japanese committed widespread atrocities on the European population), knew what they could expect from these potential conquerors. They were not happy about the prospect of being temporarily lost, temporarily murdered, or temporarily raped.

Consequently, the Australians demanded that all their troops be brought home immediately. However, Churchill could keep the one division of Australian troops in the Middle East if, in exchange, the Australians got their U.S. general. And as far as the Australians were concerned, there was only one U.S. general: Douglas MacArthur. Churchill put the whole matter to Roosevelt. Thus, on February 22, 1942, he ordered MacArthur to Australia in order to help his friend Churchill keep a desperately needed division of Australians fighting the Germans in North Africa.

All these discussions and negotiations over his fate were totally unknown to MacArthur. He was still warding off the Japanese every day, sending his imaginative communiqués, and waiting for the right moment to blow his brains out. When on February 23, he received Roosevelt's order of the previous day to "proceed to Australia where you will assume command of all United States troops," he was in shock. According to Clark Lee (1952), an Associated Press reporter who was on Corregidor at the time, MacArthur suddenly seemed "drained of the confidence he had always shown." Then he tearfully told his wife, "I am American-Army born and bred and accustomed by a lifetime of discipline to the obedience of superior orders. But this order I must disobey." True enough, he briefly toyed with the idea of disobeying the order. It was a kind of family tradition in that he often told the story of how his father won the Medal of Honor in the Civil War by disobeying an order to retreat.

TO RUN OR NOT TO RUN: THAT IS THE QUESTION

With the president's order in hand, MacArthur consulted his staff. Run away or stay and fight to the death? That was the question. Was it better to be a disobedient martyr or to depart for Australia? In one of the most self-serving recommendations in the annals of military history, the staff to a man recommended that he obey the presidential order to abandon his doomed command. This advice was so appreciated that despite no authorization to do so, when he eventually left, MacArthur took seventeen of these wise advisers with him. So, on March 11, MacArthur, his seventeen-man staff, his wife, his son, and his son's nanny departed for Australia.

When MacArthur landed in Australia, he told reporters: "The President of the United States ordered me to break through the Japanese lines . . . for the purpose, as I understand it, of organizing the American offensive against Japan, a primary object of which is the relief of the Philippines. I came through and I shall return." These last three words became one of the most stirring phrases of the entire war. They embodied America's will not to be defeated. They made it easier for MacArthur's abandoned forces to fight on. They helped to sustain the faith of ordinary citizens in all the allied nations that victory was inevitable because of the indomitable will of this one man. The phrase was a master stroke of public relations. Critics rightly contended that "we" would have been far more appropriate for a general representing a republic. However, all criticism was washed away by the public's adulation.

Upon learning of MacArthur's arrival, Curtin was thrilled. He did not know that this was a general who was only recently so depressed that he was contemplating suicide. He did not know that this was a general who had just been defeated by a force less than half the size of his own. He did not know that Roosevelt considered MacArthur's leadership in the Philippines so inept as to be "criminal." He did not know that from a psychological as well as military perspective, MacArthur was damaged goods, that he was physically and mentally

General Douglas MacArthur (center front) fulfilling his promise of "I shall return" by leading the October 20, 1944, U.S. landing on Leyte Island in the Philippines. Wading ashore with him are some of those same staff officers that ran away with him in 1942. MacArthur had wanted to land at a dock and keep his feet dry, but the naval officer serving as beachmaster insisted that the boatload of Army brass walk ashore from knee-deep water. According to William Manchester's biography of MacArthur, *American Caesar* (1978), the general's "scowl" in this picture "which millions of readers interpreted as a reflection of his steely determination, was actually a wrathful glare at the impertinent naval officer."
Source: National Archives and Records Administration.

exhausted after a harrowing journey and months of stress as a commander and creative writer. All Curtin knew was that his country was now in the hands of America's "greatest" general, that America was really and truly going to fight side by side with Australia against the Japanese menace. All Australia was jubilant. Their savior had come. And MacArthur knew that despite the efforts of certain people in Washington to see him crucified, he was just the man to play the role. And to his credit, he did—with the help of his staff

THE NATURE OF STAFF

The question remains: Why did MacArthur take his staff with him? Why did he assign scarce and sorely needed resources to transport these seventeen additional people when he had no authorization to do so? Indeed, the U.S. Army was under explicit orders to fight to the end. Roosevelt considered it intolerable that his "white" soldiers should run before a "yellow" enemy and abandon their "brown" allies. Yet MacArthur, without consulting Washington, simply ordered his staff to run away with him.

The reason becomes obvious once you understand the nature of staff. A staff allows a commander to communicate with, to plan for, and to manage a large force. A smoothly functioning staff takes years to train and to adapt to the ways and wiles of the leader. Without his staff, MacArthur was just an old guy with the rank of general. With his staff, he could function as a general. The presence of his staff would allow him to immediately take control of the new forces he expected to find in Australia. His staff made him efficient. In effect, his staff made him the general he appeared to be to the outside world. And this is true of all leaders of large organizations.

Line and staff are integral. One cannot exist without the other. Line originally referred to the "line of battle," where the soldiers of opposing armies stood before they attacked each other. The "line" was thus always a most dangerous place, but it was also the place where the prime function of the organization was performed: fighting for an army or production for a factory. Line workers today remain those who perform the services for which the organization exists. Police officers who patrol the streets, teachers who fill the classrooms, and postal service employees who deliver the mail are all line workers. Their supervisors are line managers. Much like combat officers, they are the direct link to the ancient Roman centurions. Whether they are fire captains, chiefs of detectives, or elementary school principals, they know, as did those centurions over two millennia ago, that life on the line is a daily struggle.

Help with the struggle, whether with an enemy or over production, is provided by the staff. The job of the staff, whether a single individual or a bureaucratic behemoth, is to assist the line managers in carrying out their duties. Generally, staff officers or units do not have the power of decision, command, or control of operations. Rather, they are usually restricted to making recommendations to executives and line managers. To the extent that staff recommendations carry the weight of demonstrated (via academic degrees or previous accomplishment) expertise, those recommendations are more likely to be adopted.

Staff has its origins with the young assistants of old generals. They were called "staff" in the first place because these young *aides de camp* carried the general's tent posts (or staffs) and ropes. Even today, staff officers are known by the vestigial ropes over their shoulders. Whether military or civilian, public sector or private sector, *staff* seldom refers to a single or even a few individuals. Staff is huge. Staff means personnel, purchasing, legal, medical, and dozens of other support elements of a large organization. To give a sense of just how large staff has become, consider the teeth-to-tail ratio. This term refers to the ratio of direct combat forces (the teeth) to immediate support or staff elements (the tail). For the United States this ratio is at least 10, meaning that for each front-line soldier there are ten others behind the lines providing essential support services.

On February 27, 2002, President George W. Bush told a crowd in Charlotte, North Carolina, that his presidency had been so successful to date because he selected such fine people to work for him. Bush modestly explained: "You are only as good as your team." MacArthur knew that too. He knew that so well that he would stretch his orders to keep his team—his staff—with him. Because if you are only as good as your team, it also means—as MacArthur also knew—that you are not much good without them.

FOR DISCUSSION

Was General MacArthur doing the right thing when he took his staff away with him to safety in Australia, or should he have taken wounded soldiers or U.S. Army nurses instead? How similar was MacArthur's dependence on his staff to the dependence of civilian executives on their parallel staffs?

BIBLIOGRAPHY

Beck, John J. *MacArthur and Wainwright.* Albuquerque, NM: University of New Mexico Press, 1974.

Blair, Clay, Jr. *MacArthur.* London: Futura, 1977.

Churchill, Winston. *The Second World War.* Vol. III. London: Cassell, 1950.

Dale, Ernst, and Lyndall F. Urwick. *Staff in Organization.* New York: McGraw-Hill, 1960.

Eisenhower, Dwight D. *Crusade in Europe.* Garden City, NY: Doubleday, 1948.

Huff, Sidney L. *My Fifteen Years with General MacArthur.* New York: Paperback Library, 1964.

James, D. Clayton. *The Years of MacArthur.* Vol. I. Boston: Houghton Mifflin, 1970.

———. *The Years of MacArthur.* Vol. II. Boston: Houghton Mifflin, 1975.

Karnow, Stanley. *In Our Image.* New York: Random House, 1989.

Keegan, John. *A History of Warfare.* New York: Knopf, 1993.

Lee, Clark, and Richard Henschel. *Douglas MacArthur.* New York: Holt, 1952.

Lee, Norman E. *John Curtin: Saviour of Australia.* Melbourne: Longman Cheshire, 1983.

Lowenheim, Francis L, Harold D. Langley, and Manfred Jonas, eds. *Roosevelt and Churchill: Their Secret Wartime Correspondence.* New York: Dutton, 1975.

MacArthur, Douglas. *Reminiscences.* New York: McGraw-Hill, 1964.

Manchester, William. *American Caesar.* Boston: Little, Brown, 1978.

Perret, Geoffrey. *Old Soldiers Never Die.* London: Andre Deutsch, 1996.

Rasor, Eugene L. *General Douglas MacArthur 1880–1964.* Westport, CT: Greenwood, 1994.

Schaller, M. *Douglas MacArthur: The Far Eastern General.* New York: Oxford University Press, 1989.

Stimson, Henry L., with McGeorge Bundy. *On Active Service in Peace and War.* New York: Hippocrene Books, 1948.

Whitney, Courtney. *MacArthur: His Rendezvous with History.* New York: Knopf, 1955.

Willoughby, Charles A., and John Chamberlain. *MacArthur.* London: Heinemann, 1956.

CHAPTER TWENTY-ONE

Why Advancement in Public Administration Has Always Been an Essay Contest
PROOFS FROM THE PRESIDENCY AND THE BUREAUCRACY

PREVIEW

In 1938, a teen-aged Henry Kissinger fled Nazi Germany with his family and arrived in the United States. This Jewish refugee then proceeded to write his way to the top of his new country's political and social elite. However critical one may be about the policies he espoused while he was managing U.S. foreign affairs in the administrations of Richard M. Nixon and Gerald R. Ford, it cannot be denied that he is the living embodiment of the American dream, of advancement through merit and the ability to write one's way up into high office no matter how low one started.

The contention of this chapter is that real life in the world of public policy and administration is an essay contest. Those who win very often do so by writing their way to bureaucratic or policy-making success. Kissinger not only won, he had to play the game in a foreign language. He did not learn English until high school and never lost his trademark German accent. The turning point of his youth was 1943. In that year, he became a U.S. citizen and was drafted into the U.S. Army. The army was the making of him.

It was while he was serving in Germany as a translator in military intelligence and rising to the rank of sergeant that he had his "Alexander Hamilton moment." Hamilton, as a young man on the Caribbean island of Nevis, so impressed the men he worked for that they gratuitously arranged for him to leave the island and attend Kings College (now Columbia University) just in time to join the American Revolution and earn his place on the $10 bill. In a parallel development, Kissinger so impressed the Army officers he worked for that they saw to it that, upon being discharged from service in 1946, he entered Harvard University as an undergraduate. This was a far more difficult proposition then than now, because Harvard was at that time swamped with applications from returning servicemen and, significantly, it had a quota on the number of Jews it would admit. Nevertheless, for Kissinger the Army led directly to Harvard, because his highly influential and academically connected organizational superiors were so taken with his native brilliance, engaging personality, and ability to write—in both German and English. Once at Harvard University, he never left until he left for the White House. After earning his Ph.D. in 1954, he was invited to join the faculty.

PROMINENCE THROUGH WRITING

Henry Kissinger first came to national prominence with the publication of a reworked version of his doctoral dissertation, *A World Restored* (1957), which dealt with the aftermath of the Napoleonic Wars and the impact of revolutionary change on the nineteenth-century international order. As an ambitious young professor, he wrote countless articles, conference papers, and research reports that established him as a "comer" in foreign policy analysis. Then he literally came out as one of the world's leading strategic analysts with two landmark books: *Nuclear Weapons and Foreign Policy* (1957), in which he seemed to embrace the possibility of limited nuclear war; and *The Necessity for Choice* (1960), in which he backed away from some of his ideas on the tactical use of nuclear weapons and argued, like many other nuclear strategists of the period, for more emphasis on conventional forces, especially in Europe.

Kissinger's main concern as a strategist was with devising ways to make U.S. Cold War policies more effective. Even as an academic, he saw his role less as an analyst and more as a policy adviser. His writing led to more opportunities to organize conferences, where he met and impressed increasing numbers of the members of the foreign policy establishment. By 1968 he was the national security advisor to Governor Nelson Rockefeller of New York, Richard Nixon's chief rival for the Republican Party's presidential nomination that year. After Nixon won both the nomination and the election, Rockefeller strongly recommended Kissinger to Nixon.

Richard Nixon, already familiar with Kissinger's ample writings, invited him to serve as the next National Security Adviser. Finally, Kissinger would be able to move away from just writing about foreign and defense policies; he would be able to help make them from his pivotal position in the White House. From 1969 to 1973, Kissinger, as National Security Advisor, eclipsed Secretary of State William Rogers; eventually, in 1973, also replacing him as Secretary of State. He also presided over major changes in U.S. foreign policy, including the disengagement from Vietnam, the opening to China, and the development of détente with the Soviet Union. His style was one of secret diplomacy based on a shrewd appreciation for power considerations. Some of his most effective policies were in the Middle East, where he skillfully disengaged Egypt from its close relationship with the Soviet Union and helped facilitate the armistices between Israel and its neighbors that ended the 1973 Yom Kippur War. Because Nixon was weakened by the Watergate scandal during the last two years of his presidency, and his successor, Gerald Ford, deferred to his more experienced Secretary of State, Kissinger dominated U.S. foreign and security policy as no Secretary of State had ever done before.

Although Ph.D.s are quite common among the Washington elite, Kissinger was one who was almost always "Doctor" Kissinger. Perhaps it was the accent? It so reminded people of the archetypal German professor, the avuncular mentor so beloved in early twentieth-century operettas, before Germany went bad and later went humble.

The lesson here is that Dr. Kissinger got his doctorate in the first place because he could write and then rose to be the physician of U.S. foreign policy because he could write prescriptions better than anyone else close enough to the powerful to be recognized and appointed. Why him? You might as well ask why someone becomes a movie star when the competition is so vast and so many others have equal talent. Kissinger auditioned for his part with his writings. Personality counts. Looks count. However, in the world of high-level policy making, your writings—whether books, articles, consulting reports, or internal memoranda—get you to the audition. Then it is your turn to be an actor.

THE OLDEN DAYS

In days of yore, leaders were also doers. Thus the great leaders of the past led from the front. From ancient times until the last few hundred years, leaders such as Alexander the Great, Julius Caesar, Charlemagne, and even George Washington often led from the front, risking their own lives right alongside those of their lowest-ranking subordinates. However, as firearms became more accurate during the era of the American and French revolutions, leaders learned to stay behind the front lines, where they could wield a weapon for more deadly than any rifle: the pen. Yes, both Washington and Napoleon did their fair share of front-line leadership, risking their lives sword in hand; but in the end, they were far more effective with pens than with swords.

With the vast expansion of theaters of war and sizes of armies, victory would go to the great organizers, coordinators, and, above all, logisticians. Both Washington and Napoleon left a vast correspondence on logistics matters. Why? Because it is effective logistics, the adequate provision of food and all the other accoutrements of war, that wins battles in the end. Armies must eat before they can fight. This is why, Napoleon so famously said that "an army marches on its stomach." This is why, it was said then as well as now that amateur soldiers talk about strategy while professionals talk about logistics. And logistics is an administrative enterprise requiring the massive writing of memoranda, letters, orders, and contracts.

It is comparatively easy to find brave soldiers who will risk their lives in battle, but these battles can only be won by officers who can draw up and implement plans of action. They must be able to write clearly and succinctly under the pressure of time as well as the pressure of battle. There is much wisdom in the military maxim that an order than can be misunderstood will be misunderstood. It is not the bravest general who wins modern battles, but the general who above all else can write (or dictate) unambiguous orders.

A famous example will illustrate this. During the U.S. Civil War, Union and Confederate forces suffered more than 23,000 casualties during a two-day battle near Shiloh in central Tennessee along the Tennessee River. The Union Commander, General Ulysses S. Grant, was surprised by Confederate forces and suffered devastating losses on the first day. With his back to the river, everybody thought that Grant would withdraw his remaining forces on river boats and leave the field to the enemy, a clear defeat. Instead, Grant—with the dead piled up and the wounded moaning about him—dictated and wrote his way to victory.

Under tremendous pressure in a time of great desperation, he created the clearest prose: orders for the bringing up of more troops by river boats, orders for the placement of troops before the dawn, and orders for how his subordinate generals would proceed with the battle at first light. All major biographies of Grant recall this famous incident: As Grant sat that night under a tree in a pouring rain, General William T. Sherman walked over and said, "Well, Grant, we've had the devil's own day, haven't we?" Grant responded by puffing on his cigar and agreeing: "Yes. Lick 'em tomorrow, though." And he did.

To the astonishment of many, Grant's plan worked. The rebels were forced back, lost ground was retaken, and Grant established his reputation as a general who could win a major engagement. Had he withdrawn after the first day of battle, he surely never would have been given another major command. And it is unlikely that his career would have ended with two terms in the White House. What made all the difference—what differentiated Grant from so many other brave officers—was his ability to give and write orders under the most unimaginable pressure.

Grant's story of a career-making achievement obtained because of the ability to write is not unique. The one great example from the ancient world in which writing made a major career difference was Julius Caesar's *The Gallic Wars,* his personal propaganda about his exploits in what is now France, which made him a hero to many of the people of Rome. However, the real era of the writer as hero in both the military and civilian contexts began with the revolutionary era of the late eighteenth century, when far-flung operations in government, business, and the military had to be managed in writing. People were increasingly becoming winners in government, business, or on the battlefield because of their ability to write. This is why, the core contention of this chapter is that real life in the organizations of the modern age, since the age of revolution, is an essay contest. And the winners of this contest are rewarded with political appointments, prestige, and high office—sometimes even the presidency itself.

THE ADAMS–JEFFERSON DIALOGUE

There is a famous dialogue from the start of this age that is a perfect example of our point. American Revolutionary leader John Adams (later to be president) recounted in a July 1776 letter (printed in Colbert [1997]) how it was that Thomas Jefferson and not himself came to write the Declaration of Independence:

> The committee met, discussed the subject, and then appointed Mr. Jefferson and me to make the draught, I suppose because we were the two first on the list.
> The sub-committee met. Jefferson proposed to me to make the draught. I said, "I will not."

"You should do it," he said.

"Oh! No."

"Why will you not? You ought to do it."

"I will not."

"Why?"

"Reasons enough," I said.

"What can be your reasons?"

"Reason first—You are a Virginian, and a Virginian ought to appear at the head of this business. Reason second—I am obnoxious, suspected, and unpopular. You are very much otherwise. Reason third—You can write ten times better than I can."

"Well," said Jefferson, "if you are decided, I will do as well as I can."

Yes, Adams was accurate in describing himself as "obnoxious" and "unpopular." The Continental Congress rapidly reached consensus on this. However, he was wrong to say that Jefferson could write "ten times better than" he could. The political fact of the matter is that the proposed declaration of independence had to come from someone representing a colony outside of New England. Adams, an extraordinarily skillful scribbler, was demurring to and flattering Jefferson because he wanted a Virginian to do the drafting, the better to consolidate support for the cause of independence. This is the same reasoning that led Adams to nominate George Washington to be the commander-in-chief of the Continental Army. Nevertheless, Jefferson made the most of this opportunity with a draft that the Continental Congress only partially mauled.

This was certainly a jump-start to the shy 33-year-old Jefferson's career. For the rest of his life and into the pages of U.S. history, he would always be the one who wrote the Declaration of Independence—even though he essentially produced a first draft that was significantly revised by others. Search into the career of any major figure in a leadership position, and you will probably find that it was jump-started by an ability to write well.

WOODROW WILSON YEARNS

The same thing happened just over a hundred years later to another well-known future president. In 1885, Woodrow Wilson, having not yet completed his doctoral program at Johns Hopkins University and being desperately poor as well as recently married, began his teaching career at the newly founded Bryn Mawr College for Women. According to Ray Stannard Baker's eight-volume biography of Wilson (1927), he would have preferred a better appointment. He would have preferred to teach men. But, as he wrote his future wife, "beggars cannot be choosers." In the following year, he returned briefly to Johns Hopkins to pass the final examinations for his Ph.D. and wrote to his wife, "Hurrah—a thousand times hurrah—I'm through I'm through—the degree is actually secured! Oh, the relief of it!"

Young Woodrow was not happy with his situation at Bryn Mawr. His salary was barely adequate for a growing family. Reportedly a lecturer of genius, he resented having to teach women. As he told an associate, such an activity "relaxes one's mental muscle." In 1887, Baker reports, he summed up his life by saying, "Thirty-one years old and nothing done!" In retrospect, Wilson seems to have been like many another ambitious academic seemingly stuck in a post that did not do justice to talent. And he chose as the way out the now traditional road to high academic fame, fortune, and position: He wrote and published and was saved!

During this time, he worked on several textbooks (eventually completed, but now long forgotten); wrote fiction under a pen name (it was all rejected); and wrote a few political essays, one of which remains his most enduring contribution as a political scientist.

In June 1887, the fledgling *Political Science Quarterly* published Wilson's article, "The Study of Administration." It attracted slight notice at the time, but over the years it has become a distinguished and much-honored essay—so much so that it is now customary to trace the origins of the academic discipline of public administration to it.

And what happened to the young Wilson, who, Baker says, wrote plaintively in 1888, "I have for a long time been hungry for a class of men"? Shortly thereafter, he took up an appointment at Wesleyan University in Connecticut. From there he went to Princeton, made good, and became president of that university; then governor of New Jersey. In later life, he found a job in Washington—and all because he could write. Not entirely, of course. Writing alone can't do it, but, as for Kissinger, the writing got him the audition.

WINNING WITH A GHOST

Sometimes you can win the essay contest of life without doing much writing at all. Just hire a ghost writer to produce a draft, which you can edit lightly and make your own. This tactic has a long tradition. Alexander Hamilton, first as an *aide de camp* and then as Secretary of the Treasury, wrote many of the drafts of General and then President George Washington's letters and speeches. Secretary of State John Quincy Adams wrote the Monroe Doctrine (declaring the Americas free of future European colonization) that President James Monroe incorporated into his 1823 message to Congress. This was no secret, and it solidified Adams's credentials as a presidential candidate the following year. He won.

Then there is the case of a lightweight senator who wanted to appear to be an intellectual heavyweight in preparation for a presidential bid. In the early 1950s, a young senator from Massachusetts, John F. Kennedy, knew he wanted to run for president but also knew that he had no substantial record of accomplishment on which to run. So he and his father, Joseph P. Kennedy, one of the richest men in the country, arranged for young John to win the prestigious Pulitzer Prize for biography. That'll show them!

First they found a talented staffer (Theodore Sorensen) to ghost-write most of the book, *Profiles in Courage* (1955), a collection of essays on eight senators who behaved courageously at the risk of their political careers. In *Counselor,* a memoir Sorensen wrote more than half a century later, he admitted that he wrote "a first draft of most chapters" in *Profiles in Courage.* (Kennedy then revised the chapters himself.) Second, the Kennedys arranged for—paid for—significant purchases of the book to quickly make it an acknowledged best-seller. Then the elder Kennedy used his considerable influence on the Pulitzer Prize committee to effectively buy his son the prize. Result: instant gravitas for an otherwise insignificant junior senator.

Could the Pulitzer Prize really be bought? Not for crass cash, but in that period it could be influenced by those with massive amounts of money or elevated social connections. There is at least one heavily documented parallel case at roughly the same time when who got the prize was dictated by an outsider. In his autobiography, *The World Is My Home,* novelist James A. Michener (1907–1997) tells the story of how he won the 1948 Pulitzer Prize for Fiction. Until 1948 there was only the Pulitzer Prize for the Novel. Michener's book, *Tales of the South Pacific,* did not qualify because it was a collection of short stories. The book had sold a respectable few thousand copies and Michener, who had recently returned from wartime Navy service, was resigned to resuming his career as a textbook editor in New York. However, Alice Roosevelt Longworth (1884–1980) had read the collection of the loves and exploits of U.S. servicemen in World War II Polynesia, and she was determined that it win the Pulitzer Prize. She was not on the selection committee, but as the eldest daughter of President Theodore Roosevelt, the cousin of President Franklin Roosevelt, and the wife of a Speaker of the House, she was the uncrowned queen of Washington society for sixty years. She was famous for her biting wit and was not a woman to cross. And she would not take no for an answer when her friends on the Pulitzer committee told her they could not award Michener the prize for the novel because it was not a novel. So she demanded they change the rules. And they did. Thus in 1948 there was no prize for the novel; the category was abolished. And Michener received the first Pulitzer Prize for Fiction, thanks to a then-secret patron who just loved the book. The book became famous enough to be adapted into a Broadway musical, *South Pacific.* The point here is that if a stranger could influence the award for a merely deserving author, then Kennedy senior could also influence the award for, in his own eyes, an even more deserving son.

With his now award-winning best-seller in hand, John F. Kennedy was considered a serious candidate for vice president at the 1956 Democratic National Convention. Although he lost his bid for the nomination and his party lost the subsequent presidential election, the concomitant favorable publicity about this handsome prize-winning war hero senator laid the foundation for his successful presidential campaign four years later in 1960.

Sometimes having the credential (a best-seller, a Pulitzer Prize, etc.) as a fine writer is just as good as being one—especially if you have a rich father who will buy you a literary reputation. Unfortunately for Kennedy, word leaked out about his ghost, and a prominent Washington columnist (Drew Pearson) asserted that the senator had not written his prize-winning book—at least not by himself. As soon as the senior Kennedy heard of this, he threatened to sue for $50 million unless an immediate retraction was forthcoming. He got his retraction and chilled any future allegations for decades. And to prevent other outbursts of the truth, Senator Kennedy effectively bought Sorensen's silence. Concerned that Sorensen might be put out by not getting any credit for a Pulitzer Prize–winning book or by not getting any royalties for a major best-seller, Kennedy, according to Sorensen, "unexpectedly and generously offered, and I happily accepted, a sum to be spread over several years, that I regarded as more than fair." The financial terms were formalized by a legally binding agreement. Sorensen did not acknowledge this until his 2008 memoir.

Not every president has had a reputation as a fine writer, either real or "store-bought." Nowadays, however, all presidential candidates make the effort to publish a book or two. And unlike in Kennedy's time, they don't even make the pretense that they wrote it themselves. Indeed, today it is fashionable to list the person who wrote the book for you as your co-author. Of course, none of these books has won the Pulitzer Prize since Kennedy's. Of course, no candidate since Kennedy has had a father as rich as his was.

WRITING AS PERSONAL ADVERTISING

People in bureaucratic careers tend to rise or fall on how well they can write. In a game of shuffling paper, the person whose memorandum ends up on top wins. It is a legendary truism in the U.S. State Department that nobody who is good writes his or her own memos. If you are considered talented enough, you will be asked to write your boss's memos. Then, because you are too busy writing the boss's memos, you find a younger talent to write yours. When your boss gets that big promotion, you go along for the ride with your own promotion. And, of course, you bring along the person who has been writing for you.

This essential story of a successful writing opportunity leading to bigger things in one's career is common. For example, when General Douglas MacArthur was head of the U.S. Army in the 1930s, a young major wrote the general's reports and speeches. Co-workers knew that Dwight D. Eisenhower was an officer who was going places, because he could write. When President-elect Ronald Reagan was seeking cabinet members in 1980, he read an article by Jeanne Kirkpatrick, on the basis of which she got an audition and was made ambassador to the United Nations.

This tradition of writing to advertise your intellectual wares to the powers that be is not new. Many of those op-ed articles in the *Washington Post*, the *New York Times*, and the *Wall Street Journal* on pressing public issues are written by those with a pressing need to get into the policy-making arena as a new assistant secretary of this or that. The man who pioneered this tactic of writing to draw attention to one's administrative and/or policy skills lived during the Italian Renaissance; he was Niccolo Machiavelli (1469–1527), the most quoted, most read, most interpreted, and most misunderstood public policy advisor who ever lived. By the time William Shakespeare wrote *Richard III* in 1592, Shakespeare could assume that his audience would be familiar with Machiavelli's diabolical reputation. Thus Shakespeare could have his title character introduce himself as being so evil that he could "set the murtherous Machevil to school." Similar references to Machiavelli as the personification of evil doings abound in the plays and literature of Shakespeare's time and have continued ever since.

The real Machiavelli, however, was an exemplar as a public administrator and policy analyst. Born into a family of ancient nobility but persistent impoverishment, he was educated well enough to become a civil servant, sometime ambassador, for Florence beginning in 1498. He was an honest, truthful, and competent employee. However, his was a patronage position (there being no merit system then), and he lost his job and nearly his life with a shift in the political winds of 1512. Thereafter, he eked out a living on a meager farm left to him by his father.

Machiavelli's greatest desire was to go back to work for his beloved Florence, now in the control of the Medici family. So like many a high-level political appointee out of power, he wrote a book (indeed, several) to demonstrate his usefulness to potential employers. In his most famous private letter (dated December 10, 1513), quoted by biographer Giuseppe Prezzolini (1967), he expresses hope that "if it [his book, *The Prince*] were read they [the Medici] would see that for . . . fifteen years I have been studying the art of the state." He even offers proof of his honesty as a past and potential employee: "[A]s a witness to my honesty and goodness I have my poverty."

Because Machiavelli, despite constant efforts, never did get the government job he so coveted, he had the time, after hard days working the fields on his farm, to work at night on the most enduring books of political philosophy produced by the Italian Renaissance. *The Prince* (1532) and *The Discourses* (1531) were important political and military analyses that led to the use of the term *Machiavellianism* to refer to cunning, cynical, and ruthless behavior based on the notion of the end justifying the use of almost any means.

What Machiavelli actually noted in *The Prince* was that a ruler would be judged by results: "So let a prince set about the task of conquering and maintaining his state; his methods will always be judged honorable and universally praised." Machiavelli, as one of the first policy advisers, developed a set of prescriptions and proscriptions for his prince that were designed to ensure that the prince would flourish politically. His introduction summarizes his methodology: "I have long pondered and scrutinized the actions of the great, and now I offer the results . . . within the compass of a small volume."

Alas, Machiavelli's books failed in their initial purpose to get him into a job and out of poverty. Although his manuscripts circulated privately among his friends, *The Prince* was not published until five years after his death. Only then did it become a sensation. Posthumously, however, Machiavelli has been a great success.

REWARDING GRACEFUL PROSE

Oral presentation skills are also essential for career advancement. Because more people can speak than write effectively, writing is more decisive in determining whose ideas get advanced. All organizations place great value on the person who can write succinctly in times of stress. That is the person who will be turned to when an important opportunity comes up. This is why, public administration is an essay contest: because your writing reputation creates your administrative persona of winner or loser. According to a U.S. Department of State report, the Foreign Service "has prized drafting ability above almost all other skills. We emphasize this skill in recruitment and reward it generously in our promotion system. The prize jobs in the service are the reporting jobs." Donald P. Warwick, in his analysis of the State Department's bureaucracy, found that "following the classic model of the gentleman generalist, the Foreign Service exalts graceful prose and the well-turned phrase." Other agencies with fewer "gentlemen" are equally anxious to reward "graceful prose."

If you examine the personal histories of the best-known and most influential members of the George W. Bush administration—Vice President Richard Cheney, Secretary of State Condoleezza Rice, and Secretary of Defense Robert Gates—you will find that when they were lowly bureaucrats, they each jump-started their careers because of their ability to write. Of course, their boss, President Bush, was widely known not to be one to whom "graceful prose" came naturally, but he overcame that handicap through the combination of leadership skills and by being born into a political dynasty of great wealth and influence. Unless you are similarly well born, you have no choice but to enter the essay contest to advance in a public administration career.

As for the Obama administration, just look at the top. Senator Barack Obama had an even more modest legislative record than Senator John F. Kennedy. So he took a page from Kennedy's book and wrote himself some gravitas. Unlike Kennedy, Obama had to do all the work himself. That is one problem with starting out poor in life: You lack a readily available ghost writer. Nevertheless, Obama soon had millions from his book sales. Poor no more.

With two best-selling books (one a memoir and the other a romp for policy wonks), Barack Obama was suddenly a serious contender for the Democratic nomination for president. Obama could not only write books, he could write speeches, too— and deliver them in a compelling fashion. That is a winning combination. That attracts campaign donations and volunteers. One who volunteered was Theodore Sorensen, the same man who about sixty years earlier had "helped" Kennedy write *Profiles in Courage* and because of that was able to help him write his inaugural address ("Ask not what your country can do for you. . . ."). Now Kennedy's ghost was ghosting for Obama. How sweet! Not only had the Kennedy torch been passed, so had the ghost. Sorensen, the old ghost, was a young lawyer from Nebraska who, through his own writing, under his own name or not, won more wealth and esteem than he had ever dreamed of as a boy. He saw a kindred soul in Obama—a fellow contestant in the essay contest of life. And a winner, too.

FOR DISCUSSION

Can you name other prominent leaders in public policy and administration whose careers took off because of their ability to write the kind of graceful prose that attracted positive attention? What can you do in your own career to ensure that your writing is recognized and helps to advance you toward your long-term aspirations?

BIBLIOGRAPHY

Baker, Ray Stannard. *Woodrow Wilson, Life and Letters: Youth 1856–1890,* Garden City, New York: Doubleday, 1927.

Colbert, David. *Eyewitness to America.* New York: Pantheon, 1997.

Cordery, Stacy A. *Alice: Alice Roosevelt Longworth, from White House Princess to Washington Power Broker.* New York: Viking, 2007.

Dallek, Robert. *Nixon and Kissinger: Partners in Power.* New York: HarperCollins, 2007.

Grant, Ulysses S. *Memoirs and Selected Letters.* New York: Library of America, 1990.

Hitchens, Christopher. *The Trial of Henry Kissinger.* New York: Verso, 2002.

Isaacson, Walter. *Kissinger: A Biography.* New York: Simon & Schuster, 2005.

Martin, Daniel W. "The Fading Legacy of Woodrow Wilson." *Public Administration Review* 48 (March–April 1988).

Michener, James A. *The World Is My Home.* New York: Random House, 1992.

Obama, Barack. *Dreams from My Father.* New York: Crown, 1995.

———. *The Audacity of Hope.* New York: Crown, 2006.

Prezzolini, Giuseppe. *Machiavelli.* New York: Farrar, Straus & Giroux, 1967.

———. *Niccolo Machiavelli, The Florentine.* London: Putnam, 1928.

Smith, Jean Edward. *Grant.* New York: Simon & Schuster, 2001.

Suri, Jeremi. *Henry Kissinger and the American Century.* Cambridge, MA: Belknap, 2009.

Sorensen, Theodore. *Counselor: A Life at the Edge of History.* New York: HarperCollins, 2008.

U.S. Department of State. *Diplomacy for the 70s.* Washington, DC: U.S. Department of State, 1970.

Van Riper, Paul. "The American Administrative State: Wilson and the Founders—An Unorthodox View." *Public Administration Review 43* (November–December 1983).

Warwick, Donald P. *A Theory of Public Bureaucracy: Politics, Personality, and Organization in the State Department.* Cambridge, MA: Harvard University Press, 1975.

Wilson, Woodrow. "The Study of Administration." *Political Science Quarterly* 2 (June 1887); reprinted 50 (December 1941).

CHAPTER TWENTY-TWO

The Case for Mentoring Junior Managers with Executive Potential

HOW GENERAL FOX CONNER SET A YOUNG DWIGHT D. EISENHOWER ON THE PATH TO THE PRESIDENCY

PREVIEW

Dwight David ("Ike") Eisenhower (1890–1969) was elected president of the United States in 1952 and reelected in 1956. He initially earned the confidence of his fellow citizens the same way George Washington, Andrew Jackson, and Ulysses S. Grant did: by being a victorious general. Eisenhower commanded all U.S. and Allied forces in Western Europe and the Mediterranean region during World War II. This case tells the story of how a now-obscure mentor taught Eisenhower what he needed to know to advance as a career military officer and eventually to the presidency. Both historians and Eisenhower himself agree that without this mentor's efforts at a critical point in Eisenhower's early career, D Day would have had a different commander and Eisenhower would not now be admired as one of the better presidents of the United States.

A MEMORABLE DINNER

Dinners have often been pivotal events in the history of the world. One immediately thinks of the Last Supper that Jesus shared with his twelve apostles as described in the *New Testament*. In ancient Egypt, Cleopatra had a famous dinner with Mark Anthony that led to her being pregnant with twins and his instigating a civil war in the Roman Empire. Then there was the 1790 meal over which Alexander Hamilton and Thomas Jefferson agreed that the new national government of the United States would assume the revolutionary war debts of the states in exchange for moving the capitol from New York to a swamp on the Maryland side of the Potomac River–later to be called Washington, D.C. Our present concern, however, is with a September 1920 meal at Fort Mead, Maryland, where three U.S. Army officers unknowingly started Dwight D. Eisenhower on the path to becoming president of the United States.

The host for this gastronomical event was Major George S. Patton, Jr., who was later to win fame during World War II as the U.S. tank commander par excellence. Because Patton was personally rich, snobbish, and an ambitious social climber with an equally rich, snobbish, and social climbing wife, Beatrice, he frequently hosted dinners that might advance his military career or social aspirations. On this day the guest of honor was Brigadier General Fox Conner. Two years earlier, Conner had been the chief of operations for the U.S. Army in France. This meant that he was in charge of the planning for all the major U.S. military actions of World War I. Other generals may have bravely led their man in battle; but Conner told those generals when, where, and whom to fight. He was widely considered to be the "brains" of the U.S. Army in France. So Conner was a highly desirable dinner guest for a middling officer of burning ambition.

At Fort Mead, Majors Patton and Eisenhower were the two senior officers among those who were then part of the experimental U.S. tank corps. Because they were both close friends and neighbors, Major and Mrs. Eisenhower were also invited to dinner with Conner. In those days, dinner was what we now call lunch; so afterwards there was plenty of daylight and time for the two younger officers to show Conner their tanks and discuss how these mechanical beasts might best be employed in battle.

Conner knew Patton from France. This was his first opportunity to meet Eisenhower, and he was impressed. The peacetime U.S. Army between the world wars was not overburdened with brilliant officers. In that afternoon of talking about and playing with tanks, Conner saw that Eisenhower, who was stuck in stateside training assignments throughout World War I and thus, unlike Patton, never saw combat, had incredible potential as an officer. So, toward the end of 1921, when Conner was given a new assignment to command a brigade of troops in the Panama Canal Zone, he arranged for Eisenhower to join him as his executive officer.

THE MENTOR STEPS UP

This took some doing and illustrates just how much trouble Conner was willing to go to for Eisenhower's sake. Eisenhower's commanding officer at Camp Meade was not pleased at the prospect of losing his services—especially as a very successful part-time football coach. So when Eisenhower, at Conner's request, sent his application for transfer to the War Department, it was rejected. Upon learning this, Conner went to the top, to General John J. Pershing, then the Army Chief of Staff, and had Eisenhower's transfer to Panama approved effective January 1922. Thus began a pattern that would continue for the next two decades: Some of the most senior, most respected, and most competent officers in the U.S. Army would take an interest in and advance Eisenhower's career. This was not because of his political or family connections (as it certainly was the case with Douglas MacArthur) but because of the general recognition of his competence and potential. Conner felt strongly that if he had Eisenhower, a highly talented but relatively uneducated officer, under his wing for a few years, he could turn him into one of the finest officers in any army.

The questions now to be asked are these: (1) What did Conner do for Eisenhower? (2) How did he do it? (3) Why did he do it? And finally, (4) What difference did it make?

What Conner did for Eisenhower was to consciously decide to become his mentor and a counselor on learning the skills of high command and career advancement. Now it has always been the obligation of senior officers to mentor their juniors for the good of the organization. Indeed, mentoring as a function is as old as humanity. Did not old Merlin the Wizard mentor the young King Arthur? Have not rulers always mentored their sons and successors? Have not mothers of the premodern age traditionally mentored their daughters on being good wives and household managers? And do not modern mothers use their mentoring skills to guide their daughters into graduate programs in law, medicine, and public administration?

THE ORIGINS OF MENTORING

The word *mentoring* itself predates English, coming from ancient Greek. When Odysseus (or Ulysses) in Homer's *Odyssey* left home for the war in Troy, he put his home and family in the care of a trusted friend, Mentor. When things got rough at home for Odysseus's family, Athena, the goddess of wisdom, assumed the shape of Mentor and provided Telemachus, the son of Odysseus, with some very helpful advice about how to deal with the problems of his most unusual adolescence.

Although mentoring relationships have always existed, there was not much analysis of them as an organizational phenomenon until the advent of the modern women's movement that began in the late 1960s. Organizational analysts, concerned with the limitations on the careers of women, noticed that many successful men had their careers advanced by informal mentoring: An experienced worker or manager would take under his wing, so to speak, a more junior member of the organization. Then, through the processes of friendship and informal interaction (lunches, golf dates, after hours drinks, etc.), the mentor would share with the mentee the "tricks of the trade" by which he could eventually advance in his career.

The key here is that mentoring has traditionally been a spontaneous process. Friendship cannot be ordered. You cannot be told to "take pleasure" in someone's company. Senior people can be directed to train their juniors, but mentoring, which may include training for specific tasks, goes far beyond training to become a unique variant of management development. This can truly happen only when there is an element of genuine affection involved, when the mentor finds joy in the company of a gifted apprentice. It is the same kind of joy—love, if you will—that a teacher finds with the best students. All teachers, including college professors, know that instructing—mentoring—eager and capable students is the greatest joy of their professional life.

This is what Conner saw in Eisenhower: an eager, capable, personable, and determined young officer who could be developed into one of the country's great captains. That one dinner at Patton's home was all Conner needed to grasp Eisenhower's potential.

Decades later, after Eisenhower became president, historians started looking at how this obscure lieutenant colonel in 1941 could rise to full (four-star) general by 1943 and command of all the Allied forces in World War II's European Theater of Operations. The trail—the answer as to how—led back to Eisenhower's duty with Conner in the 1920s. This is why, later historians have referred to Conner as "the man who made Eisenhower."

"Made" in this context means mentored. So how was the making—the mentoring—undertaken? There was extraordinary talent on both sides. First, the mentor, Conner, was widely considered the most brilliant officer in the army. After all, John J. Pershing, the commanding general of the U.S. Army in World War I France, trusted Conner enough to make him his chief of operations, effectively his second in command. In 1929 Conner would be Pershing's choice for Army Chief of Staff. (Conner lost out to Douglas MacArthur, but it was close.) Conner was not only brilliant, he was intellectually inclined. A natural student and teacher of military history, strategy, and tactics, he traveled to his new assignment in Panama with a large professional library. Knowing that the duties of a U.S. general in 1920s Panama were minimal, he also knew that he needed a student to make his tour of duty enjoyable, a protégé, someone who would share his zeal for military history and for analyzing campaigns of the past and those he saw coming in the future.

Second, comes the mentee. Eisenhower was no intellectual. He graduated from West Point in 1915 a respectable 61st in a class of 164. However, Eisenhower excelled at sports, horsemanship, and field exercises. Although he was obviously bright, he was not a serious student; indeed, he disdained military history as it was then taught at West Point as a turgid mush of names and dates. Eisenhower found rote memorization to be a dull drill when the course lacked strategic focus, tactical analysis, and historical perspective.

Nevertheless, Eisenhower was an inherently gifted writer, engaging at oral presentations and obviously ambitious for himself and his service. There was also that wide Eisenhower smile, which charmed Conner just as it would eventually charm the nation's electorate. As the afternoon grew to evening on that fateful day in 1920, Eisenhower explained to Conner how tanks should be used in the next war: not as portable artillery for the infantry, but as armored columns that would break through enemy lines and disrupt his rear. Conner saw that there were depths to Eisenhower beyond the grin, which could be delved into for the Army's benefit. For example, though neither of them knew it at the time, Eisenhower had just laid out for Conner the very *Blitzkrieg* tactics that the Germans would use twenty years later to achieve their initial victories in World War II. This young officer had insight.

However, Eisenhower's insights on tank warfare were not appreciated by most of his superiors in the Regular Army. In 1920 he published "A Tank Discussion" in *Infantry Journal*. Then he drafted another article on tank doctrine, "Tanks with Infantry," offering new ways to employ tanks in battle. According to Mark Perry (2007), "Eisenhower's arguments were widely viewed as heretical. His beliefs did not pay proper obeisance to current Army doctrine, a nearly liturgical faith in massed infantry attacks." His unpublished draft aroused so much antagonism that he was literally called before the Chief of Infantry and, as he wrote more than fifty years later in *At Ease* (1967),

"I was told that my ideas were not only wrong but dangerous and that henceforth I would keep them to myself. Particularly, I was not to publish anything incompatible with solid infantry doctrine. If I did, I would be hauled before a court-martial." His fellow tank enthusiast, George S. Patton, Jr., found himself in similar trouble for the same offense of publishing an article that challenged current doctrines. Both determined to lay low intellectually, believing that their time would eventually come and their ideas would certainly prevail.

A MENTOR IN ACTION

Eisenhower, upon reporting for duty in Panama, was surprised to find that his new job came with homework. A pattern soon developed. Conner would loan Eisenhower a book from his extensive library and expect an oral critique shortly afterwards. Almost every day they would ride out on horseback to inspect their troops and plan for a defense should an enemy attack. However, this did not take long, and much of the day was devoted to an analysis of the previous evening's reading. Conner did not start with a formal course of instruction. He knew that Eisenhower's time at West Point had prejudiced him against military history, so Conner started by loaning him novels set in a military context such as the Napoleonic Wars. Evenings in the Panama of the 1920s left much time for reading. As they discussed the historical events described in the novels, Conner recommended (and provided copies of) real histories of those times. Thus Eisenhower was gradually seduced through historical fiction into becoming a real student of military history.

Eisenhower was gradually given a comprehensive education in military history and its classical writers. And his tutor, Conner, acknowledged as one of his nation's most experienced masters of strategy and tactics, was not satisfied with summaries of the works of Thucydides, Caesar, Machiavelli, Jomini, and Clausewitz. He required Eisenhower on a daily basis to apply the concepts of these and other great strategic thinkers to battles in the far past, the recent past, and the future. Together they refought all of the critical battles of world history, with a special emphasis on the U.S. Civil War and the just past World War. To Conner, a battle was far more than the traditional mass slaughter. Equally and sometimes even more important than having troops ready to fight were the political and logistical considerations that had to be addressed prior to battle. Conner was convinced that the Versailles Peace of 1919 would buy only a twenty-year respite before the war would begin anew. And he knew that his country would then desperately need officers of Eisenhower's quality.

According to F. Douglas Mehle (1978), "the general taught Ike the real meaning and value of military history. He taught the younger officer the art of reading, thinking and talking about what was read." Mehle concludes that Eisenhower's "three years of postgraduate education under Fox Conner in the isolation of Panama were the most formative of Eisenhower's entire military career."

There is an apt and eerie parallel to Eisenhower's informal but nevertheless highly structured education. Eisenhower's World War II near-peer, Winston Churchill, the British Prime Minister, had a decidedly similar experience when he was a young army officer in isolated outposts in India. Without a mentor, however, beginning in 1896 when he was twenty-two years old, Churchill pursued a conscientious course of reading on history, politics, and philosophy. Eisenhower literally could not afford to buy books and thus was dependent on Conner's informal lending library, but Churchill simply sent long lists of book titles from India to his mother in England, who dutifully (and at annoying expense) bought and shipped them to him.

Over the ensuing few years, Churchill made himself not only an accomplished historian but arguably the best-selling military historian of the twentieth century, ultimately winning the 1953 Nobel Prize in Literature for his six-volume history, *The Second World War*. The point here is that both Churchill and Eisenhower were thoroughly schooled in military history, strategy, and tactics, so when it came time for them to collaborate during World War II, they spoke the same language—and not just English. Eisenhower had Churchill's respect not just because Eisenhower represented the power of the United States, but also because Churchill soon learned that Eisenhower had an intellect and background much like his own. They were united by their mastering of military affairs even though the older man was self-taught and the younger man was fortunate enough to have had the mentoring of Conner.

Conner was absolutely certain of three things: A renewed war in Europe was inevitable; senior officers with a broad historical perspective and logistical sophistication would be needed to develop the grand strategies needed to vastly expand the army and fight the war; and when war came, it would be a war of allies and coalitions calling for generals who understood how to wage war in this context. This latter concern reflected Conner's widely shared opinion that one of the greatest Allied failures of World War I was the inability of the allied powers to cooperate fully. Because there never was a single overarching command or commander, many lives were lost unnecessarily as a result of inadequate coordination of effort.

Eisenhower studied under Conner for three years (1922–1924), but it wasn't all book learning and two-person seminars. As Conner's confidence in Eisenhower grew, Conner increasingly allowed him to do the job of the general in handling troops and in writing plans, reports, and orders. So Eisenhower had the rare opportunity while still a major to effectively function as a general. Conner was so pleased with his protégé's progress that he used his influence to get Eisenhower assigned to the Command and General Staff School at Fort Leavenworth, Kansas. This was the Army's most important assignment on the way to promotion to general. Because of his mentoring by Conner, this mediocre West Pointer graduated first in a class of 275. Over the next decade Eisenhower worked closely with Generals Pershing and MacArthur. Soon he had the reputation as one of the most competent staff officers in the U.S. Army.

THE ORGANIZATION BENEFITS FROM MENTORING

Now for the payoff, the reasons why Conner's tutelage of Eisenhower was so important to all of us who benefited from the Allied victory in World War II. On the day that the Japanese attacked Pearl Harbor, December 7, 1941, and brought the United States into World War II, George C. Marshall was the head of the U.S. Army. Shortly thereafter,

Marshall ordered then–Brigadier General Eisenhower to the War Plans Department. Eisenhower was not happy about this assignment. He had spent World War I writing training manuals and was not happy to leave his position with troops in the field to become an army scribe for the duration.

Marshall had met Eisenhower personally on only a few occasions in the previous fifteen years, but Marshall knew that three of the army's leading generals (Conner, Pershing, and MacArthur) had only the highest praise for him. And Marshall knew that Eisenhower, even as a lowly major, had done much of MacArthur's job (currently Marshall's job) as Chief of Staff of the Army, writing most of MacArthur's speeches, reports, and letters. Marshall desperately needed an officer with sound policy judgment who could back up his recommendations with supporting paperwork.

As soon as Eisenhower got to Washington, he headed to Marshall's office. The situation was bleak. Germany and Japan were making sweeping advances and seemed invincible. Things were only going to get worse, because U.S. forces in the Philippines under MacArthur were on the verge of being overrun. Much of the U.S. Navy had been sunk at Pearl Harbor. There were few troops to be had, and fewer that were properly trained and equipped. In his memoir of World War II, *Crusade in Europe* (1948), Eisenhower quoted Marshall as saying to him as he reported for duty, "We have got to do our best in the Pacific and we've got to win this whole war." Then he bluntly asked, "Now, how are we going to do it?" With only the briefest hesitation, Eisenhower answered, "Give me a few hours."

This was the payoff for all those evenings reading and all those mornings on horseback with Conner discussing military strategy, logistics, and coalition warfare. Eisenhower understood the situation in the Pacific because he had recently spent almost four years there as MacArthur's chief of staff. He knew personally most of the officers who were still there with MacArthur; he even knew their wives and children. Nevertheless, within a few hours he came back to General Marshall with the tough decision that had to be made.

MacArthur could not be reinforced. The United States had nothing in the way of naval or land forces that could readily come to his rescue. The only logical thing to do, besides ordering a few submarines or bribing a few merchant ships to attempt to break through the Japanese blockade with meager supplies, was to start building up men and material in Australia, the base from which a counterattack would eventually have to come. The U.S. forces in the Philippines would simply have to fight on until the end. Marshall immediately concurred with this harsh judgment. They then presented it to Secretary of War Henry R. Stimson, and he concurred. Stimson's diary entry for February 2, 1942, read: "There are times when men must die." Despite his smiling demeanor, Eisenhower could be a hard man, made harder by his understanding of the necessities of history.

Shortly thereafter, Marshall told Eisenhower that he wanted a plan for the reconquest of Europe. Because of the career path he had followed after his initial nurturing by Conner, Eisenhower had the strategic vision, historical perspective, and personal confidence to produce a U.S. plan for liberating Western Europe. Eisenhower's plans and his ability to write and articulate them convinced Marshall to send Eisenhower to England to start their implementation. The rest is well-known history, as Eisenhower became the Supreme Commander whose allied forces successfully invaded North Africa, Sicily, Italy, and Northern Europe. The public was oblivious as to where Eisenhower came from, but all of the senior officers of the Army knew he was a Conner man.

A MENTOR'S INFLUENCE

It is never possible to truly know how influential a mentor has been. All we know for sure is that Eisenhower always freely acknowledged his intellectual and professional debt to Conner, and that because of that debt Eisenhower played a pivotal role in saving the world from tyranny. A grateful nation later elected him for two terms as president (1953–1960). Eisenhower is usually rated as one of our better presidents; however, he is also ranked as one of our greatest generals. Mentors and mentees come in all sizes. Conner and Eisenhower were two of the largest.

How much credit should a mentor be given for the eventual success of the mentee? Historian Stephen E. Ambrose concluded in *Ike* (1973) that "under Conner's direction, Eisenhower found a sense of purpose. For the first time he became a serious student of his profession." This begs the question of whether Eisenhower would have "found a sense of purpose" without Conner's mentorship. Eisenhower was so disappointed by his post–World War I assignments and career prospects that he seriously considered leaving the Army. Had he done so, he certainly would never have played the role he later did on the world's stage. So did Conner "make" Eisenhower by encouraging him to aspire to be and become one of the best professional officers of his era? All any mentor can do is act like a spice in a stew and bring out the flavor that is lurking within; but without the subtle influence of the mentor to spice things up, the stew tastes flat and the mentee may fail to achieve his or her full flavor.

Just how pivotal is the mentor's role? All of Eisenhower's biographers as well as Eisenhower himself agree that Conner's role was critical. Toward the end of his life, after he had met and worked frequently with all of the major military and political leaders of his time, Eisenhower wrote in his informal memoir, *At Ease* (1967): "In a lifetime of association with great and good men, he [Conner] is the one more or less invisible figure to whom I owe an incalculable debt." Eisenhower hit on two common themes in mentor/mentee relationships: (1) the successful mentee is the protégé of an effectively "invisible figure"; and (2) the mentee knows that he or she owes "an incalculable debt." The case of Conner and Eisenhower is especially interesting because of its effect on a great historical figure, Eisenhower; but the phenomenon of successful "invisible" mentoring is both common and critical to our understanding of how people rise to the top of their organizations and professions. Conner did "make" Eisenhower. And he had good reason to be pleased with his handiwork, because he lived until 1946—long enough to see Eisenhower triumph as a soldier during World War II.

In the history of the world there seems to be only one parallel to the Conner/Eisenhower relationship. In the fourth century BCE, Aristotle, the great sage of ancient Greece, was brought north to Macedonia to tutor the teenage Alexander, soon to be the great conqueror of the ancient world. Both pupils went on to be the most successful, influential, and admired military leaders of their time. How much credit should we give to their mentors? Aristotle's reputation remains preeminent among all of the intellectuals of the ancient world. How does Conner compare? All we can say on this is that after Eisenhower retired from the presidency and understood his end was near, he reflected on all the great men of the twentieth century whom he had met as a general, as a university president (Columbia University), and as president of the United States. He concluded, as he personally told his biographer, Stephen E. Ambrose (1973), "Fox Conner was the ablest man I ever knew."

Eisenhower benefited from mentoring in the classical style, one on one with a wise elder who undertook the task mainly out of the sheer joy of engaging an apt pupil. However, mentoring in today's world has been institutionalized and thereby trivialized. Now that the power of mentoring has been recognized, younger organizational members are assigned mentors who may or may not be enthusiastic about the mentee's prospects. We have here the difference between an arranged marriage of strangers and spontaneous true love. The organizational world is full of such arranged marriages. No doubt many of them prove to be effective at fostering nascent talent. However, those like Eisenhower, who find a skillful mentor informally, will have an advantage in the quality of instruction, in gaining success in their careers, and, just possibly, in saving the world.

FOR DISCUSSION

How has the role of the mentor changed through the ages, or is it essentially the same as it was in ancient Greece? Do you think that current technology and instant communications will inhibit or facilitate modern mentoring?

BIBLIOGRAPHY

Ambrose, Stephen E. Eisenhower: Soldier, General of the Army, President-Elect 1890–1952. New York: Simon & Schuster, 1983.

———. Ike: Abilene to Berlin. New York: Harper & Row, 1973.

David, Lester, and Irene David. Ike and Mamie. New York: Putnam's, 1981.

D'Este, Carlo. Eisenhower: A Soldier's Life. New York: Henry Holt, 2002.

Eisenhower, Dwight D. "A Tank Discussion." Infantry Journal, November 20, 1920.

———. At Ease: Stories I Tell to Friends. Garden City, NY: Doubleday, 1967.

———. Crusade in Europe. Garden City, NY: Doubleday, 1948.

Kingseed, Cole C. "Mentoring General Ike." Military Review, October 1990.

Korda, Michael. Ike: An American Hero. New York: HarperCollins, 2007.

Manchester, William. The Last Lion: Winston Spencer Churchill: Visions of Glory 1874–1932. Boston: Little, Brown, 1983.

Mehle, F. Douglas. "Sponsorship." Army 28 (March 1978).

Perry, Mark. Partners in Command: George Marshall and Dwight Eisenhower in War and Peace. New York: Penguin, 2007.

CHAPTER TWENTY-THREE

Brown Reverses the Plessy Doctrine

HOW THURGOOD MARSHALL CONVINCED THE U.S. SUPREME COURT THAT SEPARATE IS INHERENTLY NOT EQUAL, LAID THE LEGAL FOUNDATIONS FOR THE MODERN CIVIL RIGHTS MOVEMENT, AND EARNED HIMSELF AN APPOINTMENT AS THE FIRST AFRICAN AMERICAN JUSTICE ON THAT SUPREME COURT

PREVIEW

When Barack Obama was elected president of the United States in 2008, many people and organizations were pleased to take partial credit for the advances in civil rights that had led to the first African American president. Outside of the political efforts of Martin Luther King, Jr., and his associates, one man and one institution stand out as the leading fighters who created the legal foundation of civil rights for all Americans. That man is Thurgood Marshall, and that institution is the National Association for the Advancement of Colored People (NAACP). This is the story, the case of, their greatest victory in the Supreme Court decision of *Brown v. Board of Education of Topeka, Kansas,* which became the bedrock of further legal advances in civil rights.

APPOINTMENT TO THE SUPREME COURT

In June 1967, President Lyndon B. Johnson had a vacancy to fill on the U.S. Supreme Court. This president, who did more for the civil rights of minorities than any other in the twentieth century, had decided to appoint the first African American to the Court. He had asked his former Attorney General, Nicholas Katzenbach, a professor at the Yale Law School, to prepare a list of possible appointees. As they reviewed the candidates, they came to Thurgood Marshall (1908–1993). Juan Williams, in his biography of

Marshall (1998), quotes the president as saying, "Marshall's not the best—he's not the most outstanding black lawyer in the country." Katzenbach replied, "Mr. President, if you appoint anybody, any black to that court but Thurgood Marshall, you are insulting every black in the country. Thurgood is *the* black lawyer as far as blacks are concerned—I mean there can't be any doubt about that." Marshall, who was made a federal judge by President John F. Kennedy in 1961 and made Solicitor General by Johnson in 1964, was to be elevated once again. On June 13, President Johnson announced that Marshall was his nominee. Despite strong opposition by some senators from Southern states, Marshall was confirmed by a vote of 69 to 11 and joined the Court on October 2.

Why was Marshall "*the* black lawyer"? Because he had spent most of his career (1939–1961) as the director of the NAACP's Legal Defense and Education Fund. In that role he won 29 of the 32 civil rights cases he argued before the U.S. Supreme Court. His overall legal strategy was bit by bit to whittle down the "Jim Crow" laws that sanctioned the segregation then prevalent in the U.S. South. This culminated in one of the true landmarks of Supreme Court history, the case of *Brown v. Board of Education of Topeka, Kansas* (1954).

THE "SEPARATE BUT EQUAL" DOCTRINE

The essence of the *Brown* decision was whether black and white children should attend the same schools. Prior to *Brown* the prevailing doctrine on civil rights was "separate but equal." This meant that blacks did not suffer an infringement of their constitutional rights as citizens if they were not allowed to use the same facilities as whites, so long as "separate but equal" facilities were also provided. This may have sounded fair on the surface, there were two insurmountable arguments against this doctrine. First, there was the simple reality that what was provided separately was hardly ever equal. Second, there was the inherent stigma of being treated differently. How could you be equal if you were not treated equally? There was no doubt that this made second-class citizens of African Americans.

What made this doctrine particularly insidious was the fact that it derived not just from custom and the Jim Crow laws (laws requiring racial segregation) of the South; it was famously promulgated by the U.S. Supreme Court. In *Plessy v. Ferguson* (1896), the Court held that segregated railroad facilities for African Americans, facilities that were considered equal in quality to those provided for whites, were legal. This case didn't just happen. Homer Plessy, at the time a thirty-year-old shoemaker from New Orleans, volunteered to test an 1890 Louisiana law providing for "equal but separate accommodations for the white and colored races" on railroads. So on June 7, 1892, Plessy bought a first-class ticket on the East Louisiana Railway. Plessy was so white-looking (he only had one black great-grandparent) that he had to inform the train conductor that he was "a colored man." As expected, the conductor then asked him to transfer to the "colored" car. When Plessy refused, in one of U.S. history's first sit-ins, he was duly arrested for crimes "against the peace and dignity of the state."

Four years later, Plessy's case reached the U.S. Supreme Court. His lawyers urged the Court to reject the "equal but separate" law because it violated the equal-protection clause of the Fourteenth Amendment. However, the Court saw no such violation. The majority opinion stated that "the object of the [Fourteenth] amendment was undoubtedly to enforce the absolute equality of the two races before the law, but in the nature of things it could not have been intended to abolish distinctions based upon color, or to enforce social, as distinguished from political, equality."

The Court felt that reasonableness was the essence of the case:

> [T]he case reduces itself to the question whether the statute of Louisiana is a reasonable regulation. . . . Gauged by this standard, we cannot say that a law which authorizes or even requires the separation of the two races in public conveyances is unreasonable, or more obnoxious to the fourteenth amendment than the Acts of Congress requiring separate schools for colored children in the District of Columbia, the constitutionality of which does not seem to have been questioned.

The Court even denied the plaintiff's "assumption that the enforced separation of the two races stamps the colored race with a badge of inferiority. If this be so, it is not by reason of anything found in the act, but solely because the colored race chooses to put that construction upon it." The *Plessy* case was a disaster for civil rights. Instead of striking down a Jim Crow law in one state, it allowed the Supreme Court to formally sanction the doctrine. This made it easier for race-based legislation to be expanded and sustained.

Plessy put the stamp of inferiority on every American of African descent. One justice saw this clearly. In his lone dissenting opinion, Justice John Marshall Harlan (1833–1911)—ironically, a former slave owner from Kentucky—wrote: "We boast of the freedom enjoyed by our people. . . . But it is difficult to reconcile that boast with a state of the law which, practically, puts the brand of servitude and degradation upon a large class of our fellow citizens, our equals before the law. The thin disguise of 'equal' accommodations for passengers in the railroad coaches will not mislead anyone, or atone for the wrong this day done."

UNDOING THE "WRONG THIS DAY DONE"

More than half a century later, Thurgood Marshall of the NAACP led the legal team that urged the Court to overturn the "wrong this day done" in the *Plessy* decision and nullify this doctrine when it asserted that separate was "inherently unequal."

Linda Brown was a seven-year-old girl in Topeka, Kansas, when her famous case started winding its way to the high court. She lived just a few blocks from a local elementary school, but that school was for whites only, so she attended a "colored" school on the other side of town. This required that she cross railroad tracks and then take a long bus ride. Her father, Oliver, joined a group of African Americans who sought for three years to get Topeka to improve the "colored" schools. Finally, they filed a lawsuit and Brown found his name as the first of the plaintiffs.

In *Brown,* the Court decided that the separation of children by race and according to law in public schools "generates a feeling of inferiority as to their [the minority group's] status in the community that may affect their hearts and minds in a way unlikely ever to be undone." Consequently, it held that "separate educational facilities are inherently unequal", and therefore, violate the equal-protection clause of the Fourteenth Amendment. Chief Justice Earl Warren (1891–1974), in delivering the unanimous opinion of the

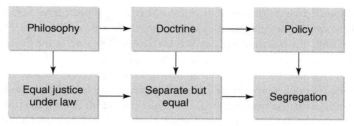

Figure 23.1 Schematic of the *Plessey* Doctrine of Segregation

Court, stated that public education "is the very foundation of good citizenship." It was so important to the nation that considerations of the original intent of the Fourteenth Amendment were less important than remedying the present situation. So the Court effectively brushed aside the question of whether the Fourteenth Amendment was ever intended to cover public education. Warren stated: "In approaching this problem we cannot turn the clock back to 1868 when the Amendment was adopted, or even to 1896 when *Plessy v. Ferguson* was written. We must consider public education in the light of its full development and present place in American life."

Then Warren proceeded to dismantle the doctrine of separate but equal. "We come then to the question presented: does segregation of children in public schools solely on the basis of race, even though the physical facilities and other 'tangible' factors may be equal, deprive the children of the minority group of equal educational opportunities? We believe that it does."

Warren acknowledged that the Court accepted the validity of various psychologists that segregated schools damaged minority students by creating "a feeling of inferiority." Finally, he concluded that "in the field of public education the doctrine of 'separate but equal' has no place."

Carved in stone on the front of the U.S. Supreme Court building are the words "Equal Justice Under Law." Those words epitomize the philosophic foundation of U.S. government, yet they once sustained a doctrine that some citizens were less equal than others. Figure 23.1 illustrates this.

The *Brown* decision kept the philosophy but revised the doctrine so that a new policy of integration emerged as illustrated in Figure 23.2.

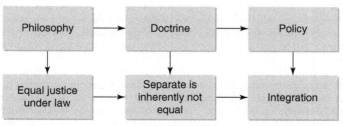

Figure 23.2 Schematic of the *Brown* Doctrine of Integration

The *Brown* decision was one of the most powerful legal precedents in U.S. history. It made the complete desegregation of U.S. society only a matter of time. Though the time seemed long, the march of equality was inexorable. The man at the forefront of the legal march to change the doctrine of separate but equal was Thurgood Marshall. Martin Luther King, Jr., marched in the streets to demand civil rights and became the personification of the civil rights movement. Marshall marched into federal court and, far more often than not, when he marched out, the civil rights of all Americans had been expanded. This is why, by 1967, Marshall was considered "*the* black lawyer" in America and the obvious choice for the first black seat on the U.S. Supreme Court. Unfortunately, Marshall has all but disappeared from American consciousness today, but Barack Obama knows that he would not be where he lives today if Marshall had not gone before him to pave the legal way.

The victors: Thurgood Marshall (center) puts his arms around two members of his legal team (George F. C. Hayes and James Nabrit, Jr.) in front of the U.S. Supreme Court on May 17, 1954, the day the Court ruled in *Brown v. Board of Education* that segregation in public schools is unconstitutional. It was Nabrit who got off the best rhetorical flourish of the proceedings when he echoed George Orwell's *Animal Farm* (1945) in telling the Court: "Our Constitution has no provision across it that all men are equal but that white men are more equal than others. . . . [W]e believe that we, too, are equal." The high drama of this case was made into a TV docudrama, *Separate but Equal* (1991), which is readily available in video stores. Sidney Poitier portrays Marshall with scrupulous accuracy as to the facts of the case. Especially fascinating is the dramatization of the behind-the-scenes politicking, cajoling, and maneuvering by Chief Justice Warren to convince all the members of the Court to join in a unanimous decision. He knew that the decision would be so controversial and difficult to implement that it needed the impetus of a united Court. *Source:* © UPI/CORBIS. All Rights Reserved.

FOR DISCUSSION

Why is the *Brown* decision generally considered to be the legal foundation of the modern civil rights movement? Was Chief Justice Earl Warren right to delay the *Brown* decision until he could get a unanimous vote on it in order to make it more acceptable to the American public?

BIBLIOGRAPHY

Kluger, Richard. *Simple Justice: The History of Brown v. Board of Education and Black America's Struggle for Equality.* New York: Knopf, 1976.

Williams, Juan. *Thurgood Marshall: American Revolutionary.* New York: Times Books/Random House, 1998.

Woodward, C. Vann. *The Strange Career of Jim Crow.* New York: Oxford University Press, 1974.

CHAPTER TWENTY-FOUR

Government Regulation of Sex
TOWARD GREATER SOCIAL EQUITY AT WORK THROUGH REMEDIAL LEGISLATION, JUDICIAL PRECEDENTS, AND SEXUAL HARASSMENT PROHIBITIONS WRITTEN INTO MANUALS OF PERSONNEL RULES

PREVIEW

Few people think of the public policy implications of their sexual activities. After all, a common enough and not unreasonable attitude is that "it is none of the government's business." However, they could not be more wrong. In the United States, the government has been in the "business" of sex from the very beginning. Even before independence from England, colonial-era governments mandated innumerable restraints on sexual display and behavior. Remember that Hester Prynne, the heroine in Nathaniel Hawthorne's 1850 novel of seventeenth-century Boston, *The Scarlet Letter*, was not forced to wear an embroidered red letter A on her breast because of her excellence in athletics. And A was not the only letter to be seen in Puritan towns during the colonial period. P had to be worn by paupers living on public relief. This policy helped the children learn their letters and improve their vocabulary as they saw alphabetically humiliated people on a daily basis: A is for adulterer; P is for pauper, and so on. Just like *Sesame Street!*

REGULATING SEXUAL ACTIVITY

"Blue laws," special legal restraints on commercial and moral behavior, have enjoyed great longevity. Although adulterers are no longer stoned to death (at least not in the Western world) or forced to have their sins symbolized alphabetically on their clothes, sexual morality is still enforced by a vast array of state and local blue laws (so-called because the 1781 Sabbath dress codes mandated by the town elders of New Haven, Connecticut, were originally printed on blue paper). Thus the first women who wore the French-inspired Bikini swimsuits on public beaches in the United States in the 1950s were often arrested under local statutes forbidding indecent exposure. (They were called Bikinis after the late 1940s Pacific Ocean atoll atomic bomb tests, because they were also so "explosive.") Even today, municipalities severely restrict (to certain locations), or prohibit altogether, beach bathing in the altogether.

Until the 1960s, it was illegal for anyone, even married couples, to use birth control devises in some states. Then the U.S. Supreme Court, in the case of *Griswold v Connecticut* (1965), held that the state regulation of birth control devices was an impermissible invasion of privacy. Justice William O. Douglas wrote, in the majority opinion: "Would we allow the police to search the sacred precincts of marital bedrooms for telltale signs of the use of contraceptives? The very idea is repulsive to the notions of privacy surrounding the marriage relationship." Nevertheless, prior to 1965, it was public policy that the state be allowed to be so intrusive, repulsive or not.

And what about homosexual behavior? "The love that dare not speak its name," in the words of Oscar Wilde, did not speak up because if you did, you got arrested. Maybe even hanged. At least that was the case in South Carolina until 1868. In 1986 the U.S. Supreme Court upheld Georgia's sodomy law in *Bowers v. Hardwick*. Thus homosexual activity was illegal even if it involved consenting adults in the privacy of their homes. However, all such laws banning "consensual sodomy" were overturned in Georgia and in more than a dozen other states that still had them on their books at the time when the Supreme Court, in *Lawrence v. Texas* (2003), reversed *Bowers*. Finally, after being persecuted since Biblical times, America's highest court had declared that homosexuals "are entitled to respect for their private lives. The State cannot demean their existence or control their destiny by making their sexual conduct a crime."

In addition to regulating sexual activity, governments have long sought to influence the number of children that their citizens or subjects produce. Many governments throughout history have offered financial incentives for married couples to have more children. The United States does this in a modest way thought the income tax system: the more children, the more tax deductions. This is an indirect cash subsidy for larger families. All of Western Europe has long had even more generous programs of family allowances. In 2000, Singapore, concerned about its declining birthrate, announced a multibillion-dollar program of cash bonuses for couples who have a second and third child. In marked contrast, in China today there are draconian laws against couples having more than one child. Couples who create a baby brother or sister for their first-born child face fines, loss of employment, and even expulsion from their public housing.

The regulation of the myriad aspects of sexual activity extends even to just talking about it. Nowadays you cannot make sexual allusions or tell sex-related jokes at work without suffering possible legal consequences if a co-worker complains. How "dirty" jokes, suggestive language, or a friendly slap on the back at work became a federal offense is an interesting tale of how public policy is often made by accident. And it is a story that is old. So old that we find it in the Bible.

JOSEPH AS THE HARASSEE TRIUMPHANT

Joseph, the Bible tells us, was sold into slavery by his older brothers for "twenty pieces of silver" (Genesis 37:28). Taken to Egypt by a slave merchant and sold to Potiphar, the captain of Pharaoh's guards, Joseph's talents served his master so well that Potiphar "made him overseer over his house."

Joseph, a natural administrator, was on the fast track, as slavery goes, until his career was derailed by an unfounded claim of sexual harassment. Potiphar's wife "cast her eyes upon Joseph." One day when they were alone in the house, "she caught him by his garment, saying lie with me." Joseph immediately fled, leaving "his garment in her hand."

Poor Joseph. He goes to work one day and the next thing he knows he's running away. But where to? In those days there was no Equal Employment Opportunity Commission to whom Joseph could complain about workplace sexual harassment. Besides, slaves did not have the right to complain about anything anyway—sexual intimidation least of all. It is bad enough to be harassed; it is worse to be framed and jailed—which is just what happened next to Joseph. Potiphar's wife claimed that Joseph had approached her and ran away when she cried out, leaving his garment behind as evidence. When Potiphar heard this false accusation, "his wrath was kindled." And Joseph was put into prison.

Fortunately, this particular story of sexual harassment has a happy ending. While he was in prison, Joseph's skills in long-range business forecasting came to the attention of the Pharaoh, who needed a dream interpreted—something about seven thin cows eating seven fat cows. Joseph's warning of a coming famine so impressed the Pharaoh that Joseph began his rise to the top of the Egyptian bureaucracy. This just goes to show that sometimes an ex-convict can be a very effective employee.

Just about 3,000 years later, Joseph's problem with sexual harassment at work arrived on the docket of the U.S. Supreme Court. Though it was too late to help Joseph, the Court ruled in 1986 on a case similar to his. How this came about is a long story. To make it manageably short, we will arbitrarily skip many centuries during which women suffered from sexual harassment, sexual oppression, and sexual domination and jump to the fight for civil rights in the United States of the early 1950s.

DEATH TO JIM CROW

The Civil Rights Movement is the overarching phrase for the continuing effort of minorities and women to gain the enforcement of the rights guaranteed by the Constitution to all citizens. The modern Civil Rights Movement is often dated from 1955, when Rosa Parks (1913–2005), a black seamstress, refused to sit in the back of a bus, as was then required by local segregation laws. Her refusal led to her arrest (she was charged with a misdemeanor) and to a year-long bus boycott by the black citizens of Montgomery, Alabama. This gave the boycott leader, Dr. Martin Luther King, Jr., national exposure, which he used to good effect.

The law that Rosa Parks violated, by refusing to move to the back of the bus where blacks were required to sit, was a "Jim Crow" law. This was the name given to any and all legal requirements for segregation of the races. Many Southern states had laws mandating separate drinking fountains, separate rest rooms, separate sections of theaters, and so forth, for blacks and whites. The term is derived from a nineteenth-century minstrel character typically played by a white man in blackface makeup. "Jim Crow," essentially a clown, became so popular and well known that his name was applied to many things having to do with blacks. Thus there was Jim Crow food and a Jim Crow part of town. Most of all, Jim Crow became the designation for all Southern laws designed to keep blacks separate and economically deprived. Consequently, the overarching goal of the Civil Rights Movement was to kill Jim Crow, repeal all segregation laws, and allow blacks to participate equally in U.S. social and political life.

The political turmoil and agitation of the Civil Rights Movement, with its demonstrations and boycotts, led eventually to three new laws. The first two would take tiny bites out of Jim Crow. The third, thanks to the efforts of Dr. Martin Luther King, Jr., and millions of others in the Civil Rights Movement, would kill him entirely.

The Civil Rights Act of 1957 was the first federal civil rights legislation enacted since the post–Civil War Reconstruction period and was significant primarily as an indication of renewed federal legislative concern with the protection of civil rights. The act essentially accomplished three things: It established the U.S. Commission on Civil Rights to investigate civil rights violations and make recommendations; it created the Civil Rights Division in the U.S. Department of Justice; and it enacted limited provisions to enforce the Fifteenth Amendment guarantee of the right to vote.

The Civil Rights Act of 1960 included limited criminal provisions related to racially motivated bombings and burnings and to obstruction of federal court orders; a clause to enlarge the powers of the Civil Rights Commission; and a section providing for the desegregated education of children of U.S. military personnel. The most important new provision made a remedy available to those improperly denied the right to vote: a voter-referee procedure enforced by the federal courts.

Neither the 1957 nor the 1960 act amounted to much. They were largely symbolic sops given by the congressional Southern conservatives of the Democratic Party to their liberal colleagues from other parts of the country. The core problem of civil rights was segregation legally enforced by Jim Crow laws in the South. The question here was simple: When would the rest of the country develop the legislative will to force the South to desegregate? The answer was 1964. In the wake of President John F. Kennedy's assassination on November 22, 1963, succeeding President Lyndon B. Johnson, formerly the leader of the Southern conservatives in the Senate, used all his political skills to get a real civil rights act passed.

The Civil Rights Act of 1964 was the real thing; it was the legal death of Jim Crow. The act consists of eleven titles, of which the most consequential are titles II, VI, and VII. Title II bars discrimination in all places of public accommodation whose operations affect commerce. This includes hotels and other places of lodging of more than five rooms, restaurants and other eating places, gasoline stations, theaters, motion picture houses, stadiums, and other places of exhibition or entertainment. In Title VI, the Congress made broad use of its spending power to prohibit racial discrimination in any program or activity receiving federal financial assistance. More important, Title VI goes on to provide that compliance with the nondiscrimination requirement is to be effected by the termination or refusal to grant federal funds to any recipient who has been found guilty of racial discrimination. Title VII makes it an unfair employment practice for any employer or labor organization engaged in commerce to refuse to hire, to fire, or to otherwise discriminate against any person because of race, religion, sex, or national origin. Title VII is enforced by the Equal Employment Opportunity Commission, which was also created by the act.

It is Title VIII and the little word "sex" that was included in the list of personal characteristics that the law says should be free from discrimination that is our concern. How did it get there? What have been its implications?

SEX DISCRIMINATION

Sex discrimination is any disparate or unfavorable treatment of a person in an employment situation because of his or her gender. The Civil Rights Act of 1964 makes sex discrimination illegal in most employment, except where a bona-fide occupational qualification (a good-faith exception to EEO provisions; a job requirement that would be discriminatory and illegal were it not necessary for the performance of a particular job) is involved.

Sex discrimination in employment was by no means a significant concern of the civil rights advocates of the early 1960s. Its prohibition only became part of the Civil Rights Act of 1964 because of Congressman Howard "Judge" Smith (1883–1976) of Virginia. As chairman of the House Rules Committee in 1964, Smith was one of the most powerful men in Congress—and as unlikely a hero as the women's movement will ever have. As the leader of the South's fight against civil rights, he added one small word—sex—to prohibitions against discrimination based on race, color, religion, and national origin. Why did he do that? Smith was an "old-style" bigot: To his mind the one thing more ridiculous than equal rights for blacks was equal rights for women.

The "sex discrimination" amendment was opposed by most of the leading liberals in Congress. They saw it as nothing but a ploy to discourage passage of the new civil rights law. Remember that the goal was to kill Jim Crow. Anything that did not focus on that goal was a distraction that would delay, dilute, or harm the main effort. What better proof that "sex" here was a distraction could there be than the fact that the major support for adopting the amendment in the House came from the reactionary Southern establishment of the day. There was no discussion of sex discrimination by the Senate. The momentum for a new civil rights law was so great that Smith's addition not only failed to scuttle the bill, it went largely unnoticed. The legal foundation for the modern women's movement was passed with almost no debate or media attention.

The question remains, why? It has long been thought that Smith was opposed to the addition. After all, he had spent decades in Congress opposing all civil rights legislation and often said scurrilous things about black people in general. Furthermore, in his comments at the time of the amendment's insertion, he made a big joke of it. He sought to ridicule it, and this was a tone taken by many of his House colleagues—conservative Southern gentlemen all—as the debate went on. Quoted below is Smith's statement from the *Congressional Record* of February 8, 1964, directly after he proposed that "sex" be included as an amendment. Note how Smith does not seem to be taking this discussion at all seriously, despite the fact that he says, "Now I am very serious about this amendment."

Chairman, this amendment is offered to the fair employment practices title of this bill to include within our desire to prevent discrimination against another minority group, the women, but a very essential minority group, in the absence of which the majority group would not be here today.

Now I am very serious about this amendment. It has been offered several times before, but it was offered at inappropriate places in the bill. Now, this is the appropriate place for this amendment to come in. I do not think it can do any harm to this legislation; maybe it can do some good. I think it will do some good for the minority sex.

I think we all recognize and it is indisputable fact that all throughout industry women are discriminated against in that just generally speaking they do not get as high compensation for their work as do the majority sex. Now if that is true, I hope that the committee chairman will accept this amendment.

That is about all I have to say about it except, to get off of this subject for just a moment but to show you how some of the ladies feel about discrimination against them. I want to read you an extract from a letter that I received the other day. This lady has a grievance on behalf of the minority sex. She said that she had seen that I was going to present an amendment to protect the most important sex, and she says:

"I suggest that you might also favor an amendment or a bill to correct the present 'imbalance' which exists between males and females in the United States."

Then, she goes on to say—and she has her statistics, which is the reason why I am reading it to you, because this is serious—

"The census of 1960 shows that we had 88,331,000 males living in this country, and 90,992,000 females, which leaves the country with an 'imbalance' of 2,661,000 females."

Now another paragraph:

"Just why the Creator would set up such an imbalance of spinsters, shutting off the 'right' of every female to have a husband of her own, is, of course, known only to nature. But I am sure you will agree that this is a grave injustice."

And I do agree, and I am reading you the letter because I want all the rest of you to agree, you of the majority—

"But I am sure you will agree that this is a grave injustice to womankind and something the Congress and President Johnson should take immediate steps to correct— [laughter]."

And you interrupted me just now before I could finish reading the sentence, which continues on:

"immediate steps to correct, especially in this election year."

Now I just want to remind you here that in this election year it is pretty nearly half of the voters in this country that are affected, so you had better sit up and take notice.

She also says this, and this is a very cogent argument too:

"Up until now, instead of assisting these poor unfortunate females in obtaining their 'right' to happiness, the Government has on several occasions engaged in wars which killed off a large number of eligible males, creating an 'imbalance' in our male and female population that was even worse than before.

"Would you have any suggestions as to what course our Government might pursue to protect our spinster friends in their 'right' to a nice husband and family?"

I read that letter just to illustrate that women have some real grievances and some real rights to be protected. I am serious about this thing.

There are now two schools of thought on Smith's motivations: (1) He wanted to ridicule the whole bill so it would be defeated; and (2) knowing that the overall civil rights bill would pass the House and eventually be signed into law no matter how much he and his fellow Southerners opposed it, he wanted to be sure that sex discrimination was as forbidden as race discrimination. He, as well as others such as Representative Martha Griffiths of Michigan, was concerned that under the new law, if the word "sex" were absent, employers would end up discriminating against white women so as not to seem to be discriminating against black women.

So sex was inserted not in an effort to ameliorate the workplace sex discrimination that was widespread, but to deny a possible advantage to black women. Later that same day, during the debate over the amendment, Smith confirmed this:

> I put a question to you in behalf of the white women of the United States. Let us assume that two women apply for the same job and both of them are equally eligible, one a white woman and one a Negro woman. The first thing that the employer will look at [unless the Smith amendment is approved] will be the provision with regard to the records he must keep. If he does not employ that colored woman and has to make that record, that employer will say, "Well, now, if I hire the colored woman I will not be in any trouble, but if I do not hire the colored woman and hire the white woman, then the [Equal Employment Opportunity] Commission is going to be looking down my throat and will want to know why I did not. I may be in a lawsuit."
>
> That will happen as surely as we are here this afternoon. You all know it.

All that is absolutely certain here is that the amendment, "sex," stayed in the bill, put there by a man with an established record as a vicious racist in order to (1) help white women or (2) hurt black women. In the end he helped all women, but his motives were so impure that he hardly warrants credit for this landmark legislation. Nevertheless, he did a good deed—even if for a bad reason.

Although the sex discrimination prohibition was included in the new civil rights law almost in secret, word quickly got out. The new law brought into being the Equal Employment Opportunity Commission to enforce its various provisions. During the first year of the new commission's operation, over one-third of all of the complaints it received dealt with sex discrimination in employment. Typical complaints included inadequate consideration of female applicants for promotion, "help wanted" ads for separate male- and female-labeled jobs, and higher retirement benefits for male workers. All these practices and more were made illegal by Title VII. Over the next four decades, Judge Smith's unintended gift to the nation's women became the judicial reference for countless court cases and out-of-court settlements.

SEXUAL HARASSMENT

When the Civil Rights Act of 1964 prohibited sex discrimination in employment, it would not have occurred to anyone to say or imply that the new law had anything to do with sexual harassment. The phrase "sexual harassment" was not even in the language.

Today, however, for all legal purposes, sex discrimination includes sexual harassment—the action of an individual in a position to control or influence the job, career, or grade of another person and who uses such power to gain sexual favors or punish the refusal of such favors. Sexual harassment on the job varies from inappropriate sexual innuendo to coerced sexual relations.

Although there was universal agreement that sexual harassment was bad, there was no agreement as to where the normal give and take between the sexes ended and sexual harassment began. An old maxim of the common law in such situations was that "there is no harm in asking," but the harm was always there. Countless women left jobs rather than submit to persistent sexual requests. Countless others, out of sheer economic necessity, continued on in humiliation, fear, and silent outrage.

Of course, even prior to passage of Title VII of the Civil Rights Act of 1964, the kind of sexual harassment that was tolerated was limited to social interaction harassment—talking, cajoling, and threatening to a degree. Once harassment went beyond these limits and became physical, it was no longer mere harassment but a case of criminal physical assault, which has always been illegal. Sexual harassment can be viewed as a continuum with relatively innocuous wordplay such as calling someone "honey" or "sweetie" at one end and the brutality of rape at the other. At some point along this continuum, perfectly appropriate behavior can turn into harassment. Crossing that line can subject you and your organization to extensive litigation. However, this situation was not obvious at the beginning.

Then a few courageous women enlarged the meaning of the law because they were mad enough about unwarranted sexual pressures to "go public" and test their novel interpretation of sex discrimination in federal court. In 1974 Paulette Barnes started the first major case linking sexual harassment to violations of the federal civil rights law. She was an administrative aide in the Environmental Protection Agency when her supervisor began a "campaign to extract sexual favors." This included suggestions that sexual cooperation would advance her career and repeated requests for dates despite her consistent refusals.

After Barnes's supervisor finally gave up hope of seducing her, he initiated an "administrative consolidation" of his office that, as a by-product, eliminated the need for her job. A federal judge ruled that it was sex discrimination to abolish a woman's job because she refused her male supervisor's sexual advances. The Court of Appeals left no doubt that sexual harassment was sex discrimination when a woman's job "was conditional upon submission to sexual relations—an exaction which the superior would not have sought from any male." Consequently, in 1977 Paulette Barnes was awarded $18,000 in damages.

Over the next few years, a variety of similar cases were successfully brought to trial. They all involved women who had lost their jobs because of sexual harassment. These women were not suing their actual harassers; they were going for the deep financial pockets and suing the organizations that had employed them.

In 1980, after the lower federal courts had decided that sexual harassment was sex discrimination in a variety of cases, the Equal Employment Opportunity Commission (EEOC) issued legally binding rules that defined and prohibited sexual harassment. According to the EEOC, unwelcome sexual advances, requests for sexual favors, and other verbal or physical contact of a sexual nature constitute sexual harassment when:

1. Submission to such conduct is made either explicitly or implicitly a term or condition of an individual's employment;
2. Submission to or rejection of such conduct by an individual is used as the basis for employment decisions affecting such individual; or
3. Such conduct has the purpose or effect of unreasonably interfering with an individual's work performance or creating an intimidating, hostile, or offensive working environment.

Finally, in 1986, the U.S. Supreme Court issued its first ruling on sexual harassment. In *Meritor Savings Bank v. Vinson*, sexual harassment that creates a hostile or abusive work environment, even without economic loss (wages foregone because one is unjustly fired, disciplined, or not promoted) for the person being harassed, was declared illegal because it was in violation of Title VII of the Civil Rights Act of 1964.

This case sought to establish ways by which to judge whether sexual harassment exists in any given set of circumstances. Thus the court held that Title VII is violated when the workplace is permeated with discriminatory behavior that is sufficiently severe or pervasive to create a discriminatorily hostile or abusive working environment. The standard laid down by the Court is that of an objectively hostile or abusive environment, one that a reasonable person would find hostile or abusive. Whether an environment is "hostile" or "abusive" can be determined only by looking at all the circumstances: the frequency of the discriminatory conduct, its severity, whether it is physically threatening or humiliating (or only an offensive utterance), and whether it unreasonably interferes with an employee's work performance. The effect on an employee's psychological well-being is also relevant in determining whether the environment is abusive.

However, this standard was not detailed or clear enough to provide sufficient guidance to employers and the lower federal courts, so the Supreme Court expanded upon the 1986 standard in the 1993 case of *Harris v. Forklift Systems*. Teresa Harris worked as a manager at an equipment rental company for more than two years. Throughout Harris's time of employment, the male president of Forklift Systems often insulted her because of her gender and often made her the target of unwanted sexual innuendos. For example, he said to Harris on several occasions, in the presence of other employees, "You're a woman, what do you know?" and "We need a man as the rental manager." Again in front of others, he suggested that the two of them "go to the Holiday Inn to negotiate [Harris's] raise." He even asked Harris and other female employees to get coins from his front pants pocket.

When Harris complained about this conduct, the company president said he was surprised that Harris was offended, claimed he was only joking, and apologized. He also promised he would stop. Based on this assurance, Harris stayed on the job. A few weeks later, however, the problem began anew. Harris quit, then sued Forklift Systems, claiming that the president's conduct had created an abusive work environment for her because of her gender. The lower federal courts held that the situation had not created an abusive environment. The courts found that the comments would offend any reasonable woman, but that they were not "so severe as to be expected to seriously affect [Harris'] psychological well-being."

The Supreme Court agreed to hear this case to resolve the conflict over just what constituted a sexually abusive work environment. Associate Justice Sandra Day O'Connor, in writing the majority opinion of the Court, asserted that Title VII's protections necessarily had to "come into play before the harassing conduct leads to a nervous breakdown." Victims do not have to prove "concrete psychological harm," only that the offending conduct "would seriously affect a reasonable person's psychological well-being."

Thus the new standard holds that "so long as the environment would reasonably be perceived, and is perceived, as hostile or abusive, there is no need for it also to be psychologically injurious." In effect, there is no need to wait for it to lead "to a nervous breakdown." O'Connor concluded that "while psychological harm, like any other relevant factor, may be taken into account, no single factor is required" because this is not, and by its nature cannot be, "a mathematically precise test."

The story of the Biblical Joseph may be the first recorded instance of on-the-job sexual harassment. More than three millennia later, the issue is still being fine-tuned by the courts. Progress has certainly been slow. Nevertheless, the Court continues to add precision to the myriad subtleties of sexual harassment law. For example, in *Oncale v. Sundowner Offshore Services* (1998), the Court held that same-sex claims of harassment are permissible. Overall, the odyssey of sexual harassment jurisprudence is also a good example of how the federal courts make public policy—how they can take a piece of legislation and make it out to be something that nobody ever thought it would be.

FOR DISCUSSION

If sexual harassment has been a problem dating from Biblical times, why is it that it has become a significant legal issue only in recent decades? Have you ever been subjected to, or been an instigator of, sexual harassment, even without realizing it at the time?

BIBLIOGRAPHY

Brauer, Carl M. "Women Activists, Southern Conservatives and the Prohibition of Sex Discrimination in Title VII of the Civil Rights Act.," *Journal of Southern History,* February 1983.

Dierenfield, Bruce J. *Keeper of the Rules: Congressman Howard W. Smith of Virginia.* Charlottesville, VA: University of Virginia Press, 1987.

Gregory, Raymond F. *Unwelcome and Unlawful: Sexual Harassment in the American Workplace.* Ithaca, NY: Cornell University Press, 2004.

MacKinnon, Catharine A., and Reva B. Siegel, eds. *Directions in Sexual Harassment Law.* New Haven, CT: Yale University Press, 2003.

McAllister, Bill. "The Problem That Won't Go Away: A New Survey Finds Complaints of Sexual Harassment Are Still Widespread in Federal Offices." *Washington Post National Weekly Edition,* November 20–26, 1995.

Mink, Gwendolyn. *Hostile Environment: The Political Betrayal of Sexually Harassed Women.* Ithaca, NY: Cornell University Press, 2000.

Reese, Laura A., and Karen E. Lindenberg. *Implementing Sexual Harassment Policy: Challenges for the Public Sector Workforce.* Thousand Oaks, CA: Sage, 1998.

Robinson, Robert K., et al. "Sexual Harassment in the Workplace: A Review of the Legal Rights and Responsibilities of All Parties." *Public Personnel Management* 19 (Spring 1993).

CHAPTER TWENTY-FIVE

Take Me Out to the Ball Game and You Buy the Ticket

THE CASE FOR PUBLIC STADIUM FINANCING

PREVIEW

They are America's sports cathedrals. Mammoth in size and grandiose in design, baseball and football stadiums have become centerpieces of the urban landscape in the United States. Unlike the towering religious cathedrals that have marked American and European cities for centuries, stadiums are generally not venerated for their historic value. Instead, they are often denigrated for being too old and out of date to accommodate how modern games are played and viewed. In the sporting world, newer and bigger beats historic and intimate.

Nowhere was this scenario more true than in the case of the downfall of venerable Yankee Stadium in 2009. Built in 1923, New York's Yankee Stadium evolved as the most famous and historic sports site in the nation. In addition to being the home of the most successful sports franchise in U.S. history, Yankee Stadium has hosted events featuring Pope John Paul II and Nelson Mandela, and was the site of the famous Joe Louis–Max Schmeling Depression-era boxing match. Even with this unparalleled history, the stadium met the wrecking ball in 2009 when a New Yankee Stadium was opened across the street in the Bronx.

The new Yankee Stadium, though designed to look like the original one, had at least one big difference from its predecessor: The public paid about half a billion dollars for it. Back in 1923, the original Yankee Stadium's $2.4 million price tag was covered completely by the Yankees' owners. During the construction of the new stadium in the Bronx, the Yankees ownership did pony up about half the construction costs ($400 million) but turned to the public to cover the rest. Far from an exception, the public financing of Yankee Stadium is the latest in a series of cases in which the public has been asked to cover the costs of construction for sports venues that host privately owned sports franchises and their highly compensated athletes. And just as the games in the new stadiums display the finest of sports strategy, the deals that were made to pay for the new digs involved an equal amount of strategic maneuvering on the part of the franchises and the governments they dealt with.

THE OPENING PITCH

Large U.S. cities of the late twentieth and early twenty-first centuries have almost universally engaged the issue of the construction of sports facilities to house professional sports franchises. From the construction of the new Yankee Stadium to a bitter debate in hurricane-ravaged New Orleans regarding the future of the Superdome, the nation's urban areas have regularly wrestled with a topic of considerable controversy. Although the issue of public involvement in funding can be viewed from a number of perspectives, it essentially remains a game in which primarily privately owned sports franchises attempt to maximize their bottom line by securing public funding from political officials, who seek to keep franchises in their cities at the lowest cost to their constituents. In many cases, these games are played out in the realm of public elections, in which citizens decide the fate of deals developed through negotiations between the franchises and government.

The securing of public funds for the construction of professional sports facilities can be achieved through two broadly defined approaches: public approval or nonelectoral negotiations. In the most common approach, sports franchises can gain the support of government financial backing through nonelectoral avenues. In these approaches, the sports organization and government institutions agree on a "deal" in which the sports franchise agrees to operate in the geographic confines of the city, county, or state in return for a set level of financing for the construction or renovation of the venue that houses the team. Of the eighty venue deals struck in the past two decades, about 60 percent have been finalized through the negotiated mechanism without direct approval of the public.

In some cases, final approval through negotiation came without the public ever getting a chance to vote on the use of public funds (e.g., the new Yankee and Mets stadiums that opened in 2009); in other cases, a negotiated settlement between organizations and government came after voters declined to support the use of public revenues for venue construction (e.g., Milwaukee's baseball stadium in 1995). A quote in the *Phoenix Gazette* by former Chandler, Arizona, Mayor Jay Tibshraeny in 1995 regarding renovations to a spring training facility in his city nicely demonstrates the dynamic associated with the process of getting deals done even without direct public support. Tibshraeny stated: "I believe the citizens should have a say in this issue. If the voters pass this, we'll move forward. If the voters don't pass this, we'll still move forward."

MAKING THE CALL

Avoiding public votes on the question of sports venue financing can be seen as an attractive option for sports franchises, but it can be a less positive option for policy makers. For the sports organizations, the opportunity to secure funds from the public without having to mount a campaign to sway public opinion may seem less risky and thus a first choice when seeking to raise revenue for a project. Although it is less risky for sports franchises, the risks for elected officials concerned about the political liabilities associated with the transfer of public funds to private sports entities helps explain why many political figures seek public ratification before allocating funds. Thus in 40 percent of stadium construction projects involving public funds, the public has been asked to weigh in on the matter by voting at the polls.

It may seem at first that the movement of a stadium finance decision from legislative chambers to the ballot box would place the organization's quest to secure public funding in peril, but the track record demonstrates that the electoral approach usually bears fruit for a franchise. Of the thirty-one plans that have been put to the voters, a vast majority (84 percent) were eventually approved. The remaining five (or 16 percent) that did not receive voter support were eventually approved with either a combination of public–private financing or completely private financing. A more detailed examination of the four cases sheds some insight into the resolution of these situations.

In the cases of stadium projects in Milwaukee, Seattle, and Pittsburgh, public referenda failed to gain public approval, with the projects in Milwaukee and Pittsburgh failing by nearly 2-to-1 margins and the proposal in Seattle failing by a narrow 51.1 to 49.9 percent. Nevertheless, substantial public funding was secured for the eventual construction of these venues through measures passed by the state legislatures in Wisconsin, Pennsylvania, and Washington. In the case of Columbus, Ohio's, attempt to build an arena to house a professional hockey franchise, voters rejected a proposal for stadium financing by a 56-to-44 percent margin in 1997. Following the failure of this plan at the polls, private financing by the Nationwide Insurance Company and other private investors allowed for the construction of an arena and the creation of the expansion Bluejackets franchise in the National Hockey League.

THE GAME WITHIN THE GAME

For elected officials, the presence of a major league sports franchise in their city is a sign of prestige and economic vitality. Thus cities and states seek to both retain and attract sports franchises to their confines. While valuing the presence of sports teams, elected officials would rationally prefer to have their presence at the lowest possible cost to the public. In essence, the ultimate scenario for an elected official (such as a mayor) would be a vibrant sports franchise in his or her city with the public paying none of the cost for the venue in which the team plays. This situation is optimal for elected officials because it would allow them to avoid entering the realm of revenue raising to finance a stadium or redistributing revenue from other areas while maintaining the benefits of the franchise's presence.

For the sports franchise the situation is even simpler. As profit-maximizing entities, an organization would like to receive as much public financing as possible for the construction and operation of the venue housing its team, thus allowing it to maintain a healthier bottom line and a more competitive position within the league it inhabits.

With such conflicting goals present, it helps to consider the negotiation between the franchise and government officials as a zero-sum game. This is a perspective that views potential gains for one side as a loss for the other; for one player to win, another must lose. With stadium funding negotiations, any movement toward greater public funding is preferable to the franchise and any movement toward greater private funding is preferable to government officials. With this scenario in mind, we can turn our attention to the relative bargaining positions of the negotiating parties and the impact of those positions on the setting of the ballot referendum question. In terms of bargaining strength, the relative power each party holds during negotiations, the sports organization clearly has the upper hand because of its ability (at least perceived) to relocate to another city. As long as cities publicly court the relocation of franchises, elected officials are held within the confines of a prisoner's dilemma. Former Washington, D.C., Mayor Sharon Pratt Kelly clearly describes this situation:

> The mayors of American cities are confronted with a prisoner's dilemma of sorts. If no mayor succumbs to the demands of the franchise shopping for a new home, then the teams will stay where they are. This, however, is unlikely to happen because if Mayor A is not willing to pay the price, Mayor B may think it advantageous to open up the city's wallet. Then to protect his or her interest, Mayor A often ends up paying the demanded price.

The threat of moving gives the franchise an enormous advantage in the negotiation, but the strength of an elected official's desire not to use public funds is also modified by the very presence of the ballot question. More specifically, given the cover of citizen ratification of the use of public funds, elected officials may not feel the urgency to strike a deal in which the franchise pays a larger share of the facility costs. Other than the opportunity costs for the revenue being directed to the sports venue, and the possibility of diminished reputation due to a failed referendum, an elected official can justify a large public contribution to the construction of a sports facility through voter ratification as a case of "the will of the people."

In the event, new sports cathedrals have risen from coast to coast, with palatial luxury boxes to host high-paying corporate sponsors in climate-controlled environments. Meanwhile, the soaring price tag on tickets to these state-of-the-art stadiums has left many fans stuck outside the gates. For although the average fan's taxes may have helped build the new palaces, there is no government subsidy to help them buy tickets to go see the games. The original Yankee Stadium was commonly referred to as the "House that Ruth Built," because Babe Ruth's fame and ability to generate ticket sales gave the Yankee owners the funds to build a bigger stadium. Today's stadiums can be called the "House that You Built," because your taxes helped make them real. And unlike many of the taxpayers who will never set foot in the houses that they built, Babe Ruth at least got to play in his for many years.

FOR DISCUSSION

Why do local and state governments direct public funds to the construction of stadiums and arenas when those venues are used primarily by privately owned sports teams? Do cities get back their investment in sports venues through added revenue from economic activity generated by the stadiums and arenas?

BIBLIOGRAPHY

Baade, Robert. "Professional Sports as Catalysts for Metropolitan Economic Development." *Journal of Urban Affairs* 18(1), 1–17 (1996).

Bagli, Charles V. "Stadium Deals Give Yankees and Mets Benefits and Breaks to Be Borne by Taxpayers." *New York Times,* June 19, 2005.

Fort, Rodney. "Direct Democracy and the Stadium Mess." In *Sports, Jobs and Taxes,* edited by Roger Noll and Andrew Zimbalist. Washington, DC: Brookings, 1997.

———. "Stadium Votes, Market Power and Politics." *University of Toledo Law Review* 30(3), 419–441 (1999).

Owen, Jeffery G. "The Stadium Game: Cities Versus Teams." *Journal of Sports Economics,* August 2003.

Quinn, K., P. Bursik, C. Borick, and L. Raethz. "Do New Digs Mean More Wins? The Relationship Between a New Venue and a Professional Sports Team's Competitive Success." *Journal of Sports Economics,* August 2003.

Rosentraub, M. *Major League Losers: The Real Cost of Sports and Who's Paying for It.* New York: Basic Books, 1999.

CHAPTER TWENTY-SIX

The Fall of the House of California

HOW THE RICHEST STATE IN THE COUNTRY CRATERED INTO BUDGETARY CHAOS AND A FISCAL NIGHTMARE[1]

PREVIEW

California is not just any state. If it were a country, it would be the world's eighth biggest economy. However, it is not a country, so it faces the same public financial test that all subnational governments face in the United States. Each year it must submit and pass a balanced budget. What the state of California experienced from 2008 to 2009 is widely regarded, according to *The Economist* (July 11, 2009), as "America's worst budget crises." This fiscal collapse actually began with a tax revolt through voter referendum, Proposition 13, over thirty years ago, which altered local government financing and led to a budget situation in which projected deficits reached almost half of expected revenues, the state's credit rating fell to barely above junk bond status, and IOUs were issued to pay contractors and creditors. The actual day-to-day events of this continuing crisis, frequently producing front-page headlines, have left California residents wondering whether they were reading a horror story in the style of Edgar Allen Poe's masterpiece, *The Fall of the House of Usher* (1839)—an eerie tale of dire events as a once-wealthy family falls into decline and madness.

IN THE BEGINNING

The first seeds of California's present budget problems were planted in 1978, when a voter referendum, Proposition 13, passed by large margins, rolled back the property tax as a source of revenue for local governments. As housing values rose dramatically in California in the economic expansion of the 1960s and 1970s, so did assessments and property taxes.

---

[1]This chapter was written by Albert C. Hyde, an independent advisory consultant on strategy and innovation.

Homeowners in many cities found themselves living in properties valued far above their initial purchase price, and county tax offices appropriately raised assessments and thus required higher tax payments. A tax resistance movement spread that led to putting a referendum on the ballot that would roll back assessments to previous levels and limit the amount that future assessments (no more than 2 percent per year) could rise. Its passage also included provisions requiring supermajority votes to raise taxes in the future.

This did not mean, of course, that local governments could never raise property taxes, but it changed the foundation of the property tax to one under which the assessed value would only be raised to true market levels when the property was sold or was new construction. This is what Robert Bland, a local government finance expert, has called "acquisition-based valuation." One would expect that, over time, property tax levels would catch up, especially as home prices continue to rise and new construction increases. There is a catch, though; in fact, there are two.

Acquisition-based valuation assumes that housing prices, especially in the nation's richest and most populous state, will always increase. In economic terms, property taxes are highly elastic, because they track the rising value of real estate and everyone knows that real estate values, especially in California, only go up. And this was true, at least until 2008, when the housing bubble finally caught up with California. When housing values plummeted, foreclosures rose, and new housing starts were abandoned, property taxes did not just decline; they crashed. The California Department of Equalization reported in late 2008 that the annual change in revenues went from plus 12.5 percent in 2006 to plus 4.8 percent in 2008 to minus 6 percent projected for 2009. Revenues were not expected to be positive again until 2012. That's bad, of course, but in California it is especially bad because property taxes are normally designed to be stable sources of revenues for local governments. In short, acquisition-based valuation has made difficult economic conditions even more catastrophic for California's local governments.

Then there is the second catch. Proposition 13 altered "diversification" of state and local tax systems in California. Normally, states and local governments rely on different sources of revenues, with different levels of elasticity (i.e., stability in light of changing economic conditions) and economic effects, but each is supposed to be self-sustaining. State and local governments share some burdens for public services. State governments, with a larger base of resources, use intergovernmental transfers to supplement and support local government basics such as education and social services. What has happened in California, as Robert Bland notes, is that more and more fiscal resources in the state and local system have been coming from the state. At the time of Proposition 13, the ratio of state funding for local government assistance was 1.9 to 1.0. By 2009 it has risen to 3 to 1. In effect, over 70 percent of the California state budget passes through to local governments. This, in essence, is why the state government budget crisis is not limited to the state; it is a state and local government budget crisis.

To be fair, it should be noted that this situation is not all attributable to Proposition 13. Various coalitions of California taxpayers have been active in securing state funding for basic services. For example, in 1988, Proposition 98 was passed, which required that 40 percent of the state's general fund must be allocated to schools (K to 12). So, given that the state's budget contains a 40 percent spending mandate for education, 70 percent overall for local governments is not such a reach.

One other fiscal dimension of the House of California's budget should be examined before proceeding. Critics often refer to California's spending patterns as "boom and bust" budgeting. What this refers to is the state's heavy reliance on a highly progressive income tax as its main source of income. Over half of the state's approximately $90 billion in annual revenues comes from the personal income tax—with the greatest share coming from the top 1 percent of earners. An even more significant share of income tax revenues is derived from capital gains and stock options taxes. California, at the center of the new high-tech economy, reaped a huge windfall in stock tax gains, which went from $2.8 billion in 1995, at the start of the tech stock boom, to over $16 billion in 2000. At the high point, over 20 percent of California's annual revenues came from taxes paid on stock gains and from stock options being cashed in, enabling the state to pile up seemingly endless budget surpluses with little fiscal effort or spending discipline. Needless to say, this reliance on potentially highly variable taxes on equities made the highly progressive income tax (normally a virtue) a more unbalanced and volatile revenue source.

When the tech stock market first fell in 2001, California went into another round of budget chaos. The former governor's attempt to raise revenues by tripling the car registration fee and accusations that rampant spending had been used to bolster his reelection campaign were major reasons for the governor being recalled in a special election. Politics aside, however, this episode was just another small incident in a state that had allowed its budgetary revenue to be based on the highly variable but somehow always rising U.S. market forces. When the U.S. economy went into recession in the early 1980s, the early 1990s, and even after the dot-com bust, the state would cut back expenditures, reduce workforce, delay spending and salary increases, and borrow from the credit markets to balance budgets—and then spend aggressively to catch up when the economy recovered. Table 26.1 presents the major categories of California's revenues and expenditures.

IT'S NOT JUST ECONOMICS

The student of budgeting can also learn much about governance from California's budget crises. Budgeting today in the public sector usually requires joint action by the executive and legislative branches. Mayors and city managers, governors, and presidents assemble spending plans, a series of recommendations on the levels of expenditure for each program or department in government along with forecasts of what the levels of revenues will be to keep the budget in balance.

State and local government budgets are expected to be balanced at the end of each fiscal year, but there are numerous ways for governments to balance the budget on paper at that point in time yet still have an unbalanced budget in the end. One can collect revenues in advance, delay paying bills until the next fiscal year, make unrealistic or simply incorrect estimates of what revenues will be—the list of possible "budget adjustments" is extensive. Another tactic used by governments over the years has been to borrow funds for the short term from the credit markets—called tax or revenue anticipation notes— to even out revenue collections and expenditure payouts. However, the practice of financial

Table 26.1 A Quick Glance at California's State Budget: 2008–2009 General Fund

Revenue (Dollars in Millions)			*Expenditures* (Dollars in Millions)		
	2008–2009	*Percent*		*2008–2009*	*Percent*
Personal income tax	46,807	51.4	Legislative, judicial, executive	3,779	4.1
Sales tax	27,778	30.5	State and consumer services	566	1.0
Corporation tax	10,197	11.2	Business, transportation, and housing	1,466	1.6
Motor vehicle fees	26	0.0	Resources	2,030	2.2
Insurance tax	1,831	2.0	Environmental protection	79	0.1
Liquor tax	599	0.7	Health and human services	29,996	32.5
Tobacco taxes	113	0.1	Corrections and rehabilitation	10,432	11.3
Oil severance tax	358	0.4	K–12 education	35,499	38.4
Other	3,408	3.7	Higher Education	11,745	12.7
			General government: reimbursements for revenue warrants	−4,102	−4.4
Totals	91,117	100.0		92,413	100.0

Source: Summary Charts—California Budget FY 2008–2009.

management has evolved to a point at which good accounting can usually identify the consequences of these budget tricks of the trade and provide a reasonable accurate assessment of what the state of the budget is. What accountants and economists cannot do is reconcile the politics of the budget process.

The legislative and executive branches do their annual budget confrontation with different perspectives and indeed different powers. Legislatures must approve all of the tax and revenue decisions, recommendations of the executive branch; this process delineates the funding of government programs and the final obligations, the spending decisions for each program. The executive branch has the responsibility for compiling the budget requests from each agency or program, usually after it has given some guidance about budget expectations and higher priorities, and putting it into one overall budget request.

In some states (and especially the federal government), the legislature has the power to rewrite the entire budget, to decide how much funding it wants to provide for each program after it has decided what the level of tax effort and revenue collection will be. In other states, the executive has stronger powers and can reject any additional spending recommendation made by the legislature that exceeds what the executive has recommended. This is called a line-item veto. Of course, if the legislature reduces spending levels or cuts taxes, that cannot be overridden.

However, it is in the nature of government budgeting—it is indeed one of the core budget objectives for executives and legislatures—to work out their differences on the highest priorities, to sustain basic levels of funding support for essential programs and services, and to negotiate a new budget each year. Where it gets difficult, and this is where the California budget crises is so instructive, is when there are fundamental political and philosophical differences about taxation capacity, spending levels for public services, and debt levels.

Looking at California's budget crises of 2008–2009, one sees a budget process that has been severely affected by politics and political preferences. For starters, there is California's famous "democratic populism": It is relatively easy to place on the state ballot a proposition that can change taxation levels (as in Proposition 13) or spending mandates (as with Proposition 98). Admirable as it may seem to have the public so directly engaged in budgeting, the result is often not the compromise and coordination needed to make governance better, but rather extreme requirements and inflexibility that make budgeting harder to accomplish and respond to new environments. California voters have raised "budgeting by initiative," as former state senator Patrick Johnson (2009) calls it, to an art form, approving referendums that have earmarked tobacco taxes first to preschools programs (1993) and then to health programs (1998), sales taxes for local public safety (1993), restricting sales taxes on fuel to transportation (2002), or the "millionaires tax" for certain mental health programs (2004).

Another factor is "supermajorities" that may be needed for the passage of revenue measures. Many states require 60 percent or two-thirds supermajority votes to raise taxes. California has a two-thirds requirement for the budget itself. This has, in a perverse demonstration of the law of unintended consequences, empowered the much smaller Republican minority in the state's budget process. When California recognized that its projected 2009 deficit would be over $40 billion (that's almost half of total revenues), a small group of Republican lawmakers in the state senate voted for tax increases to deal with the worst budget crises in the state's history. The reward for the six Republican lawmakers who voted for the budget deal accepting tax increases was having their campaign funding cut off by the party. One of them, the Republican minority leader, was booted out of his post. Two of them faced recall in their districts. Needless to say, when the legislature returned to negotiate a second budget deal, no Republican broke ranks to vote for any tax increase. Party discipline had triumphed.

THE BUDGET CRISES OF 2008–2009

The full story of the 2008–2009 budget crises played out in the headlines of California's major newspapers and on nightly news shows could be a book of its own, true to Edgar Allen Poe. As noted, the seeds were sown with a budget dependent on constantly rising revenues tied to bullish estimates of what the U.S. economy was capable of doing with California as its chief engine of growth. California had convinced itself that it could weather the occasional recession, and it had, basically playing the role of first state in, first state out in the recessions of the early 1980s and 1990s.

So when the first dark clouds began gathering after the dot-com bust and the tragic aftermath of the terrorist attacks on September 11, 2001, there was only a little concern. The previous governor had been recalled, and the new Republican governor, Arnold Schwarzenegger, had positioned himself as a fiscal conservative. He kept his campaign promise to repeal the raise on the vehicle license tax and then proceeded to deal with a looming $15 billion deficit (not trivial, but not significant) by backing a voter bond proposition that would refinance the state's shortfall. His message was that this would be a last-time remedy, akin to tearing up one's credit cards, and the state would live hence-forth within its means. The propositions passed, and California continued to finance its services and then add more debt financing (through voter-approved referendums) for transportation, hospitals, and other infrastructure projects so that California could con-tinue in its place at the vanguard in the growth in the now global economy.

After Schwarzenegger was reelected in 2006, the governor and the state's econo-mists began to notice that the dark clouds pointing to a possible economic downturn seemed to be hovering over the Golden State. Unemployment nationally hovered at 4.5 percent, while California's rate jumped to nearly 6 percent by the end of 2007. Housing starts sputtered, dropping by two-thirds statewide. Some magazines, such as *The Economist,* questioned whether California might already be in recession. So, in January 2008, the governor announced that the state faced a possible budget deficit of over $10 billion, which would have to be dealt with through spending reductions. Declaring the first of what would be three "fiscal emergencies" in the next eighteen months, the governor asked for $17.5 billion in cuts. He also requested in his proposed budget that $2.5 billion be set aside as a reserve fund and focused most of his attention on suspending the Proposition 98 requirement for schools. Other spending adjustments were proposed, along with a 10 percent across-the-board reduction in all state programs.

The final budget, approved in September 2008, after months of wrangling, pleased no one, though education was left untouched and half of the remaining $5 billion in deficits was kicked into the next fiscal year. By the end of the following month, however, the dark clouds had turned into a maelstrom. No one in California was remotely pre-pared for this type of economic meltdown. Worse, California's finances were set up to be more severely affected than those of any other state. Estimates of the budget deficit jumped on a month-to-month basis—anywhere from $15 billion to $50 billion. From this point on, California would have two budget deficits to contend with: The nagging little $5 billion leftover deficit that never seemed to go away would now require $10 bil-lion to $12 billion to close the Fiscal Year 2008–2009 books, and on the horizon loomed a colossal $30 billion to $40 billion deficit that would have to be dealt with by June 2010 to balance the next year's budget. To keep a sense of perspective, a deficit of $45 billion would be about half of the total average revenues that California collects annually.

The governor jump-started the latest budget process by declaring a fiscal emer-gency in early December 2008, bringing the legislature into special session to confront what he called "financial Armageddon." (See Table 26.2 for a chronology of the key

Table 26.2 A Fiscal Chronology for California: A Walk on Budgeting's Wild Side

2007 Fall: prequel Projected deficit: $5 billion	In the previous year's budget, the state had a recurring fiscal shortfall of over $5 billion, which was projected to "reemerge" in the next fiscal year.
2008 January Projected deficit $14.5 billion	Governor's proposed budget notes major worsening of fiscal deficit projection by June 2009, estimated at $14.5 billion. Governor declares state fiscal emergency and calls for special legislative session. Governor's budget calls for $17 billion in new spending cuts and establishment of a $2.8 billion reserve fund.
February	Agreement with the legislature yields $7 billion in spending adjustments, with $3 billion coming from deficit financing bonds to address budget shortfalls.
May Projected deficit: $17.2 Billion	New projections for deficit set at $17 billion by June 2009, setting the stage for major conflict in legislative passage of budget.
Summer Budget finally signed on September 24	Brutal political confrontations among legislative parties and governor's office finally resolved with a budget that is 85 days late but sets sufficient changes (no broad-based tax increases, but some increased revenue charges and numerous expenditure cuts).
November Projected FY 2009 deficit: $10 billion Projected FY 2010 deficit: $27.8 billion	As the U.S. economy crashes into its most severe recession in fifty years, with financial indices losing more than a third in value, California's budget situation deteriorates rapidly. Expected declines in tax revenues re-raise projected deficit levels.
December Projected FY 2009 deficit: $11.2 billion Projected FY 2010 deficit: over $40 billion	Governor declares second fiscal emergency, warning of impending "financial Armageddon" and calling for a special legislative session. State legislative Democrats propose a "budget-neutral" plan that raises taxes by $9 billion but requires only a simple majority vote for approval. Governor indicates he would veto the plan.
2009 January–February California's credit rating lowered	U.S. economy worsens, and California's unemployment rate rises above 10 percent. Legislature and governor negotiate over budget designed to close a $40 billion spending gap (January 2009–June 2010). Governor proclaims furlough plan for state workers. After being upheld in court, over 200,000 state employees begin taking semimonthly furloughs equating to 9 percent pay reduction.

Table 26.2 (*continued*)

	On February 3, rating agencies reduce California's credit rating to one level above non-investment-grade or "junk" status. California now has lowest credit rating of all fifty states.
February 19 Deficit close to $6 billion. Special election called.	Governor and legislature agree on budget package of temporary tax increases ($12.8 billion in sales tax, vehicle licensing fee, and income tax), $15 billion in spending cuts, and $11. 4 billion in borrowing (lottery, short-term notes). Six ballot measures are set up for a May special election to shift spending, establish spending caps and reserve funds, and borrow against lottery revenues.
April Projected deficit: $15 billion	U.S. economy reaches bottom of recession; California unemployment rate now at 12 percent. Tax revenues fall $8 billion below expected.
May Projected deficit: $24.3 billion	On May 19, voters reject ballot measures on budget except for a proposition that prevents legislature from raising salaries in deficit years.
July Projected deficit: $26.3 billion	Governor declares third fiscal emergency and re-opens budget negotiations. State controller announces that state will run out of cash on July 28 and begins issuing $3.6 billion in IOUs to contractors and local governments.
July 24 Second budget plan agreement	Governor and legislature budget deal closes $26.3 billion gap with $15.6 billion in spending cuts ($8.8 billion in education cuts and $1.3 billion in state worker furloughs, $4.7 billion in reductions and borrowing from local government funds, and $2.9 billion in spending adjustments and tax withholding).

California's budget year runs from July 1 to June 30.

events in this story.) Consequently, budget negotiations in early 2009 were conducted with enormous additional pressures and political influences in play. The staggering size of the deficit precluded any major new borrowing. The credit rating agencies quickly downgraded the state's credit rating; then they downgraded the state again, giving California in the end the lowest rating of any state in the country. The state could still borrow, but not much and at very high cost. Cash management became a real issue. The state now recognized that at current spending levels and lower revenue accumulations, it would simply run out of money by early summer. The state controller laid out plans to issue IOUs to major creditors and local governments. These IOUs paid interest, of course, but it was still uncertain whether banks would accept them and when the state would be able to redeem them.

Additionally, the governor took a further drastic step and announced mandatory furloughs or pay cuts for over 200,000 state workers. In the previous summer, the governor had sparred with the controller when he announced that he would lower wages to minimum-wage levels for temporary hires and would lay off seasonal hires. Upheld by the courts on this, the governor now targeted a planned $1.3 billion in spending reductions by closing state offices twice a month (the first and third Fridays of each month), in effect reducing state worker salaries by 9 percent. Challenged again but upheld by the courts, the furlough plan went into effect in February while budget negotiations were proceeding.

A budget deal of rather unprecedented proportions was reached on February 19. Six Republican senators, despite the party's pledge to vote against any broad-based tax increase, agreed to temporary tax increases in personal income tax rates, sales taxes, and vehicle registration fees amounting to one-third of the deficit reduction deal. These tax increases would expire after 2011 or if the economy improved and the deficit receded. Likewise, another third of the deal approved major cuts in state spending to include almost all programs and especially local government assistance and education. The final third of the deal required short-term borrowing and amortizing the state lottery (contracting it out to private management and borrowing against future revenues). This latter arrangement may seem a bit bizarre, but governments have often done this, most notably in the area of tobacco litigation, where many states have chosen to take a lump sum for litigation proceeds that are to be paid over time by tobacco companies.

Part of the budget deal also required setting up six ballot initiatives to get voter approval on a range of budget solutions for the future. The lottery proposal required voter approval, but initiatives were also to be voted on that established spending caps, established financial reserves, and adjusted spending allocations across various social programs from education to mental health. Looking forward to a May election date with expected low voter turnout, many political observers were skeptical that the public and the numerous special interests in California would support this package, even if it did avert "financial Armageddon." However, the temporary tax increases and spending cuts were in place regardless.

Public perception of the budget provisions was at best annoyance that the governor and legislature could not simply fix the budget situation. Special interests were ferocious in their contempt and in their campaigns against the provisions. On election day, May 19, 2009, all of the initiatives were defeated except Proposition F, which prevented the legislature from raising salaries in a deficit year. However, the size of the projected deficit began to decline, even as unemployment in California soared to over 12 percent—a 40-year high. As the governor proclaimed his third fiscal emergency and prepared to reopen budget negotiations, there was a slightly more optimistic mood.

As the summer began, nothing was now more pressing than the cash shortage situation. The comptroller announced he would begin issuing IOUs in the first week in July. The state legislative Democrats proposed a partial solution, setting aside $5 billion to avoid the IOUs, but the governor threatened to veto anything except a complete solution. Legislative Republicans locked up a "no tax increase" front, and the negotiations got down to finding $25 billion-plus in spending reductions. Slightly complicating things, the governor asked for new spending management reforms and powers to control fraud and waste, but these were discarded later as bargaining chips. In what ended up as one of the earliest-passed budgets in a decade, all three sides—the governor, legislative Democrats, and legislative Republicans—came up with about $15 billion in spending cuts, another $5 billion in reductions and borrowing from local government funds, and $3 billion in spending adjustments and tax withholding. The spending cuts were particularly difficult because they affected most social programs, prisons, and education. Budgets for higher education were cut by over $2 billion, resulting in unprecedented faculty furloughs. Local governments also found themselves hit hard as the state announced it had to either borrow or delay obligatory payments.

Thus the fiscal crises of California played out in the summer of 2009 to include three fiscal emergencies, two budget agreements, and one failed special election. Of course, the story continues. Despite the July final budget deal, several local governments were reported as being ready to sue the state for the "diversion" of their designated funding. Republican lawmakers threatened to vote against the package because the cost reductions in state prisons would require an inmate release program (called "alternatives to incarceration"). Health care advocates threatened legal action against reductions in a child health insurance program that would place new applicants on a waiting list until June 2010. Another suit was announced as mental health advocacy groups prepared to go after the governor for tacking on another $455 million in spending reductions as part of the governor's line-item veto power after the budget deal was voted on and signed. The suit contends that the governor exceeded his power and that the cuts in the budget deal were the most allowed.

Meanwhile, back at the economy, many economists announced that the recession probably ended in the second quarter of 2009 and that although economic recovery would be slow, the bottom was past. In mid-August 2009, the ratings agencies took California off of their "credit watch with negative implications" list, making it possible—or at least making it easier—for the state to borrow. The state controller announced that he would stop issuing IOUs and hoped to redeem them a month earlier than planned. The state treasurer's office announced that bank financing for a $1.5 billion loan had been secured to bridge the state's finances until September, when the state would sell over $10 billion in short-term notes.

The economics of the House of California's budget now seemed destined to slide into the background, disaster averted, for this recession, this time. Nevertheless, this is a crisis that would be continued in the next budget cycle. Stay tuned for more exciting adventures in fiscal years to come.

> ### FOR DISCUSSION
>
> Some economists point out that although California's tax revenues are "unstable" during times of severe economic downturn, the system has other benefits: It is highly progressive (i.e., more equitable in terms of who pays taxes), and the state raises most of the revenues for local governments, which are often less efficient in collecting taxes and which use more regressive tax sources. Those who lament the passage of Proposition 13 often fail to note that the property tax gets low marks for fairness and progressivity. Given that economic recessions like the one spawned by the financial meltdown are rare, should more states emulate California's tax system?
>
> California is different. When a state is this big in terms of both population and wealth, should it even be required to have a balanced annual budget? Would it have made a difference if California had to balance its budget, say, every second or third year, and have the budget focus instead on ensuring that the deficit stayed below a fixed percentage of state wealth (as in the European Union, the deficits of whose members are required not to exceed 3 percent of gross domestic product).

BIBLIOGRAPHY

Beacon Economics. "An Economic Backdrop for Fiscal Reform in California." Sacramento, CA: California Forward, November 2008.

Bland, Robert L. "Tax Policy Lessons from California's Proposition 13." Washington, DC: *ICMA Newsletter,* www.dentonrc.com, August 7, 2009.

"California's Budget: Crimson Tide." *The Economist,* January 10, 2009.

"California's Budget Crises: Meltdown on the Ocean." *The Economist,* July 11, 2009.

"California: Sliding into the Sea." *The Economist,* November 2007.

Hyde, Albert C. *Government Budgeting: Theory, Process and Politics,* 3rd ed. Belmont, CA: Wadsworth, 2002.

Johnson, Patrick. "California's Sad Budget Saga Has Many Authors." *California Journal of Politics and Policy,* June 2009.

Legislative Analyst's Office. "California Spending Plan 2008–09." State of California Report, www.lao.ca.gov, November 2008.

Legislative Analyst's Office. "July 2009 Budget Package." State of California Report, www.lao.ca.gov, July, 2009.

McCaffery, Jerry, and John H. Bowman. "Participatory Democracy and Budgeting: The Effects of Proposition 13." *Public Administration Review,* November–December 1978.

Poe, Edgar Alan. *The Fall of the House of Usher and Other Tales.* New York: Signet, 2006.

Media sources: California newspapers cover and update the California budgeting situation extensively. Three of the state's newspapers do especially comprehensive reporting and interviewing of the key participants: the *Sacramento Bee,* the *Los Angeles Times,* and the *San Francisco Chronicle.*

CHAPTER TWENTY-SEVEN

Why Florence Nightingale, the Famous Nurse Who Pioneered the Graphic Presentation of Statistical Data, Is the Now-Forgotten "Mother" of Program Evaluation and PowerPoint® Illustrations

PREVIEW

Today the Crimean War of 1853 to 1856, fought by Great Britain, France, and Turkey (then the Ottoman Empire) against Russia, is all but forgotten save for two things: the classic poetic description of military incompetence, and a nurse. The 1854 poem, "The Charge of the Light Brigade," by Alfred Lord Tennyson (1809–1892) still resonates as a "tribute" to misunderstood military orders and the sacred duty of obedience notwithstanding the stupidity of the orders: "Theirs was not to reason why, theirs was but to do and die." Many generations of young men had this poem as their mantra as they traveled "into the jaws of death, into the mouth of hell" when it became their duty to charge during the wars of the twentieth century.

However, this poem, perhaps the most memorized and most influential of all war poems, pales in significance compared to the incomparable nurse and the inspiring story of her professional accomplishments and self-sacrificing personal example. We speak, of course, of the women whose name has come to epitomize both the invention and practice of modern nursing, Florence Nightingale (1820–1910).

THE CALLING

She was rich, a respected member of the aristocracy that ruled England and the British Empire. This fact more than any other explains how Florence Nightingale defined herself as the archetypical nurse, secured the opportunity to demonstrate her professional prowess, and inevitably succeeded as a political and institutional reformer.

Unlike Elizabeth Bennett, the fictional heroine of Jane Austen's *Pride and Prejudice* (1813), young Miss Nightingale felt no need to marry a dramatically handsome and exceedingly wealthy Mr. Darcy as Miss Bennett did in the novel. The Nightingale family's wealth was such that she could easily afford to reject the formal proposal of a real-life Mr. Darcy, every bit as attractive in appearance and pocketbook as his fictional contemporary.

From a young age, Nightingale felt that she had a calling. Yes, a calling from God. Although she never professed to hearing voices from above, as Joan of Arc had, she was determined on a career caring for the infirm. Such a calling precluded marriage no matter how brilliant and lucrative the match. Her parents were as appalled as they were furious when Nightingale finally turned down Richard Monckton Milnes (1809–1885), later to be a member of Parliament and minor poet, after nine years of flirtation with traditional domesticity. She was determined to enter nursing instead. This was unthinkable to her family. Hospitals in those days were filthy places fit only for the dregs of society, who were attended by their own kind. Many of the nurses in those places had the social status of prostitutes; it was certainly not a job for a decent woman, much less for a brilliant child of the aristocracy.

Nightingale's family, especially her father, though totally opposed to her aspirations to be a nurse, was indirectly quite supportive of her eventual career. Mr. Nightingale, part of the landed gentry and a gentleman (meaning that he never had to work), nevertheless became one of England's pioneering statisticians. Recognizing that his daughter had a receptive mind, he introduced her to statistical analysis.

This unusual statistical competence for her time and her sex would be a critical factor in her future success, as was her father's introducing her to many of the most influential men in the realm. After all, the Prime Minister lived on down the road a bit. So, because of her family's wealth and social status, Nightingale was from an early age conversant with the movers, shakers, and maintainers of English society. Quite simply, by the time she reached adulthood, she knew almost everyone worth knowing in upperclass English society, from the Prime Minister on down. Thus she developed the confidence that she, too, could be a social mover and shake things up.

LESS A NURSE THAN A HOSPITAL ADMINISTRATOR

Why nursing? First of all, every other profession was closed to her. In her day, women could not aspire to be doctors, lawyers, or military officers. Nor did members of her class go into business. The women of her time who worked outside the home were all in low-status, low-wage occupations such as textile mill workers, seamstresses, governesses, or worse. Such drudgery was not for her, nor was traditional nursing, which offered, at best, a kind of morally uplifting drudgery. Ultimately, she was no more a nurse than a general was a simple soldier or an admiral an ordinary seaman.

She was thoroughly experienced in the work of a nurse, but this was merely an apprenticeship. The work she did that made her famous was not nursing but nursing and hospital administration. She advanced medicine not by tending to individual patients, though she did do so in passing, but by creating systems by which large numbers of patients would get better care than before her reforms. It is perhaps best to think of her as the first modern hospital administrator.

Nightingale's career really began with a nursing apprenticeship at a medical establishment, the Kaiserwerth Institute in Germany. Her family considered themselves so humiliated by this that they felt it was better to tell people that she had had a nervous breakdown with the breaking off of her engagement to Mr. Milnes than to admit the truth of her consorting with the lowly sick—and foreigners, too! After almost a year gaining experience on the Continent, she returned to England.

In 1853, the year the Crimean War started, she became the superintendent of the Institution for the Care of Sick Gentlewomen. This meant that by the time word of the terrible conditions in British Army hospitals reached the British public, she was thoroughly experienced as a nursing and hospital administrator. And she was so socially acceptable to the upper classes that ran the government that she could be given a leadership position in alleviating the conditions of those soldiers who had been effectively dumped at an immense but old and filthy Turkish army barracks in Scutari, a suburb of Constantinople. Why Constantinople? Because the war was fought in the part of Russia (the Crimea) that bordered on the Black Sea, the wounded and sick were simply and quickly shipped across the sea to Turkey, Britain's ally in the war.

Conditions were appalling. Those who did not die on the "middle passage" between Sebastopol and Scutari arrived at a hospital complex that had 4 miles of corridors but hardly any of the supplies that make such a place a fount of healing. The place was so filthy, vile, and infectious that far more were dying from their unfortunate living conditions—filth and vermin prevailed—than from their wounds. The situation was a scandal of enormous proportions made all the more notorious by publicity created by the first modern war correspondents.

War correspondents have often been troublemakers as far as governments have been concerned; and that was certainly the case here. The London *Times,* through its correspondent, William Howard Russell (1820–1907), published such appalling accounts of how the sick and wounded were treated at Scutari that there was a general call that something should be done and immediately.

SAILING TO DESTINY

The Secretary of State for War, Sidney Herbert (1810–1861), because of his social connection to her, wrote to Nightingale to ask if she would lead a nursing mission to Turkey. Nightingale, who read the same newspaper accounts as Herbert, wrote volunteering to do just that. The story goes that their independent letters crossed in the mail. In any event, within a week, Nightingale and a team of thirty-eight nurses, along with a shipful of supplies, were sailing off to her destiny as "The Lady with a Lamp." This famous title came from an 1857 poem by Henry Wadsworth Longfellow, in which he wrote:

Lo! In that hour of misery
A lady with a lamp I see
Pass through the glimmering gloom,
And flit from room to room.

Upon arrival, the legend began. At first, the Army officers in charge of the immense barracks hospital were disdainful of her and her cadre. The women were civilians, however, and there at the behest of the Secretary of State for War, so they were tolerated. And the men soon began to revere them. According to Hugh Small (1998), "The world's most powerful industrial nation was filling its steamships with unheard-of quantities of supplies for dispatch to the hospitals—bandages by the ton, and 15,000 pairs of sheets . . . but for some reason none of it was arriving at the right place." It was a demonstration of the grossest incompetence on the part of the War Office—a complete breakdown of medical logistics. And nobody noticed or cared until soldiers began to die in large numbers. Lytton Strachey (1963) summarized the essence of all the "administrative incapacity," the "confused systems," and the "petty bungling of minor officials" when he concluded that "the evil was in reality that worst of all evils—one which has been caused by nothing in particular and for which no one in particular is to blame."

Fortunately, the nurses had brought with them the basic elements of hygiene, from clean sheets to toothbrushes. They would not be dependent on the War Office's wholly inadequate logistical efforts in medical supply. Unfortunately, the officials in charge of the hospital were not always as appreciative as the patients. Strachley reports that the commanding officer incredulously asked, "with a growl, what a soldier wanted with a tooth-brush?"

The nurses could not do much medically for the men, but the patients were cleaned up and given a much improved diet because Nightingale had sufficient funds to buy more nutritious food. Nightingale and her nurses were empowered because they did not need supplies, food, or money from the career Army officers who managed the hospital. They brought their supplies with them and had ample funds to buy food and whatever else they needed from local sources. Thus the nurses succeeded in radically improving the well-being and morale of the suffering soldiers, most of whom were sick, not just from battle wounds, but from preventable diseases as well.

The reports of the war correspondents, supplemented by letters written home by ordinary soldiers as well as some officers, sang the praises of Nightingale and the other nurses. Her ensuing reputation as a self-sacrificing nurse and hospital administrator *par excellence* has never been equaled. Just as Napoleon will always be "the" general, Nightingale will always be "the" nurse.

Nevertheless, despite the best efforts of the nursing team, the death rate did not decline significantly. The problem did not become clear to Nightingale until after she returned to England and began to analyze her statistical data. The death rate from disease did not start to decline until more than four months after the arrival of the nurses. It was at that point that a sanitary commission arrived to clean out the clogged-up toilets and sewers. The hospital complex was situated atop an enormous stopped-up cesspool. Because she had neglected to attend to this elementary sanitary precaution, she felt responsible for the unnecessary deaths of thousands of men. This was a considerable torment to her. Hugh Small, a recent biographer, even suggests that the guilt from this led to a nervous breakdown that kept her largely bedridden for years. Of course, this made her all the more committed to hospital reforms and proper sanitation.

THE NEW MODE OF PRESENTATION

Our concern here is not with the legend or the good works that Nightingale did in the Crimea, but with what she did afterwards, when she returned to England as the most famous and admired Englishwoman of her time, second only to Queen Victoria herself. What she did was to write a program evaluation of the events at the hospital and summarize these events in a way that had never been done before. Her summary, a report that ran to almost 1,000 pages and was submitted to the British Parliament, was radical in two different ways. First, it was a legislative report written by a woman. Although she could not do so openly because of her gender, she ghosted it for the Secretary of State for War, who submitted it as if it was his own work. However, it was hardly a state secret who the real author was. The report was radical, not only in its recommendations to clean up all military hospitals, provide adequate supplies, ventilation, and nursing; but also in its mode of presentation.

Knowing that members of Parliament (then as well as now) were disinclined to read a lengthy report, Nightingale summarized her findings with an innovative diagram, a kind of pie chart, with the slices of the pie being of different sizes, which she called a rose diagram. Each petal or slice of pie illustrated monthly death rates by cause. As conditions improved over time, the deaths declined and the petals or slices became progressively smaller. Thus, at a glance, policy makers (the members of Parliament) could see what lifesavers the proposed reforms had been at Scutari and could be throughout the British Empire—after all, the diagram clearly showed their effectiveness during the war. Implementing these reforms at home in Great Britain and throughout the worldwide British Empire could save countless lives, and could save significant money as well.

Nightingale was not the first person to use graphic images to illustrate data. Pie charts and bar graphs, for example, had been around for decades. However, she was the first to use such illustrations for political effect, to specifically influence and change public policy. She is the great unsung pioneer of governmental program evaluation, the systematic assessment of the effectiveness of a program, project, or procedure after it has been completed. This information is then fed back into the decisional or legislative process so that revisions and improvements can be achieved. This is exactly what her report and its famous illustration sought to do. Even before she arrived at the theater of war, she was insisting that the progress of patients be charted, that statistics be created and analyzed to better understand the effectiveness of medical treatment. Her father, the famous statistician had taught her well.

Nightingale was obsessive about gathering data and subjecting it to statistical analysis. Everything that could be counted would be counted; then analyses would be made and conclusions could be drawn. This was literally her dogma. As she said, "To understand God's thoughts we must study statistics, for these are the measure of His purpose" (Kopf, 1916). Her life-long penchant for counting data points ("to understand God's thoughts") was now applied to hospitals. This gave her the ingredients for a potent recipe of policy analysis that she fed to policy makers with lengthy prose highlighted by digestible illustrations.

She was an advocate of program evaluation before program evaluation was cool. More than a hundred years before Edward Suchman published the first major work on evaluation theory, *Evaluation Research* (1967), she was applying evaluative criteria to hospital care. By measuring whatever factors she could (diet, space between beds, frequency of laundry service, etc.), she sought to answer the eternal question: Which procedure is best? Though she never used the term, she endeavored to proceed systematically. Nightingale's credo was succinctly summarized by Alice Rivlin in her classic critique of program evaluation, *Systematic Thinking for Social Action* (1971): "Put more simply, to do better, we must have a way of distinguishing better from worse." Nightingale could not have said it better.

In today's world of personal computers, PowerPoint® presentations of complex data have become common, yet it was Nightingale, the nineteenth-century icon of the nursing profession, who first demonstrated the enormous utility of the graphic presentation of statistical data. So whenever you come across statistics presented in a graphic manner, remember that the famous "lady with a lamp" was also the lady with a chart, gathering data to be turned into a diagram for easy intellectual digestion.

In 1858 Florence Nightingale became the first woman to be elected to the Royal Statistical Society, a tribute to her pioneering efforts in making quantitative data more visually appealing and instantly understandable—even by legislators!

FOR DISCUSSION

Why is it fair to suggest that Florence Nightingale is the "mother" of PowerPoint® illustration, when all she did was invent a variant of a pie chart, a rose diagram, to influence public policy? How did Nightingale's fame and writings influence nursing throughout the world?

BIBLIOGRAPHY

Bostridge, Mark. *Florence Nightingale: The Making of an Icon.* New York: Farrar, Straus and Giroux, 2008.

Gill, Gillian. *Nightingales.* New York: Ballantine, 2004.

Goldie, Sue M., ed. *Florence Nightingale: Letters from the Crimea.* Manchester, UK: Manchester University Press, 1997.

Gordon, Richard. *The Private Life of Florence Nightingale.* London: Heinemann, 1978.

Kopf, E. W. "Florence Nightingale as Statistician." *Journal of the American Statistical Association,* 15:388–404 (1916).

Rivlin, Alice. *Systematic Thinking for Social Action.* Washington, DC: Brookings Institution, 1971.

Small, Hugh. *Florence Nightingale: Avenging Angel.* New York: St. Martin's, 1998.

Strachey, Lytton. *Eminent Victorians.* New York: Capricorn, 1963.

Suchman, Edward. *Evaluation Research.* New York: Russell Sage, 1967.

Woodham-Smith, Cecil. *Florence Nightingale 1820–1910.* New York: McGraw-Hill, 1951.

CHAPTER TWENTY-EIGHT

The Often Ridiculous Nature of Public Policy and Its Analysis

WHY IT IS SO IMPORTANT TO ALLOW FOR RIDICULE AND TO CONSIDER THE RIDICULOUS

PREVIEW

Remember Oedipus? In the ancient Greek tragedy by Sophocles (*Oedipus Rex*), he is the man who unknowingly kills his father, then, by an equally strange set of convoluted circumstances, marries the victim's widow, his own mother. This is why, more than two millennia later, Sigmund Freud, the "father" of psychotherapy, would say that a boy who loved his mother too much had an Oedipus complex. Meanwhile, back at the tragedy, the widow, now wife, after having had four children with Oedipus, discovers the truth and kills herself. Oedipus, upon learning that he had been, until recently, happily married to his now-dead mother, pokes out his own eyes. This isn't called a tragedy for nothing!

And then there are the sequels. In *Oedipus at Colonus,* the blind Oedipus is led about by his daughter Antigone as they discuss the great issues of philosophy and incest. With Oedipus dead at the end of this second episode in the life and times of this dysfunctional family, Sophocles completes his trilogy by making Antigone the star of her own tragedy.

In *Antigone,* the heroine defies the king who has ordered her dead brother's body to lie unburied, because he was a traitor who died in a revolt against the state. Now this is the point at which the play gets really interesting and contemporary. Antigone defies the king, citing a higher law—a higher obligation to the gods—and buries her brother, thereby forcing the king, in order to maintain his authority and uphold the law, to have her killed. With Antigone dead, her fiancé, the king's son, overwhelmed by grief, kills himself. Thereupon the boy's mother, the king's wife, kills herself over the loss of her son.

The law has been upheld, but at a huge cost to the king. This story has resonated with relevance ever since. *Antigone* offers the classic justification for defying the laws of the state: There is a higher law that must be obeyed. The core question here is which is more ridiculous; obeying a law that you consider immoral or disobeying the law and suffering the consequences. Many ordinary and some famous people have been subject to considerable ridicule for doing the latter.

THE TRADITION OF THE HIGHER LAW

One of the time-honored techniques for reforming public policies is to espouse a belief in a higher law—the notion that no matter what the laws (the policies) of a state are, there remains a higher law, to which a person has an even greater obligation. A higher law is often appealed to by those who wish to attack an existing law or practice that courts or legislators are unlikely or unwilling to change. Martyrs throughout the ages have asserted a higher law in defiance of the state, thus earning their martyrdom. Because the courts of any state will enforce the law of the land, appealing to a higher law is always chancy.

Civil disobedience is the higher-law approach in action. This is Henry David Thoreau's (1817–1862) notion from his essay, *On the Duty of Civil Disobedience* (1849), that one should not support a government (by paying taxes) if it sanctions policies (slavery) with which one disagrees. Thoreau's civil disobedience implied a willingness to stand up publicly and accept the consequences of one's disobedience, such as going to jail.

Indeed, Thoreau did go to jail in 1846 for refusing to pay his local taxes, in protest against the national government's policies concerning the Mexican War and slavery. Many of his friends and neighbors thought his insignificant protest was ridiculous, even silly. A famous exchange supposedly occurred, when the essayist and poet, Ralph Waldo Emerson (1803–1882), visited his friend in jail and asked, "Henry, why are you here?"

Thoreau responded, "Waldo, why are you not here?" Obviously, Thoreau thought that all right-thinking citizens should extend his protest and join him in jail. This famous exchange is quoted in many biographies of Thoreau, such as that of Henry S. Salt (1896), but is probably aprochryphal.

In the event, someone paid Thoreau's taxes anonymously, and he was released from jail after one night. His protest was a failure, but it did inspire him to write his famous essay, in which he created the phrase that is used to refer to acts of lawbreaking designed to bring public attention to laws—meaning public policies—of questionable morality and legitimacy. The most famous practitioners of civil disobedience in the twentieth century were Mohandas K. Gandhi (1869–1948) in India and Martin Luther King, Jr. (1929–1968) in the United States.

Interestingly, there are direct lines of influence among these three. Biographer Louis Fischer (1954) quotes Gandhi's opinion that Thoreau's *Civil Disobedience* (which he read, appropriately enough, during an early jail stay) was a "masterly treatise" that "left a deep impression on me." King, shortly after his initial involvement with the civil rights movement in the United States in the mid-1950s, traveled to India (in 1959) to study Gandhi's techniques of nonviolent civil disobedience, inspired in part by Thoreau. Here is King's Thoreau-inspired justification for civil disobedience from his *Why We*

Can't Wait (1964): "I submit that an individual who breaks a law that conscience tells him is unjust, and who willingly accepts the penalty of imprisonment in order to arouse the conscience of the community over its injustice, is in reality expressing the highest respect for the law."

Many people at the time considered King's actions and words to be ridiculous. Yet with time both the man and his words grew less and less ridiculous, until now the man is generally considered to be a secular saint and his words accepted wisdom. Public policies can outgrow ridicule; they can go from ridiculous to reverence in a generation, sometimes less.

EXAMINING PUBLIC POLICIES

The examination of public policy issues go back as far as we can trace civilization. Policy issues can be found in the Old Testament, in Genesis 4:9 ("Am I my brother's keeper?"); in the New Testament, in Matthew 22:21 ("Render therefore unto Caesar the things which are Caesar's . . ."); in Homer's *The Iliad* ("It is not unseemly for a man to die fighting in defense of his country."); in Aesop's fable of "The Rats and the Cat" ("Who shall bell the cat?"); and in the works of countless other ancient storytellers, philosophers, and historians. Indeed, the only really new thing about public policy is the self-conscious study of it: the attempt to assign methodological techniques retroactively to what was always done instinctively or as a matter of common sense.

Yet despite common sense, public policy analysis in the United States often appears to be ridiculous, silly or absurd. Worry not about the fate of the republic. This is a good and essentially healthy aspect of the policy-making process and has been since ancient times. But why is it desirable that something as important to the lives of every citizen as public policy be routinely subjected to ridicule? To begin to answer that question, it helps to get organized.

ORGANIZING TYPOLOGIES

A *typology* is a systematic organization of categories. Typologies are commonly used in the study of public policy and other social sciences and have a long historical tradition. They conveniently create neatness out of chaos; consequently, they make it easier to remember the essence of complex intellectual arguments.

For example, Aristotle (384–322 BCE), the ancient Greek philosopher, wrote of the three forms of government, kingship, aristocracy, and polity (majority rule); and the three perversions into which they typically degenerated, respectively; tyranny, oligarchy, and democracy (mob rule). German sociologist Max Weber (1864–1920) wrote that there are three pure types of legitimate authority: charismatic (in which the personal qualities of a leader command obedience), traditional (in which custom and culture yield acquiescence), and legal (in which people obey laws enacted by what they perceive to be appropriate authorities). More recently, American political scientist Theodore J. Lowi (1931–) classified all domestic public policies into distribution, regulation, or redistribution.

The study of public policy offers enormous scope for the creation of typologies. Textbooks and scholarly monographs sag with lists, categories, and classifications of public policies and ways to analyze them. The study of public policy is a chaotic world that cries out for organization, for definitive classification, and for a unified approach.

However, this is a cry that is unlikely to be heeded. Chaos rules because there is no power—neither U.S. president nor university president—who can tell the scholars of those academic disciplines concerned with public policy (political science, public administration, economics, international relations, etc.) how to ply their trade. Textbooks in science (biology, chemistry, physics, etc.) at least agree on the subject matter they cover. Public policy texts, in contrast, are far less in agreement. There is considerable overlap, of course, but it is minimal compared to that in the sciences. This is so largely because the various disciplines that study public policy have different traditions and approaches.

Typologies are also used to explain different approaches to the same problem. For example, there are three major approaches to decision making (rational, incremental, and mixed scanning). Looking at the differing approaches to common problems is particularly useful when comparing different cultures or organizations. A typology of how things are done in different cultural environments is often instructive. Consider this story, often told in the Pentagon. Each of the military services is told to secure a building. The Navy makes sure that all the doors and windows are watertight and locked. The Army posts guards at all the entrances and exits. The Marines stage an assault on the place and arrest everyone inside. The Air Force seeks out the owner of the building and negotiates a five-year lease. Each service has secured the building—in its fashion.

The analysis of public policies also has its fashions. As with all fashions, some are logical and utilitarian while others are, quite frankly, ridiculous. To appreciate fully just how ridiculous some fashions can be, we must first examine what passes for the normal, the acceptable, and the mundane. Thus we have created an artificial typology of approaches to understanding, analyzing, and presenting public policies. In the end—literally at the end—the approach becomes ridiculous; and that is a good thing. However, you cannot fully appreciate just how good and how important it is until you understand our arbitrary and capricious typology of the traditional approaches into three categories: everyday policy analysis, formal policy analysis, and policy analysis as dissent.

EVERYDAY POLICY ANALYSIS

Policy analysis, ridiculous or not, is ubiquitous. You can hardly go through the day without bumping into it. You wake up to a talk radio show spewing vitriolic opinions on a new presidential proposal. As you eat breakfast while reading the local morning newspaper, you are exposed to more analysis on regional issues such as school taxes and crime rates. At work, your officemates freely give you their analyses of the behavior of a political leader caught in the latest financial or sex scandal. Returning home from work, you review your mail and find more analyses in the magazines to which you subscribe and in the unsolicited junk mail from public-interest groups and political parties. Then perhaps you turn on your computer and surf the Internet for even more news and analysis

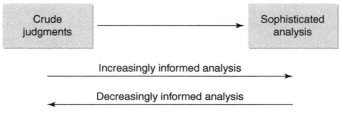

Figure 28.1 The Policy Analysis Continuum

of current affairs. Finally, you conclude your day by falling asleep while watching even more analyses on TV news and talk shows. It seems that almost everybody is constantly explaining or complaining about something.

If journalism represents the first rough draft of history, it is also the first policy analysis that most people hear or read on a new issue. The powers that be make policy, but it is then reported and explained to the public by the journalistic media. All the major news organizations, both print and TV, have reporters who specialize in various policy areas. Thus there are White House, congressional, Supreme Court, education, medical, consumer, and financial correspondents, among others. It is these specialists who are almost always the first analysts to tackle a new policy issue. Scholarly analysis is usually years behind—unless, of course, it is done by the relatively small group of academics who also write for journalistic sources. The op-ed pages are full of college professors and think tank denizens telling the public what the implications are of any new policy.

All this—from the current buzz at work to the latest blogs and weekly news magazines—is informal policy analysis. These "quick and dirty" critiques of current issues are both ubiquitous and essential to a flourishing democracy. They may be made with style, wit, and true depth of feeling, but they tend to lack the methodological rigor of a formal policy analysis.

To the extent that we make judgments on governmental policies from affirmative action to zoning variances, we all do policy analysis. Any judgment on a policy issue requires an analysis, however superficial. Policy analysis can be viewed as a continuum from crude judgments made in a snap ("The governor is an idiot and all his policies are stupid.") to the most sophisticated analysis using complicated methodologies ("I have just administered an IQ test to the governor and he really is an idiot."). Policy analysis is like sex: Almost everybody does it; but there is a relatively small group that does it professionally. See Figure 28.1 for a graphic presentation.

FORMAL POLICY ANALYSIS

A man driving his sport utility vehicle (SUV) is lost in a desert when he spots another SUV, driven by a woman. The man approaches her and asks, "Where am I?"

She responds, "You're in the middle of the desert."

He then observes, "You must be a policy analyst."

She answers, "Why yes, how did you know?"

He concludes, "Because you just told me something that is absolutely accurate and totally useless."

The story is not true, but it does tell a profound truth: Much that passes for policy analysis is viewed as "totally useless" by many public-sector decision makers. That is because so much that passes for analysis is really just opinion or biased advocacy. Opinion, however flip and accurate, won't cut it: Someone lost in the "desert" of indecision needs a formal structured policy analysis to find his or her way home.

Formal research is the end product of a methodologically rigorous effort to test the utility of a given policy. It essentially reports the result of formal research involving techniques such as data gathering and analysis, sample surveys, benefit–cost analysis, and game theory, among others. Much of the academic world is dedicated to policy research that presents new evidence regarding factors such as the effectiveness of public policies or the causes of policy adoption. Even research in areas that seem far afield from public policy can have vast public policy implications. For example, new medical research might mean that government has to take action to make a new treatment widely available. New findings about crop productivity might mean that government has to revise its agricultural policies. And new investigations about how a law has been administered might mean that a government must pay out vast sums to remedy past injustices.

A common aspect of policy research conducted in academic or nonpartisan settings such as government agencies is tight adherence to rigorous scientific methodology. To sustain the scrutiny of review by peers, the press, and the public at large, policy researchers must incorporate processes that meet the accepted standards of social science research. Failure to follow accepted research practices casts doubt on the validity of the policy research.

Formal policy analysis uses a set of techniques that seeks to answer the question of what the probable effects of a policy will be before they actually occur. A policy analysis undertaken on a program that is already in effect is more properly called a program evaluation. Nevertheless, policy analysis is used by many to refer to both before- and after-the-fact analyses of public policies.

Neutral competence is a long-standing concept in public policy and administration. It refers to a continuous, politically uncommitted cadre of bureaucrats at the disposal of elected or appointed political executives. This ethic of neutrality has now been borrowed by the policy analyst.

Policy analysts should be unbiased when they first approach a problem. An open mind is essential for systematic compilation and interpretation of facts. Once the analytical task of the analyst is complete, however, analysts may be transformed by their conclusions and attendant circumstances from analysts to advocates. This is dangerous. Presenting the results of a policy analysis allows an analyst to pose as a neutral, nonpartisan, disinterested professional. Prescribing public policy on the basis of an analysis takes the analyst into the realm of politics. The advocate may then become a lobbyist and risk his or her reputation for objectivity.

A policy paper is a formal argument in favor of (or opposing) a particular public policy. It may incorporate formal research or may be merely a legal, political, or administrative

---

NEUTRAL COMPETENCE IN ACTION

The Budget Bureau keeps humble and if it ever becomes obsessed with the idea that it has any work except to save money and improve efficiency in routine business it will cease to be useful in the hands of the President. Again I say, we have nothing to do with policy. Much as we love the President, if Congress, in its omnipotence over appropriations and in accordance with its authority over policy, passed a law that garbage should be put on the White House steps, it would be our regrettable duty, as a bureau, in an impartial, nonpolitical and nonpartisan way to advise the Executive and Congress as to how the largest amount of garbage could be spread in the most expeditious and economical manner.

Source: Charles G. Dawes, *The First Year of the Budget of the United States.* New York: Harper Bros, 1923.

---

analysis of the validity of a proposal. Political candidates typically generate a variety of policy papers on issues of importance to their constituents. Political campaigns often become a "battle" of opposing policy papers. And the modern battleground for these opposing policies is frequently in cyberspace, on the websites of political candidates. Such websites promote not only the candidate but also the policies of that candidate. Consequently, they usually include white papers (formal statements of an official policy) about where the candidate stands on various issues and why. In theory, voters can read these thoughtful papers on a wide range of policy issues. However, there is little evidence that many voters take the time to read these thorough policy positions and instead receive most information from short political commercials that lack detailed policy material.

No matter how astute and detailed the arguments are for or against a particular policy, the media tend to distill them into a few words. Thus an extreme and thoughtful review of the utility of capital punishment often comes down to the fact that the candidate is "for" or "against" the death penalty. Voters prefer to think that their favored candidates have given great thought to all the subtle aspects of their policy positions. Consequently, it is more important that such policy papers exist than that they be read. However, policy papers put out by advocacy groups and academics—and not related to political campaigns—tend to be both more sophisticated and better received.

Policy papers today are almost always written, but they have an ancient unwritten tradition. In the Old Testament, Moses says to Pharaoh (Exodus 5:1), "Let my people go." In *The Iliad*, Ulysses tells the Greeks besieging Troy to build a wooden horse. These are both policy "papers," even though there was not yet any paper. There is still a strong oral policy paper tradition, but the modern version of a would-be Moses or Ulysses is most likely to be found giving a speech on the campaign trail—either running for office or as the representative of a public-interest group. For example, Charlton Heston (the actor who played Moses in the 1955 film, *The Ten Commandments*), as president of the National Rifle Association, frequently spoke against further government regulation of firearms. However, the place where you will find this oral tradition flourishing every hour of every day is on TV and radio talk shows. There the most pressing public policy issues of any given day are dissected, criticized, and/or supported *ad nauseum*. Academic policy papers are published in professional journals and read by few. Talk show hosts publish little and may be relatively ignorant, but they can be immensely influential.

POLICY ANALYSIS AS DISSENT: NOW IT GETS RIDICULOUS

Finally, now that we have presented the traditional aspects of policy analysis, our analysis can get ridiculous. Understand that public policy analysis has a long literary tradition. For example, Aristophanes (445–380 BCE), another ancient Greek playwright, wrote *Lysistrata,* a play with a famous analysis of how to end the then twenty-year war between Athens and Sparta: All the women of both cities would refuse to have sex with their men until peace was concluded. Although this technique has never been successfully implemented, the play is still often produced—proving the popularity of at least examining the proposed policy.

Lysistrata is a comedy that is often performed on college campuses today. Not only is it the oldest antiwar play, it offers many excellent parts for both men and women. While the women get to talk a lot about the relationships between war and sex, the men are directed to show their earnest need for resuming sexual relations by holding or wearing oversized phalluses in front of them while they discuss the great issues of war, peace, and marital connubiality. The overall effect is quite ridiculous while at the same time being serious, indeed timeless; public policy issues are presented in a highly digestible and wonderfully salacious manner.

Another follower in this tradition was the English satirist Jonathan Swift (1667–1745), the self-described misanthrope whose best-known work is *Gulliver's Travels* (1726), his masterpiece of political analysis that is so entertaining on the surface that it is considered a children's classic. It is in this book that Swift introduces the Yahoo, a race of humanlike creatures enslaved by Houyhnhnms, a race of horses. The Yahoo would later achieve fame as the name of one of the most useful websites on the Internet.

Swift's most outrageous satire, however, was probably a brief pamphlet written while he was resident in Ireland as Dean of St. Patrick's Cathedral in Dublin. Entitled *A Modest Proposal for Preventing the Children of the Poor People in Ireland from Being a Burden to Their Parents or Country, and for Making Them Beneficial to Their Publick* (1729), this masterpiece of irony tinged with bitterness offered a logical solution to the problem of overpopulation in Ireland: Eat the young. The excess children of the poor should be sold for sustenance because "at a year old [they make] a most delicious, nourishing, and wholesome food, whether stewed, roasted, baked or boiled." It has long been a British tradition to serve a whole suckling pig with an apple in its mouth for a holiday feast. Why not a suckling child? The apple would fit in either case.

Swift's extensive list of arguments why this "wholesome food" would be beneficial to the nation, like Aristophanes' suggestion for achieving peace, has been widely read but never implemented, at least as far as we know. Swift's proposal was deliciously ridiculous but hardly modest; it was radical in its intent, to call attention to the plight of the Irish poor. It was a best-seller in its time and continues to be read by anyone who has ever seen a child "good enough to eat."

A final example is this tradition is Al Franken, a *Saturday Night Live* alumnus and, since 2009, U.S. senator from Minnesota, who noted two facts in his best-selling book, *Rush Limbaugh Is a Big Fat Idiot* (1999): "30 percent of Medicare expenditures are incurred by people in the last year of their lives," and "NASA spends billions per year on astronaut safety." So Franken asks, "Why not shoot the elderly into space? . . . Just think how many more manned space operations NASA could undertake if they didn't have to worry about getting the astronauts back. Now, I'm not saying we don't try to get them back. We just don't make such a big deal about it."

Now that Senator Al Franken is one of the overseers of NASA, he might have even greater influence in foisting his "elderly astronaut" plan on the space program—as a cost-saving measure, of course. Fortunately, Franken himself is a member of a group of potential elderly space volunteers. Remember that the word *senate* has the same Latin root as *senile*. *Senate* is a noun meaning an assembly of the old. *Senile* is an adjective referring to the behavior of the elderly. Franken's colleagues are probably not senile enough to volunteer for his unsafe but cheap space travel initiative. After all, they are supposed to be an assembly of wise old people.

What these three examples have in common is that they are all theoretically possible but hardly practical. The difficulties of implementation immediately defeat these ideas, but they do represent a type of policy analysis that will always be—must always be—with us. What one generation perceives to be outrageous or even satire (as all three examples clearly are), another may find feasible.

This is already happening with Senator Franken's "elderly astronaut" proposal. It is gradually losing its ridiculous aspect and becoming a real possibility as NASA considers the problems of sending humans to Mars. The voyage would be so dangerous and so long that it might be logical if the astronauts stayed on Mars to the end of their lives. Consequently, older astronauts whose longevity is inherently limited might be the best candidates for the trip. Accordingly, Lawrence M. Krauss of Arizona State University, writing in the *New York Times* in 2009, argued that: "To boldly go where no one has gone before does not require coming home again." The Mars voyage is so much more feasible when it is designed as a one-way trip that the elder option will be seriously considered.

Major policy innovations often sound ridiculous at first. Many continue to sound ridiculous. Others, however, gradually lose their comic aspect and actually become policy. This is most obviously true with advancements in science and technology. It once seemed ridiculous that steam would replace sail on the world's oceans, a human heart could be transplanted, or men could walk on the moon.

In the realm of politics, it once seemed ridiculous that people could live without kings, slavery would be illegal, convicted murderers would not be executed, or women would have the right to vote. The ridiculous policy analysis has value because it is very much like the minority opinion of an appellate court. Minority opinions issued by the U.S. Supreme Court have sometimes been extremely significant because they have so often established the intellectual framework for subsequent reversals of decisions. Chief Justice Charles Evans Hughes (1862–1948) wrote that these dissenting opinions are "appeals to the brooding spirit of the law, to the intelligence of a future day, when a later decision may possibly correct the error into which the dissenting judge believes the court to have been betrayed."

Few public policy issues were initially considered as ridiculous as the idea of same-sex marriage. In all societies, ethical traditions and cultural influences affect how public policy issues are analyzed. Societies differ on what they consider to be appropriate sexual mores. Historically, the core problem of dealing with the civil rights of gays and lesbians is that the activity that defines them (physical intimacy with a member of the same sex, otherwise known as consensual sodomy), had been long considered a crime in many states. In 2003, the Supreme Court, in *Lawrence v. Texas,* declared unconstitutional the Texas ban on consensual sodomy and in effect asserted a broad constitutional right to sexual privacy. Justice Anthony M. Kennedy wrote in the majority opinion that the case concerned "two adults who, with full and mutual consent from each other, engaged in sexual practices common to a homosexual lifestyle. The petitioners are entitled to respect for their private lives. The State cannot demean their existence or control their destiny by making their private sexual conduct a crime."

In an extremely strong dissenting opinion, Justice Antonin Scalia said that the ruling "effectively decrees the end of all morals legislation" and could possibly pave the way for "judicial imposition of homosexual marriage, as has recently occurred in Canada." This case overruled a 1986 decision in which the court upheld Georgia's sodomy law (*Bowers v. Hardwick*). The 2003 decision effectively nullified sodomy laws in the thirteen states besides Texas that still had such laws. The 2003 *Lawrence* decision on homosexual rights has its origins in the 1965 case of *Griswold v. Connecticut,* which first asserted that there was a constitutional right to bedroom privacy even though the word "privacy" does not appear in the Constitution.

One needs to look no further than the recent policy debates surrounding same-sex marriage in the United States for confirmation of the contention that what starts out as ridiculous often ends up as settled law. In November 1993, a Massachusetts Supreme Court decision granted marriage rights to same-sex couples in that state, initiating months of hectic political activity well beyond the borders of the New England commonwealth. Most notably, President George W. Bush became an active participant in the debate, arguing for a constitutional amendment that would preserve marriage as a union between two people of opposite sex. In defending his position, President Bush argued in a February 25, 2004, speech that "the union of a man and a woman is the most enduring human institution, honored and encouraged in all cultures and by every religious faith," and therefore, "cannot be severed from its cultural, religious and natural roots without weakening the good influence of society."

The president's position on the matter reflects long-standing hesitancy and opposition on the behalf of many Americans to accept homosexual relationships as part of the nation's mainstream culture, essentially because they believe such relationships to be immoral, wrong, and frankly, just ridiculous. Conversely, supporters of same-sex marriage in places ranging from San Francisco to New Paltz, New York, engaged in acts of civil disobedience against restrictions on gay marriage, largely because they believed such restrictions of rights on the basis of a citizen's sexual preference are both immoral and wrong. Both sides in the debate claim the moral high ground, with any resolution through the policy-making process likely pleasing neither side completely. Nevertheless, what once seemed ridiculous is gradually becoming mainstream as more and more states allow for same-sex marriages. This is not yet settled law, but it now seems headed in that direction. What is most decidedly settled is the question of whether same-sex marriage is ridiculous. Not if it's legal!

FOR DISCUSSION

What elements of the institutional framework of the U.S. political system allow new, seemingly preposterous ideas to travel from the lunatic fringe to mainstream thinking? Can you think of any policy proposals that are currently considered ridiculous that are likely candidates for mainstream acceptance?

BIBLIOGRAPHY

Aristotle. *Politics.* Translated by B. Jowett. Chicago: Great Books, Encyclopedia Britannica, 1952.

Emerson, Ralph Waldo. *Essays: First and Second Series.* New York: Vintage Books, 1990.

Fischer, Louis. *Gandhi.* New York: New American Library, 1954.

Franken, Al. *Rush Limbaugh Is a Big Fat Idiot.* New York: Dell, 1999.

Gladden, E. N. *A History of Public Administration.* 2 vols. London: Frank Cass, 1972.

Hughes, Charles Evans. *The Supreme Court of the United States: Its Foundation, Methods and Achievements: An Interpretation.* New York: Columbia University Press, 1936.

Krauss, Lawrence M. "A One-Way Ticket to Mars," *New York Times,* September 1, 2009.

Lowi, Theodore J. "American Business, Public Policy Case Studies and Political Theory." *World Politics* XVI (July 1964).

Plato. *The Republic.* Translated by B. Jowett. Oxford, UK: Clarendon Press, 1925.

Salt, Henry S. *Life of Henry David Thoreau.* London: Walter Scott, 1896.

Tichy, N. M., and D. O. Ulrich. "The Leadership Challenge—A Call for the Transformational Leader." *Sloan Management Review* 26 (1984).

Tichy, Noel M., and Mary Anne Devanna. *The Transformational Leader.* New York: Wiley, 1990.

Weber, Max. *From Max Weber: Essays in Sociology.* Edited and translated by H. H. Gerth and C. Wright Mills. New York: Oxford University Press, 1946.

Index

A

Abbate, Janet, 149
Academic and professional public
    administration, corruption, 20
Acquisition-based valuation, 243
Adams, Guy B., 94–95
Adams, John, 24
Advanced Research Project Agency
    (ARPA), 147
The Adventure of the Noble Bachelor, 9
The Adventure of the Six Napoleons, 6
The Adventures of Sherlock Holmes, 4
The Age of Reform, 14
Aid to Families with Dependent
    Children (AFDC), 66
Al Franken, 268
Ambrose, Stephen E., 185, 218
Ambrose, Steven E., 135
Anderson, Martin, 48
Animal Farm, 141, 144, 224
Ansoff, H. Igor, 180–181
Antigone, 260
Appleby, Paul, 81
Arendt, Hannah, 90
Aristocracy government, 262
Aristotle, 107
    forms of government, 262
ARPAnet, 148
Asymmetrical warfare, 105
At Ease, 214, 218
Atlantic Alliance, 159
Atlas Shrugged, 51–52
Attack!, 137
Away All Boats, 136–137
A World Restored, 201

B

Balfour, Danny L., 94–95
Baltimore Sun, 127

Banality of evil, 90
    Arendt's concept of, 90
    Eichmann's trial (*See* Eichmann, Adolf)
    ethnic cleansing and, 93
    gas chamber of Philadelphia and, 93–94
    Hilberg's examination of *Reichsbahn*'s
        operations and, 91–93
    Milgram experiments on, 90–91
    public administration and, 94–95
Baran, Paul, 148
Beeton's Christmas Annual, 2
Bentham, Jeremy, 39
Berlin Airlift, 159
Berlin blockade, in Cold War, 158–159
Bertalanffy, Ludwig von, 107
Beschloss, Michael R., 163
Big Democracy, 81
Biological evolution concept, 17
Bismarck, Otto von, 55–56
Bland, Robert, 243
Blitzer, Wolf, 150
Blitzkrieg formation, 32
Boom-and-bust business cycle, 31
Boscombe Valley Mystery, 10
Bowers v. Hardwick case, 227, 269
Brady Handgun Violence Prevention
    Act, 72
Branden, Barbara, 52
Brodie, Bernard, 169
*Brown v. Board of Education of Topeka,
    Kansas,* 222–224
Brushfire wars, 169
Buchanan, James M., 52
Bunyan, John, 11
Burke, Edmund, 39
Burns, Robert, 154
Bush, George H. W., 28
Business consultants, 7
Byrne, John A., 110

C

California
  budget crises, 244
    of 2008–2009, 246–251
  California Department of Equalization, 243
  child health insurance program, 251
  "democratic populism," 246
  diversification of state and local tax
    systems in, 243
  and economy, 242
  fiscal chronology for, 248–249
  fiscal crises of, 251
  fiscal emergency in, 247
  health programs, 246
  House of California's budget, 244
  inmate release program, 251
  mandatory furloughs/pay cuts, 250
  "millionaires tax" for mental health
    programs, 246
  preschools programs, 246
  sales taxes for local public safety, 246
  sales taxes on fuel to transportation, 246
  state budget and general fund, 245
  stock market, fell of, 244
  unemployment and, 247
Capitalism, The Unknown Ideal, 51
Card, Andrew, 130
Carnegie, Andrew, 20
Carter Doctrine, 28
Cassidy, John, 48
Castle doctrine, 75
"Chain of circumstance", concept by Nicolson,
    147. *See also* Internet
Chamberlain, John, 191
Chaos theory, 111–112
Churchill, Winston, 187
Circumstantial evidence, 9
Civil disobedience, 261
Civil Rights Movement, 228
  Civil Rights Act of 1957, 229
  Civil Rights Act of 1960, 229
  Civil Rights Act of 1964, 229–230
Civil War and abolition of slavery, 17
Clinton, Bill, 28
Closed system, 108
Coates, James, 105
Cold war, 153–154
  and Soviet Union, 36

Confident organization, 185
Confucius in ancient China, 27
Conspiracy, 89
Consultant
  definitions, 5–6
Corporate default, 98
Corruption, academic and professional public
    administration, 20
Cosmopolitan
  series of articles and President Theodore
    Roosevelt, 12
Counselor, 205
Counsels of War, 172
Crimean War of 1853 to 1856, 253
Crusade in Europe, 217
Cuba by Cuban exiles, United States
    sponsored invasion, 39
Cybernetics, 109

D

Dahlberg, Jane, 20
Danger and Survival, 161
Darwin, Charles
  concept of biological evolution, 17
Davis, Richard Harding, 127
Default. *See* Orange County investment
    scandal
Democratic National Convention, 26
Deregulation, in United States, 48
Dickens, Charles, 4
Distributed communications, Baran's concept
    of, 148–149
District of Columbia v. Heller case, 74, 78
Doctrine
  definition, 23
  innovations, 31–32
  and policy development, cyclical
    nature of, 32
  of republicanism, 23–24
  template, 32–33
Donne, John, 104–105
Doomsday machine, 172
Douglas Aircraft Company, 167
Down and Out in Paris and London, 144
Downs, Anthony, 173–174
Doyle, Arthur Conan
  consultant, inventor of, 5–6
  creater of Holmes, 2–3

imagination of characters, 3
literary dinner by U.S. editor of *Lippincott's
Monthly Magazine,* 2–3
short stories in U.S., 2
Strand Magazine, stories in, 4
Drucker, Peter, 184

E
Easton, David, 107
The Economist, 247
EEOC. *See* Equal Employment Opportunity
Commission (EEOC)
Eichmann, Adolf
capital punishment for, 89
*Eichmann in Jerusalem, A Report on the
Banality of Evil,* 90
kidnapping of, 87–88
trial in Israel, 88–89
Einstein, Albert
theory of relativity, 37
Eisenhower career, role of mentor in
benefits from mentoring, 216–218
Conner role, as mentor, 212–214
education in military history by
Conner, 215–216
Eisenhower as mentee, 214–215
influence of mentor, 218–219
meeting with Conner at dinner, 211–212
Eisenhower, Dwight
Eisenhower Doctrine, 27
Emerson, Ralph Waldo, 261
Enola Gay, 36
Enthoven, Alain, 169
Equal Employment Opportunity Commission
(EEOC), 233
Evaluation Research, 258
Everyday policy analysis, 263–264. *See also*
Public policy

F
Facebook, 145
Facial recognition technology, 142
The Fall of the House of Usher, 242
FCRA. *See* Firearms Control and Regulation
Act (FCRA)
Federal Aid Highway Act of 1956, 164
Fiduciary responsibility, 101–102

"Financial Armageddon," 247–248
Firearm regulations, in United States,
71–73, 77–78
attack on presidents, 71–72
in New York, 76–77
in Texas, 74–76
in Washington, 73–74
Firearms Control and Regulation Act
(FCRA), 73
Fiscal chronology for California, 248–249
Fischer, Louis, 261
Foreign Affairs, 156
Formal policy analysis, 264–267. *See also*
Public policy
For-profit think tanks, 177
Franklin, Benjamin, 112
French Revolution of 1789, ideology
and, 24
Freud, Sigmund, 260
Friedman, Milton, 48
Fussell, Paul
Thank God for the Atom Bomb, 37

G
Gabriel, Richard, 110
Galbraith, John Kenneth, 37
The New Industrial State, 38
Gandhi, Mohandas K.
techniques of nonviolent civil
disobedience, 261
Garnett, John, 171
Georgia's sodomy law, 269
G.I. Jane, 132
Gingrich, Newt, 133
Gleick, James, 112
Goodbye, Darkness, 36–37
Goodnow, Frank J., 80
Grant, Ulysses S., 15
Great Depression, 60–61
of 1930s, 28
Greek tragedy by Sophocles, 260
Griswold v. Connecticut case,
227, 269
Gulliver's Travels, 267
Gun Control Act of 1968, 72
*Guts and Glory, Great American
War Movies,* 133

H

Hafner, Katie, 148
Hamburger, Tom, 82
Hands-off style of governance, 28
Harris v. Forklift Systems case, 234
Havemann, Judith, 66
Hayek, Friedrich A., 43
  Hayek's economic philosophy, 43
    California electric utility industry
      and, 51–52
    economic crisis in 2008 and, 52–53
    and George H. W. Bush approach, 49
    and Goldwater's presidential bid, 46–47
    public-choice doctrine and, 49
    Reagan revolution and, 47–48
    Thatcher and, 44–45
    and U.S. economic policy, 45–46
Heavy Losses, 105
Herbert, Sidney, 255
Herken, Gregg, 172
Herring, E. Pendleton, 82
Herzfeld, Charles, 148
Higher law, 261
High-Performance Computing
  Act of 1991, 151
Hilberg, Raul, 91
Hirohito, Japanese Emperor
  effectiveness of bombs, 36
Hiroshima, atomic bomb, 36
History of the Internet, 147
Hobbes, Thomas, 153
Hofstadter, Richard, 14
  The Age of Reform by, 14
"Homeless army" of children, 21
Hoogenboom, Ari, 15
How the Other Half Lives, 21
Hughes, Charles Evans, 268–269
Hull House, 19

I

Ideology, 23–24
Ike, 218
The Iliad, 262
Inmate release program in California, 251
In Search of Excellence, 121
Inside Bureaucracy, 174
Inside the Whale and Other Essays, 140

Internet
  ARPAnet, birth of, 148
  from ARPAnet to Internet, 148–150
  as child of cold war, 147–148
  Gore effort in development of, 150–151
  history of, 147
  Websites, 141
Inventing the Internet, 149

J

James, D. Clayton, 127
Jigsaw puzzle approach, 6
"Jim Crow" law, 228–229
Joe Louis–Max Schmeling Depression era
  boxing match, 237
Johnson, Patrick, 246
Johnson Doctrine, 28
John Wayne, American, 133
Jomini, Antoine Henri, 127
The Jungle, 13

K

Kadet, Anne, 142–143
Kahn, Herman, 170–171
Kanigel, Robert, 7
Kaplan, Fred, 172
Kelly, Sharon Pratt, 240
Kennan, George F., 156–157
Kennedy, John F., 21
Kilian, Michael, 105
King, Martin Luther Jr., 261
Kingship government, 262
Kissinger, Henry, 201
Krauss, Lawrence M., 268
Kuhn, Thomas S.
  The Structure of Scientific Revolutions, 30

L

Lawrence v. Texas case, 227, 269
Learned helplessness, 185
Lee, Norman E., 195
Legal authority and technical ability, 38–39
Leviathan, 153
Light, Paul C., 63
Lincoln, Abraham, 49
Line-item veto, 246
Line workers, 198

Lippincott's Monthly Magazine, 2
Lippmann, Walter, 81
Literary piracy, 2
Little Dorrit, 61
Longfellow, Henry Wadsworth, 256
Lorenz, Edward, 112
Lowi, Theodore J., 262
Luttwak, Edward N., 111
Lyon, Matthew, 148
Lysistrata, 267

M
MacArthur, Douglas, 190
    as Chief of Staff of U.S. Army, 191
    and decision to take his
        staff, 197–198
    departure to Australia, 196–197
    early life of, 190–191
    and Eisenhower's recommendation,
        194–195
    fighting Japanese invaders in Philippines,
        191–192
    as general supreme in rhetoric, 193–194
    and order to command troops in Australia,
        195–196
    stand-and-die orders, from Roosevelt,
        192–193
Machiavelli, Niccolo, 207–208
Makers of Nuclear Strategy, 171
Management by objectives (MBO)
    concept, 184
Management consultants, 7
Manchester, William, 36–37
Marshall, George C., 157
Marshall Plan, 157–158
Marshall, Thurgood,
    220–222, 224
Master and Commander, 137
MBO. *See* Management by objectives (MBO)
McClure's Magazine
    muckraking and, 19
McCullough, David, 37–38
Mehle, F. Douglas, 215
Memoirs of Sherlock Holmes, 4, 6
Mentoring power. *See* Eisenhower career,
    role of mentor in
Meritor Savings Bank v. Vinson case, 234

Michener, James A., 206
Microsoft Explorer, 150
Milgram, Stanley, 90–91
Military Maxims, 110
Milnes, Richard Monckton, 254
Monroe Doctrine, 27
Montgomery, Bernard L., 186
Mosaic, 150
Muckraking, 12
    kinds of, 20
    McClure's Magazine and, 19
    to reform, 13–14
Mysak, Joe, 100

N
NAACP. *See* National Association for
    Advancement of Colored People
    (NAACP)
Napoleon, 110
National Aeronautics and Space
    Administration Act of 1958, 165
National Association for Advancement of
    Colored People (NAACP), 220–222
National Commission on Social Security
    Reform, 64
National Defense Education Act of 1958,
    164–165
National Oceanographic and Aeronautics
    Administration (NOAA), 84
National Review, 46
National welfare system, 33
NATO. *See* North Atlantic Treaty
    Organization (NATO)
Neal, Steve, 128
Netscape Navigator, 150
Neutral competence, 265
    in action, 266
New Deal, 26
The New Industrial State, 38
Newman, James, 171
Newsweek International, 24
Newton, Isaac
    concepts of physics, 31
New York Bureau of Municipal
    Research, 19
New York Review of Books, 90
Nicolson, Harold, 147

Nightingale, Florence
aspirations to be nurse, 254
and Crimean War, 255
as hospital administrator, 254–255
invention and practice of modern
nursing, 253
legislative report on military hospitals
graphic images use for data illustration,
257–258
quantitative data making, pioneer
of, 258
statistical analysis and, 254
suffering soldiers, well-being and
morale of, 256
"The Lady with a Lamp," 255–256
Nineteen Eighty-Four, 140–141, 144
Nixon, Richard M., 15
Nixon Doctrine, 28
NOAA. *See* National Oceanographic and
Aeronautics Administration (NOAA)
Nonprofit think tanks, 177
North Atlantic Treaty Organization (NATO),
159–160
Novick, David, 172
Nuclear Weapons and Foreign Policy, 201

O

OASDI. *See* Old Age, Survivors, and Disability
Insurance (OASDI)
Obedience to Authority, 91
Old Age, Survivors, and Disability Insurance
(OASDI), 62
Olson, James, 133
Olson, Mancur, 50
Oncale v. Sundowner Offshore Services
case, 235
One Party Country, 82
On Escalation, Metaphors and Scenarios, 171
On the Duty of Civil Disobedience, 261
On Thermonuclear War, 171
Open systems theory, 108–109
Oppenheimer, J. Robert, 39
Optimism, 185, 188
optimistic leaders, 186
Orange County investment scandal, 98–99
Citron, role of, 99
fiduciary responsibility, neglect of, 102

guilty of six felony counts, 100–102
risky investment strategy of Citron,
99–100
Organizational policies, strategic
implementation, 179
hierarchy of doctrine, levels
grand strategic, 180
operational, 182–183
strategic, 180–182
tactical, 183–184
and optimism, 185–186, 188
Organization development
at command level, 136–137
leadership, style of, 133–134
three acts of group development, 135–136
in war movies
G.I. Jane, Moore in, 132–133
The Sands of Iwo Jima, Wayne in,
132–133
Wayne role in, 134–135
Organization of categories, 262
Orwell, George, 144
conception of "Big Brother," 141–142
Nineteen Eighty-Four by
on all-intrusive government, 140–141
surveillance technologies, use of, 142–143
implications of, 143–145
on totalitarian states, 140–141
Outlawing the Spoils, 15
Oxford English Dictionary, 5–6

P

Paget, Sidney
illustrations by, 4
Parker v. District of Columbia case, 74
Parsons, Talcott, 108
Paths of Glory, 137
Patton, 136
Pax Romana, 154
Pendleton Act of 1883, 16
Peterson, John, 100
Peters, Tom, 121
Phillips, David Graham, 12
Philosophy, doctrine and policy, relationship
among, 24–25
Phoenix Gazette, 238
The Picture of Dorian Gray, 3

Pilgrim's Progress, 11
Planks of political party platform, 25
Planning Programming Budgeting Systems
    (PPBS), 173
Plato, 107
Plessy v. Ferguson case, 221–222
Poe, Edgar Allen, 242, 246–247
Poe, Sheryll, 143
Policy advisors, 39–40
Political party
    doctrines, 25
    platform, planks of, 25
    comparison, 26
Politician–administrator nexus, in
    U.S., 81–82
Politics, 107
Polity government, 262
Ponzi, Charles, 61
Poor Richard's Almanac, 112
Post–Civil War reform era, 14
Potsdam declaration, 35–36
PPBS. *See* Planning Programming Budgeting
    Systems (PPBS)
Presidential doctrines, 28
Presley, Elvis, 165
Price, Don K., 38
Pride and Prejudice, 254
The Principles of Scientific Management, 9
Professional education in public
    administration, 20
Professional public administration advent, 19–21
Profiles in Courage, 205
Program budgeting, 172
Progressive movement, 17–18
Public administration, as essay contest. *See*
    Writings, importance in policy
    making world
Public-choice theory, 49–51
Public funds, gambling with, 99, 101–102
Public interest, 81
Public policy
    evolution of, 147
    examination, 262
        creation of typologies, 263
        everyday analysis, 263–264
        literary tradition of, 267–270
        Policy Analysis Continuum, 264
        policy papers, 265–266

Public service, social advancement
    through, 15–16
Public stadium financing, 237–240
Pure Food and Drug Act of 1906, 13
Pygmalion effect, 186

R

Rand, Ayn, 51–53
RAND Corporation
    birth of nuclear theory, 169–170
    and doomsday machine, 172
    expansion of, 172–174
    Kahn as superstar of, 170–171
    as nonprofit think tank, 177
    project, beginning of, 167–169
Reagan, Ronald, 21
    Reagan Doctrine, 28
The Red-Headed League, 6
Reform movement, 14–15
Republic, 107
Republicanism doctrine, 23–24
Republican Party split, 18
Rhodes, Richard, 40
Riis, Jacob A.
    How the Other Half Lives, 21
Rivlin, Alice
    *Systematic Thinking for Social
        Action,* 258
Roberts, Randy, 133
Rockefeller, John D., 13
Romeo and Juliet, 147
Roosevelt, Franklin D., 28
Root, Elihu, 126–127
Rove, Carl, 82
Rove Doctrine, 82–83
    and environmental preservation, 83–84
    on issue of global warming, 84
    legacy after "Rove era," 85
    natural resource policy and, 83
    and patronage firings, 84–85
"Rugged individualism" philosophy, 49
Rush Limbaugh Is a Big Fat Idiot, 268
Russell, William Howard, 255

S

Sassoon, Siegfried, 128
Saturday Night Live, 268

Savage, Paul, 110
Scalia, Antonin, 269
A Scandal in Bohemia, 9
Schick, Allen, 173
Schwarzenegger, Arnold, 247
Scientific American, 171
Scientific management
   Homes as "father" of, 7–9
   theory, 4
Self-conscious consulting firm, 5
Self-described consultant, 5
Seligman, Martin E. P., 185
Senate, 268
Senile, 268
"Separate but equal" doctrine, 221–222
   in field of public education, 222–223
Sexual activity, regulation of, 226–227
   Jim Crow, killing of, 228–230
   Joseph story of sexual harassment, 228
   sex discrimination, prohibition
      of, 230–232
   sexual harassment, claims of, 232–235
Shakespeare, William, 114
   on bureaucracy and hierarchy
      concept of division of labor, use of, 116
      in *Henry V,* 115–116
      in *Troilus and Cressida,* 115
   characters in plays and, 38
   on human behavior in organizations, 117
   on leadership, 119–120
      in *Coriolanus,* 120
      in *Henry V,* 119
      in *King Lear,* 120
   on managers role in motivating
      employees, 116
      informal norms, importance of, 117
      in *King John,* 118
      in *Macbeth,* 116
      in *Measure for Measure,* 116–117
      in *The Merchant of Venice,* 117–118
   on personnel management, 120–123
      in *Henry V,* 122
      in *Julius Caesar,* 121
      in *Much Ado About Nothing,* 121
   on systems analysis, 118–119
      in *Macbeth,* 119
      in *The Merchant of Venice,* 119
The Shame of the Cities, 12–13, 19

Sherlock Holmes character
   as consultant, 5–6
   fame for, 5
   illustrations of, 4
   invention, 1–2
   success, 3–4
   as system analyst, 6
"Shop management," 8
Showdown, 133
The Sign of the Four, 3
Silver Blaze, 6
Sinclair, Upton, 13
Slevin, Peter, 142
Slums conditions in New York City,
     documentation, 21
Small, Hugh, 256
Smith, Adam, 116
"Snoopware" programs, 143
Social advancement through public
     service, 15–16
Social insurance, 61–62
Social networking sites, 144
Social Security, 29, 62–64
Sorensen, Theodore C., 39
Spencer, Herbert
   "natural selection" and "survival of the
     fittest," working on, 17
Spoils system, 14–15
Spoke-and-wheel administrative structure, 128
Sports franchises and policy
     makers, 238–239
Stadium finance decision, 239
Staff concept, 125
   general staffs in U.S. Army, creation of,
     126–128
   hierarchical staff system *vs.* spoke-and-wheel
     approach, 128–130
   influence of, 130
   Napoleon defeat, by Prussian general staff,
     125–126
   nature of, 198
Steffens, Lincoln, 12–13
   Autobiography by, 18
   McClure's Magazine in
     article on corruption in St. Louis, 19
   and muckraking, 19
Stivers, Camilla, 19
The Stock-Broker's Clerk, 9

Stoddart, Joseph Marshall
  editor of *Lippincott's Monthly Magazine,* 2
Stowe, Harriet Beecher
  Uncle Tom's Cabin by, 2
Strachey, Lytton, 256
Strand Magazine, 1, 4
Strategic Air Command (SAC), 170
Strategic management, 154–155, 181–182
  planning in, 182
  public sector and, 184–185
"Street arabs," 21
The Structure, 31
The Structure of Scientific Revolutions, 30
A Study in Scarlet, 2, 5
Suchman, Edward
  Evaluation Research, 258
Suid, Lawrence, 133
The Sullivan Act, 76–77
Summary of the Art of War, 127
Sun Tzu, 105
  The Art of War by, 105
  system for training chinese concubines,
    105–107
Survivable communications system, 148
Swarns, Rachel L., 68
Swift, Jonathan
  Gulliver's Travels, 267
Swope, Herbert Bayard, 154
Systematic Thinking for Social Action, 258
Systemic approach to problem, 6
Systems. *See also* Chaos theory
  adaptations in making of, 110–111
  analysis, 109–110
  approach, utility of, 107
  definition of, 107
  as open systems theory, 108–109
  structural-functional approach for social
    systems, 107–108
  theory, 107–108

T
Taft, William Howard, 18
Tales of the South Pacific, 206
Tarbell, Ida M., 13
Taylor, Bob, 148
Taylor, Frederick W., 7
The Ten Commandments, 266

Tennyson, Alfred Lord, 253
Thank God for the Atom Bomb, 37
Thatcher, Margaret, 44–45
The Absolute Weapon, 169
The Art of War, 105
The Caine Mutiny, 137
The Calculus of Consent, 50
The Congress of Vienna, 147
The Conscience of a Conservative, 46–47
The Cowboys, 134
The Crisis Years, 163
The Cruel Sea, 136
The Fountainhead, 51
The General, 128
The Guns of August, 90
The Last Samurai, 137
The Logic of Collective Action, 50
The Man Who Captured Eichmann, 89
The Necessity for Choice, 201
The Passion of Ayn Rand, 52
The Path to Power, 44
The Practice of Management. MBO, 184
The Prince, 208
Thermonuclear war, 171
The Road to Serfdom, 43
The Sands of Iwo Jima, 132–133
The Second World War, 216
The Wizards of Armageddon, 169, 172
The World Is My Home, 206
Thinking About the Unthinkable, 171
Think tank, 174–175
  for-profit, 177
  governmental, 176
  nonacademic, 175–176
  nonprofit, 177
Thomas, Norman, 57
Thoreau, Henry David, 9
  On the Duty of Civil Disobedience, 261
  Why We Can't Wait, 261–262
Three Musketeers, 135
Thriving on Chaos, 121
Tibbets, Paul W. Jr., 40
Tibshraeny, Jay
  Phoenix Gazette, 238
Time-honored techniques for reforming
    public policies, 261
"Time lag" phenomenon, 31
Totalitarian state, 140

Toynbee, Arnold J., 31
Transformational leader, 119
"Treason" argument, 12
The Treason of the Senate, 12
Truman, Harry S., 29
    Truman Doctrine, 27, 155–156
Tuchman, Barbara W., 90
Tullock, Gordon, 52
Twelve O'Clock High, 136

U

Uncle Tom's Cabin, 2
Unemployment insurance law, 65
United States
    "America's worst budget crises," 242
    "big government" in, 26
    Civil War and President Abraham
        Lincoln, 2
    democracy and, 24
    economy during nineteenth century, 16
    experience in Vietnam, systems analysis
        and, 109–110
    founders of, 24
    governing doctrine, 24
    policy of containment
        in Berlin, 158–159
        and dismantling of Berlin
            Wall, 163–164
        domestic implications of, 164–166
        Kennan and, 156–157
        Korean War and, 160–161
        and Marshall Plan, 157–158
        and NATO, 159–160
        objectives of, 163
        strategic planning, usefulness of,
            154–155
        Truman Doctrine and, 155–156
        and Vietnam War, 161–163
    progressive movement in, 18
    sponsored invasion of Cuba by Cuban
        exiles, 39
    terrorist attacks on September 11,
        2001, 247
    U.S. Interstate Commerce Commission
        (ICC), 8
    U.S. Social Security Administration, 56
Unmasking Administrative Evil, 94

V

The Valley of Fear, 6
Vegetius, Renatus, 27
"Vietnamization," 29
Vietnam War, U.S. involvement in, 29
Vobejda, Barbara, 66

W

Wallsten, Peter, 82
Walton, Richard J., 128
War movies. *See also* Organization
        development
    G.I. Jane, Moore in, 132–133
    The Sands of Iwo Jima, Wayne in,
        132–133
War on terror, 180
Warren, Earl, 222–223
Wealth of Nations, 116
Welfare
    aid to families with dependent
        children, 66
    change in welfare doctrine, 66–68
    evolution of, 57–58
    Great Depression and, 60–61
    old-age pensions and, 62–63
    social insurance approach
        to, 61–62
    Social Security Act of 1935 and, 62
    and Social Security reform, 64
    traditional approach to, 59–60
    and unemployment insurance, 65
Welfare-state policies, 29
Western society, urbanization and
        industrialization, 17
Why We Can't Wait, 261–262
Wiener, Norbert, 109
    model of organization as adaptive system,
        108–109
Wilde, Oscar, 3
    The Picture of Dorian Gray by, 3
Williams, Juan, 220
Willoughby, Charles A., 191
Wills, Garry, 134–135
Wilson, James Q., 32–33
Wilson, Woodrow, 18
Winthrop, John, 21
Wohlstetter, Albert, 170

Woodward, John D., 142
World War II summit meetings, 35
Writings, importance in policy making
    world, 200
  Declaration of Independence draft by
    Jefferson, 203–204
  examples of, impact on career, 202–203
  ghost writer, winning with, 205–207
  and Kissinger prominence, 201–202
  as personal advertising, 207–208

  rewards, in public administration
    career, 208–209
  Wilson's writing, importance
    of, 204–205

Z
Zakaria, Fareed
  Newsweek International, editor, 24

9 780205 607426